ENGLISI

ENGLISH
PASTS

ESSAYS IN HISTORY
AND CULTURE

Stefan Collini

OXFORD
UNIVERSITY PRESS

OXFORD

UNIVERSITY PRESS

Great Clarendon Street, Oxford OX2 6DP

Oxford University Press is a department of the University of Oxford.
It furthers the University's objective of excellence in research, scholarship,
and education by publishing worldwide in

Oxford New York

Athens Auckland Bangkok Bogotá Buenos Aires Calcutta
Cape Town Chennai Dar es Salaam Delhi Florence Hong Kong Istanbul
Karachi Kuala Lumpur Madrid Melbourne Mexico City Mumbai
Nairobi Paris São Paulo Singapore Taipei Tokyo Toronto Warsaw

with associated companies in Berlin Ibadan

Oxford is a registered trade mark of Oxford University Press
in the UK and in certain other countries

Published in the United States
by Oxford University Press Inc., New York

© Stefan Collini 1999

British Library Cataloguing in Publication Data

Data available

Library of Congress Cataloging in Publication Data
Collini, Stefan, 1947- .
English pasts: essays in culture and history/Stefan Collini.
p. cm.
Includes bibliographical references (p.) and index.
1. Great Britain—Historiography. 2. England—Civilization—
Historiography. 3. Nationalism—England—Historiography.
I. Title.
DA1.C85 1999
941—dc21 98-47247

ISBN 0-19-820779-4
ISBN 0-19-820780-8 (pbk.)

3 5 7 9 10 8 6 4 2

Typeset in 10/12 pt Sabon
by Cambrian Typesetters, Frimley, Surrey
Printed in Great Britain
on acid-free paper by
Biddles Ltd., Guildford and King's Lynn

To John Thompson, ideal reader

CONTENTS

Nothing succeeds in which high spirits play no part.
Friedrich Nietzsche, *Twilight of the Idols*

Introduction

THE essays in this book are addressed to any reader interested in history and literature, in England and 'Englishness', and in that ill-defined constellation of activities we call, with increasing unsteadiness these days, 'culture'.

Within these broad limits, the arrangement of the contents is intended to emphasize three related clusters of issues. The essays in Part I are primarily concerned with ways of situating ourselves in our history, including the understanding yielded by a comparative perspective (which is one reason why contrasts with France are a substantial presence in this book despite its title). Here, I particularly try to suggest some of the political reasons, in the largest sense of the term, why it matters that we, whoever that dangerous pronoun is taken to refer to, should have available to us more adequate characterizations of the past than the stereotypes peddled by many journalists and most politicians. Part II focuses on individual biography in an attempt to explore, in a relatively gentle and untheoretical way, the relations between ideas, sensibility, and background in several leading English writers and thinkers. A secondary part of my purpose here is to show how some of the most substantial or forbidding forms of modern scholarly publication—a comprehensive 'Collected Works', a thoroughly researched biography, an annotated edition of correspondence—can yield interest and insight to non-specialist readers beyond the austerer purposes that such learned publications are mainly intended to serve. The essays in Part III are all, in different ways, explicitly concerned with the relationship between academic research and wider publics, variously conceived. I here engage in more directly critical and polemical ways with certain forms of oversimplification, exaggeration, mis-characterization, and (a particular *bête noire*) the baneful consequences of binary or dichotomizing categories. Some of my targets here are official or institutional, some are individual and idiosyncratic, some may be conventionally classified as on 'the Right', others as on 'the Left', but all seem to me symptomatic of a wider failure to acknowledge the nature and distinctiveness of intellectual or scholarly activities in their own terms.

These essays are almost all based on pieces which have already been published in other forms, often initially in response to an invitation to write about a particular book or occasion. These earlier versions have here been revised, extended, and combined so as to be read as essays in their own right, but I have not attempted to 'update' the references and allusions. At the start of each chapter, I have given details of the book or books whose publication first prompted the writing of the main sections of that chapter, so that its focus should be evident to the reader at a glance. For the most part, I have tried to retain only those passages of appraisal and judgement which may possess a boader force, omitting that kind of critical comment whose function is confined to a review in the strict sense. There are parts of every essay (with the exception of Chapter 12, for reasons which I explain there) which have not appeared in print before; in addition, the greater part of Chapter 2 on Anglo-French contrasts has hitherto only appeared in French, and Chapter 16 on the idea of a 'non-specialist public' has not previously been published in any form.

The writing of such 'occasional' pieces presumes that there is a kind of general cultural conversation about these matters which goes beyond, though it to some extent builds upon, the activity of the professional historian or literary critic (or philosopher or whoever) whose work is largely addressed to other members of the relevant scholarly sub-community. In the concluding essay I attempt to explore a little of the history of this assumption and try to suggest how it may be best understood in our present circumstances. But whatever the misgivings we may now quite properly have about what has variously been called 'the general reader', 'the non-specialist public', and so on, these labels point towards a concern that will, it seems, simply not go away. I realize that to attach this last phrase to the concern may seem to give it little more status than the neighbourhood cat we resolutely refuse to feed, but at least it accurately records an autobiographical fact. That's to say, across many, perhaps most, areas of intellectual and literary activity I certainly spend more time reading *about* books and ideas than I do reading the original works themselves; review essays in publications like the *Times Literary Supplement* or the *London Review of Books* have for years been a chief staple of my education. One way in which I may differ from some others of whom this is true is that I long ago stopped feeling guilty about these proportions. After all, I would never read all those fat books, and nor, if you're honest about it, will you. But it matters how we, in our various roles as friends, colleagues, readers, reviewers, or writers of other books, talk about them: it matters in itself, and it is also one of the ways we express and embody some of the intellectual and other values that help make us who we are. But, that being so, we need at least the sustaining illusion of something like the idea of a 'non-specialist public'.

The attempt to realize that idea in practice can, it's true, generate its own peculiar deformations. There can, for example, be a kind of philistinism involved in the over-eager adoption of a robustly plain-man style, a danger not always avoided by, among others, some of the leading book-reviewers in the English 'quality' press. 'Come off it!' can, occasionally, be a telling and quite proper critical response, but it can also, and more frequently, serve as the battle-cry of mere prejudice and intellectual defensiveness. In such cases, invoking an imagined audience of 'general readers' may simply mask an unwillingness to learn or to be stretched. Worse still, in some ways, is the ease with which the notion lends itself to over-dramatization, turning into one of those bleak, irascible philippics about the 'disappearance of the reading public' and the 'degeneration of modern culture'. The essays in this book are not designed to give comfort to either of these comfort-seeking tendencies. Rather, they are committed to the continuing possibility of writing for a sophisticated and probably highly educated, but still in the relevant sense non-specialist, audience, an audience interested in the serious discussion of serious matters without being given to heroic or unrealistically strenuous efforts at self-improvement. In this respect, it can be salutary for those who sometimes attempt to *write* for non-specialists to recall what goes on in the far more frequent experience of *reading* as non-specialists.

As in my title itself, I have up to this point been deliberately speaking of 'England' and 'English' rather than using the more general,

and for many purposes the more correct, 'Britain' and 'British'. I
trust it will become obvious that I am very far from endorsing
many of the traditional assumptions of English cultural nationalism. My reasons for preferring the more restrictive term here are,
first, that it was the established usage during much of the period I
am concerned with; second, that there have been real differences of
social and institutional structure, and to some extent of intellectual
tradition as well, among the countries of the British Isles, and it can
sometimes be important to isolate what features of the situation
commonly classed as 'British' are more properly to be seen as
'English' (when talking of higher education, for example, it is
always important to distinguish the historically different Scottish
pattern); third, that it underscores the intimacy of the connection
with 'English literature' which has, for better or worse, played such
a large part in shaping the identity of English culture (though this,
needless to say, begs many questions, including that of the silent co-
opting of Irish, Scottish, and Welsh writers into 'Eng. lit.'); and
fourth, that the entities involved in the frequent comparisons with
France and French culture have most often been 'England' and 'the
English' (Halévy, for example, called his masterpiece *Angleterre en
1815* not *Grande Bretagne en 1815*, though that, in practice, was
its subject-matter). At the same time, there are many cases—such
as, for instance, the comparisons between British and American
academic culture referred to in Chapter 16—where 'Britain' and
'British' are clearly appropriate. Probably no usage here can be
entirely consistent and satisfactory: this is inherently, and rightly, a
contested matter.

In terms of content, these essays, as I have already indicated, are
concerned with ways of understanding, characterizing, and inhabiting the cultural continuities and intellectual traditions that constitute so much of the texture of life for the review-reading classes.
Inevitably, this recurrently takes the form of a preoccupation with
what others like to call 'Englishness'. I do not believe, perhaps I
had better make clear straight away, that there is *an* English tradition in these matters or that it makes any sense to look for a mythical entity called 'the English mind'. Of course, there are
continuities and patterns, in the plural, which have given intellectual life in England a certain distinctiveness in the past and which
still inform, though they certainly do not altogether determine, our
relations to the legacies we have inherited from that past. But that

distinctiveness, such as it may be, can only be determined by analysis that is, implicitly if not always explicitly, comparative, and such analysis will, and should, always tend to be corrosive of cosy pieties and parochial prejudices.

It seems important to emphasize my rejection of coercive fictions like 'the English tradition' in case the very fact of my having cultivated a pretty intimate familiarity with the small print of English intellectual life in the nineteenth and twentieth centuries should be interpreted as indicating that I basically endorse what may be thought of as its dominant values, or even that I desire, as part of some polemical nostalgia, to reactivate or restore some of these values in the present. I don't. But the fact is that in much of the so-called 'serious' journalism and popular textbook writing of recent decades it has been almost *de rigeur* to pillory the shortcomings of what is alleged to have been the pervasive tone and character of intellectual life in England—its political complacency, its disdain for theory, and so on. In so far as these dispositions *have* been marked features of English culture (they are not unknown elsewhere, of course), they have often expressed an anti-intellectualism which I detest even more than I am irritated by the self-righteousness of its would-be 'radical' critics. But such trading in stereotypes, for it is usually little more than that, does us all a disservice. The hostile characterizations are mostly offered from too far away. Notoriously, getting too close runs the risk of losing sight of the limits, and hence the limitations, of what one is looking at. But there has been no shortage of voices eager to remind us of those, and so these essays are an attempt to get a little closer.

I
HISTORIES

1

Writing 'the National History': Trevelyan and After

I

It is hard for the historian not to feel ambivalent about the sort of public fuss that accompanies the significant anniversaries of great moments in English history. While it ought, in some ways, to be gratifying to find one's professional concerns receiving a little public attention, in practice one more often ends up feeling an unsettling lack of connection with the kind of 'history' that serves as so much raw material for the television producers and postage-stamp designers. Perhaps one thing that adds to the historian's sense of the artificiality of it all is that, in England at least, so many of these commemorated episodes do not seem to have any real presence in our collective consciousness until they are briefly lodged there by the publicity surrounding some significant anniversary. The celebration does not involve the intensification of interest in an issue which is normally part of the texture of our cultural or political life: it is an entirely fabricated moment when the public has its attention drawn to some previously ignored historical event which then becomes the focus of that kind of detached and transient curiosity normally aroused by the rare moments of media coverage accorded to the annual rituals of the minor sports.

David Cannadine, *G. M. Trevelyan: A Life in History* (HarperCollins, 1992).
Ross McKibbin, *Classes and Cultures: England 1918–1951* (Oxford University Press, 1998).

I found myself reflecting on this feeling after having spent some time in Paris in the late 1980s observing the anticipatory tremors already being caused by the approaching Bicentenary of 1789, and then returning to see if our politicians, leader-writers, and other pundits were getting similar mileage out of the impending Tercentenary of our own Glorious Revolution of 1688. But apart from an isolated bit of official huffing and, implausibly, puffing, the event seemed singularly lacking in resonance: old wounds showed no signs of being reopened, and the streets were marked by a notable absence of Jacobite marches. And yet it would on the face of it be rather paradoxical to suggest that we do not live in a history-conscious country: to foreign observers we often seem to be a history-drenched people, even to the point of drowning in our own history. Why does it seem so certain that the anniversary of any of the most decisive moments in our political history will be merely a media event and not genuinely a political event?

This question came back to me in a different form when, not long after, I visited Wallington Hall, the Trevelyan family home in Northumberland now owned by the National Trust. Clearly, the inhabitants of this house in its heyday between the mid-nineteenth and the mid-twentieth centuries had had no difficulty in being stirred by the mere thought, let alone the anniversaries, of the decisive moments in 'the national history', and one of them, the historian G. M. Trevelyan, had devoted much of his life and his literary energy to trying to communicate this excitement to his compatriots. In recent years the English historian David Cannadine has on more than one occasion exhorted modern historians to try to do the same, and he has written a biographical study of Trevelyan strongly informed by a sense of identification on this score. But the more I ponder Trevelyan's example and Cannadine's exhortations, the more I come to feel that the late twentieth-century historian needs to think about 'the national past' and its place in contemporary British culture in other terms. Ross McKibbin offers a striking example of a historian who has indeed attempted to deal with a slice of the English past in utterly different terms, terms which are intended to give pride of place to the lives of the 'ordinary people' who make up the vast bulk of the population. Yet here, too, the forcefulness of the example serves to highlight the limitations of the approach, and considering these books in the context of the official promotion of certain anniversaries has the effect of making me feel more acutely than ever just how problematic the whole enterprise of writing 'the national history' has now become.

II

In France the approach of 1989 provoked political controversy, not least because of the impossibility of making any neutral decision about *what* to commemorate when dealing with an episode that was so multifaceted and, on at least one view of the matter, still unfinished. Not the least of the questions needing to be faced was whether an official celebration of 1789 would be seen as constituting an endorsement of the principles of 1793. In 1889 the Third Republic encouraged the cult of Mirabeau and Danton who, at a time when contemporary politics were dominated by the conflict between Church and State, could be portrayed as the true heirs of the anticlerical Voltaire. But in 1989 it was more difficult for a right-wing government to know how to handle Robespierre and Saint-Just, putative inheritors of Rousseau's still-challenging theory of a radically egalitarian democracy.

Of course, one of the many ways in which the French Revolution ultimately differed from 1688 was that the latter was self-consciously a conservative 'revolution', made not in the name of a radical programme of universal rights but as a way of restoring a tradition that had become corrupt or been subverted. A justification of this sort, even if it is not entirely to be accepted at face value, inevitably reduces the event's long-term resonance in one way at least: it makes it harder for subsequent centuries to draw any relevant inspiration from the informing principles of a set of actions which were themselves so determinedly backward-looking. It doesn't much matter whether the 'ancient constitution' James II was held to have abrogated was or was not largely a fiction created by Whig lawyers and antiquaries: it would still go down like a lead balloon if invoked from the platform at a Labour Party conference. (An invocation of the Levellers and other radical groups from the Civil War might be another matter.)

As it turned out, 1988 was made the occasion for official invocation of the virtues of constitutional compromise and peaceful change. It is perhaps illustrative of a general point about our alleged low temperature in these matters that this characterization

of 1688 should be so little contested, so that as an animating allusion or reference-point it packs all the political punch of a stiff shot
of Trevelyan-and-water. After all, one wouldn't have to be terribly
knowledgeable about the murky constitutional goings-on of that
year to present a rather different picture of the sequence of events
whereby an hereditary monarch claiming divine endorsement is
kicked off his throne by a temporary alliance of party godfathers
who then draw up the terms of the contract for bringing in a
complete outsider who had made quite a name for himself by the
aggressive style in which he had run a foreign outfit.

There was even less likelihood of 1688 being marked by any very
vigorous assertion of the essentially Protestant identity of the English
nation. In the middle of the nineteenth century this still mattered a
great deal, and the public that bought so many copies of Froude's
vindication of the English Reformation could also get very steamed
up about the Pope's pretty notional reintroduction of Catholic dioce-
ses into England in 1850. But one of the more effective bits of 'incorporation' that took place in the next half-century or so was the way
it came to be taken for granted that Catholics were pretty decent
sorts really and there was no question but that they would be loyal
subjects of a monarch who was, and is still, head of the Established
Protestant Church and who still declares on her coins that she is 'the
defender of the faith'. Is it remarkable, or is it a sign of our collective
tepidity of feeling about both the Monarchy and the Established
Church, that in specifying the qualifications of any future occupant
of the throne, we take for granted a job-description that would get
you roasted alive if you worked for most London boroughs?

Approaching the matter a little more systematically, stirred by
the French comparison, one might begin by distinguishing between,
on the one hand, the mere presence of historical residues, however
abundant, and, on the other, the active resonance which certain
aspects of the national past have and which can be exploited for a
variety of current purposes. In principle, two of the most obvious
ways in which versions of English history could effectively and self-
consciously be mobilized in contemporary public life are, first, in
expressions of nationalism (which is not quite the same thing as a
sense of national identity), and second, in the partisan or sectarian
appropriation of those few historical episodes the (suitably selective) evocation of which might still be thought capable of yielding
some political advantage.

It was for a long time an unspoken premiss of much English historiography that nationalism was something that happened to other people. The Hungarians were inevitably nationalists; the Indians were understandably nationalists; the Irish were tiresomely nationalists; but the English weren't nationalists—they were just naturally patriotic. Partly, this way of putting it fitted in better with the preferred, evasively genteel, register of the Higher Flannel, but partly, of course, there were a few undeniable facts about Britain's position in the world that made it easier to sustain this assumption. Indeed, there was implicit recognition that these other chaps had first to find or construct, and then assert and give political embodiment to, a sense of their collective identity which in England could, if you didn't look too closely, pretty much be taken for granted. But the crucial condition for this asymmetry was that self-conscious nationalism is largely a matter of asserting an identity against someone or something, whether colonial masters or the claims of rival states to bits of one's territory or similar affronts to one's dignity, and in modern English history these have not exactly been the most pressing problems (those fearful of closer European integration may wish to use the past tense here).

However, the experience of political and economic decline understandably makes available an atavistic kind of nationalism, and it has also stimulated a tendency to over-invest in the glories of distinctively English cultural achievements—what one might call 'British Council nationalism'. These two forms are all too easily run together, and it is noticeable how Britain's twentieth-century wars, large and small, have invariably been accompanied by renewed celebrations of the achievements of the Elizabethan period, without, in their most popular form, exhibiting any very firm hold on the distinction between William Shakespeare and Sir Francis Drake.

The other major way in which interpretations of aspects of the national past can in principle figure actively in contemporary public life—as valuable weapons in the verbal battles between political parties—is in practice often thought to be more noticeable by its absence in this country. The lines of division between the parties in British politics in the twentieth century have not essentially been structured around rival accounts of significant episodes in English history (Irish and, to some extent, Scottish history are another matter). There are some tricky chicken-and-egg questions here about the relation between the relatively narrow range and muted form of political conflict and the limited role played by explicit invocations of great contested moments in the past. The course of subsequent politics can itself deprive certain episodes of their partisan resonance, just as the declining power of historical memories and allusions can in turn help to bring about a quieter form of political life. This symbiotic relationship between memory and political conflict can tell in the opposite direction, too, of course: it is clear that in France the 'Revolutions' of 1830, 1848, and 1871 helped keep the significance of 1789 alive and relevant at least as much as they were themselves nourished by it.

The comparatively restrained nature of political conflict in twentieth-century Britain can, of course, be exaggerated: no one could say that the General Strike, for example, was not about very deep structural divisions in British society, and references to rival versions of that event have not been entirely absent from subsequent political debate. One also has to resist any temptation to see this as a timeless feature of the English 'national character'. The political life of the seventeenth century could not, after all, really be said to have been conducted along the lines of Butskellite consensualism, and the great constitutional and political conflicts of that century still had a vibrant political resonance down to at least the middle of the nineteenth century. But by the time Lecky, in 1892, delivered his celebrated aphorism that 'We are Cavaliers or Roundheads before we are Conservatives or Liberals', this association was already ceasing to have any publicly mobilizing power, and it has surely not been effective on any significant scale during the twentieth century.

Of course, having a deeply divided political life in which the past is charged with sectarian significance can be extremely nasty, and those who bemoan the lack of excitement in British politics might reasonably be reminded of what life is like under such circumstances. After all, the saying 'May it be your fate to live in interesting times' began life as a Chinese *curse*. In Ulster, for example, 1688 did indeed have a rather different resonance, not least for having taken place only two years before 1690. If, *per impossibile*, by 1990 the apprentice-boys' march could have been led by the Duke of Norfolk and the Archbishop of Canterbury, the whole show kitted out by Hardy Amies and commented upon by David Dimbleby, would we all complain that it had become boringly consensual? And if we did, wouldn't we deserve to be told to grow up?

III

The question of the contemporary resonance of the historian's work, and, if only in passing, the contrast in this respect between the situation in France and in this country, has in recent years received a good deal of journalistic attention, thanks not least to the energetic efforts of David Cannadine himself. In considering this question, it may therefore be helpful to begin by briefly returning to what has become one of the most widely cited pronouncements on this theme, his 1987 *Past and Present* lecture on 'British History: Past, Present—and Future?' I certainly find myself very much in sympathy with Cannadine's desire for history to play a larger role in our 'general culture' rather than for it to be confined within the inappropriately narrow limits of the most specialized kind of academic discipline, and I enjoyed a good deal of his vigorous indictment of the vices of what he calls 'the cult of professionalism'. But I fear that the manner in which he presents his argument about the decline in the material position and public standing of professional historians may make it easier for others to trade in crude schematizations of this aspect of recent British cultural history, and it may thereby weaken rather than strengthen the case that can be made for the distinctive contribution of a properly nuanced history to our self-understanding.

One has, to begin with, to be careful not to exaggerate the extent to which historians can determine their own fates merely by writing a different kind of history. Any lack of realism here runs the risk of being a poor advertisement for what ought to be regarded as one of the chief virtues fostered by an historical training, namely a shrewd sense of the relative power in any given situation of different kinds of historical forces. The explanation for the sadly reduced position of academic historians in this country, as of nearly all groups in state-financed higher education and research, has in the first instance to be found in developments in the world economy and Britain's declining position in that economy, and secondly in the nature of the budgetary policies followed by Conservative governments after 1979. It would encourage an

implausibly intellectualistic level of explanation to suggest (as I
fear Cannadine was immediately taken to suggest) that if only
professional historians had been seen to be offering 'bold' and
'relevant' interpretations of British history they might have
exempted themselves to any significant extent from the impact of
these larger forces.

Even if the entire historical profession had incorporated itself as
Sceptr'd Isle Productions PLC with nightly spots on prime time, it
is hard to see how it could have had much effect on the rate at
which oil was extracted from the Mexican Gulf or the Arabian
desert, nor is it likely that the Cabinet would be brought to its
knees if flying pickets from the Royal Historical Society were
dispatched to every Record Office in the land. And, turning to the
most local level of explanation, even if, most improbably, history
were ever to acquire the same perceived utility and public regard as
technology and applied science, the fate of institutions favouring
those subjects in the apparently senseless carve-up of university
funding in the 1980s is hardly encouraging.

The more general and more interesting issue raised by
Cannadine, however, concerns the part that history, and especially
interpretations of the national past, can play in a society, and, more
immediately, the role it might be realistic to expect British historians to play in this society now. Again, the historian has a particular responsibility not to encourage crudely dichotomous ways of
thinking about this question. It is just not true, as Cannadine seems
to imply at certain points, that the choice has to be between having
either 'a vision of the national past' (and note the singular) which
is 'highly usable and very relevant to contemporary Britain', or
accounts which 'are rarely more than one thing after another'. To
see it thus would be sadly to oversimplify the variety, complexity,
and interest of the many ways in which historians' accounts of
periods, episodes, and characteristics of English history can have
some purchase on our collective self-understandings in the present.
The quality of some of the best work in English history published
in recent decades (one could cite books as different as, for example,
Keith Thomas's *Man and the Natural World*, John Brewer's *The
Sinews of Power*, or J. W. Burrow's *A Liberal Descent*) should
remind us that trivial antiquarianism is not the only alternative to
those crudely present-minded or propagandistic uses of the past
that sometimes masquerade as 'history'.

It is also important to remember that different cultural traditions play a part (though only a part) in accounting for the different fates of historians in different societies, and this takes us back to the comparison with the situation in France which Cannadine himself introduces at one point, where he speaks enviously of 'the high profile of some French historians and the astonishing success of their books'. The awkward fact about this comparison for the purposes of his argument is that there has been just as much specialization and detailed research in French as in English historiography in the last few decades; indeed, the system of the *thèse d'état* (which has only recently been replaced by a more modest thesis on the British or American model) might seem to have been designed to keep French historians locked in the archives until they had entirely lost the power of human speech. But of course not only have some French historians continued to enjoy a level of attention from the educated public that their English counterparts have perhaps never known in this century, but, notoriously, works of history can often carry a political resonance in France that is practically unknown here. To understand these contrasts we would need to go to a much deeper and longer-term level of explanation than that which Cannadine's argument draws upon.

Without getting too entangled in the notorious difficulties of such large-scale cultural comparisons, two points can be made very briefly. First, contemporary French historians are not themselves the creators of that extraordinarily febrile, often extraordinarily fertile but sometimes extraordinarily daft, form of life which is the French (in practice, the Parisian) intellectual scene. In terms of receiving public attention, they are beneficiaries of it, but so, it hardly needs to be said, are philosophers, anthropologists, literary theorists, and others. It is a classic case of cart-before-horse-ism to suggest that because French historians write a more 'relevant' kind of history they therefore receive more public attention. It is, rather, that, for a variety of complex historical reasons, the French educated public pays more attention to certain kinds of intellectual activity than is the case in Britain, and so French historians (among others) can contribute to a tradition of *haute vulgarisation* and enjoy, in return, a kind of public esteem that the cultural traditions of this country have for the most part not encouraged. This does not mean that the situation in Britain could never change in this direction, nor that historians could not play a part (but only a part) in helping to bring about some change; but thoughts of that kind only make it more, not less, necessary to characterize the nature of the differences properly in the first place.

The second point goes back to my opening reflection on the respective anniversaries of 1688 and 1789. Historical allusions and reference-points do indeed play a far greater part in French political life than is the case in England (an issue which I discuss in more detail in the following chapter), but it is not within the power of historians, even in their most hubristic moments, to bring about the conditions for such resonance. It is because there were *already* far deeper and more explicit cleavages in French politics, and because these cleavages often originated in or were structured around particular historical episodes, that historians' accounts of these episodes continue to arouse such strong partisan emotions. It is not because French historians propound 'bolder hypotheses' that, say, a new account of collaboration under the Vichy regime would be bound to arouse a level of public interest in France greater than an account of any aspect of life in Britain during the Second World War would do in this country: it is because existing political passions in France already have a very direct and very intense relation to the events of that period, and the knowledge that a degree of political significance will inescapably be attributed to any account of the matter combines with other traditions in French intellectual life to induce a general self-consciousness about the political bearing of even ostensibly very recondite researches.

Obviously, there is much more to be said about the matter than this, and the tendency of a fuller analysis might well be to diminish the sharpness of the contrasts between these two necessarily crude and selective sketches of certain cultural patterns. But that is the point. One of the services that the historian renders to society is to help prevent its members becoming the prisoners of any tendentious or partisan versions of 'the national past'. This involves, among other things, providing a properly complex characterization of those features of its cultural life within which a discussion such as this about the role of history in shaping our collective self-understanding is itself located. There can be an unhelpful element of platform oratory in calling for more 'bold hypotheses' and less 'detailed research', not least because it may unwittingly encourage that kind of crude dichotomizing from other quarters which tells us that if we do not happen to endorse the theoretical flavour of the month we must be 'mindless empiricists'. We sell our intelligence short when we allow such alternatives to be presented as exhaustive.

The qualities of imagination, sensitivity, judgement, accuracy, and so on that are exhibited in good historical writing of whatever level of generality are themselves antidotes to the narrowing and distorting of our self-understandings that so many forces in our— or, let it be recognized, any other—society constantly press upon us. If we think that these qualities are in practice undervalued in the policies which public opinion allows governments and official bodies in this country to pursue, and if we are minded to try to do something about it directly, we would presumably do better to embody some of these qualities in giving an illuminating account of how this situation has come about and how far it might be realistic to think that things could be otherwise, rather than to try deliberately to create a 'relevant' interpretation of the national past that may—and, there again, may not—appeal to those who at any given time control the ladling out of our mess of pottage.

IV

The questions of what is or should be going on in the official celebrations referred to earlier and what is or should be the public role of the historian entail further questions about what the story of 'the national past' should include and in what senses such a story might be 'relevant' to the experience of living in contemporary Britain. As always, the attempt to answer such questions requires in turn some scrutiny of who 'we' are and what connections we acknowledge between that past and ourselves. As I reported earlier, the modern visitor to Wallington Hall, the Trevelyan country seat in Northumberland, is constantly prompted to remark the sense of national and family destiny which it imparted to the young George Macaulay Trevelyan, and reflecting on this example may, indirectly, help us to identify some possible answers to these questions.

Wallington Hall had been built in the late seventeenth century for the Blacketts, early Newcastle industrialists, and then inherited by their distant relatives, the Trevelyans, who were West Country gentry. In the course of the nineteenth century, these two social threads were interwoven with a third, as the Trevelyans became

central to that 'intellectual aristocracy' which occupied so many of
the high places in Victorian Britain. Sir Charles Trevelyan set the
pattern, both by marrying Macaulay's sister and by his distinguished career as a civil servant in London and in India. Indeed, he
created one of the conditions for the flourishing of that self-
described 'aristocracy of talent' by helping to open the Civil Service
to entry by competitive examination rather than by patronage. His
son, Sir George Otto Trevelyan, became a prominent Liberal
Cabinet minister in Gladstone's governments as well as a noted
historian, and presided at Wallington for over forty years. Sir
George had three sons, of whom the historian, born in 1876, was
the youngest. The eldest, Charles Philips Trevelyan, followed his
father into politics, eventually serving as Education Secretary in the
first two Labour governments. The overlapping of the brothers'
worlds was nicely illustrated when in 1941 Charles made
Wallington over to the National Trust, on whose behalf it was
received by the Chairman of the Estates Committee, his brother
George.

The house in which Trevelyan grew up now seems full of pointers to his later vocation. In the study, the desk bears the simple
legend 'Lord Macaulay wrote his *History of England* at this desk'.
One of Trevelyan's earliest literary memories is of his mother reading to him Macaulay's third chapter; seventy-eight years later, as his
daughter, Mary Moorman, recalled in her *George Macaulay
Trevelyan: A Memoir*, he had some of that same chapter read to
him the day before he died. All his work was written, a reviewer
was later to complain, as if he had 'a bust of Lord Macaulay upon
his desk'. The house also contains a display of the meticulously
detailed lead soldiers with which the three brothers used to conduct
the elaborate and long-drawn-out battles, complete with contour
maps, lovingly described by Trevelyan in his autobiography.
Military history was to be at the heart of many of his best works,
and he endearingly confessed when writing his *England Under
Queen Anne* trilogy that he was 'terrified of its becoming a "drum
and trumpets" history, . . . especially as I like drums and trumpets
so much, provided they were blown a good hundred years ago'.

But Wallington contains a yet more striking clue to the young
Trevelyan's sense of his destiny. The frieze in the great saloon
depicts eight scenes of Northumberland history, interspersed with
portrait medallions of famous Northumbrians, culminating in the

mid-nineteenth-century Trevelyans. The design not only suggests the historian's frequently displayed sense of how the national past was but the family history writ large, but also his sense of himself as a Northumbrian and, in a favoured term, 'a countryman'. As a product of Harrow and Trinity College Cambridge, who spent much of his early manhood in London, he was even less of a 'countryman' than most of the English landed classes. But he felt he was in his natural habitat when walking and shooting in the surrounding fields and moors (during food rationing in the Second World War he would often, when expecting an important visitor in the Master's Lodge at Trinity, go out into the Cambridgeshire countryside with his gun to get something for the pot), and his projection of this identity was surely a crucial element in the popular success of his history books in the age of *Country Life* and the Council for the Preservation of Rural England.

Reaching that audience by means of what he always regarded as 'the family tradition of literary history' gave Trevelyan's life its purpose and its structure. After early academic successes, he was duly elected to a Fellowship at his old college, but when his modest teaching duties threatened to drain energy from his writing, he resigned his Fellowship and for the next twenty-four years lived as an independent scholar, until in 1927 Stanley Baldwin, a friend and fellow 'countryman', appointed him to the Regius Chair of History at Cambridge. By then he had published fourteen books, including the pre-war Garibaldi trilogy and in 1926 his single-volume history of England. These books had certainly reached their intended audience: in 1911 the third Garibaldi volume sold out its first printing of 3,000 copies in two days, while the *History of England* enjoyed a steady sale most novelists would envy, passing 200,000 copies by 1949. But even these impressive figures were to be eclipsed by the phenomenal success of his *English Social History*, published in Britain (after being delayed by paper rationing) in 1944. It sold over 100,000 in the first year, and passed the half-million mark in the early 1950s. Thereafter his place on the shelves of second-hand bookshops was never in doubt.

David Cannadine's *G. M. Trevelyan: A Life in History* is intended to rescue him from this dusty domain. The book does not present itself as a biography (his daughter's *Memoir* remains the fullest picture of the life) but as 'the first sustained analysis of his work, his attitudes, his influence and his achievement, based on a thorough examination of the appropriate and available sources'. The very identification of some of these sources is part of the book's achievement. Trevelyan destroyed his own papers, decreeing that no biography of him should be written, but Cannadine has tracked down substantial remains of his correspondence in fifty-seven different archives spread between Newcastle upon Tyne and Austin, Texas.

The book is most successful in tracing the relations between the different phases of Trevelyan's large output and those develop-ments in national and indeed European politics which he felt so deeply. As presented here, Trevelyan was always illustrating the truth of Croce's epigram that 'all history is contemporary history'. As the pre-1914 'liberal internationalist' gives way to the 'Whig constitutionalist' and finally to the 'rural elegist', all of Trevelyan's major books are illuminated by fresh thematic analyses or sugges-tive juxtapositions, and this is no mean feat. Among the plums (and it is a Plumby book), pride of place must go to the extremely perceptive discussion of the *English Social History*, not just as a thinly disguised broadside against mass society and a threnody for a lost England, but as a welcome displacement of attention from the world of politics that had become so unendurably alien and threatening by the 1940s. For this and each of the other major works the relevant contexts are deftly pencilled in. In linking the books to Trevelyan's extensive work for the National Trust Cannadine writes with particular authority (as befits the historian of the aristocracy) on the changes after 1918 not just in the pattern of landownership but also of the land's cultural significance, as the aristocracy ceased to be seen as 'the exclusive owners of "the land", [and] became instead the altruistic protectors of "the coun-tryside" on behalf of the community as a whole'.

One of Cannadine's strengths is that he knows all about anybody who was anybody, and since Trevelyan seems to have been either related to or acquainted with everybody who was anybody, this command of earlier editions of *Who's Who* is much in evidence. Cannadine's vigorous expository manner means there is no danger of not being able to see the wood for the family trees, and his acquired familiarity with the social elite does enable him to bring out very tellingly just how extraordinarily well-connected and fortunate Trevelyan was. Thus, he 'had friends or relatives in every British cabinet—whatever its political complexion—until

1955', and he was related to '*every* Master of Trinity this century except the present incumbent'. (One of the few illustrations of this theme Cannadine does not mention occurred in 1915 when Trevelyan wanted to ship the vehicles of the entirely unofficial Friends' Ambulance Unit over to France en route for Italy: he led them, as his daughter records, to Southampton 'where a friend in the Admiralty . . . had seen to it that a ship was at their service to take then across to Havre'.) His private income generally exceeded his needs, enabling him to support his favoured causes with more than his time and his reputation: in later life, for example, he bought land in his beloved Lake District expressly in order to donate it to the National Trust.

In addition, 'he never applied for a job he did not get: indeed, with the exception of his Trinity Fellowship, he never applied for a job at all' (in fact, he turned down things which would have seemed the crowning glory to half a dozen careers). Almost inevitably, the Regius Chair was followed by the Order of Merit and the Mastership of Trinity, and he could presumably have had other honours had he not followed the practice shared, according to Cannadine, by 'Cambridge men of Trevelyan's background and generation' who 'only accepted honours which came after their name, but not before it'.

Trevelyan's sensibility and moral temper are touched upon more briefly, though they distance him from us at least as much as his social advantages. He lived according to what he called in 1899 'the gospel of love', interpreted in markedly puritanical terms: self-ishness was the doom always to be avoided. To 'live for others' was a moral duty as well as a psychological need, and the ground of this creed he found best expressed in certain poems by Wordsworth and Meredith (whose work he read to members of his ambulance unit during shelling on the Italian front). To his credit, Cannadine avoids easy mockery here, with the result that the reader is neither surprised nor too glibly amused to find the hugely productive 62-year-old Trevelyan reproaching himself in 1938: 'I must discipline myself again. . . . I have been living too much for pleasure.'

The impact of his writings is harder to gauge, and this study does not inquire about the social make-up of his readership. It seems likely that the sales of Trevelyan's books both nourished and depended upon the widespread nostalgia so many scholars have identified in Britain since the end of the First World War. He thought of himself

as out of tune with his times: in many ways he was a survivor from
another age even when quite young, but this possibly made him all
the more palatable to a readership which located its ideals of 'essential Englishness' firmly in the past. For by the 1920s his was a
Whiggism turned autumnal. The unique political achievement of
English liberties was still to be venerated and to be seen as the expression of the national character; but that character was formed by
conditions which were now disappearing. He contributed freely to
the cultural pessimism so common among the educated classes in this
period: in 1947 he spoke of living in 'an age that has no culture
except American films and football pools. . . . The advent of real
democracy . . . has cooked the goose of civilization.'

English history as told by Trevelyan was rather like a tour of a
beautiful country house conducted by one of the last surviving
members of the family. Taxes and modern attitudes have between
them destroyed the agreeable life which used to be led within its
walls (at least above stairs), yet there it still stands, able to tug at
the hearts of all but the most resistant visitors. On this analogy, the
appeal of the *English Social History* may in part have been that it
was obviously a tale told by a toff.

Certainly, there can be no disputing that 'Trevelyan lived and
moved in a world very different from that of the average professional historian of today'. None the less, Cannadine, an accomplished professional historian who has recently emphasized his
own 'lower middle-class' background, wants not only to understand him: he wants to defend him, to speak up for the virtues of
the kind of history which Trevelyan wrote, perhaps even to write
its modern equivalent. With some flashing swordplay, he disposes
of several of the dismissive criticisms levelled at Trevelyan in recent
decades, though he perhaps wins a too-easy victory by taking
Geoffrey Elton and Jonathan Clark as representative critics. But
there are deeper objections which have to be faced by anyone aspiring to emulate Trevelyan now, and here we need to consider points
of departure very unlike Wallington Hall and all it stood for.

V

It is a pretty safe bet that the National Trust will never attempt to
acquire the graceless 1950s bungalow on the edge of the Shirley

Hills beyond Croydon in which I grew up. Nor can I believe that some latter-day Pevsner will ever feel obliged to catalogue its few distinctive features ('large "lounge" giving on to pretentiously balustraded "terrace" '). Still, in its way even that taciturn structure communicated some sense of the fortunes of the Collini dynasty: my grandfather had graduated from a respectable terrace in Penge to a solid villa in Anerley, but my father's instinct, typical of those who managed to prosper between the 1930s and the 1950s, was to move further out and acquire as big a plot of land as he could afford.

Perhaps that beshrubbed and greenhouse-cluttered spot could even have stirred, in a more perceptive schoolboy than I was, a sense of the course of recent English history: that ribbon of settlement represented the second wave of suburban expansion, fed by car-ownership rather than the railway, and the choice of site and style of building expressed the values of individualism, privacy, and ruralist nostalgia. In his work for the National Trust, Trevelyan was always trying to limit the damage done to places of natural beauty like the Shirley Hills by the kind of development which represented the fulfilment of my parents' aspirations. But, ironically, his writings may indirectly have helped to feed the appetite that drove such expansion, that blend of middle-class tea-service gentility and the fantasy of graceful country living that craved well-rolled lawns and well-stocked kitchen gardens.

Obviously, Trevelyan's own origins and upbringing stirred *his* historical imagination, but it is a nice question whether such a background might not ultimately be more disabling for the historian of modern Britain than the perspective available from the Surrey bungalow and its like. Trevelyan was able to write with an easy familiarity about the families who had for so long ruled England, and yet in some ways his inherited sense of destiny was a handicap: there were certain kinds of questions it didn't dispose him to ask. For all his implicitly comparative dwelling upon the uniqueness of the island story, English history just seemed so *natural* to him. Moreover, he was not prompted to be critically reflective about the assumptions and concepts he brought to the writing of history. In an important sense, Trevelyan was not an intellectual.

To take Trevelyan as one's model may, for all his virtues, too easily lead one into the cul-de-sac of middle-brow blandness.

Despite his constant swooning over the beauties of English literature, there was a strong philistine streak in him. He couldn't be
doing with cultural innovation, and is reported as having remarked
that 'all novelists since Conrad are cads'. In always speaking with
distaste of 'intellectuals', he was partly following a widespread
pejorative use of the term in the early twentieth century, but he was
also insistently claiming a 'healthier' and more down-to-earth identity for himself.

His historical judgements reflected some of the limitations of
this identity, as, for example, in his view that the Great Reform Act
of 1832 was 'an affair of which Englishmen of all classes and
parties may be proud, and it was a characteristically English business from beginning to end', or again his claim that eighteenth-
century England was marked by 'humanity, moderation, and
cooperation', a society in 'perfectly beautiful equilibrium between
man and nature'. Cannadine does not comment on the culpable
smugness of these remarks, but even allowing for difference of
idiom it is hard to regard their author as that 'master' of the historian's craft which he is here described as being. There was too little
irony and scepticism, too little probing the weak spots of received
descriptions, too little grasp of the structural constraints upon
action of which the historical actors were unaware. Surely the
reviewer of the *English Social History* in *Annales* was right to
complain of its tone of 'complaisance et d'autosatisfaction'.

Cannadine's wholehearted endorsement of Trevelyan's determination to address a wide audience also raises some complex issues.
He presents the alternative as the production of 'articles and monographs [which] have a readership of twenty and a shelf life of five
years', but this is perhaps to let the mind rest too easily in a convenient contrast. The limiting assumptions at work here are embed-
ded in Trevelyan's description of his aim as 'scholarly but readable
history'. The 'but' may be misplaced defensiveness: accurate or
well-informed history is not necessarily any less readable than its
opposite. And in present circumstances, over-insistence on the
priority of being 'readable' may, as I hinted in the Introduction,
concede or gloss over too much. When works of history are praised
by reviewers as 'readable', it can mean that you can keep turning
the pages without having to do any thinking. The real question is
who is doing the reading and for what purpose.

There are, anyway, not just two homogeneous audiences: that is to let the booksellers' categories of 'trade' and 'academic' override the variety and subtlety of the decisions which historians, like other writers, make about tone, allusion, nuance, and so on. Moreover, the size and character of the audience reached by history books these days has at least as much to do with publicity, marketing, and the 'public profile' of the author as with the style of the prose or the number of footnotes. The danger inherent in declaring oneself firmly on the 'readable' side of some supposed division between 'readable' and 'academic' is that one lets literary agents and Sunday reviewers determine one's intellectual ambition.

Aspiring to emulate Trevelyan may also encourage too strong a taste for drama, emphasis, significance. Cannadine himself is a bit of a superlative-junkie: he seems to be afraid that if he goes too long without a 'most important' this or an 'outstanding' that, he may lapse into a coma of academic caution and dullness. But if we worry too much about the presumed difficulty of holding the attention of an easily bored non-professional reader we risk falling into adman's hype. Thus, the preface to this book calls Trevelyan 'one of the towering figures' in the political as well as the intellectual life of twentieth-century Britain. Well, he knew a lot of important people and received a lot of honours, yet he was surely a pretty small tower in political life. Trevelyan's books have often been praised for their 'epic sweep', but 'epic' suggests something more Hollywood than Homer these days, and the fate awaiting the historian too infatuated with 'sweep' is to end up as scriptwriter for *English History: The Movie*. History has its share of wet Monday afternoons when nothing much seems to have happened, and whatever audience is being aimed at, the historian needs a register adequate to the demanding task of describing them, too.

And this is where we come back to the symbolic contrast between the Northumbrian mansion and the Surrey bungalow. Trevelyan could, without artificiality or self-deception, aspire to write the kind of history Macaulay wrote: even allowing for a century of social change, the two men stood in a not dissimilar relation to their society, and the younger man's sense of continuity was not merely piety. The main outlines of *the* 'national story' were never in doubt. But for a professional historian like Cannadine writing at the end of the twentieth century, a distancing self-consciousness cannot help but supervene, and with it should surely come a sense of the contingency of so much that a well-connected

Victorian gentleman took to be natural. In practice, this inescapable reflexivity has contributed to the manifold merits of Cannadine's study, and it would be a pity to let those merits be obscured by polemics about 'readability' or the echoes of tired debates over 'narrative' versus 'analysis'. It is not just historiographical fashion which says there can be no one authoritative narrative of the national past: no historian formed by modern British culture could write it without a kind of wilfulness or bad faith. Nor is this all loss. There may, after all, be good reason to believe that, even leaving aside the disparity in evidence, it is easier for a Cannadine to understand a Trevelyan than vice versa.

VI

In the Preface to his *A Short History of the English People*, first published in 1874, J. R. Green declared that he aimed above all to avoid what, in a phrase which Trevelyan's later usage suggests may have enjoyed greater longevity than the book itself, he called 'mere drum and trumpet history'. He warned his readers that he was therefore omitting much that had been the staple of the old histories—the court intrigues, the wars, the diplomatic manoeuvres, and so on—in order to concentrate instead on those aspects of 'social advance in which we read the history of the nation itself'. Before the book's publication, his close friend and fellow-historian E. A. Freeman had voiced what was to become a common objection to its chosen historiographical strategy when he observed that Green's determinedly unconventional focus meant that his account of the English past 'will have no meaning save to people who already have a knowledge of the matter a good deal above the average'. Attempting to drive his point home, Freeman pointed out that Green's idiosyncratic account of the Reformation, for example, gave the reader no clue to the eventual fate of Thomas, Lord Seymour (who was in fact beheaded in 1549). But Green was as unrepentant about 'Tommy Seymour' as he was unmoved by the general objection: 'His intrigue and death have in my mind no bearing whatever on the general current of our history.'

This exchange between two of the nineteenth century's leading Whig historians hints at some of the further questions that have to be faced by anyone aspiring to chart 'the general current of our

history'. Implicit in it is the contrast between what another school
of history was to call *l'histoire événementielle* and *l'histoire de la
longue durée*, and thereby the contrast between focusing on the
doings of prominent individuals and attending to the lives of the
anonymous mass. And, of course, beneath such decisions can lie
larger philosophical convictions about whether reigns, wars,
discoveries, elections, and so on are to be regarded as the decisive
forces in history or as essentially epiphenomenal, the spume
thrown up by the deeper movement of the tides. But the exchange
about 'the Tommy Seymour problem' also crystallizes the expository difficulties faced by any historian attempting to shift the centre
of historiographical attention away from the political and military
deeds of individuals: does such a history always have to presuppose
some familiarity with the chief chronological landmarks and
events, gleaned at some stage from a different and more orthodox
kind of history book? Is such a history, therefore, inevitably parasitic upon a more conventional narrative account, or does it wholly
replace it, reordering our sense of significance and slicing up the
past in accordance with different criteria and into different units of
measurement?

If Ross McKibbin were to interest himself in the doings of such
'elite' figures as Green and Freeman, he would, presumably, be
wholly of Green's party. For, in *Classes and Cultures: England
1918–1951*, which was initially commissioned to be part of the
New Oxford History of England (to which series I shall return), he
has deliberately set out to give us the history of the English *people*
in his assigned period. And numerically speaking, at least, the
English people were overwhelmingly working class: that class,
broadly defined, accounted for approximately 78 per cent of the
population at the start of the period and declined only to 72 per cent
at its end. The concept of 'the middle class' notoriously presents
delicate definitional problems, but, after a judicious discussion of
these, McKibbin concludes that this class made up approximately
21 per cent of the population at the beginning of the period and
about 28 per cent at its end. During the same period, the upper class
(another tricky category) constituted somewhere between 0.1 per
cent and 0.05 per cent of the population. Experts may wish to take
issue with the details of his calculations, but the overall proportions
are plain. As McKibbin roundly declares: 'England was one of the
most working-class countries in the world'.

In his initial chapters surveying the economic conditions and ways of life of the three classes, he maintains roughly these proportions: his two chapters on the working class, for example, are together about twice as long as the two on the middle class. These surveys are then followed by long chapters on education, on religion, and on sexuality, and then a set of slightly briefer, but still very substantial, chapters on the chief forms of recreation, especially sport, popular music, cinema, and radio. But on all these topics, his concern is with the ways of life shared by the vast majority of the population, making this, in its distribution of attention as well as in its informing sympathies, a determinedly democratic history.

As McKibbin frankly, perhaps proudly, acknowledges at the outset, this involves the omission of two subjects or dimensions of the past that one would normally expect to find in any period survey: 'the first is "formal" politics: high politics, party politics, England's relation with the empire and the rest of the world'; and 'the second . . . is "high culture" ', on which, McKibbin says, so much has been written anyway and in which he professes himself not to be very interested. The reader must, therefore, be prepared for what is not discussed in the (approximately) quarter of a million words devoted to these thirty-three years. For example, Winston Churchill, no mere spear-carrier during this period, is only mentioned three times, and then primarily in connection with such matters as the 1944 Education Act and the guest lists of leading Society hostesses. Clement Attlee appears less often than Marie Stopes. Figures who determined the country's history in other ways, such as J. M. Keynes or Alan Turing, get even more cursory mention, while a whole galaxy of leading intellectual and artistic figures from Rutherford to Wittgenstein and from Eliot to Moore mostly do not appear at all. Emblematic of the pattern of McKibbin's decisions is the fact that the index, in a book dealing with the period around the Second World War, contains the film star Douglass Montgomery but not the Allied commander Bernard Montgomery. McKibbin has been even less tempted than Green by 'mere drum and trumpet history': the military defeats and victories surrounding Britain's 'finest hour' find no place in his book, and the Second World War chiefly figures as the cause of a sharp downturn in working-class unemployment. (It is perhaps only the faintest of ironies that the period which gave us 'the Few' should be so insistently written about in terms of 'the many'.) All of this is by no means necessarily a fault in a book focusing on the working class and its culture, but it can initially be disconcerting if one is expecting a more wide-ranging survey.

The book largely takes the form of a series of descriptive analytical (rather than chronological) accounts of its chosen topics, which cumulatively builds a richly textured picture of life in inter-war England (the period on which it tends to concentrate). McKibbin is excellent on matters as diverse as 'ribbon development' in inter-war housing, the different forms of male and female sociability in the working class, the impact of Hollywood films, the nature and appeal of betting, and much else besides. The book occasionally exhibits some of the characteristics associated with the 'labour history' of a generation or so ago: a similar concern to recover ordinary working people's experience combined with just the hint of frustration that ordinary people did not always sufficiently share the political commitments of the historian; a similar registering of the appalling conditions in which so many lived and worked combined with a faintly pleasurable nostalgia for the world of pigeon-fancying and the works outing. But this is social history that has built upon its labour history base, that has been greatly enriched by feminism (McKibbin is at every point alert to the ways the social, economic, sexual, and cultural life of women tended to differ from that of men), and that has been broadened by the kinds of researches that tend to be published in *Twentieth Century British History* as much as by those that tend to appear in *History Workshop Journal*. The result is expressed in a prose that is relaxed and jargon-free but quietly argumentative: statistics are fully digested into the text, footnotes are used sparingly, amusing snippets and quotations are not wholly eschewed. In all these respects, this is a people's history that many people might actually enjoy reading.

And what view of their society's history during this period does McKibbin present to his readers? It is a view, above all, of how class remained the chief determinant of individuals' life-chances and experience. Whether talking about employment or sociability, about education or family size, about reading habits or sport watching, he over and over again affirms that class proved to be a stronger determinant than region or religion or any number of other variables, rivalled in its structuring power only by gender and then only in certain aspects of life. It is, in addition, a view of an intensely class-conscious and class-antagonistic society, and would-be celebrants of English history as being somehow inherently peaceful and harmonious might ponder his persuasive claim that 'the 1920s experienced more severe class conflict than at any other time in modern British history'. His balance sheet of the class war is that, roughly speaking, in the inter-war period the middle class made marked economic and social gains at the expense chiefly of the working class (and, secondarily, of the upper class), but that in the 1940s the working class registered the biggest gains in their standard of living and their political influence. He emphasizes the huge long-term social and economic impact of the Second World War, which rescued large swathes of the working class from the long night of un- or under-employment and disturbed many of the assumptions of deference and politeness on which pre-war social relations had been based. (He also observes that between 1939 and 1941 'the number of private domestic servants declined by nearly two-thirds and was never to recover'.)

Trevelyan famously described social history as 'history with the politics left out'. McKibbin's is certainly history with the politicians left out, but there can be no doubting that this is a profoundly political book. In so far as it is held together by a set of recurring concerns or motifs (inevitably in some tension with the obligation to survey and synthesize), it is a book about the social and cultural bases of political attitudes and allegiances among the working class and certain sections of the middle class. For the book is, implicitly, concerned to explain why, in such an overwhelmingly working-class society, there was so little effective challenge to the fundamental injustice of the distribution of wealth and power, and why 'those who had authority in 1918 still had it, more or less, in 1951'. As so often, such questions arise from an implicit contrast with a supposed European norm, which breaks through to the surface at one point when McKibbin returns, as he does often, to the fact that 'throughout the interwar years about half the working class voted Conservative . . . [I]n no other country did such a large proportion of the industrial working class vote for a right-of-centre party instead of, as people in the 1920s expected, voting for one committed to the destruction of the status quo.' The implicit strategy of the book is to send us to its analyses of the cultures of work and of leisure, or of family and of film, in search of an answer. Although neither his name nor the concept figures explicitly in the book, the ghost of Gramsci's 'hegemony' walks the battlements at every turn.

A book of this kind inevitably has to struggle with difficulties with which any historian who has ever contemplated writing a period survey can only sympathize. There is, to begin with, the problem of keeping strictly to 'England': only a few pages into the book there begin to be examples from Scotland, and the miners of South Wales figure prominently in his discussion of the working class. These and other cases are not negligently introduced, but they highlight the problem of writing the history of something that during this period was so far from being a separate or wholly distinctive political, economic, or cultural unit. No less challenging is the problem of remaining within one's allotted period when attempting to deal with the *longue durée*. That the division of domestic responsibilities along strict gender lines in working-class households obviously did not begin or even necessarily take a distinctive form in 1918 raises one awkwardness of this kind, while another is provided by McKibbin's decision to illustrate a point about the powerful loyalties of football supporters by referring to the reaction to the loss of almost half of Manchester United's team in the Munich air crash of 1958.

A further familiar if equally intractable problem is knowing what to expect of one's readers and hence what to explain and not to explain. McKibbin's is a book for people familiar with English life and already informed about the main outlines of English history during this period. The equivalent of Green's 'Tommy Seymour problem' is constantly in evidence: the bearers of such proper names as appear in these pages are generally not thought to need introduction, and the writing presupposes that the reader already knows vital things such as who won which elections or roughly what happened when in the Second World War. He remarks in passing that the humour of *The Goon Show* was 'perfectly recognizable to anyone acquainted with English cultural traditions', but that it 'was not and could never have been popular' in the United States. *Mutatis mutandis*, it is possible that similar judgements may apply to McKibbin's book—and for not wholly dissimilar reasons.

The calm intelligence with which McKibbin explores and draws significance out of a wide range of social experience is not the least of the book's attractions, but just occasionally we bump sharply up against the limits of his imaginative sympathy. Anything that smacks of 'elite values', for example, tends to get pretty short shrift. It is good to have a historian who devotes so much space to sport, but the significance of its cultural role is surely not fully understandable, perhaps not even properly describable, without some feel for the emotional and stylistic appeal, operative in many areas of English life, of 'the amateur ideal'. McKibbin chronicles the predictable idiocies of 'Gentlemen' and 'Players' at cricket coming out to bat through separate entrances and so on, but he can only really see snobbery at work in the notion of amateurism. Again, he is very good on the social significance of the inter-war boom in 'listening to the wireless', but he rather understates the achievement of the BBC, and he is perhaps a little too predictably dismissive of the Third Programme. Launched in 1946, this service soon became what one later defender rightly called 'the envy of the world', but McKibbin briskly describes it as 'remorselessly intellectual' and 'heavily biased to continental European "high culture" '. 'Biased' made me wince a little.

Classes and Cultures will presumably not be the runaway commercial success that Green's *Short History* was in the 1870s, as much because of large-scale changes in the marketing and reading of scholarly history as because of differences between the books themselves. But it deserves to be widely read, and for some of the same reasons as Green's work did. It attempts to move closer than much of the conventional historiography of the previous generation to giving us a history of 'the English people'. This cannot, and does not, pretend to be '*the* national past', though it is a substantial part of the nation's past, and one in which a large number of readers can, as it were, recognize themselves and their concerns under the sign of time. How far it is the best way to assist those readers to *understand* that past and their relation to it will necessarily remain a matter of dispute, and here we must return to the origin of the book as a contribution to a series surveying the entire 'national history'.

VII

This volume had been long announced as part of the New Oxford History of England, designed to replace the series edited by G. N.

Clark a generation or two ago, but it seems to have been decided that it would be more appropriate for the book that McKibbin has actually written to stand on its own rather than as an instalment of that History. This is entirely understandable: books have a way of asserting their own identity in the writing, and a book such as *Classes and Cultures* does not need to be either cosseted or corseted by a series format. None the less, it retains the marks of its genesis and clearly aspires to be a history of what its author thinks are the most important characteristics of this period.

Just how radical is McKibbin's departure from earlier models becomes apparent if one returns to the corresponding volume in the original Oxford History of England, A. J. P. Taylor's *English History 1914–1945*, first published in 1965, where one enters a dramatically different historiographical universe. Taylor was, of course, principally a diplomatic and European historian, and this, combined with the slight but hugely consequential difference of his allotted period embracing both world wars, means that military and political history, *l'histoire événementielle*, predominates over social and economic history, though these latter are far from neglected. Churchill's name occurs hundreds of times; Marie Stopes makes one brief appearance.

But one does not have to turn to the historians of a generation ago for a comparison which brings out the distinctive features of McKibbin's enterprise; one can place it next to the recent twentieth-century volume in the new Penguin History of Britain, Peter Clarke's *Hope and Glory: Britain 1900–1990*, published in 1996. Clarke ranges much more widely than McKibbin, not just chronologically but also in his coverage of different kinds of history. Although its backbone is provided by an account of the political responses to the problems thrown up by changes in the economy and Britain's international economic situation, Clarke's book does attempt to provide something like a synthesis, incorporating high and low culture as well as high and low politics and much else besides. And it takes stock of 'the national past' in different terms, too—terms, indeed, among which 'hope' and 'glory' have their proper place. It repudiates the fashionable focus on 'decline', it points to real gains both in the standard of living and in the liberalization of social attitudes, and it ends with a look forward at Britain as politically and culturally as well as geographically a part of Europe. Such a survey inevitably lacks the depth of McKibbin's analysis, but this may be perhaps as near as a contemporary historian can come to doing for the present generation some, at least, of what Trevelyan or Taylor did for theirs.

One of the most interesting questions raised by *Classes and Cultures* is essentially one about the relative causal power of different historical forces and agents. McKibbin wants to write his history in terms of the experience of the vast majority of the population. But what if much of what has determined that experience is actually the work of small elites and even of individuals, whether in politics, science, thought, or whatever? One would neither be returning to old-fashioned political history nor endorsing newly fashionable narrative history by suggesting that the intelligibility of the changes in the circumstances of much working-class life across the period cannot be found within the confines of the history of that class alone.

And this raises in another form the same large and controversial question hinted at earlier: how far is a history which concentrates on the everyday doings of the vast majority of the English population the same thing as the history of 'England' during that period? We can no longer have the confidence of earlier generations that we know how to write the story of 'the national past', partly because of a salutary sensitivity to the historical complexities of the relation between 'the English people' and 'the British state', but partly also because of a heightened awareness of multiple perspectives and of the existence of a range of appropriate expository and narrative techniques. There will no doubt always be a demand for large overviews, and the nation, however defined, will presumably long remain one of the more obvious organizing categories. But by comparison with the histories written by Taylor or Trevelyan, let alone those of Freeman and Green, future narrators of 'our island story' will probably opt for forms that are more essayistic, more frankly selective, more visual, and perhaps in some ways more overtly polemical and self-reflexive as well.

But perhaps Trevelyan should, after all, be allowed the last word. As a reminder of how we should never underestimate our predecessors' awareness of problems we too easily tend to think of as distinctively modern, we may turn to his 1930 review of Lewis Namier's *England in the Age of the American Revolution*. In addition to throwing down a challenge to the 'Whig interpretation of English history', Namier's structural and prosopographical approach represented, as Trevelyan clearly recognized, a sharp contrast to his own cherished narrative style. Whatever other inspiration we may choose to draw from Trevelyan's example in general, we may at least hope to emulate the generosity of his response in this case. 'There are so many different ways in which things happen, or can be truly described as happening', wrote Trevelyan. 'Gibbon's is one, Carlyle's another, Macaulay's a third. Each is true, yet taken by itself each is false, for no one of them is the whole truth. In Mr Namier's narrative things "happen" in yet another new way—the Namier way. And it is one of the truths...'.

2

French Contrasts: From the Panthéon to Poets' Corner

❦

I

Commemoration fever now seems to be endemic in advanced societies. This is clearly both a broader and more international phenomenon than the invocation of the shaping moments of Britain's 'national history' discussed in the previous chapter. Scarcely a month, let alone a year, passes without our being 'reminded' that some round number of years has elapsed since an event or birth or death which we are urged to celebrate. Anxieties about oblivion and forgetting play a part here, as do the needs of the 'culture industries' to create self-justifying activity. But above all, as more and more aspects of our way of life appear to become matters of choice, matters of tapping in the appropriate code on some on-line cultural menu, so we look to the past for given, inherited connections that can help to provide a sense of identity.

Durkheim famously described religion as society worshipping itself. From this perspective, 'heritage' or 'la patrimoine' functions as a modern religion, providing occasions for ritual, reverence, and revivalism. Solidarity across the generations is evoked to paper over the feebleness of the affective bonds which survive in the highly individualistic public sphere of modern societies. Arguably, France has led the way in the elaboration of this cult, as evidenced,

Pierre Nora (ed.), *Les Lieux de Mémoire*, vol. i: *La République*; vols. ii–iv: *La Nation*; vols. v–vii: *Les France* (Gallimard, 1984–92).
Daisy Goodwin (director), *The Trollopians*, BBC 2, 4 October 1993.

for example, by the establishment some years ago of a separate
government department charged with co-ordinating 'les célébra-
tions nationales'. But it has become a Europe-wide phenomenon:
the one new Ministry created by John Major after his election
victory in 1992 was the National Heritage Ministry. Comparisons
between Britain and France have long been a staple of historical
reflection, but perhaps we now also need to compare the different
ways in which what we might call 'public memory' operates in the
two countries. Is it true that, to modify the old adage, they remember these things differently in France?

II

The date is 21 May 1981. The place is the Panthéon, in the heart
of the Latin Quarter. The man is François Mitterand. A photo-
graph reproduced in the first volume of Pierre Nora's *Les Lieux de
Mémoire* shows him ascending the steps with self-conscious
dignity, flanked by a Guard of Honour. What is he doing? On the
face of it, he may seem to be engaging in a piece of public ritual for
which there would be recognizable equivalents in most modern
states: the newly elected President inaugurates his term of office by
paying homage at a shrine which traditionally represents the unity
and continuity of his country. In this case, the frieze over the
portico under which he is entering bears the legend 'Aux Grands
Hommes, la Patrie Reconnaissante', its resonant pomposity apparently expressing the kind of eirenic sentiment appropriate to such
occasions.

But, as Mona Ozouf explains in a captivating essay on the
Panthéon in the same volume, it is not quite as simple as that. In
choosing, against all recent precedent, to hold this ceremony at the
Panthéon, the Fifth Republic's first Socialist President was in fact
reopening an old debate about the sectarian, as opposed to national,
significance of the concept of 'Les Grands Hommes' embodied in
this gloomy monument. The limitations of the Panthéon as an
expression of national consensus can be brought out by contrast
with the ceremony that followed as M. Mitterand crossed to the
Right Bank of the Seine to be received by the then Mayor of Paris,
Jacques Chirac. At the Panthéon, M. Mitterand evoked the spirit of
the place by means of certain key representative figures: Carnot,

embodiment of the citizen army of the Revolution; Hugo, celebrant
of the suffering poor; Jaurès, the people's tribune; Jean Moulin,
martyr of the Resistance—all radical, even populist, figures, a kind
of Popular Front of Heroes, the great names who represent the
claims of the anonymous masses. But across the river the presences
summoned by M. Chirac were Sainte Geneviève and Sainte Jeanne
d'Arc, Henri IV, and Général de Gaulle, none of whom is represented in the Panthéon. On one side, 'les grands hommes'; on the
other, saints and heroes; on the one side the Republic and the
Revolutionary tradition; on the other, the monarchy (including
republican monarchs) and Christianity. The great divide of modern
French history is expressed in the resonances of this contrast. The
paradox of the Panthéon is of a monument intended to embody the
shared patriotic emotions of pride and gratitude, which has
throughout the nearly two hundred years of its history obstinately
retained a deeply partisan significance.

Ozouf's exploration of this paradox concentrates on the early
history of the Panthéon (which, following a *mot* of André Billy, and
evoking the traditionally radical intellectual elite of the nearby rue
d'Ulm, she nicely refers to as 'l'École Normale des Morts'). She
argues persuasively that we need to begin by recovering an understanding of what the cult of 'les grands hommes' meant in the late
eighteenth century. That conception of 'un grand homme' was
intended to exclude monarchs and the great chiefs of the aristocracy and even heroes in the conventional sense; 'un grand homme'
was likely, rather, to be a citizen of the Republic of Letters, a figure
whose labours were solitary and extended, but whose achievements
were recognized by his peers and who could be admitted to that
timeless club whose cachet transcended even that of the most aristocratic of earthly institutions. Thus, as Ozouf points out, it was
easy for the Revolution to appropriate this conception as
'naturellement démocratique'; it represented the apotheosis of the
ideal of 'la carrière ouverte aux talents'. But how to commemorate
such figures? The eighteenth century had engaged in a prolonged
debate about 'l'efficacité pédagogique relative des différentes
formes d'expression', but for the purposes of commemorating 'les
grands hommes' a privileged place came to be assigned to the
statue, the pre-eminent art of 'éducation civique'. Ozouf touches
interestingly on the way a recognizably Enlightenment sensibility
was expressed in the preference for a lifelike statue, which creates

an eternal presence, with the Great Man in characteristic pose, as against a tomb or urn or other non-representational block of stone which serves as a conventional prompt to pious memory.

The eighteenth century's deliberations about establishing an 'Élysée visible' were overtaken by the Revolution, so that when the idea was once more revived in 1791 and the existing church of Sainte Geneviève was selected for the purpose, the conception of *who* was to be carved into the memory naturally took a yet more radical turn. The decision to place Mirabeau, the first of the leading revolutionaries to die, among the pedestalled luminaries signalled that the Panthéon was about to become quite explicitly a monument to the Revolution (including those retrospectively press-ganged into its ranks like Voltaire and, improbably, Descartes). By linking the immortals of the Revolution not just to their putative French predecessors but to their ancient forebears—the self-conscious classicizing of the Revolution at one point led to the proposal to costume the statues, with Mirabeau 'en Demosthène', and so on—the Panthéon could become, as Ozouf puts it, 'le lieu d'une Révolution installée, éternisée . . . qui a oublié, ou voulu oublier, son histoire'.

Ozouf then gives an elegant sketch of the ways in which the political complexion and historical self-description of each of the succeeding regimes in the nineteenth century were reflected in their handling of this sensitive site. The Revolution itself began the business by instituting rituals of 'dépanthéonisation' for those who were no longer ideologically correct: appropriately, the first to suffer in this way was Mirabeau, whose statue left by a side door as Marat's was carried in solemn procession through the main entrance. Almost from the start, therefore, what had been conceived as a shrine to that impartial harmony of qualities epitomized by 'les grands hommes' was exploited to reinforce the legitimacy of a particular regime or faction, and where the eighteenth century had conceived of eternity as the appropriate time-frame for these exemplars of the human spirit, in practice many of the statues enjoyed a rather shorter life-span. Under Napoleon, the Panthéon reverted to being a Catholic church but also retained its role as a temple of national worthies; under the Restoration, it became simply a church again, and the frieze reverted to bearing an ecclesiastical inscription in Latin. The July Monarchy restored both civic inscription and secular function, but, by now predictably, the

Second Empire removed both. As in so many domains of French
life, the Third Republic was the decisive period for the stabilization
(or, more often, creation) of the official version of the memory of
'La République radicale'. The building itself was, as it were
'pantheonized' by being chosen as the setting for the massive
display of republican theatre that was the funeral of Victor Hugo
in 1885 (the subject of an interesting essay in its own right in the
first volume of *Les Lieux de Mémoire*); this provided the occasion
for reverting to the inscription 'Aux Grands Hommes', since when
the form and function of the building have not substantially
changed.

   Some of the deep divisions within French society at the turn of
the century continued to disturb its inmates, of course. In 1889 the
family of the impeccably revolutionary general Hoche refused to let
him be pantheonized on the grounds that it was unthinkable that
he could lie in peace next to the remains of the opportunistically
Bonapartist general Carnot; in 1908 the descendants of Lannes
were so outraged by the pantheonization of Zola, that they
demanded the right to carry the ashes of their ancestor off to lie
amidst more respectable company in Montmartre cemetery, and so
on. These wrangles have become less common in the twentieth
century, barring a notably heated controversy at the time of the
Liberation, but even so it is clear that the gathering of 'grands
hommes' on the hill of Sainte Geneviève still does not constitute
any kind of neutral or comprehensive national symbol. The radical
resonances of its identity as 'l'École Normale des Morts' can only
have been reinforced by the pointed pilgrimage of the Socialist
President.

   However, as Ozouf observes in her conclusion, it is extremely
unlikely that the Panthéon will henceforth engage our political
emotions in the way it did those of earlier generations. This is
partly, she suggests, because we have become more sceptical about
the whole notion of the 'grand homme' who in his blameless
labours for human welfare embodies those universal qualities of
the human spirit which will ineluctably lead to a better society. But
it is even more because we no longer believe in the educative power
of such public monuments. The material expression of the cult of
'les grands hommes' presupposed a faith in 'la solidarité spontanée
de l'esthétique et de la morale, dans la nécessaire docilité du
publique à la leçon des sens et dans l'éfficacité d'un art pédagogue'.

With the decline of this conviction, the Panthéon is becoming more and more a memorial to memory itself; the collective ardour which responded to the propaganda of stone has cooled, and, in Gibbonian vein, one observes that its chill, gloomy spaces are now chiefly disturbed by the uncomprehending chatter of citizens of Atlanta and Osaka.

III

I have dwelt so long on this one essay not only because it is a very fine piece of historical writing on an interesting subject, but also because so many of the contributions to the seven large volumes of *Les Lieux de Mémoire* are, like Ozouf's, 'essays' in the best sense, extended meditations or explorations that are not easily reducible to a briefly stated argument. The character of the whole collection is therefore probably better represented by attempting to convey something of the intellectual subtlety and cultural range of one particular piece rather than by providing a series of one-sentence summaries. But the variety and richness of these volumes also have to be signalled, however baldly.

To begin with, the sheer scale of the enterprise is impressive. Seven large volumes, over 5,500 pages, more than 1,100 illustrations, 134 essays, some 110 contributors, among them practically all of the leading French historians. Then, the fine quality of design and production puts most British publishers to shame, or would if they seemed at all susceptible to that emotion. On a broader front, the very existence of these volumes, bulging with writing by distinguished scholars that has neither withdrawn into professional inaccessibility nor, with one or two exceptions, become the willing victim of trend and jargon, might be taken as a sign of a notable vitality in this area of French intellectual life, the reports of whose death have been greatly exaggerated following the nearly simultaneous disappearance of the famous *maîtres à penser* of the 1960s and 1970s. In more immediate terms, the credit for this impressive enterprise belongs to Pierre Nora, who is a walking *conjoncture culturelle* in himself. In his professional role as editorial director at the house of Gallimard he has been responsible for initiating and overseeing the whole project, while, wearing his hat as a trained historian and directeur d'études at the École des Hautes Études en

Sciences Sociales, he has also contributed three learned essays to
these volumes as well as an elegant introduction and conclusion to
each part (lest time should hang heavy on his hands he is also editor
of the general cultural review *Le Débat*).

In one respect, the title of this collection may give a misleading
impression of the range of its contents (and clearly poses problems
for an English translation). Neither term should be taken too literally. The Panthéon, it is true, is a 'site' in the literal sense, and so
are 'Le Mur des Fédérés' (treated with great brio by Madeleine
Réberioux), 'Les Monuments aux morts' (Antoine Prost), 'Reims,
ville du sacre' (Jacques le Goff), and several others. But the majority of the essays deal with symbols, moments, or books which are
not historical monuments in this literal sense. In the first volume,
there are fascinating pieces on, for example, the Tricoleur (Raoul
Girardet), 'La Marseillaise' (Michel Vovelle), and 'Les Centenaires
de Voltaire et de Rousseau' (Jean-Marie Gulemot and Eric Walter),
while the three volumes making up *La Nation* range even more
widely (the subject does not, after all, bring with it the same
chronological constraints as does *La République*), embracing
pieces on representations of the countryside, conceptions of the
national boundaries, ideas of the national heritage, expressions of
the taste for glory, embodiments of the tyranny of the word, and so
on.

Nor should 'memory' be construed too narrowly, especially
since Nora explains in his introduction to the collection that as
used here it goes beyond mere 'recollection' and includes 'forgetting' also. 'Memory' in this sense is not to be equated with
'history', which is something more precise and locatable, grounded
in evidence and subject to correction: memory as treated here is
more a matter of associations, allusions, symbols. It is the collective semi-consciousness. It is popular to the extent that it is part of
a common culture, not something that is the arcane preserve of a
professional group; but it is far from popular in the sense in which
the term 'popular culture' is used now (it may be another interesting sign of the way the intellectual breeze is blowing among French
historians that so much of this collection is devoted to what, in
English-speaking countries, has often been referred to in recent
years, with pejorative intent, as 'high culture'). So the terms of the
title ought rather to suggest a very heterogeneous set of sources of
resonance, rather than an inventory of historic monuments. At the

same time, this does not mean that these volumes contain any very sustained inquiry into the ways the past operates in the consciousness of the present; this is not a survey of contemporary attitudes. Instead, they offer a series of historical explorations of the ramifications of the major (and some of the minor) evocations of the past in French life, where that past includes the ways in which the symbols involved have come to have an effective reality of their own.

In his introduction to the volumes on *La Nation,* Nora makes some pretty large claims for the novelty and significance of the kind of 'history of symbolism' represented here. In fact, the approaches preferred by most of his contributors will seem perfectly familiar to Anglo-Saxon cultural and intellectual historians (and are none the worse for that); the greatest novelty lies in the highly imaginative selection of topics and their juxtaposition, and in the perceptiveness of the contributors. In another respect, these volumes may be seen as symptomatic of a more general reassertion of the independence of the 'political' at the expense of the 'social' in French intellectual life: in their central themes, such as questions of political identity and nation-building, no less than in their unapologetic concentration on the activities of exceptionally articulate members of the educated class, these volumes would probably have been disparaged as old-fashioned fifteen or twenty years ago. As Nora remarks with tangible satisfaction: 'L'histoire "totale" s'était définie contre l'histoire politique et son étroitesse. Et voici que le politique resurgit comme l'instrument d'une histoire plus englobante encore.'

A recurring motif of the collection is the way in which institutions or symbols which are sectarian in their origins become in time national possessions. This is particularly well brought out in the first volume, since of course initially, and recurrently through the nineteenth century, the republican tradition represented but one half of a divided nation. However, the opening decades of the Third Republic saw a concerted and in some ways successful attempt to identify republicanism with Frenchness itself, and the years between 1875 and 1895 provide the effective chronological focus of this volume. The early Third Republic (sometimes referred to as 'La République des Professeurs') was a self-consciously pedagogic regime, attentive to the variety of ways of teaching the inhabitants of the Hexagon that they were French and that they were citizens, two novel notions that could still, as has been amply demonstrated by the work of Eugen Weber and Theodore Zeldin, be regarded with suspicion by peasants in the more remote parts of the country. At a symbolic level, the years between the centenary of the deaths of Voltaire and Rousseau in 1878 and the anniversary of the Revolution in 1889 were marked by several significant steps in the Republic's consolidation of its position. In 1879 'La Marseillaise' became the national anthem, in 1880 the Fourteenth of July was decreed to be 'La Fête de la Nation' and the seat of Parliament was transferred from Versailles to Paris, and so on.

This process of the installation of the heritage of the Revolution as the essence of the national tradition is illuminated from an unusual angle in the essay on the centenaries of Voltaire and Rousseau. In 1878, with the new Republic's anticlerical campaign gathering momentum, Voltaire still evoked violently partisan feelings. It is also illustrative of belief in 'the power of the word', another recurrent theme of these volumes, that there was an official proposal to distribute free copies of his selected works, on the grounds that 'quand il y a un Voltaire dans chaque famille, les églises se videront'. His centenary was turned into a republican carnival, with Victor Hugo wheeled out to claim that the Enlightenment and the Revolution represented the true France; Catholics held counter-celebrations in memory of Jeanne d'Arc.

Thereafter, however, as Goulemot and Walter bring out splendidly in their essay, the sectarian exploitation of both Voltaire and Rousseau tended to give way to a more consensual invocation of their national status as great writers, 'magiciens de la langue, investi . . . de la mission d'incarner face au monde le génie universel de la France'. By 1912, the bicentenary of Rousseau's birth, all parties except Action Française could join in the government-led homage to this hero of 'La Culture Française', and when in 1944 the Liberation coincided with the 250th anniversary of Voltaire's birth, the celebrations drew enthusiastic support not only from all shades of political opinion but also from self-conscious representatives of the national heritage such as the Bibliothèque Nationale and the Comédie Française. As Goulemot and Walter observe: 'Au prix de mille ambiguités, l'unanimité de la célébration veut dire la patrie retrouvée et restaurée, les Français réunis et réinscrits, par l'héritage littéraire, dans une nation fraternelle'.

In his conclusion to the first volume, Nora ruminates interestingly on the outcome of this process. Once the point had been reached where a conservative general supported by a right-wing party could present himself as the living embodiment of 'La République', it became harder to think of 'La République radicale' as still having any effective mobilizing power in the party-political contest. The failure of Vichy may have discredited the anti-republican tradition for good. Those overlapping totalities of State, Nation, and Society all now seem viable and sufficient in their own right, and the presence of 'La République' in the consciousness of the citizen of modern France, concludes Nora, is above all as 'un lieu de mémoire'. Although this is true enough in one sense, it is a claim which perhaps needs to be treated a little sceptically or even to be seen as a polemical move in itself. While it is true that the republic is no longer faced with a serious challenge from any rival *form* of polity, the capacity of the republican *idea* and its history to stir the passions still seems to the outsider to retain a remarkable vitality. The bicentenary of the Revolution remained, after all, as I remarked in the previous chapter, a highly charged and politically contested event.

For all kinds of reasons, 'La Nation', unlike 'La République', can hardly be expected to disappear by assimilation, not least because it was both more and less than a doctrine or regime in the first place. Inevitably, an exploration of its 'sites of memory' will be more diffuse, as is also indicated by its expansion into three stout tomes. But although these volumes do not have such a definite organizing theme as their predecessor, it is noticeable that they, too, have an unannounced chronological focus. Where the essays in the previous volume constantly return to the early years of the Third Republic, here they go back time and again to the Restoration and the July Monarchy. The modern idea of the French nation was largely a creation of the Romantic enthusiasms of the historiography of the 1820s and 1830s. Of the leading historians of that period, only Augustin Thierry receives a separate essay to himself; the omission of his more prominent rivals, Guizot and Michelet, is defended on the grounds that their presence in these volumes is pervasive. Nora notes with satisfaction that Guizot 'reprend ici sa figure centrale de grand organisateur de la mémoire', while Michelet, more extravagantly still, is hailed as 'l'âme' of the whole book, a figure 'qui transcende tout lieu de mémoire possible'. In this, as well as in some less direct ways, these volumes may reflect and contribute to the largely favourable revaluation of the liberal historians and political theorists of this period which seems to be taking place in French intellectual life at the moment.

For all the variety of topics and treatment in these volumes, the standard still seems to be remarkably high and the choice of topics is, if anything, even more admirably imaginative than in the first volume: the almost ritualized pattern of 'La Visite au Grand Ecrivain', for example, yields some interesting material for Olivier Nora. Another far from obvious topic is treated in Jean-François Sirinelli's essay on the institution known as 'La Khâgne', the class, usually at one of the crack Parisian *lycées*, of an additional year or two's study after the Baccalauréat for that small group preparing for the competitive entrance examination for l'École Normale Supérieure or other *grandes écoles*. Sirinelli makes many interesting suggestions about the influence of this formative experience on the French intellectual elite, not least in its transmission of a very conservative notion of 'culture générale' against which so much of the self-conscious iconoclasm of recent years can be seen as a reaction.

IV

In his conclusion to the last of these volumes, Nora remarks that it would require comparisons with the formation of the national memory in other countries really to bring out the distinctiveness of the French experience. Certainly, the English reader is bound to reflect that they do indeed remember these things differently in France. As one starts to imagine what a comparable collection by English historians would look like (apart from scruffier and dearer), some obvious contrasts leap to the mind's eye. Not only, of course, could there be no equivalent volume to that on 'La République', but it is hard to see what might be substituted in the English case. 'The Kingdom' would be pretty vacuous for the parallel period of modern history: there would be plenty of ceremonial and symbolism to study (much of it, as has been recently pointed out, invented in the late nineteenth century), but even though the monarchy has enjoyed an increasingly wide popularity in this century, it could not be said that English life has been significantly informed by 'monarchical values'. Some unwieldy abstraction like 'the representative system' might come a bit nearer the mark: it can boast a stirringly long pedigree, some great historical moments, a bit of civic ritual, and a few resonant slogans, as well as that great spur to historical awareness, a current decline. Yet it would all seem a bit strained: the anniversary of the passing of the Great Reform Bill is an unlikely candidate for a national holiday, and old ballot boxes make dull shrines.

Some may find in this further evidence to support the now-familiar complaint that in Britain we suffer from what might be called a 'National Trust' model of political memory, which muffles the sound of conflicts in our political history by admitting only those episodes and individuals that can be spoken of with the proper Dimbleby-in-the-Abbey reverence (see the discussion in Chapter 1). More fundamentally, one is led back to the unoriginal conclusion that many of these political symbols retain a greater resonance in France than in Britain because French history has been so much more overtly and fundamentally divided than that of Britain in the last two centuries. As Nora nicely observes: 'Le paradoxe de l'histoire nationale française a été de localiser sa continuité essentielle dans ce qui, par nature, est le moins continu, la politique'. So, where Marianne is on the barricades, an exposed nipple pointing the way to a contested future, Britannia is sedately seated, perhaps a co-opted member of some ad hoc committee. We exaggerate the contrast, however, by concentrating on political topics: one could imagine a no less rich collection of essays on the sources of the English 'national memory' by shifting the attention to literature or the countryside or even sport.

Although the historical constitution and symbolic expression of our sense of national identity is a subject that has been receiving increased scholarly attention just recently, nothing on this scale has yet been attempted for England. Some very suggestive comparative points were made in the collection edited by Eric Hobsbawm and Terence Ranger, *The Invention of Tradition*, and, from a quite different perspective, the literary representation of England in the twentieth century is explored in David Gervais's *Literary Englands*. But although both Patrick Wright's *On Living in an Old Country* and *Englishness: Politics and Culture 1880–1920*, edited by Robert Colls and Philip Dodd, contain much of interest, for the most part both of these books seem too preoccupied with the Marxisant project of 'unmasking' the ways in which ideas and symbols of national identity are essentially ideological forms designed to shore up the position of the dominant class. By comparison, Nora's contributors seem much more flexible and sensitive in their response to the plurality of meanings and uses involved.

This comparison may seem to conjure up the teasing picture, itself a stimulus to flexibility in dealing with the supposedly characteristic intellectual styles of the two societies, of a historian a hundred years hence using all these books to illustrate some by-then familiar stereotypes about the contrast between the sceptical, untheoretical French and the dogmatic, politically over-excited English. But, as ever, things are not that simple, and in particular we have to recognize that for all the disinterested or even elegiac tone in which the essays in *Les Lieux de Mémoire* treat some of the most fundamental divisions in French history, they represent further instalments in a continuing debate, and not its closure. After all, it *was* the Panthéon that M. Mitterand chose to visit: *la lutte continue.*

V

When the first four volumes of Pierre Nora's *Les Lieux de Mémoire* appeared in 1984 and 1986, they were in constant danger of being recruited to the craze for commemoration that I referred to earlier. Some reviewers in France said that Nora was animated by nostalgia or was casting himself as a latter-day Michelet attempting to stir up a kind of nationalist piety. And since then, the term 'lieu de mémoire' itself has been accorded official recognition: not only has it entered the dictionary, but the 'Loi de 1913' concerning the preservation of historical monuments has been modified to allow classification under the heading 'lieux de mémoire'.

Reading those first volumes with an outsider's eye, their sophistication and professional coolness seemed to resist rather than encourage the all-engulfing stream of 'patrimoinialisation'. The subsequent appearance of the final three sumptuous volumes on *Les France* should have made clear even to the most obsessive centenary-hunters that Nora always intended his project to be an antidote to celebration mania rather than a contribution to it. Indeed, I imagine that for Nora the kiss of death would have been the kiss bestowed by Jack Lang, the then Minister of Culture, had he been awarding him a medal 'pour la patrimoine'.

For, although Nora has been portrayed as a modern Lavisse, organizing his generation of historians in the service of civic duty, all of this overlooks another strand in his allegiances, one which stretches back, via Foucault, to Lavisse's contemporary in the late nineteenth century, Nietzsche. This suggestion may puzzle those who do not associate the offices of Gallimard with experiments in radical 'immoralism', but the work which Nora set his pack of historians to do bears a clear resemblance to Nietzsche's characteristic enterprise of 'genealogy', of uncovering that hidden history through which our modern pieties and truisms acquired their aura of timeless naturalness. In Nora's hands, history is as much a means of corrosion as of construction. By showing, with unchallengeable scholarly authority, how the 'eternal' symbols of Frenchness have their own history, in which contingency, self-interest, and sheer misunderstanding have their part, these volumes inevitably relativize the cherished expressions of national identity even as they appear to burnish them for service in a new century.

In this sense, Nora is at best an ambivalent rather than a whole-hearted believer in the cult of a distinctive 'Frenchness'. Certainly, the concern here is passionately hexagonal, and in his own elegant opening and closing essays in the final set of volumes he takes the temperature of the national culture with an attentiveness to minute variations of symptoms which borders on love. Moreover, the informing conception of that culture is in some ways quite traditional—it is, for example, literary and philosophical rather than scientific and technological. But at the same time, Nora is a professional sceptic, delighting in the ironies by which the unforeseen and the inappropriate become transmuted into the universal and the representative.

These volumes are not, therefore, a great national parade, orchestrated by a more learned Goude: they are rather a series of expertly conducted cross-examinations which reveal that France has not always been telling the truth about its past behaviour. They leave their readers vastly better informed about the ways in which 'memory' has become lodged in certain buildings or writers or concepts, and they may stir that most valuable form of civic curiosity, the desire to see behind the official regalia of national identity. But it is no part of their purpose to produce romantic patriots or edified citizens.

The modernity of the enterprise is evident in another way. This is a history of France for an age that does not believe there can be *one* 'history', *one* narrative, *one* perspective which has a monopoly on truth. It may seem strange to describe as 'modest' a project that now fills seven fat volumes, but there is an epistemological modesty here that marks a decisive break with the great systems of even the recent *maîtres à penser*. This is 'post-everything' history. The choice of topics bespeaks a creative historical imagination at work, but the reader is deliberately left free to rearrange the pieces to highlight different connections. *Les Lieux de Mémoire* is not the testament of a school, still less of a sect: there is an essential open-ness in *histoire à la bricolo-Norasque*.

Inevitably, this means the contents of the final three volumes can at first appear miscellaneous, perhaps even more so than those of their predecessors: sixty-four essays on an engagingly diverse range of subjects—'Francs et Gaulois', 'Le Département', 'La Galanterie', '*L'Histoire de la langue française* de Ferdinand Brunot', 'Vézelay', 'Liberté, Égalité, Fraternité'. In addition, one or two of the players seem to have followed a different tempo from that set by the *chef d'orchestre* or to have played flat. But overall, what is surprising is not the occasional raggedness but the sustained ensemble playing. And without at all descending into jargon or methodological sectarianism, nearly all the contributors seem to have been touched by the Nietzschean as well as the Lavissian spirit of the enterprise.

One sees this, for example, in the brilliant analysis by Antoine Compagnon of the process by which Proust, initially marginalized as the snobbish, Jewish, homosexual author of self-indulgent, inac-cessible novels, emerged as the pinnacle, the very model, of French literature itself. (Compagnon has some shrewd remarks here about Proust as the figure onto whom are projected collective fantasies about 'becoming a writer'.) Or again, this same probing, unsenti-mental spirit is evident in the very learned and nicely ironic essay on 'Descartes' by François Azouvi, tracing the steps by which the man who spent nearly his entire writing career in Holland, at odds with the dominant forces of official French intellectual life, became not just the chief philosophical glory of France, but the incarnation of Frenchness itself, the presiding spirit of 'un peuple cartésien'. (At this point, readers may submit themselves to a little test in their knowledge of French 'national memory': as I remarked earlier, the Revolution proposed to install the remains of Descartes, Voltaire, and Rousseau in the Panthéon—which of them is not there?)

These and similarly authoritative essays on 'La Droite et la Gauche' by Marcel Gauchet or on 'Paris-province' by Alain Corbin are minor masterpieces in the historical analysis of how symbols and traditions establish themselves. The effect of such sober, detailed analyses is bound to be demystifying rather than celebratory. And of course, the more the analysis reveals the mechanisms by which 'lieux de mémoire' are created, the more the French experience is seen to partake of a larger pattern. Indeed, one of the least obvious forms of national pride which these volumes might excite is the awareness of what a stimulus and model they provide for historians in other countries to explore their own national memory. Nora's founding notion of a 'lieu de mémoire' has proved fertile, revitalizing the understanding of the apparently familiar, and re-directing attention, like any successful historiographical concept, to otherwise neglected topics or unrecognized evidence. Debate will doubtless continue over whether there is something distinctive about the presence of the past in contemporary France or whether the conflicts and divisions of French history have deposited a sediment of allusion and residue not matched by other countries. But there can be no question that, with the completion of these volumes, France can now boast the most imaginative and stimulating attempt to capture the processes through which a complex national identity is formed and transmitted.

VI

England, as I suggested earlier, is the country for which it would, at first glance, seem easiest to compile an inventory of 'lieux de mémoire' that could attempt to rival the richness and significance of the seven volumes assembled by Pierre Nora. Obviously, any complex and long-established society could yield a certain amount of comparable material, but the French volumes make clear that it requires a historically rare conjunction of elements for the cultural landscape to be so crowded with reminders of the action of the past in the present. An exceptional degree of political continuity and territorial stability is one precondition; a long habit of collective self-consciousness about the world-historical significance of one's national history is another; and the survival of remarkably complete and detailed documentary records stretching back through the centuries is a third. In the absence of these conditions, the existence of certain symbols and monuments deriving from earlier periods in a given geographical region may possess an anti-quarian or touristic interest without generating that animating power, that intricate layering of association and resonance, of a genuine 'lieu de mémoire'.

No less comparable has been the French and English (though here one needs to insist on 'British') experience of declining into, at best, second-rank powers in the twentieth century. In both coun-tries the writing of what was once confidently called 'the national story' has been affected by similar factors—the loss of empire, the continuing illusion of an independent world role, intractable economic and social problems, the shock of immigration, and so on. They both now stand as awkward members of a larger Europe (Britain far more awkward than France, to be sure), without a distinctive world-historical mission, reduced to investing national-ist emotion in trade figures, sporting records, and the marketing of 'heritage'. At this level of analysis, the similarities between these two endlessly contrasted societies may well seem by the end of the twentieth century to be more significant than the differences.

However, although these circumstances may have produced a comparable obsession with 'celebration' and 'patrimoine', there perhaps remain instructive contrasts when one focuses on the notion of a 'lieu de mémoire' itself. That is to say, the functioning of 'memory' in Nora's sense requires there to be something in the present that keeps alive or confers significance on something in the past other than its sheer pastness. Once something becomes simply the object of nostalgia, or is self-consciously cherished as an element of 'heritage', it ceases to function as an active 'lieu de mémoire'. In this respect, the divisions of France's political history have done more than any other single factor to keep these 'lieux' alive. Those great structuring divisions of royalist and republican, Left and Right, and so on, were so fundamental to modern French culture that few things could be neutral or indifferent; for two centuries now, there have always been two names for the village square just as there have always been two histories of the Revolution. For these reasons, it was inevitable that the Third Republic should bulk so large in Nora's volumes (and perhaps also in his affections, dare one guess?): rarely can a modern state have seen such a sustained and wide-ranging attempt to use 'memory' as the chief instrument with which to fashion its ideal citizens. But the very conception of *Les Lieux de Mémoire* indicates that the Owl of Minerva is following its usual flight schedule: only because the living, conflict-fed vitality has for some time been ebbing away from these divisions and their power in French public life could these volumes even have been contemplated.

English history, at least since the end of the seventeenth century, has been marked by much greater apparent continuity and agreement (the gap between the appearance and the reality is what keeps historians in business). Hence Nora's *mot* 'les Anglais ont la tradition, nous avons la mémoire'. A tradition, in this sense, is something lived in, not something retrieved: it presumes an intimate, unbroken contact with a past, but the constant adaptation which is vital to its continuation requires an element of amnesia. The essence of tradition is to confer the legitimacy of continuity on what is in practice always changing; the essence of memory is the willed attempt to recover and fix a source of significance which is perceived to be in danger of being forgotten. To this extent, memory presupposes discontinuity even as it attempts to establish persistence over time. But the remembered element from the past has, once recovered, to possess some animating significance in the present: in this respect, an inventory of 'lieux de mémoire' is inevitably an exploration of the needs, disputes, and imaginings of the present.

This contrast can be drawn too sharply, but perhaps a more subtle way to explore the differences involved may be to consider degrees of explicitness. In the pure (if historically rare) notion of tradition, action is guided by precedent without this basis requiring any principled defence. One of the things that threatens to bring an end to a living tradition is the growth of self-consciousness: once a community's actions are carried out *because* there is an explicit commitment to preserving and extending the tradition (as opposed simply to adapting successful past practices to new circumstances), we are beginning to encounter the reflexiveness characteristic of memory. Implicitness also allows flexibility: if the relevant element of the past is etched too sharply, the ensuing stages of the practice become rigid and brittle, no longer capable of being adapted and thereby half-forgotten. Roughly speaking, the dealings of the British parliament in the two subsequent centuries with the political and religious settlement of 1689 could be said to be a case of 'tradition'; the relations right up to the present of both communities in Ulster to the events of 1689–90 are rather an example of the power, and dangers, of 'memory'.

Conversely, one could say that the euthanasia of a 'lieu de mémoire' is brought about by a decline of self-consciousness, in the sense that present doings no longer seem so charged with *this* rather than with *that* inherited meaning, and hence that there is no longer a need to parade one's paternity and affiliations so insistently. A society that was entirely harmonious, confident, and future-orientated would have no use for 'lieux de mémoire': the chief role of relics from the past would be as measuring-sticks of the progress that had been made. Thus, for a rich array of real 'lieux de mémoire' to operate at full power, a society needs, in addition to the general preconditions mentioned earlier, a combination of sustained and even repetitive discord and unsparingly reflexive explicitness—a combination strikingly present in France for almost two centuries after the Revolution, but less obviously characteristic of English history during that period.

However, although English history in the modern period may not have structured itself around the same kinds of explicit and enduring cleavages as French history, there is (as I argue in other essays in this book) none the less a large element of myth in the idea of a supple tradition being wisely adapted so as constantly to renew a fundamental national consensus. Indeed, in the twentieth century this idea of tradition—the heart of what has been called 'the Whig interpretation of English history'—has itself become an ideological resource, summoned up when needed to disguise some of the deep and unresolved conflicts that have increasingly surfaced. Just as in recent years many of the familiar polarities of French political life have started to lose their force, so, moving in the opposite direction, the allegedly consensual and gradualist nature of English political life has given way to more overt and more ideological conflict. To adapt Nora's *mot*, one could say, rather, that 'les Anglais ont la mémoire de la tradition, nous avons la tradition de la mémoire'.

Indeed, nowhere is the fiction of a continuous, unchanging identity more blatant than in the very name of the entity which has supposedly endured and triumphed through the centuries. (This was amusingly illustrated in a letter from the editor of a French journal inviting me to write an essay on this topic: I assume that no

significant distinction was intended by the fact that two of the
sentences described the requested article as being about 'l'Angleterre'
while in several other places the reference was to 'Grande-Bretagne'.)
Historically, 'England' was the name of a kingdom which in the
course of the Middle Ages also came to rule a subject people in
Wales; in 1603 the accession of James VI of Scotland to the throne
of England gave the two kingdoms the same crown. In the mid-
seventeenth century the Cromwellian protectorate showed it could
rival the Elizabethan monarchy in the severity with which it tried to
subjugate and absorb the neighbouring island of Ireland. In 1707, by
the Act of Union, England and Scotland became subject to the same
Parliament, and from a further act in 1800 Ireland, too, was
governed from Westminster. Meanwhile, the throne of this expanding kingdom had been occupied by some very un-English people: the
Glorious Revolution of 1689 saw a Dutchman, William of Orange,
installed on the throne, and then in 1714 it was occupied by a
German prince, George of Hanover, who did not even speak English.
The state which eventually conquered or otherwise assumed control
of approximately a quarter of the land surface of the globe changed
its title and character more than once, but after the Irish Free State
was granted independence in 1922 following a bloody civil war, the
correct title of the state whose passport I carry has been 'The United
Kingdom of Great Britain and Northern Ireland' (I am thus described
as a British citizen, though technically I am not a citizen but a
'subject' of the Queen).

Obviously, 'England' has always been the dominant element in
these various polities, but it is an interesting question how far a
series of volumes comparable to Nora's ought to confine themselves to 'England' rather than to 'Great Britain' (or 'the United
Kingdom' or 'the British Isles' or one of the other titles used for
different purposes). Certainly, as I shall emphasize below, part of
the conjuring trick of modern British history has been to attempt to
pass off 'English culture' as though it were a common possession of
all the inhabitants of the British Isles. Rather than engage with this
contested and tangled issue here, I shall (as I explained in the
Introduction) continue to confine myself as far as possible to
speaking of 'England', even though I realize that, as throughout
much of British history, many readers will unconsciously expand
this to refer to the larger and more heterogeneous entity of which
England has been the dominant part.

The party game of selecting symbols of national memory in England and contrasting them with their French equivalents is interminable. Imagine, for example, some possible chapter headings in the section in the comparable volumes which would correspond to Nora's 'Singularités': gardening, cricket, pubs, roast beef, 'fair play', and so on. But these are the facile contrasts, the commonplaces of the tourist guide's patter. It may, instead, be more interesting and revealing to examine in detail a topic which is beyond question at the heart of the operation of 'mémoire' in the French case and where the comparison with England may be correspondingly close and revealing, namely the lodging of nationalist emotion in the supposedly unchallengeable primacy of the nation's literature. This will inevitably lead us back to the latter part of the nineteenth century, that great period of the deliberate consolidation of the national cultural identity of so many European states. But our journey, like all attempts to uncover the working of 'mémoire' in Nora's sense, must begin in the present.

VII

At five o'clock in the afternoon of 25 March 1993 in a church in London, a group of distinguished people listened to a man reading a short address about the author of several well-known novels. Having concluded the reading, the man stepped forward and unveiled a memorial stone to the novelist.

What was happening in this scene? The church was no ordinary church: the little ceremony took place in the South Transept of Westminster Abbey, the spot known as Poets' Corner. And the reader was no ordinary reader: he was John Major, the British Prime Minister. Was this, therefore, a case of a state bestowing official recognition on a recently dead writer and intellectual who had adorned the public life of the country? It was and was not, and both the positive and the negative illustrate some interesting themes in the contemporary functioning of the English national memory.

The author being commemorated by this ceremony was Anthony Trollope. Trollope did not die in 1993 but in 1882 (see the discussion of his life in Chapter 7 below). At his death, he had been buried in Kensal Green cemetery in North London, a resting-place of no particular distinction. During his lifetime he had been a prolific and immensely successful novelist, publishing forty-seven novels. The novels had many admirers, but on the whole subsequent judges have not regarded them as being among the imperishable classics of English literature. In addition, he wrote a candid autobiography in which he revealed not only the industrial regimen that had allowed him to be so productive while for the most part having a professional occupation—the alarm clock on the desk, so many words to be completed for each quarter of an hour, and so on—but also the extent of his absorption in and recording of the financial details of his dealings with publishers. He itemized, down to the last penny, the earnings from his major novels, he emphasized the businesslike nature of his methods; it might have been subtitled 'portrait of the artist as a calculating businessman'. It was not a conception of the artist cherished by the late Victorian public, and his reputation suffered when the autobiography was published some months after his death. Whether for this or other reasons, no monument in his memory was erected at the time.

Neither his admirers nor his critics have ever described Trollope as 'an intellectual'. For a few years he edited a minor magazine, and he once stood for Parliament, unsuccessfully, but he had a gruff disdain (sometimes seen as quintessentially English) for the intrusion of abstract ideas into the practicalities of everyday affairs. Nor could he really be said to have adorned public life. He spent most of his career as an official in the Post Office, where his greatest claim to fame was that he invented the pillar box, the precursor of the red postal boxes that still decorate English towns and villages. But it was surely neither for this piece of typically Victorian inventiveness nor for reorganizing postal deliveries in the Essex district that he was being remembered by the galaxy of distinguished political and literary figures who had assembled in Westminster Abbey.

Still, even if this little ceremony came one hundred and eleven years late, one might still ask whether it represented the British state conferring official recognition on the memory of Trollope? In the obvious sense it did not, though there was a more surprising sense in which some such action was being performed. To begin with, it is entirely characteristic of English traditions of autonomous local bodies (now much diminished by the depredations of Tory governments) that the decision to bury or memorialize someone in Westminster Abbey does not rest with the Government or Head of State; it is up to the Dean and Chapter of the Abbey. Since the Abbey has long been the nearest equivalent to a national pantheon, the burial of certain eminent public figures takes place there almost as a matter of course. But formally the decision rests with the Dean, even if discreet pressure is applied by the Government, and there are well-documented cases where the request by a writer's family or admirers for such a privilege has been turned down.

This should lead us to examine the history and status of Poets' Corner more closely. When was it established? Is it restricted to poets, or even to writers? Are all Poet Laureates buried there? The answer to these simple questions is unclear where it is not simply negative. It is again illustrative of a commonly remarked feature of English traditions that the institution seems to have grown up almost by accident, and its perpetuation has relied, at least until recently, on the initiative of private individuals and groups. It is true that Geoffrey Chaucer, 'the father of English poetry', is buried there, and this might lead one to believe that the ground was consecrated to its literary-memorial purpose as early as the end of the fourteenth century (Chaucer died in 1400). But in fact, Chaucer's resting-place was not determined by any conception of establishing a Poets' Corner; he was buried in the Abbey because he had been the King's Clerk of Works and he lived in Westminster. The present monument was only erected much later, in 1556. The beginnings of the practice of commemorating poets on this spot probably came with the death of Edmund Spenser in 1599; a decision was made to bury this acknowledged prince among English poets of the time next to Chaucer. Several others, not all subsequently well known, followed in the next few decades, including Jonson and Beaumont. Shakespeare, who died in 1616, was buried at Stratford-upon-Avon; a monument was not erected in the Abbey until the middle of the eighteenth century. But from the early seventeenth century onwards, the statues and memorial stones which began to cluster in this part of the Abbey were seen as the physical expression of a poetic tradition unexampled in its richness and diversity.

None the less, the process by which a writer received this accolade remained informal and somewhat haphazard. To begin with, the initiative nearly always came from private individuals—from family, friends, or, most often, later admirers—not from official sources. This fact combined with the greater apparent continuity of modern English political history to produce another interesting contrast with France's Panthéon (and indeed with many of those state-sponsored forms of consecration in other countries). The decision to honour a writer of one political or religious inclination did not entail the need to remove those of contrary allegiances who had previously been admitted; there were no equivalents in Westminster Abbey of the vaudeville theatre scenes at the Panthéon I mentioned earlier in which the remains of the discredited worthy are hastily shunted out the back door as the coffin of the currently approved 'grand homme' is ceremoniously carried up the main steps. A different notion of the relation between cultural recognition and political regime is implied in this contrast.

Another relevant difference was the fact that England had an established church: should burial in the Abbey be reserved for members of the Anglican communion, or did its 'national' function require that distinguished Catholics, Jews, and unbelievers be granted their plots, too? And, as so often in English attitudes, it is hard to separate questions of religious orthodoxy from questions of moral orthodoxy: a little laxness in theology has generally been more readily tolerated than any laxness in sexual behaviour. Only rarely do untoward political opinions seem to have been a ground for permanent exclusion, though it is always hard to tell about cases which may have been settled by 'a quiet word' in the appropriate ear. The inclusions can now seem as surprising as the exclusions. In the seventeenth and eighteenth centuries several lesser poetic lights (such as Michael Drayton and William Davenant) obtained a place though they are not included in the modern canon of English literature. By the nineteenth century a certain acknowledged eminence was required, though in some cases literary shortcomings seem to have been compensated for by the kind of respectability and social standing that mattered so much in that period (but which have not always been attributes possessed by the most gifted poets). Thus, John Keble (1792–1866), who is now remembered far more as one of the founders of the 'Oxford Movement' in theology than for his single volume of devotional verse, is there, but John Keats (1795–1821), generally considered one of the greatest of the English Romantic poets, is not.

The kinds of criteria which have operated at different periods are illustrated by the cases of Milton, Byron, and Meredith. In his lifetime, Milton was a notorious radical and republican, detested by the Tory-Anglican hierarchy. At his death in 1674, though already recognized as the pre-eminent poet of his day, there could be no question of his burial in the Abbey (he was buried in a church in the City of London, next to his father). The enduring hostility to Milton is evident in the fact that when the little-known writer John Phillips died in 1706, the Dean of Westminster refused to allow an epitaph to be placed in the Abbey because it contained a reference to Milton (his successor admired Milton, and relented in 1714). Partisan passion had sufficiently diminished in the mid-eighteenth century for a memorial to Milton himself to be placed in Poets' Corner in 1737, though it still did not pass without comment—'I have seen erected in the church a bust of that man whose name I once knew considered as a pollution of its walls' observed one of Dr Johnson's friends. When Byron died in 1824, at the height of a European reputation few other English writers have ever achieved, there was simply no question of his being accorded a place in the Abbey. His scandalous sexual adventures were alone sufficient for him to be debarred from any ecclesiastical recognition, and a memorial to him was not erected in Poet's Corner until, remark-ably, 1969. When George Meredith died in 1909, it was said that the Prince of Wales was among those who requested burial in the Abbey. But the Dean (Armitage Robinson) declined the request: 'The Dean justified his decision on the grounds that there was not much room in the Abbey, and that in his opinion Meredith had no lasting fame and would not be read a hundred years hence'. As this illustrates, entry into 'the national valhalla' could ultimately be determined by the literary judgement of a senior churchman. Successive Deans of Westminster have been charged with the burden of literary talent-spotting on behalf of posterity.

Burial or commemoration of leading writers in Westminster Abbey has been, therefore, neither official nor automatic. None the less, this privilege has long been recognized as a form of national consecration, and in the late nineteenth century the increasingly elaborate ceremony became more and more an expression of patri-otic pride of a deliberately 'all-party' kind. At his death in 1892, Tennyson had been Poet Laureate for forty-two years, and his funeral provided an occasion for one of those orgies of national self-importance which the late Victorians were so good at. His twelve pall-bearers included two prime ministers, representatives of Oxford, Cambridge, and the United States, and sundry prominent political and literary figures (the nave was lined by men of the

Balaclava Light Brigade). These state funerals (for such they were in all but name) were the counterpart to other celebrations of the national cultural heritage which marked these years, including the compilation of the *Dictionary of National Biography*, of the *Oxford English Dictionary*, and so on.

The sense of the need to stage such showpiece events was most strikingly illustrated when Thomas Hardy died in 1928 at the age of 88. Hardy had made clear that he had no wish to be buried in the Abbey, but his grieving widow was overruled by influential friends, conscious of Hardy's national status. As Robert Gittings recounts in his biography of Hardy, a gruesome compromise was arranged whereby the heart was buried at Stinsford (immortalized as 'Melstock' in his Wessex novels) in his native Dorset, but the rest of the body was cremated and the ashes buried, with great pomp, in Westminster Abbey. The 'national' character of the proceedings was underlined by the fact that the first two pall-bearers were the Prime Minister, Stanley Baldwin, and the Leader of the Labour Party, Ramsay MacDonald, followed by representatives of Oxford and Cambridge and the leading literary figures of the day, beginning with George Bernard Shaw, Rudyard Kipling, and John Galsworthy. (It was among the more bizarre ironies of the occasion that it should have seemed to the organizers fitting for the author of *Jude the Obscure* to be carried to his grave by such embodiments of Christminster as the Master of Magdalene College Cambridge and the Provost of Queen's College Oxford.) Hardy was also a known agnostic, but the established rituals required Anglican liturgy and hymns, and so the author of the sceptical poem 'God's Funeral' was laid to rest to the accompaniment of the anthem 'Thou will keep in perfect peace whose mind is stayed on Thee'. The managers of the national identity were determined to put the final seal of approval on one of the glories of that selective tradition known as 'English literature', and he was in no position to object.

VIII

In the twentieth century the entry requirements have become more stringent, and the only poets to have received this honour since 1945 have been T. S. Eliot, John Masefield, and W. H. Auden.

How, therefore, should one interpret the fact that the Prime
Minister was among those (and was apparently, and not surpris-
ingly, the most effective among those) who pressed for a place for
the long dead and not universally admired Trollope? (The Prime
Minister's role was hinted at by the Secretary of the Trollope
Society in a revealing television programme, directed by Daisy
Goodwin, entitled *The Trollopians*, broadcast on BBC 2 on 4
October 1993.) It was doubtless important that Trollope is still a
widely read novelist: a taste for his easygoing narratives is not
confined to an artistic avant-garde or a coterie of the critically
sophisticated. It would not be altogether unfair to say that his
novels particularly appeal to those who do not like too much thinking to interfere with their reading. His recent boom in popularity
also represents a more general current of cultural conservatism that
embraces a reaction against the experiments of literary modernism
and postmodernism as well as a hostility to academic literary critics
and to intellectuals generally. The Trollope Society now boasts a
considerable number of 'Establishment' figures among its members,
including a former editor of *The Times*, a former Governor of the
Bank of England, and several ministers in John Major's government.
But more than this, Trollope's name suggests the world described in
his most popular sequence of novels—a world of the countryside
and of small cathedral towns, a world of rectories and manor
houses, of cottages and village greens, a peaceful, slow-moving,
golden world that has become synonymous with a conception of
'the real England' for which so many of the inhabitants of contemporary Britain appear to feel an unfocused nostalgia.

    In fact, Trollope's oeuvre is more varied than this, and his novels
of political life often present an unflattering portrait of politicians,
especially perhaps of the Tories of his day. But commemorations of
the kind we are discussing here do not rest on the most discriminating literary criticism, and Trollope's name clearly represents an
image of England that the Tory government needed to invoke in an
attempt to glue its individualistic and society-dissolving policies
together. That government talked a lot about this essence of
'Englishness'. John Major did so, for example, in a speech in April
1993: it was delivered on St George's day, and he exploited the
(actually very feeble) patriotic associations of the day to launch a
hymn of praise to just such a greetings-card parody of 'the real
England', complete with 'warm beer', 'the long shadows falling

across the cricket ground', and so on. The memorial to Trollope that was put up in Westminster Abbey only four weeks before this speech has to be seen as part of the same idealization of an essentially rural, 'squire-and-parson', England. Even so, this blatantly partisan exploitation of an occasion would have possessed much less power were there not already a long-established tradition of looking to English literature for the most distinctive expression of the national character.

The invocation of a (selective and shifting) tradition of 'English Literature' as the most distinctive embodiment of national identity has a long history, but its modern phase dates, as with so much about English 'traditions', from the late nineteenth century. (I am here drawing on an argument mounted in greater detail in my *Public Moralists*.) Indeed, the consolidation of a 'national' interpretation of England's *political* history in that period can be roughly paralleled in the celebratory accounts of English *literary* distinctiveness, to the point where we might get some illumination from referring to 'the Whig interpretation of English literature'. The analogy implied by this phrase suggests a relation to the national literature which was celebratory and consensual, qualities much in evidence in the late nineteenth century. But in the course of the twentieth century this relation, while remaining culturally central, has become more divided, more combative, and more troubled, thereby contributing to the situation in which literary criticism in the broadest sense has been acknowledged as the chief idiom for cultural criticism in mid-twentieth-century Britain. (This is perhaps the unstated premiss underlying the common observation, usually given the form of a complaint, that much of the elaboration of moral and political values which has been carried on in some other European countries in a more explicitly theoretical vein has been conducted in Britain in the twentieth century through the medium of the discussion of literature.)

As part of this wider cultural activity, what developed as the academic study of 'English' was thus freighted from the start with an exceptional intellectual and even moral significance, a condition attested in part by the violence of so many of its ostensibly literary-critical debates. In particular, the question of sustaining, reworking, or challenging the central 'canon' of English literature has become a crucial mode of legitimation in the cultural politics of the mid- and late twentieth century, as well, of course, as an apparently inexhaustible source of rancour among those charged with the design or reform of syllabuses. I suggest that an important dimension in our understanding of these disputes will be missing until we recognize that what we are witnessing in these debates is the disintegration of the Whig interpretation of English literature. The recent canonization of Trollope represents a very local and surely rather wilful attempt to reverse this trend.

More generally, it may seem that the chief manifestation of the increased sensitivity to questions of English cultural nationalism in Britain today is, as I mentioned earlier, a rash of publications by academic historians and literary critics uncovering, with a mixture of scorn and envy, some of the ways in which our less self-conscious ancestors derived *their* identities from *their* less complicated relation to *their* chosen past. Still, there may be some unacknowledged continuities here, too, since the seductions of nostalgia are not altogether absent even in such reflections on a lineage twice removed. In other words, the scholarly study of 'Englishness' can, in some cases, be yet another way of perpetuating that fond absorption in the alleged distinctiveness of the English past which it ostensibly desires to criticize. (It is perhaps not too impertinent to wonder whether all the contributors to Nora's volumes are exempt from this criticism.) But this sceptical observation does not entail the conclusion that we should regard the forms of self-definition discussed in this essay simply as part of a world we have lost. If it does nothing else, the fact that Kenneth Baker, while Secretary of State for Education, chose to promote his triumphalist version of 'England's' (predominantly military) history by publishing an anthology of English poetry, *The Faber Book of English History in Verse*, should at least suggest that the impulse, and perhaps the need, to address questions of national identity through the medium of literary history is likely to be with us for a while yet. After all, in reading that address about Trollope in Westminster Abbey, John Major was doing more than paying homage to a favourite author. He was drawing upon 'the Whig interpretation of English literature' to propound a Tory conception of England and Englishness.

3

Idealizing England: Élie Halévy and Lewis Namier

I

It takes a foreigner, of course, really to idealize a country, especially when to the potent mixture of selective familiarity and presumed detachment is added the yearning to find a society whose virtues might go some way to make up for the failings of one's country of origin. There has been a long tradition in European thought of idealizing the alleged achievements of England's constitutional evolution, stretching back at least to Montesquieu and Voltaire in the early eighteenth century. Two figures in the twentieth century who wrote particularly influential accounts of the distinctiveness of England's political and social development from the eighteenth century onwards were Élie Halévy and Lewis Namier. But although they concurred in their respect for what Halévy called England's 'moderate liberty', they painted intriguingly different portraits of the land they admired. Here, as in several of the essays in Part II, it seems to me that intellectual biography (fleshed out in Halévy's case with a substantial recent edition of his letters) can provide one indispensable way of approaching an understanding of their

Myrna Chase, *Élie Halévy: An Intellectual Biography* (Columbia University Press, 1980).

Henriette Guy-Loë (ed.), *Élie Halévy: Correspondance (1891–1937)*, preface by François Furet (Éditions de Fallois, 1996).

Norman Rose, *Lewis Namier and Zionism* (Oxford University Press, 1980).

Linda Colley, *Namier* (Weidenfeld and Nicolson, 1989).

contrasting achievements as historians. For they not only focused on different problems and drew upon different conceptual and literary resources: they invested different hopes and fantasies in their construction of English history in part because they stood in such different relationships to the political traditions of their respective countries of origin. To do justice to their only partly acknowledged idealizing impulses, we need to know where, in every sense of the phrase, they were coming from.

II

It is always difficult to write satisfactorily about the work of an outstanding historian—an historian, that is, who remains worth reading for other than narrowly professional reasons—without making him sound like little more than a political pamphleteer or not very scientific social scientist. For expository purposes, there is an understandable pressure to isolate his 'problem' and summarize his 'argument', or to portray him as rather laboriously 'testing hypotheses' by means of wide reading or archival legwork. In any such schematic and colourless account, the texture of his achievement as history slips from view. As a partial remedy, the quality of the unique gaze which informed that achievement may be illustrated by extensive quotation, though some effects require a Wagnerian scale for their full realization. A literary critic's eye for significant detail, recurring imagery, and the like can do something, of course, but the cumulative force of a narrative sustained and thickened through several hundred pages does not lend itself to sampling. In the end, whatever resources one employs, the most successful evocation, like the best criticism, may be that which makes us want to go and read the work for ourselves.

That Myrna Chase's *Élie Halévy: An Intellectual Biography* does not stimulate the appetite in quite this way owes more, perhaps, to Halévy's qualities as an historian than to any expository failings on her part. For in his case it would not be altogether unfair to say that history was political science pursued by other means. One can now draw on the excellent recent edition of his letters by his niece, Henriette Guy-Loë, to document this intellectual development at first hand. In a letter to his close friend

Celestin Bouglé, written when he was only 26, Halévy reported that he was studying the life of Bentham and went on to muse on where this might take him: 'Une théorie de la société? ou une théorie de la démocratie moderne? ou une histoire de l'Angleterre? L'avenir me révélera à moi-même, et me dira dans lequel de ces trois cercles concentriques je m'enfermerai.' In some ways, Halévy always remained within all three of these circles simultaneously, and the great strength of Professor Chase's book lies in showing how Halévy's interest in English history was sustained at every stage by wider political and philosophical concerns. What she gives us, in consequence, is the biography of a turn-of-the-century French intellectual, with the emphasis very much on the development and even the defence of his political 'liberalism', an account in which the enduring achievement of his *History of the English People in the Nineteenth Century* receives rather brisk notice. Chase draws upon a wide range of Halévy's occasional writings, supported by passages from his letters; quotations from the *History* itself, however, are very rare indeed. In so far as she does discuss it, her interest centres on the subsequent historiographical controversy surrounding 'the Halévy thesis' about the respective roles of religion and radicalism in the development of the English working class rather than on the work itself. This helps to clarify what had become a somewhat confused debate, but it does not produce any deepened appreciation of why *England in 1815* might be considered an outstanding example of historical literature.

That said, the biography of this particular French intellectual remains full of interest. Halévy was born, in 1870, to a half-Jewish, half-Protestant family of the Parisian *haute-bourgeoisie* with more than respectable artistic and diplomatic connections: his great-uncle was the composer of *La Juive*, and his father made something of a reputation as a popular novelist and librettist, collaborating with Bizet, a cousin by marriage, on the creation of *Carmen* among other operas. An education at the smart Lycée Condorcet hardly extended his social range: he had Mallarmé as his English master, and Proust was one of his younger brother's classmates. (Ernest Barker later recorded that Proust had been afraid of the austere and precocious Halévy, who in turn maintained a strong dislike for the novelist, though with characteristic fair-mindedness he remarked as early as 1893 Proust's 'grande somme de talent'.) In 1889 he took first place in the *concours générale* in philosophy, and entered the

École Normale Supérieure. After three years of concentrated study, he was placed second in the Agrégation, behind his friend Émile Chartier (later to write under the pseudonym of Alain). In 1893, he and a group of like-minded and equally precocious sons of the *noblesse de la plume* founded a philosophical journal which, with the slightly comic over-ambitiousness of those who were too successful too young, they hoped would provide a forum for the criticism of both Christianity and what they capaciously referred to as positivism, criticism which they hoped would contribute directly to that familiar Sisyphean task, the 'moral reformation' of the Third Republic. For something which began as little more than an undergraduate magazine, the *Revue de Métaphysique et de Morale* has done pretty well.

In prescribing to Xavier Léon, who was to act as executive editor, what he thought their philosophical position should be, Halévy declared: 'Il est nécessaire d'agir contre le misérable positivisme dont nous sortons, et l'agaçante religiosité où nous risquons de nous embourber,—de fonder une philosophie de l'action et de la réflexion—d'être rationalistes avec rage.' For the rest of his life, which always included a close involvement with the affairs of the *Revue*, Halévy's philosophical allegiances could well be described as 'rationalist with a passion'. Following the Agrégation, Halévy completed a scholarly monograph on *La Théorie platonicienne des sciences*, but by the time of its publication in 1896 he had already decided against a career as a professional philosopher, and had begun the researches which were to lead to his studies on the Philosophic Radicals, Methodism, and nineteenth-century English history. This was the great, and far from predictable, turning-point in his career: François Furet remarks in his substantial preface to the recent edition of Halévy's correspondance 'l'étonnant paradoxe qui a fait de l'auteur d'un premier livre sur Platon l'érudit passioné par l'histoire du peuple le moins philosophique de l'Europe'. Furet also emphasizes just how exceptional Halévy was among French intellectuals of his generation in combining a lifelong scholarly devotion to English history with good left-republican political principles at home. But for Halévy, philosophy and history were at this stage two routes to the same destination. In reply to Bouglé's teasing about adding yet another history of England to the already long list of such productions by French authors, Halévy revealingly replied: 'Mon cher ami, puisqu'il ne faut pas écrire une histoire d'Angleterre, je n'écrirai pas une histoire d'Angleterre. J'écrirais donc une philosophie de l'histoire, ou un examen critique des notions sociales fondamentales, ou toute aute en cet ordre d'idées'. Even when launched on his history of England, Halévy did not think he had abandoned his interest in 'cet ordre d'idées'.

This and similar remarks from the same period raise the tantalizing question, touched on only in passing in Chase's biography, of why Halévy did not join Bouglé and several others of their generation in becoming a devotee of Durkheimian sociology, just then embarking on its most successful period of intellectual and academic imperialism. He certainly had many of the requisite qualifications—a training in philosophy, an ambition to develop a secular morality, a preoccupation with the causes of social stability and an inclination to look for them in the influence of moral and religious ideas, and so on. (At the very end of his life, he began the only completed section of 'England in 1852' with a phrase which might well have introduced one of Durkheim's last works: 'If we would study the social composition of a nation, we must begin by studying its religion.') He was also a Dreyfusard *avant la lettre*, bound by ties of family and education to the liberal, secular, republican cause. Here, surely, was a model recruit for the Durkheimian *équipe*.

However, the early reputation of Durkheim's sociology for positivism and even materialism in its treatment of morality would not have recommended it to the young Halévy, deeply influenced by the neo-Kantian revival of the late nineteenth century (as, ironically, was Durkheim himself of course). Less obviously, he also seems to have been self-consciously committed to a kind of individualism in social explanation. In the conclusion to the third volume of his study of Philosophic Radicalism, published in 1904, there was a hostile and easily identifiable reference to the modern proponents of a social science 'defined as a science of collective representations', and after drawing attention to what he took to be some of the methodological difficulties of this project, Halévy concluded that 'the Philosophical Radicals were right in seeing in the individual the principle of explanation in the social sciences'. Moreover, from a very early stage he was drawn to the idea of developing a 'science of politics', whereas the whole emphasis of Durkheim's sociology appeared to be to regard political conflict as 'pathological', an ailment which would eventually be corrected by a proper application of the laws of social health, and thus not the subject-matter of a science in its own right. (For this as well as for more immediately tactical reasons, no space was found for 'political science' in the various classifications of the sciences laid out in the *Année Sociologique*.) This difference of focus is alluded to in a letter of 1903 where Halévy observes that the whole phenomenon of 'Chamberlainism' in England 'devrait retenir l'attention de Durkheim et de ses troupes, si tous étaient capables de s'occuper d'autre chose que de totem et du tabou.' In any event, his distance from, even scorn for, Durkheimian sociology is evident in his letters, where he frequently teases Bouglé about the ideas of 'ton maître Durkheim'.

More generally, Halévy was determined to remain independent of the intellectual cliques who controlled the Sorbonne, and further inquiry might shed some interesting light on his acceptance of a post outside the university system at the increasingly anti-Durkheimian École Libre des Sciences Politiques. He was invited there by Émile Boutmy, its founder and director, who may have affected Halévy's life in more ways than one since he was also a well-known historian of the English constitution, and author of one of the more respectable late nineteenth-century inquiries into the political consequences of different 'national characters', enti-tled *Essai d'une psychologie politique du peuple Anglais au 19e siècle*. At all events, Halévy remained at Sciences Po for the rest of his life, twice refusing chairs in philosophy at the Sorbonne, though one cannot, apparently, be certain what his response would have been had he been offered one in history.

III

He made his mark as an historian with the first of the two works for which he is still best known in England, his three-volume study of *The Growth of Philosophical Radicalism*, published between 1901 and 1904, and thus almost exactly contemporaneous with Leslie Stephen's *The English Utilitarians*, also in three volumes, published in 1900. Halévy had almost completed his first volume when he learned that 'un Anglais, vieux mais considérable, prépare un ouvrage qui doit, comme sujet, et comme idée maîtresse, se rapprocher du mien'. But after having read 'l'ouvrage de mon concurrent', he realized that their two works were very different, and he pressed on with his own project. He sent his first two volumes to Stephen, who replied with characteristic grace that 'I hope that I may consider myself as an ally, not a competitor'. Only a fortnight before he died, the ailing Stephen dictated a still more winning letter to Halévy on receipt of the latter's third volume: 'You have a most perfect right to compete with me, all the more if in some respects you are, as I believe, better fitted for the task. If a young man beats an elderly gentleman the event is not unprecedented. But I still hope that you will allow me to call you collaborator as much as competitor.'

That Halévy's title should refer to a doctrine whereas Stephen's referred to people was entirely apt: the Frenchman's interest lay in the development of what he saw as one of the two most significant moral and intellectual forces in nineteenth-century England, and he traced, with still recognized authority, the roots of Benthamism in eighteenth-century thought, particularly in Anglo-French sensationalism. But where the term 'Philosophic Radicals' had originally been coined (by John Stuart Mill) to describe a group in parliament in the 1830s, Halévy used 'Philosophical Radicalism' to embrace a whole range of political theorists and economists, some of whom stood in a rather oblique relation to Bentham's own doctrines, so far as anything so systematic could be elicited from his chaotic writings, and several of whom were certainly not radicals, philosophic or otherwise, in the original, political sense. This was true in particular of some of the post-Ricardian political economists whom Halévy did not discriminate all that closely. As William Thomas observed in his authoritative *The Philosophic Radicals: Nine Studies in Theory and Practice 1817–1841* (1979): 'To say that Ricardian economics formed part of philosophic radicalism is true; but to say that all Ricardians were Philosophic Radicals is not. Halévy's account of philosophic radicalism tends to blur the political distinctions which dominated the daily lives of the men themselves, substituting instead highly abstract issues which can hardly have troubled them.' From this distance, it seems as if he may have accepted rather too readily the exaggeration of both the homogeneity and the influence of the Philosophic Radicals which, partly for polemical reasons, were such features of their late nineteenth-century reputation, nurtured by, among many others, Halévy's close friends in England, Graham Wallas and the Webbs.

The other current of thought and feeling which Halévy singled out for separate analysis was evangelicalism. In Halévy's oeuvre, his controversial essays on 'The Birth of Methodism', published in 1906, occupy a somewhat similar place to that filled in Weber's work by his more famous essays on 'The Protestant Ethic and the Spirit of Capitalism'—both investigating the unique social consequences of one branch of Protestant Christianity, both confining themselves to relatively well-documented episodes, but both freighted with implications for the explanatory strategies of the major works which were to follow. Both, too, have been travestied and vulgarized by subsequent critics, especially by those who have feared that the essays might throw what they crudely see as an 'idealist' spanner in the works of a materialist interpretation of history. Both the biography and the letters help us to understand the place of the Methodism essays in Halévy's intellectual development, which has the effect of making them seem more subtle than their latter-day critics have always allowed.

England in 1815, published in 1912, gave substantial historical expression to what had been argued more programmatically in the early essays. It was entirely in keeping with his self-ascribed identity as a philosophical historian that Halévy should begin his masterpiece by showing how little resemblance the actual English constitution of 1815 bore to that account of it made famous by Montesquieu (who, in company with Tocqueville, surely ranks as one of his true masters). Here one might remark upon Halévy's distance from those in the preceding generation of French writers on England, such as Taine, who sought to discover the secret of its history in the peculiar qualities of the 'English race'. And in a longer account more could be said about the place in nineteenth-century European reflections on politics of the various meditations on England's unique experience of stability and political liberty, with Guizot and Boutmy as the Macaulay and Green of Euro-Whiggery. Halévy himself referred to his work as an exploration of 'a theory of progress in the modern state'; if it did not exactly tell the story of liberty broadening down from precedent to precedent, it certainly conveyed, with a suitably detached restraint, a reflective admiration for the achievement of peaceful political adaptation. It was not in any sense classically Whig, of course, since Halévy precisely wanted to show, in Tocquevillian vein, that the supposed perfection of the constitution only in fact derived its efficacy from

shared moral habits resulting, in large part, from England's peculiar religious history. Nor did he display much inclination to mount
Whiggish claims about unbroken continuity: there was little reference to 1688, and none at all to Magna Carta, the Conquest, the
ancient liberties of the Saxons, or any other of the episodes so cherished by English Whig historians of the preceding generations. Still,
despite its low-keyed analytical tone, the work emitted a hum of
satisfaction with the story it had to tell. As he had observed in a
letter to Bouglé in 1905, working on English history was bound to
make a person of his temperament increasingly Anglophile, if only
because 'il est certain que, depuis deux siècles, c'est l'Angleterre qui
a donné à l'Europe des leçons de politique'.

Although best known in the English-speaking world, naturally
enough, for his work on English history, in France Halévy was, and
perhaps still is, remembered for his studies in European Socialism,
an interest he had long pursued in parallel with his English
researches and a subject on which he taught a celebrated course at
Sciences Po for many years. In his earliest writings on the subject,
he had emphasized, and obviously been attracted by, the more
libertarian strains of the Socialist tradition, sometimes implying
that this had been largely a French contribution in contrast to the
more collectivist inheritance of German Socialism. Increasingly, he
adopted a tendentiously capacious definition of Socialism: he came
to regard all doctrines which advocated a greater role for the state
in the economic life of its citizens as 'Socialist' (one may wonder
how much he was influenced here by his English contacts, especially Wallas and the Webbs, with whom he maintained a substantial correspondence). Such a framework did allow him to point out
similarities which may have escaped most of his contemporaries—
he memorably described Napoleon III as 'St Simon on horseback',
which, of course, pointed to the authoritarianism in St Simon as
much as to the collectivism of the Second Empire.

The experience of the First World War gave a fiercer polemical
edge to Halévy's writings on this subject above all others. Horrified
by every aspect of the conflict and unwilling to put his pen at the
disposal of the state or even to share in the more than usually
febrile intellectual life of Paris, he followed a particularly honest,
humble, and humane course, becoming a hospital orderly in the
provinces. (Within days of the signing of the Armistice in
November 1918 Halévy found himself a place aboard a troopship

sailing for his 'seconde patrie'.) Reflection on the causes and consequences of the war made him, like many another liberal, pessimistic
about the prospects for the enjoyment of political liberty in the
twentieth century. He was attracted by neither pole of the increasingly polarized world of French politics in the 1920s and 1930s,
and when, in a paper given in 1936 shortly before his death, characteristically entitled 'The Era of Tyrannies', he pointed to the similarly illiberal features of Socialism and National Socialism, he was
vilified by both Left and Right, but particularly by several outraged
friends among the former. For someone of such heredity, he seems
to have had a surprisingly underdeveloped taste for pleasure, but it
is clear that he took a certain wry satisfaction in suffering this
representative liberal fate.

The war and its aftermath also had its effect upon his *History*.
The second and third volumes, taking the story from 1815 to 1841,
had been begun before the war but were only published after many
delays in 1923, a piece of timing which naturally led the years after
Waterloo to be compared to the years after Versailles. Increasingly
preoccupied with understanding the series of catastrophes which he
saw overtaking Europe in the twentieth century, Halévy then
decided that rather than pursue his story chronologically through
the nineteenth century, he would jump ahead to the period
1895–1914, which he saw as forming an 'epilogue' to the civilization of Victorian England, as the period in which the forces of
imperialism and democracy started the slide into the chaos of the
'era of tyrannies'. In the first instalment of this epilogue, published
in 1926, he could still remark, albeit rather wistfully, the influence
of 'that moral and religious constitution' which he had recon-
structed in England in 1815. But in the second volume, published
in 1932 under the title *Vers la démocratie sociale et vers la guerre
(1905–1914)* (rather misleadingly called *The Rule of Democracy* in
the English translation), he brooded more bitterly over the passing
of 'that great epoch during which the British people cherished the
splendid illusion that they had discovered in a moderate liberty,
and not for themselves alone but for every nation that would have
the wisdom to follow their example, the secret of moral and of
political stability'.

The sad power of 'illusion' in that sentence marks his final
distance from anything like the pieties of Whig history. But even his
unfinished story was not without its political moral. In a letter

written when he was 30—he seems never to have been young—he announced: 'Je voudrais démontrer aux populations la vanité de l'enthousiasme et l'utilité des institutions', and one can see how certain characteristic features of his *History* might have been taken to reinforce this lesson—its emphasis on the pervasive play of unintended consequences, its attention to the impact of 'the secondary virtues' on political life, its exploration of the crucial role of 'the great unpaid' in local government, and so on. It could be read as the cautionary tale of a sceptical, disenchanted liberalism, an attitude which differed *toto caelo* from the enthusiastic, romantic, Mazzinian liberalism which Halévy had seen get its come-uppance in the years between 1848 and 1914. (And it is surely this political identity which has endeared him to such self-consciously 'liberal' critics of revolutionary and Marxist orthodoxies as Raymond Aron and François Furet; in this respect the appearance of this edition of the correspondence under Furet's auspices is but another element in that recovery of liberal predecessors which I remarked in the previous essay as forming such a marked feature of French intellectual life in the past two decades.) 'A moderate liberty' is not exactly Madison Avenue's ideal of a winning political slogan, but it describes, in suitably muted terms, the achievement which Halévy's *History* was intended to explore, to celebrate, and, ultimately, to commemorate.

IV

For all his familiarity with England and things English, Halévy was unmistakably and proudly French, indeed Parisian; in that sense, his was always an outsider's view of English history. By contrast, it may at first seem odd to find a strongly local, almost parochial, interest in the scene in which, at All Souls in 1932, Lewis Namier provoked Isaiah Berlin by scornfully dismissing the history of ideas—in German, though the rest of the conversation (or rather harangue) was conducted in English—as 'what one Jew cribs from another'. After all, but for some unpredictable migrations and a few world-historical hiccups in the previous couple of decades, they might have been having the exchange—quite possibly in French—in, say, Warsaw or St Petersburg (Namier had been born in Poland in 1888 and Berlin in Riga in 1909). Pursuing fancy in this vein, one could easily imagine circumstances under which few English readers would now be interested in the opinions of Ludwik Bernsztajn Niemirowski (though in fact Namier had already changed his name twice by the time he became a British subject in 1913). Yet, apart from some obvious reflections on cosmopolitanism, what such counterfactual whimsy chiefly reveals is the extent to which the distinctive flavour of the scene depends upon the Englishness of its setting in an intellectual as well as a physical sense.

For, the context of the remark, as Berlin recounts it, was Namier's passionate exposition of a favourite theme: the contrast between the practical, sober, interest-based political tradition of England and the ideologically riven, overdramatized, ultimately catastrophic politics of continental Europe. For Namier, notoriously, this contrast has what would now be called a methodological as well as a political significance. He took English history to have endorsed, in the appropriately practical way, the unimportance of theories in moving men to action, and he made it a maxim of his own historical researches that expressions of principle were to be treated as rationalizations or, as he put it (characteristically choosing the gruff demotic of the average practical Englishman who owned 1,000 acres) in the book which most famously exemplified this view and which cast its shadow over a generation of English historians, mere 'flapdoodle'. In 1932 he was exasperated to think that a clever young man with an Oxford Fellowship (which he clearly envied) was going to waste his time by writing a book about a frothy ideas-monger like Marx, whom he dismissed as 'a typical Jewish half-charlatan who got hold of quite a good idea and then ran it to death just to spite the Gentiles'.

Up to this point, the picture of Namier which this scene discloses may appear entirely consonant with the resonances which 'Namierism' evidently has for those who have never read a word by or about the man himself—an animus against abstract ideas, sneers at intellectuals in politics, *schadenfreude* about the outcome of European revolutions, snobbery about the traditional English governing class, and commitment to a distinctive historical 'method' ('finding out who the chaps really were', as his Russian wife engagingly reported it in connection with his later study of 1848). But the very prominence and, still more, the tone of his references to Jews in both quoted remarks introduces one disturbing element into the apparent integrity of this picture, and in fact contributes to the ironies enfolded in that opening scene. For Namier was not only proudly assertive of his own Jewishness and scornful of Jews who hoped to 'disappear' into English society, but he was also, for most of his mature life, a passionate Zionist. In fact, as Norman Rose's *Namier and Zionism* shows in considerable detail, Namier was prominently and energetically involved, at times to the exclusion of all else, in various aspects of organized Zionist political activity from the mid-1920s to the mid-1940s.

Some indication of the scope of this political involvement had already been given in the biography written by his second wife, Julia, published in 1971, though since that involvement had greatly diminished by the time she met him, and since she did not draw on anything like the range of manuscript collections and official archives which Professor Rose has so profitably mined, it did not bulk very large in her account. That account certainly illumined the career and temperament of this puzzling, difficult, forceful man. The son of wealthy Polonized Jewish landowners in Eastern Galicia, he came to England in 1907, studying first at the LSE, and then at Balliol College Oxford, where he took a First in Modern History in 1911 ('all I have done I owe to Balliol', he later remarked in a characteristic mixture of exaggeration and piety). His love for his new country was to suffer many a rebuff, some rooted in the casual anti-Semitism of the period, but it was a love fortified by his reading of, among other works, Disraeli's historical novels. 'Like Disraeli,' observes Linda Colley in her excellent short critical study,

he would come to believe that 'Judaism and Christianity must in the end be reconciled' and to regard himself as a Radical Tory. Like Disraeli, he would devote adulation, nostalgia, and the bulk of his writings to the British ruling class. Like Disraeli, too, he would translate the universalism inherent in Judaism into a strong commitment to the worldwide influence of the British Empire.

He worked for the British Foreign Office during the First World War, but in the 1920s his life was disrupted by personal and financial crises, and only with his unexpected appointment to the Chair of History at Manchester in 1930 did his career begin to take something like an orthodox academic form. Lady Namier's biography brought out the uneven, harassed nature of his life up

to the publication in 1929 of *The Structure of Politics at the
Accession of George III* in a way that made the relation between
the man and the work more than usually intriguing. Throughout
the period of the gestation and writing of what was, by any standards, an austerely professional piece of scholarship, Namier had
experienced nothing like the tranquillity and freedom of a secure
academic position: he lived, by turns, on teaching, journalism,
political commissions, subsidies from remarkably faithful well-
wishers, and even a spell as a sales representative in central
Europe for English cotton interests. He complained more than
once of the strain of his divided life, yet he always tried to give
priority to his long-projected book. The politics of eighteenth-
century England clearly mattered to him in ways that were not
altogether obvious.

With the details of his commitment to active Zionism before us,
the divisions within his personality which this signalled become all
the more striking, though this is not really explored in Rose's deliberately spare account. For it meant not only that Namier's own
most sustained public activity was so largely prompted by adherence to what looked to most observers at the time to be a quite
unrealistic, Romantic, essentially doctrinaire idea—politics by the
book and a pretty funny book at that—but also that he spent much
of his life engaged in drafting manifestos, issuing protests, and
writing letters to the press; taking part, in short, in the kind of politics without power which, as the sponsor of 'Namierism', he could
be expected to despise. The extraordinary history of Zionism has a
fascination all of its own, but certainly in the form in which
Namier was involved with it this can hardly be said to be a consequence of its exercise of power. The British government, through
the terms of the Palestine Mandate, largely had that. Namier could
praise or, more often, blame its decisions, but he was constantly,
humiliatingly reminded that he had no part to play in making
them. Namier the Zionist who sat in Foreign Office ante-rooms
simmering with rage at the latest piece of duplicity or inhumanity,
only to receive a cool dismissal from some lofty junior official, may,
perhaps, have found a kind of solace in Namier the historian's
reconstruction of a very different and much more satisfactory
pattern of political behaviour, and if so he would not have been the
first, or last, political historian to find in an intimacy with those
who exercised power in the past some compensation for an often

unacknowledged frustration at being so remote from it in the present.

The tensions in this picture are heightened when one discovers that Namier had several of what he regarded as the characteristic weaknesses of the intellectual in politics: he was inept at the arts of intrigue and compromise, remote from the prejudices of the rank and file, prickly and prone to get on some very high horses. It could not, however, be said that he also had that breed's supposed squeamishness about the use of force. He always insisted, vehemently, that a Jewish state would have to fight for its existence, though even here one senses from time to time the presence of frustrated, unavowed energies and the consequent posturing and self-deception. He was, by all accounts, an aggressive man, even something of a bully, and like many such he enjoyed exaggerating his own hard-headedness: when, as Berlin recounts, he would devastatingly ask candidates for a lectureship in English at the University of Jerusalem 'Can you shoot?', the performance had, to say the least, expressive as well as strictly selectorial functions.

Whatever the sources of these tensions, the passion, sincerity, and centrality of Namier's commitment to Zionism is beyond dispute. What also emerges from his private correspondence is just how far this was bound up with the hypnotic spell cast over him by Weizmann. (Lady Namier, who seems to have disliked Weizmann and whose marriage was the cause of a serious breach with him, may have given a somewhat muted picture of her husband's consuming attachment.) It was Weizmann who drew the younger man into Zionism, and his favour was always crucial to Namier's never very popular or secure place within Zionist organizations. Namier did not always endorse Weizmann's tactical choices, but, whatever his reservations, he could usually be flattered and inspired into some fresh co-operation. In the end, Weizmann was always seen as the only possible Moses for the return journey, and that, for Namier, overrode all else. But their friendship was certainly not without its strains, as none of Namier's friendships could be, it seems, and in another scene whose Englishness is almost the most striking thing about it we find Weizmann 'cutting' Namier dead. Why did it happen? Because the latter had just become an Anglican. Where did it happen? At the Athenaeum.

V

One of the things that bound Namier and Weizmann together was a deep, almost pious, Anglophilia. This admiration on the part of European Jews for a suitably idealized picture of Britain and its history (essentially, of course, the very Whig celebration of that history which, in its more specialized form, Namier was to help to undermine) has been remarked by Berlin and others in different contexts. Certainly, for both Namier and Weizmann, as Rose observes, 'the British connection was basic', and it was surely not for reasons of practical advantage alone that Namier was for so long an advocate of the idea of a Jewish National Home in Palestine as the 'Seventh Dominion' of the British Empire. Here the different strands of his emotional allegiances could come together. As late as 1957, when the Israeli government had decided to build a new Knesset, Namier urged Ben Gurion 'to adopt the British not the Continental arrangement of benches in the House', on the grounds, among others, that, as he had put it in an earlier essay on the subject, 'the arrangement of benches in the House of Commons reproduces the layout of a playing-field and fosters a team spirit'. The more common hemicycle (which, of course, the Knesset adopted) he sneered at, in typical vein, as 'one of those clever, logical Continental "improvements" which make Parliaments "representative" and unworkable'. Much of the pathos of Namier's life, as this suggests, came from wanting to be Burke in a situation which demanded that he be Bentham.

But Namier was nothing if not complicated, and his work on eighteenth-century England suggests that he didn't really want to be Burke either—at least not Burke the Whig rhapsode of the ancient constitution. Burke plus Freud, with a dash of Pareto, would be a more accurate characterization, for Namier was that familiar figure, the iconoclast who is, almost despite himself, drawn to certain forms of piety. His two great works on eighteenth-century England—*The Structure of Politics at the Accession of George III* (1929) and *England in the Age of the American Revolution* (1930)—were sustained assaults on those familiar, celebratory narratives of how English liberties were handed down from generation to generation by the judicious adaptiveness of (Whig) statesmen, despite the attempts to reverse this natural direction of English history by the tyrannical George III and his (Tory) advisers.

But, as Colley rightly observes, even if such anti-Whiggism was by the late 1920s not unique to Namier, 'he could certainly claim that the *form* of his history writing was an experimental and innovative one—a calculated use of structural analysis rather than the grand, narrative manner favoured by the Whig historians'. This is where Freud and, in Namier's own counter-suggestible way, Marx came in, but this meant, of course, that Namier ended up interpreting the pragmatic doings of the English political elite in terms of ideas drawn from worlds that could hardly have been more alien to it.

Namier made the eighteenth century his own to a greater extent than Halévy did the nineteenth, though each invested his chosen period with something of his own characteristics. Namier, partially sublimating both his ambition and his rage, was drawn to patrician statesmen and the manipulators of aristocratic connection, where Halévy, naturally judicious rather than enthusiastic, sympathetically evoked the contributions of voluntary associations and committees of urban worthies. More snobbish than Halévy, Namier, the landless scion of landed wealth, lamented Europe's loss of a genuinely aristocratic ruling class, and lavished attention on the country and period in which such a class came nearest to monopolizing political power. More reductive than Halévy, Namier, himself psychoanalysed by one of Freud's pupils in Vienna in the 1920s, sought in individual motivation the means of dissolving the smokescreen of ideology which groups threw over the pursuit of their interests. More touchy than Halévy, Namier, 'the doyen of the rejected' as he styled himself in 1953 when already garlanded with professional recognition and public honours, was a far more combative and controversial historian. More brilliant than Halévy, Namier, surely one of the few historians whose name has given the language a verb, undoubtedly had a wider and more profound impact not just on the writing of British history, but also on the practice of historiography more generally.

Namier, however, never completed his projected multi-volume history of England in the second half of the eighteenth century, just as his massive attempt at a complete prosopography of the eighteenth-century House of Commons was left unfinished at his death (and perhaps unfinishable, at least in the terms he had conceived it). And yet although Namier's love affair with English history was stormy, inconstant, and frustrated, it was still in its way a *love* affair. The qualities that drew him to his loved one were, characteristically, stated most forcefully in an indirect, negative fashion—in his scathing analysis of *1848: The Revolution of the Intellectuals*. Here, the *doctrinaires* and the theorists had had a field day, and the result had been chaos, betrayal, and dictatorship. But, as he made very clear, the revolutions and the social type at their heart were confined to 'Continental Europe'. 1848 in England had not amounted to much more than a Chartist demonstration at Kennington that had fizzled out because of the rain. Yet the contrast that he drew in this work, and that informed his otherwise dispersed historical writings, pointed to the central contradiction in his contradiction-filled career: Sir Lewis Namier created a significant role for himself as an intellectual largely by writing about the history of a country he admired for not having intellectuals.

4

Speaking with Authority: The Historian as Social Critic

I

Historians who also venture to write as social critics exemplify in a distinctive way the tension at the heart of the intellectual's, especially the academic intellectual's, cultural authority. In general terms, the authority of such figures derives from the alchemy between two not easily blended elements: on the one hand, the professionally validated command of a specialized discipline of inquiry; on the other, the capacity and willingness to speak accessibly to non-specialists on matters which can never be settled by expertise alone. In those disciplines characterized by technical complexity or specially evolved vocabularies, the strain shows most on the accessibility-and-relevance side of this tension. But for historians, as for (pre-poststructuralist) literary critics, the reverse is true: both the manner and the matter of their trade seem, in principle, so readily within the reach of the non-specialist that it is the claim to authority which more often gets called into question. Simply possessing more information about a particular bit of the past hardly seems sufficient claim on the attention of a general audience when addressing more controversial, or simply more contemporary, topics. So what distinctive disciplinary perspective does the trained historian bring to such discussions?

Gertrude Himmelfarb, *The De-moralization of Society: From Victorian Virtues to Modern Values* (Knopf, 1995).
Raphael Samuel, *Theatres of Memory*, vol. i: *Past and Present in Contemporary Culture* (Verso, 1994).

One difficulty here is that some of the strengths of the best historians—judgement about the comparative weight to be given to
interacting causes, a sense of the complexity of motive and the
ironies of unintended consequences, a constant alertness to the
power of anachronism—translate rather poorly into the rough-
and-tumble of the controversialist's trade. None the less, I applaud
those historians who do attempt to bring the fruits of their discipline to bear on issues of contemporary concern, but, in keeping
with the general commitment of the essays in this book, I do not
believe that this laudable attempt to address a wider audience
exempts them from meeting the appropriate scholarly and critical
standards. If the performance rests on a claim to intellectual
authority, that claim must be subjected to searching critical
scrutiny. Gertrude Himmelfarb and Raphael Samuel are two scholars who, in sharply contrasting ways, have attempted to deploy
their trained familiarity with the past, and especially with the
Victorian period, in current political and cultural debates. What do
their respective performances tell us about the possibilities, and the
limits, of the role of historian as social critic today?

II

'It ain't that hard to understand', *The New York Times* reported
Newt Gingrich as saying recently, referring to the idea of using
'shame' to stamp out undesirable behaviour. 'Read Himmelfarb's
book. It isn't that complicated.' Certainly, Mr Gingrich's summary
of Gertrude Himmelfarb's *The De-moralization of Society* could
not, as reported, be called 'complicated'. His remarks indicate one,
highly influential, level of response to the book, but they are
premised on the assumption that Himmelfarb's topical argument is
backed by the authority of historical scholarship. It is worth
considering how far that assumption is justified.

　　The De-moralization of Society is Gertrude Himmelfarb's tenth
book. As an historian, she has largely concentrated on the intellectual and social history of Victorian Britain; her earlier books dealt
with the thought of leading figures such as Acton, Darwin, and
Mill, while her more recent work has tended to focus on the analysis and treatment of poverty. Most of her historical writing has also
been intended, implicitly or (increasingly) explicitly, to address

issues in contemporary American society. Thus, for example, her highly controversial interpretation of John Stuart Mill, *On Liberty and Liberalism: The Case of John Stuart Mill*, published in 1974, contained a long concluding section in which she argued that the inadequacies of Mill's conception of liberty were most manifest in, and had perhaps contributed to, the glorification of individual self-expression, and especially sexual expression, in the present. Though in substance largely devoted to an exegesis of Mill's writings, the book's animating purpose was in fact a restatement of the case for convention, tradition, and inherited order.

In recent years, she has become an increasingly overt and increasingly prominent polemicist on behalf of current right-wing causes. Several portions of this book have already appeared in periodical form over the past seven years, their provenance constituting a roll-call of influential conservative journals: *The American Scholar*, *Commentary*, *Forbes Magazine*, *The Public Interest*, *The Wall Street Journal*. And personally, too, she is placed at the heart of the neo-conservative establishment in the Unites States: Irving Kristol, long-time editor of *The Public Interest*, is her husband, and William Kristol, leading Republican strategist and publicist, is her son. Though specialist scholars have expressed strong reservations about her historical work, her public standing is considerable: in 1991 she was selected by the National Endowment for the Humanities, then chaired by Lynne Cheney, to give the prestigious Jefferson Lecture, one of the highest American honours available to a scholar in the humanities.

In his essay on Coleridge, John Stuart Mill declared that 'an enlightened Radical or Liberal' ought 'to rejoice over such a Conservative', since the serious statement of contrary views was rare and valuable. Does Himmelfarb's book suggest that something similar might be said of her? Here, after all, is a senior, widely published scholar seeking to bring some of her extensive knowledge of the past to bear on problems of contemporary culture and society. In principle, even for those who may suspect they will not agree with her conclusions, this might be an exemplary performance in the role of Historian as Public Intellectual.

The De-moralization of Society contains seven chapters on aspects of Victorian society, concentrating largely on questions of poverty and charity and of sexuality and domestic life. The prologue, 'From Virtues to Values', asserts the claim that the firmly held Victorian sense of the priority of 'the virtues' has given way to the modern relativistic sense of the variability of 'values'. A substantial epilogue, 'A De-Moralized Society', sets out her case for the devastating effect this change is alleged to have had upon modern America and, less centrally, Britain.

The historical chapters are, as one might expect, cast in a form that makes them easily accessible to the non-expert reader. Their fairly extensive footnotes might suggest that they also aspire to be taken as contributions to scholarship, though it is hard to imagine most professional historians of nineteenth-century Britain finding anything here that they would regard as both new and true. From time to time these chapters try to induce a mildly revisionist *frisson*, in, for example, suggesting that urban conditions in Victorian England were not as bad as one might think or that many women were very happy with their 'separate sphere', and so on, but neither the definition of the topics nor the level of treatment really seem to reflect the contributions of recent scholarship. Reading these chapters, one has an uneasy feeling that the agenda that has led these topics to be selected for this treatment is being determined off-stage (if being determined in Washington, for such it surely is, can ever be described as 'off-stage').

The purpose of this longish historical detour is only made fully explicit in the epilogue. Contemporary society is, we are there told, in a pretty desperate state, and only a return to something like the moral certainties of the Victorians can save it. The evidence presented to support the claim that we face this desperate and, in the strict sense, historically unique plight is, by any standards, slight. It essentially consists of two series of statistics for the United States and Britain: figures for certain reported crimes and figures for 'illegitimacy', which she calls, in a characteristic phrase, 'those two powerful indexes of social pathology'. Nobody, I should think, could be untroubled by the incidence of crime, especially violent crime, in the contemporary United States, though the matter of the alleged rate of increase over the past century or more is bedevilled by questions of definition, under-reporting, and so on. Long-term variations in crime statistics often tell us as much about altered sensitivities to certain forms of behaviour and effectiveness in policing them as they do about any objective increase in the incidence of that behaviour. Still, one does not have to accept Himmelfarb's end-is-nigh-ism to feel that there is something to worry about here.

But quite why 'illegitimacy' is supposed to be such a powerful indicator of 'social pathology' is less clear. (At another point she brackets divorce rates with crime rates, though it is hard to see them as belonging to the same category; it is anyway surely arguable that the greater availability of divorce has tended to increase rather than diminish human happiness, an argument which not even the most counter-suggestible social thinker has been tempted to make for crime.) The most plausible case has to be that the presence of two parents makes it less likely that children will grow up delinquent. Indeed, Himmelfarb asserts, a trifle ambitiously as well as imprecisely, that it has been 'conclusively demonstrated' that 'the single-parent family is the most important factor associated with the "pathology of poverty" ' (the imprecision lies in the phrase 'factor associated with' which establishes nothing about the nature of the connection). But, even supposing there were such 'conclusive' evidence for this claim, the figures for 'illegitimacy' in contemporary society would not actually isolate the key element. For example, a recent British survey revealed that 77 per cent of a sample of women who had registered an 'illegitimate' birth five years earlier were still cohabiting; conversely, over two-thirds of 'single parent families' are the result not of 'illegitimacy' but of marital breakdown. In other words, rates of non-nuptial childbearing are of limited value in telling us about the number of adults involved in child-rearing. But this only underlines, what some of her other remarks anyway suggest, that one reason why Himmelfarb sticks to the sociologically unrewarding category of 'illegitimacy' is because she is really exercised about all that 'illicit' sex. And this, of course, is where the moral example of the Victorians is supposed to help.

Quite *how* it helps is not so clear, and it is at this point that some interesting issues about the role of history in social criticism begin to make themselves felt. Himmelfarb disclaims any intention of urging us to 'emulate' Victorian society: there can be no going back to a 'different stage of economic, technological, social, political, and cultural development'. But history is still 'instructive':

The main thing the Victorians can teach us is the importance of values— or, as they would have said, 'virtues'—in our public as well as private lives. And not so much the specifically Victorian virtues that we may well value today, as the importance of an ethos that does not denigrate or so thoroughly relativize values as to make them ineffectual and meaningless.

In fact, it turns out, one need not go specifically to the Victorian period to learn this lesson: history can 'remind us of a time, not so long ago, when all societies, liberal as well as conservative, affirmed values different from our own. (One need not go back to the Victorian age; several decades will suffice.)'

It will already be apparent that more than one claim is in play at once here. In particular, there is some unsteadiness between asserting that history acquaints us with societies that held values different from our own (which is, surely, true and beyond dispute), and asserting that all earlier periods held firmly to their values, whatever they happened to be, but that ours, uniquely, does not (which is highly disputable and, surely, false). It is some version of this latter claim that Himmelfarb returns to most frequently. Seen in historical perspective, 'it appears that the present, not the past, is the anomaly, the aberration'. So, for example, 'the kind of family that has been regarded for centuries as natural and normal' is now seen, apparently, as 'pathological'; equally, the 'sexual revolution' of the 1960s was indeed, in Himmelfarb's view, 'revolutionary', and so on.

What history teaches us, therefore, is that from, roughly, the appearance of *homo erectus* down to, roughly, 1962 all societies believed firmly in 'morality', but since then the whole thing has gone to hell. This is a bizarre position for a historian, of all people, to uphold, but it is made all the odder when juxtaposed to another of Himmelfarb's repeated claims about the present. 'Today's moralists' have a 'fanatical glint in their eye'; in fact it turns out that we are surrounded by so-called 'New Victorians' who 'zealously monitor' a 'code of behaviour' that is 'at once more permissive and more repressive than the old'. These are the upholders of 'moral correctness'.

But, wait, wasn't it supposed to be distinctive of the present age that we didn't really hold *any* moral values seriously? Although she more than once *says* that that is what is distinctive of the present, the real charge, as the above passages (which are actually far more numerous) indicate, is that people hold the *wrong* values: 'casual sexual intercourse is condoned, while a flirtatious remark may be grounds for legal action'. And who are the 'people' who hold this wrong-headed mix of moral convictions? Again, we find a kind of unsteadiness: these misguided moralists are described as constituting the 'dominant' or 'reigning' culture in the contemporary United States, though they are also accused of disdaining 'the mundane values of everyday life as experienced by ordinary people'.

We have long been familiar with the concept of 'Left paranoia', but at present we are surely seeing a recurring pattern, to which this book conforms, of 'Right paranoia': it is former Vice-President Dan Quayle's 'cultural elite' who are once again the target here, and it is their views that are alleged to dominate government and what Himmelfarb calls 'the educational establishment', although they are quite out of step with the beliefs of 'ordinary people'. It is a backhanded tribute to the importance that conservatives like Himmelfarb attach to the influence of liberal intellectuals and academics that in the United States of 1995 she can still feel that the urgent task is to prosecute this kind of *Kulturkampf*. 'The counterculture of yesteryear' (i.e. the poor old sixties again) is now the 'dominant culture', and 'one of the most effective weapons in the arsenal of the "counter-counterculture" is history'.

How should we characterize this particular attempt to enlist 'history' in the service of doctrinaire moralism and barefaced Beltway opportunism? One question to ask is whether those who are trying to understand, and even perhaps some of those who are trying to govern, the United States at the end of the twentieth century will find any especially relevant lesson in pondering on Victorian Britain more than on any other society (including, for example, nineteenth-century America). Suppose Himmelfarb had happened to be a scholar specializing in eighteenth-century France or seventeenth-century Holland, or in Tang China or imperial Rome: would she then have been able to write as though her scholarly work bore directly on current concerns? Although she occasionally writes as though historical perspective per se were all that mattered, it soon becomes clear that it is certain features characteristic of Victorian Britain, as opposed to any other historical time and place, that are supposed to be vitally relevant to the United States now. And this gives the clue to why this slight and oddly constituted book should be published with such accompanying hype, and hence a clue to assessing her performance as public intellectual more generally.

III

Victorian Britain was the first society to attempt to come to terms with the social consequences of industrialism. Probably the single greatest cultural force pre-determining the nature of that response

was the legacy of Protestant Christianity, especially in the form of
the 'Evangelical Revival' of the late eighteenth and early nineteenth
centuries. And, speaking in the broadest and most schematic terms,
the form taken by that response, in public debate and policy alike,
was a combination of individualism and moralism. In fact, even to
speak of 'combination' understates the extent to which, as historians have been recently coming to recognize, the individualism was
always and already moralized, just as the moralism was fundamentally and pervasively individualistic. Questions of social and
economic policy tended to be discussed in terms which accorded
priority to individual character and duty operating in an environment that was largely taken as given or otherwise beyond analysis.

One, equally schematic, way to characterize the political
thought and policy-making of the century between, roughly, 1880
and 1980 might be to say that they exhibited a sustained, if uneven
and often inconsistent, attempt to remedy the inadequacies of this
individualistic approach. This involved, above all, identifying the
structural elements in the determinations of individual fates, and
using the power of the community as a whole to prevent or redress
some of the most inefficient or most unjust consequences of these
structural forces. The beginnings of this response are evident in the
Victorian period itself, and although Himmelfarb's picture of the
age involves no mention of these developments, those in search of
the 'relevance' of the example of Victorian England to the contemporary United States might reflect that it was in this period that we
find the beginnings of legal protection of trade union activity,
collective provision of essential services, regulation of working
hours and conditions, publicly funded schools, libraries, and museums, death duties on inherited wealth, taxes on higher incomes,
and so on. In the course of the twentieth century an extensive
network of such measures was constructed as the analysis of the
structural forces at work deepened.

These ideas and measures were, of course, developed in response
to particular circumstances, and as some of those circumstances
changed—with, for instance, the decline in importance of the traditional manufacturing industries and the transformation of the old
urban working class—there would inevitably have been a reaction
against some of these measures and the analyses they were based
on. But in both Britain and, especially, the United States, something
else has become intertwined with that social or economic reaction

in ways that have fuelled it, given it a wider appeal, and turned it spiteful, namely a cultural reaction against a series of changes symbolized, or demonized, as 'the sixties'. And this conjunction of reactions has enlisted the support of those who feel, strongly but indistinctly, that 'things have gone too far'. Some of those who now denounce the counter-productiveness of 'welfare' believe that they could have sympathized with their parents' enthusiasm for New Deal welfare policies because those policies did not disturb what now, as part of an anxious, nostalgic reaction to the speed and scope of social and cultural change, get represented as the sexual, domestic, racial, and aesthetic verities. This produces a yearning for an Edenic state before the allegedly related corrosive forces of collectivism and the counter-culture did their deadly work.

For good historical reasons, Victorian Britain can more easily be made to look like a plausible embodiment of this happy condition than most other times and places, and *The De-moralization of Society* is designed to exploit this availability for maximum ideological effect. Moreover, the Victorian period is just near enough, and can seem (though this is often an illusion) familiar enough, to allow the projection onto it of psychological longings and cultural fantasies which are actually expressive of the strains of social change and generational conflict in the present. This was made embarrassingly clear in the course of the 'return to Victorian values' episode as it played itself out in British politics and culture in the mid-1980s, an episode that seems to be being restaged under American conditions (Himmelfarb begins her book with Mrs Thatcher's invocation of 'Victorian values' in the election campaign of 1983). As I argue in the following chapter, British historians were pretty unanimous in finding only the most tenuous or superficial links between the world conjured up by Tory politicians and the realities of Victorian society. The 'Victorian values' celebrated by Mrs Thatcher actually looked much more like an idealized version of the norms of the English lower middle class between the wars.

Mrs Thatcher's elaboration of this picture came in the course of an interview, and so needed to be judged by the criteria appropriate to that genre. But Gertrude Himmelfarb is self-consciously aspiring to the role of scholar-as-intellectual, where quite different standards apply. Speaking generally, what distinguishes the most successful practitioners of this role—those whom it is worth

reading even when one does not agree with them, perhaps especially when one does not agree with them—is the ability to
suggest that, though any single piece of writing may be occasional, accessible, and brief, it embodies some of the fruits of a
genuine attempt to pursue a line of inquiry to its limits. A particular essay or book by such a figure may be passionate and partisan, and all the better for that. But the cultural authority comes
in part from the reader's sense that the scholar-as-intellectual is
drawing on or making accessible thought and research that, on
another occasion or in another idiom, have taken inquiry as far
as, for the moment, it can go. By contrast, one's sense with this
book as with some other examples of Himmelfarb's work is that
the ulterior polemical purpose imposed itself at too early a stage
in the process and short-circuited any deeper, more sustained
probing of the complexities of the issues.

   This is one reason why, one is forced to conclude, she is not a
modern version of that kind of intelligent conservative opponent
Mill urged radicals to be grateful for. But she also falls short of that
role because her allergy to the present is too strong to allow her to
give a discriminating account of it. This irritable dismissal of so
much that is active in contemporary culture, this desperate wish
that the 1960s had never happened and that one could return to the
apparent certainties of the era of one's own early adulthood, is the
negation of any genuinely historical response to contemporary
issues. A mind that comes to rest so easily, and in such a predictable
place, has little to offer to anyone not already disposed to welcome
the same nostalgic and reality-evading simplicities. So, *The De-
moralization of Society* does not, alas, provide a heartening or
edifying example of the historian as public intellectual: it is too full
of resentment, tendentiousness, and closed-mindedness for that. It
might more accurately be titled 'Portrait of the Historian as an Old
Grump'.

IV

There seems no doubt that in Britain at the end of the twentieth
century, opportunities to fulfil the role of cultural critic present
themselves to historians rather more readily than to, say, philosophers or sociologists. This clearly has something to do with the

explosion of popular interest in recent decades in what can only be called 'pastifying'. Few areas of British life seem untouched by this mania for revival, restoration, conservation, and imitation. At times it can seem as though we are all simply extras in a continuous performance staged by Olde Worlde Productions PLC. But the very strength and vitality of popular engagement with the past (or something got up to look like the past) both promotes historians to centre stage and at the same time calls their standing as cultural critics into question. When all are eager to graze on the commons of the past, professional historians can appear to be little more than avaricious enclosers.

This problem is raised in a particularly interesting and pressing way by the first of the projected three volumes of Raphael Samuel's *Theatres of Memory*. Far from disdaining or deploring the commodification of olden times encouraged by the heritage industry, Samuel (for many years Tutor in History at Ruskin College, Oxford) urges us to celebrate the fact that 'we live in an expanding historical culture'. He delights in the claim that 'history as a mass activity—or at any rate as a pastime—has never had more followers than it does today, when the spectacle of the past excites the kind of attention which earlier epochs attached to the new'. And he takes the most inclusive and determinedly democratic view: history should be thought of 'as an activity rather than a profession', and Clio's army should be run on strictly egalitarian lines so that professional historians stand alongside collectors, conservationists, photo-researchers, producers of costume dramas, and so on. This first volume is accordingly devoted to 'the ways in which history is being rewritten and reconceptualized as a result of changes in the environment, innovations in the technologies of retrieval, and democratizations in the production and dissemination of knowledge'.

Theatres of Memory, a collection of articles and occasional pieces, certainly provides a showcase for Samuel's own quite astonishing historical and cultural range, and its form displays some of that bustling miscellaneousness that it is intended to celebrate. There are pieces on 'Retro-chic' and on 'Heritage-baiting', on 'Dockland Dickens' and on 'The Discovery of Old Photographs', and on a whole host of other related topics. The tone is by turns exuberant, combative, and fond, and (as one would expect from such a champion of using visual as well verbal

records of the past), there are some striking and acutely analysed
illustrations.

Although the book ranges widely, at its heart is a preoccupation
with one remarkable cultural development: the transition from the
modernizing aesthetic of the 1940s and 1950s to the 'retro' boom
of recent decades, the explosion of enthusiasm for all things
'period' or 'authentic', whether in architecture, design, music,
'living museums', or the many varieties of collecting. Samuel documents this change in rich detail. He does not strive for any encompassing explanation of it (the old joke about Oxford history as the
'home of lost causality' comes to mind as one tries to find a path
through his throng of examples), but economic factors clearly
constitute at the very least an enabling precondition. Conservation,
whether of unproductive bits of nature or obsolete bits of architecture, is surely the stepchild of prosperity. As Samuel observes, there
have been period 'revivals' in fashion often enough before; what
distinguishes what I am calling the pastifying mania of recent
decades is that the post-war diffusion of prosperity and higher
living standards has put this degree of aesthetic choice within reach
of unprecedentedly large numbers of people. When the historic
burdens of scarcity and labour are initially lightened, the first move
is towards convenience and freedom. For a generation whose
parents had scrimped and struggled in cramped, dark little terraces,
and had endured the rigours of the Depression and the deprivations
of war-time austerity, the airy modernity and labour-saving appli-
ances of post-war architecture and design were a liberation. The
passage to utopia was finished with formica.

The vogue in the succeeding generation for stripped pine and
'farmhouse kitchens' was obviously partly a reaction, itself facilitated by further prosperity, against the evangelism of the preceding
knock-it-all-down-and-start-again period. At the same time,
Samuel is acute on how a good deal of 'retrofitting' is moderniza-
tion in disguise. 'Authentic period details' are prized selling-points
for Victorian terraced houses, but this does not usually mean a
newly restored outside lavatory, and the 'natural pine' work-
surfaces nearly always shelter a fridge and a washing machine.
Similarly, few of the fifty million people who take Sunday afternoon rides on restored steam trains each summer would be willing
to travel to work on them each day, especially if it meant giving up
their cars.

Rates of owner-occupancy are probably the chief index of the underlying changes involved: in 1952 29 per cent of all householders owned their homes; now the figure is 64 per cent. The decline of the old industrial working class is signalled by the rise of the architectural salvage merchants. It is appropriate that Samuel, one of the moving spirits thirty years ago of labour history and subsequently of the *History Workshop Journal*, should now be the chronicler of the popular taste for steam rallies and craft shops.

As represented here, Raphael Samuel is the Gibbon of the 'Georgian-style' estates and the Macaulay of the antique marts. I remember a junk stall from my youth (reading him prompts such memories) which bore the legend 'no item too small'. This could serve as the epigraph for this magpie's delight of a book. Where else would one find between the same covers references to the history of the Victorian jigsaw puzzle, articles in the *Brick Bulletin* (Samuel is fascinating on 'the revival of brick'), the information that the Jousting Federation of Great Britain is affiliated to the Sports Council or that the Royal Society for the Protection of Birds now has a larger membership than the Labour Party, a discussion of the pictures hanging on the walls of Little Chef restaurants, an analysis of the musical *Me and My Girl* as pastoral, and a confident mention of 'the demographic explosion among fourteenth-century rabbits'? And how many historians have earned the right, as Samuel surely has, to have a footnote which, in its entirety, reads: 'Wee Willie Winkie Candleholder feature in the Save the Children Christmas Catalogue, 1992'? (The footnote which may evoke most fellow-feeling among scholars, however, simply reads 'Reference mislaid.')

One clue to the otherwise elusive unity of this book is the unabashed declaration standing at the head of the Index which reads: 'Note: most references are to England unless otherwise indicated'. It is not just that, a few passing references to other countries aside, his subject-matter is English (and not even really British) history: it is, rather, that several of these essays evince a deep, at times almost Betjemanesque, fascination with details of topography and the stranger quirks of the English suburban imagination. Above all, the book seems to be the expression of a long-standing love affair with London, the more unfashionable the district the better—one of his many points of contact with Dickens (to take a literary comparison he would probably prefer).

Another detail which catches the endearing but slightly sham-
bolic nature of the book as a whole is its index entry for 'Camden'.
On closer inspection, the pages referred to turn out to contain
references to William Camden, the seventeenth-century antiquary;
to the Camden Society, the Gothic revival ecclesiologists of the
1840s; and to Camden Town, the district in London. My response
to this discovery epitomized my feeling about the whole volume: I
kept wanting to enter mild caveats about the differences between
the diverse topics Samuel brings together in unexpected and suggestive ways, while at the same time wishing, given the riches on
display here, that more time and care had been lavished on making
it a better *book*. But perhaps sceptical nominalism is as out of place
here as the desire to tidy up this dishevelled, loquacious, and deeply
engaging collection. Even if we return to the study and the library
afterwards, Samuel shows us how much we have to learn if we are
willing to make the journey from the Camden Society to Camden
Lock.

V

However, describing this book in terms which make it sound like a
hamper of yummy but oddly assorted goodies risks hitting a condescending note which would be utterly misplaced. Apart from not
doing justice to the sheer sophistication of the writing, any such
account would not be giving proper prominence to Samuel's
frequently reiterated polemical claims. These claims, which bear
directly on the role of the historian as cultural critic, demand serious consideration even though they do not, in the end, seem to me
altogether persuasive.

These polemics are structured around an antagonism to those
whom he stigmatizes as 'academic historians' (and he does seem to
use the term as a sneer). This benighted breed are in thrall to the
most narrowly positivist conceptions of knowledge; they fetishize
archival research at the expense of a more imaginative range of
sources; they disdain or neglect the efforts of those whom they
regard as making up the other ranks in Clio's army; and they cling
to old 'master narratives' inherited from the nineteenth century, in
which the national story is told almost entirely in terms of the
doings of the traditional political and cultural elite.

Although it would not be hard to think of candidates whose profile fitted this identikit picture, Samuel's strictures seem unhelpfully swingeing and—dare one say?—a little out of date. It is surely no longer true, for instance, that historians in general neglect visual sources or material culture, and although many of Samuel's own extensive references are to works by amateurs and enthusiasts of various sorts, many others testify to the imaginative work now done by 'academic historians' on a huge range of topics that are neither archive-bound nor confined to the doings of elites. Indeed, given the international and collaborative nature of much of this research, it is Samuel himself who runs the risk of a muddy-boots version of little-Englandism in regretting that historians are no longer tramping the battlefields or going on archaeological walks, but instead are 'calling up a transatlantic or Antipodean printout'. The richness of the more substantial essays in this book is the best argument against hypothetical critics who might stuffily maintain that this is not 'real history'; his irritation with 'academic historians', though in some ways understandable, is a distraction.

The distorting effect of such polemical antagonism also seems to me evident in a curious unsteadiness in Samuel's attitude towards postmodernist claims about the nature of historical knowledge. At one point he states firmly that 'history is not the prerogative of the historian, nor even, as postmodernism contends, a historian's "invention" '. But at other points, when denouncing what he continually claims is the narrow empiricism of 'academic historians', he asserts that historians 'are in fact constantly reinterpreting the past in the light of the present, and indeed, like conservationists and restorationists in other spheres, reinventing it'. In this vein, he insists that we should not attempt to draw too sharp or impassable a dividing line between 'history'—esteemed as serious, objective, systematic—and 'memory' or even 'heritage', disdained as popular, subjective, eclectic. Let a thousand flowers bloom is rather the spirit of his methodological reflections. But in wanting to defend the various forms of popular enthusiasm for the past against both 'academic historians' and those whom, with equal imprecision, he labels 'aesthetes', Samuel seems to come perilously close to endorsing the abandonment of the historian's critical function altogether.

Of course, it is true that all the while powerfully placed persons use the claim that 'the facts must be allowed to speak for themselves' to support positions which are ultimately anti-intellectual (and which at present tend to go along with reactionary politics), then it can be worth pointing out how all history involves selection, preconceptions, artifice, and so on. But it seems to me that Samuel is being false to his own political as well as historical best self when he exaggerates these truisms into the claim that historians, like other restorationists, 'reinvent' the past.

A similar anxiety is raised by the interesting and in some ways surprising political argument carried by these essays. Samuel wants to reclaim 'heritage' for the Left. However, it is hard to say quite what 'Left' stands for in this case. He chiefly insists, as we have seen, on a democratic inclusiveness when it comes to recovering the past: we are all historians now. There is no trace here of the proletariat as a revolutionary force: if the people were ever to storm Buckingham Palace, they would presumably be in search of bits of architectural salvage with which to retro-chic their recently bought council houses. Stressing the vital, popular energies at work in current dealings with the past, he pooh-poohs 'accounts of the heritage industry which see it as a kind of ruling-class conspiracy', and, strikingly for a stalwart of the old New Left, he at one point writes dismissively of 'such abstracts as "capital" and "consumerism" '. He is critical of the work of the Birmingham Centre for Contemporary Cultural Studies 'popular memory' group, and he even takes issue with Raymond Williams's analysis of the reactionary function of 'ruralist nostalgia'. This undogmatic openness is welcome, but it again leaves one wondering about the standards by which the critical historian might be empowered to expose the phonier or more pernicious manipulations of the past.

One expression of Samuel's apparent permissiveness (as well, perhaps, as a sign of the times) is the very slight part played in these pages by the notion of 'ideology'. And yet it seems hard to get by without some such analytical tool when, for example, one encounters politicians trying to cover the nakedness of a narrow individualism by invoking images of village greens, warm beer, and the historical kitsch of consumer-friendly Englishness. Samuel would presumably take issue with those particular representations elsewhere, but in this volume he seems to replace familiar Left *Ideologiekritik* with democratic inclusiveness in both politics and aesthetics.

However, this is precisely what raises the issue of cultural authority in such an acute form. There was a time, of course, when Marxism seemed to provide one theoretically satisfying resolution of the dilemma faced by anyone who wanted to be at once a critical intellectual while remaining impeccably democratic in their practice and sensibilities. But for those who are no longer persuaded, as for those who were never persuaded, by classical Marxist theory, some acknowledgement of the authority of the standards of scholarship seems inevitable, even if it risks being pilloried as 'elitist'. For the truth surely is that Samuel himself is an accomplished 'academic historian', skilfully drawing on a disciplined understanding of the past and profiting from analyses and perspectives worked out in those very learned journals and graduate seminars he mocks.

Samuel concludes by urging professional historians to engage with the whole range of contemporary dealings with the past rather than standing aloof: with all that is at stake in education and public debate, 'it would be absurd for historians to abandon the field of moral and political argument; to attempt to return to history with a capital "H"—that is, a single master narrative—or to try to retreat to the cloistered seclusion of a library carrel'. This is well said, but some of his other pronouncements leave it a little unclear just what the historian *qua* historian has to offer that retrofitters, heritage specialists, and old-print dealers do not. Samuel is clearly drawn to the markets of the Portobello Road and Camden Lock, drawn to them as places to browse but drawn to them also for what they symbolize about the democratization of historical taste. His writing suggests that he would like to set up his stall there, too, selling history to a broad public. But surely the historian could not for very long live in peace with his fellow stallholders, because the chief product he has to sell is the trained scepticism that says 'it wasn't like that'. There are many passages and some whole pieces in this volume which demonstrate beyond any cavilling that Samuel can be a wonderful historian in this vein—alert, shrewd, resourceful, and funny. But those are just the qualities which, when applied to the claims made for their 'authentic' wares, would be bound to make his fellow stallholders edgy.

To put the point in another way, one could say that some of the best things in this collection—such as the analysis of the staged spontaneity of some of the social-realist documentary photography of the 1930s, or the passionate attack on the 'contrived

authenticities' of certain adaptations of Dickens, or the revelation
that the original of the 'Edwardian Lady' of *Country Diary* fame
'was not in fact a country lady at all but a Birmingham Socialist,
and an artist, somewhat akin, in origins, occupation, and outlook,
to the Miriam of D. H. Lawrence's *Sons and Lovers*'—not only
suggest that it cannot be right (for any but the bluntest polemical
purposes) to speak of the historian 'reinventing' the past; they also
exemplify precisely the intellectual authority which the good
historian brings to the role of cultural critic. It would be all the
greater pity, therefore, if the go-with-the-flow inclusiveness of
some of Samuel's polemical remarks were taken, at face value, as
an abdication of this authority. At a time when policies on matters
ranging from the National Curriculum to 'family values' bear the
impress of a politics of nostalgia, nourished by the marketing of
'heritage', we more than ever need historians, like Samuel at his
best, who will, with authority, say 'it wasn't like that'.

5

Victorian Values: From the Clapham Sect to the Clapham Omnibus

I

Who's afraid of 'Victorian values'? And, as the exam question traditionally adds, if not why not? For the phrase, as deployed by Mrs Thatcher and her colleagues in the 1980s, expressed something which those who believe in the informing values of the intellectual life have good cause to fear. The real emotional dynamic behind the phrase and the policies it purportedly informed was laid bare, indecently bare, by (as usual) Norman Tebbit. On the eve of the Tory Party conference in 1988, he was reported as explaining how he represented 'the man in the pub' whose values, he claimed, were superior to those of the upper-class 'cocktail set'. This 'man in the pub' (none other, presumably, than our old friend 'the man on the Clapham omnibus' consoling himself for the fact that the service has been cut) is, according to Mr Tebbit, 'far more attached to our traditional values than . . . [are] his social superiors, so called, and intellectual betters'.

Perhaps it ought to be cheering to find the then Chairman of the Conservative Party sneering at the traditional possessors of wealth and privilege, but the consequences of this resentful pseudo-populism are too dismal even for those with a taste for historical irony to be able to take much satisfaction from the spectacle. None

James Walvin, *Victorian Values* (André Deutsch, 1987).
Susan Pedersen and Peter Mandler (eds.), *After the Victorians: Private Conscience and Public Duty in Modern Britain* (Routledge, 1994).

the less, such remarks do represent much of the ethos and idiom of modern popular 'Conservatism', and thus they do indirectly help us to understand the otherwise bizarre ideological appropriation by Mrs Thatcher and her successors in the 1990s of so-called 'Victorian values'. They also suggest the pitfalls of trying to co-opt bits of the past into party propaganda, since it was precisely the continuance of Victorian cultural attitudes that right-wing commentators, speaking in another voice, blamed for the paternalist and 'do-gooding' policies that hampered the efficient operation of British capitalism. In public debate, 'the Victorians' have simultaneously figured as the source of lost virtue and the cause of our recent discontents. Clearly, the whole function of the representation of the Victorian period at the end of the twentieth century merits further exploration.

II

If the shades of the severer kinds of Victorian moralist take any interest in our goings-on, the one cause for satisfaction they may have found in the whole shabby episode of the appeal to 'Victorian values' will have been the way in which it could be said to have provided professional historians with a lesson in humility. Initially, the transparently selective and tendentious nature of the ministerial references appeared to create an opportunity for historians to deploy their expertise in the public arena; this was their 'subject', after all, and such a high-handed appropriation of it needed to be challenged. The task could even be spiced with the piquant thought that here was a chance to show how one of the most anti-intellectual administrations of modern times had slipped up on an intellectual banana-skin of its own peeling. Weighty rebuttals were accordingly forthcoming, demonstrating conclusively that the Tory version of this aspect of our collective past was, from a strictly historical point of view, pure hogwash.

The lesson in humility came with the realization that this scholarly victory did not appear to make much difference. Judging by the recurrence of these historical allusions in platform speeches, it does not seem that before the 1987 election campaign Conservative Central Office had alerted candidates to their doubtful standing, nor, judging by the results, does it seem that the electorate was particularly bothered by the slipshod nature of the politicians' scholarship. This may be irritating rather than genuinely surprising, and perhaps it has suggested the need to think a bit more searchingly about the place of historical allusion in modern British culture generally, as I suggest in Chapters 1 and 2 above. But even at the level of superficial propaganda, there has always been some implausibility in trying to revive and make effective the values of an age that had very different moral and cultural suppositions, to say nothing of vastly different material circumstances.

To appreciate the barriers to such moral revivalism, consider an aspect of the difference between the two periods that is basic and pervasive in its effects, namely the extent to which the public language and private behaviour of Victorian England incorporated a far greater explicit inegalitarianism than could ever be avowed today. It may help if we begin by reminding ourselves that in the middle of the nineteenth century domestic servants still constituted the largest single occupational group in the country. Moreover, the deeply ingrained habit of talking *de haut en bas* was the natural foundation of many of the 'social welfare' measures of the period: there is a revealing difference in this respect between the values expressed in projects for 'missions' and 'settlements' in the East End, and those embodied in plans for 'task forces' for the inner cities. 'Duty' largely referred to the duties of one's station, and most of those stations have since been closed. For example, the immense positive valuation of 'charity' as a mode of relationship between individual members of the comfortable and the destitute classes is hardly likely to survive the transition from the world of the acknowledged social gradations of the Victorian city to that of the new 'I'm-as-good-as-the-next-man' skilled workers in the Tory marginals.

Or, to take a specific if obvious example, consider the value of 'thrift', much dwelt upon by the moral instructors of Victorian England. What does thrift really mean, what can it mean, for a generation scarred by the corrosive effects of high inflation and bombarded with invitations to take advantage of a variety of loans and deferred payments? An 'enterprise culture' is not only one where it may be economically rational to be in debt, but one where it is actually sanctioned by the implications of the official rhetoric. Invocations of thrift today may express a largely aesthetic distaste for waste and for conspicuous consumption, and they may even cast a glow of righteousness over the puritan doomsayers who want to believe that the whole *Wirtschaftswunder* of continuously rising living standards is about to blow up in our faces. But that's a far cry from the likes of Samuel Smiles intoning 'better to go to bed supperless than to rise in debt'.

However, the more successful we are in bringing out these alien features of Victorian social and moral attitudes, the more puzzling and intractable becomes the question of why it might seem to be in anyone's interest, politically speaking, to represent themselves as embodying the 'values' of this relatively distant period. The virtues of industry or thrift or patriotism could, it might be thought, perfectly well be argued for in their own terms: why turn the whole thing into a costume ball and deck the policies out in crinolines and side-whiskers? In one sense the question, thus put, answers itself. The historical fancy-dress hides the hard edges and appeals to the imagination. Notoriously a selective nostalgia of this kind, a nostalgia for something that its bearers could never have known, is a response to insecurity, and especially to the disorientating sense of being swept along by rapid changes that defy comprehension or control.

But even so, why *Victorian* values, why (lack of alliteration notwithstanding) not Edwardian or Elizabethan or Jacobean values? Obviously part of the answer lies in the area of policy that requires these touches of historical make-up. At times of overseas adventures like the Falklands expedition, there is a bull-market in references to Elizabethan sea-dogs and all that. In the present case a usury-friendly government needs to put the best face on policies that manifestly make the rich richer and the poor poorer, and one way to do this is to try to mobilize some kind of moral sanction for the view of life expressed in these measures. However, the resources of our present public language are a little thin in this direction, whereas the subtle, and sometimes not so subtle, blending of moral and economic arguments could be seen as a very pronounced, if not altogether distinctive, feature of Victorian political apologetic. It is still only a vague resonance rather than a literal application that is in question; even Lord Young, chief ministerial flag-waver for 'entrepreneurship', probably couldn't swallow whole the full Carlylean notion of 'Captains of Industry' as 'moral heroes' (and invocations of that dour sage can prove a touch inconvenient anyway: one can easily imagine his characterization of the moral status of overpaid, cocaine-sniffing, yuppie bond-dealers in the City). But none the less, the borrowed vocabulary, even in its diluted form, brings with it the politically congenial suggestion of the wholesome discipline exercised by the market. Moreover, if attempting to make one's way in the world can be presented as an extended course in moral education, then it becomes easier to apply notions of 'desert', with its full ethical weight, to those who fail as well as to those who succeed.

As I suggested in the previous essay when discussing the American version of this phenomenon, and as James Walvin observed of the British case in his *Victorian Values*, the whole ideological construction of 'Victorian values' was formed in reaction to some equally hypostasived notion of the 'permissive society' of the 1960s and 1970s. One could perhaps extend this a little further and suggest that a crucial element in the emotional dynamic of this reaction was the sense that people—other people, of course—might be getting things they didn't 'deserve', whether it was money or sex. Since it seems pretty clear that in Britain allusions to 'Victorian values' have actually been refracted through memories of lower-middle-class childhoods between the wars, what they essentially express is a mean-minded petty-bourgeois *ressentiment* that anyone—anyone else, of course—might get something for nothing.

A little light of a similar kind may be cast on the appeal of these allusions by reflecting that in so far as they do bear any relation to the actualities of Victorian attitudes, they call up those attitudes that were given political expression by the Liberal rather than the Tory Party. It is not in itself particularly odd to find today's Conservative Party aligning itself with its predecessors' opponents: yesterday's radicalism is always becoming tomorrow's conservatism. More interesting in the present case is the way in which some rather similar emotions may seem to find gratification in ostensibly similar policies. Some of the targets of the 'radicalism' of recent Tory governments could, after all, seem familiar to the mid-Victorian Liberal: entrenched municipal aldermen, over-endowed and under-producing universities, restrictive trade practices, and the like. If there is one Victorian political figure for whom the present Conservative Party should feel a natural affinity, it is not one of those traditional Tory stalwarts like the Duke of Wellington or Lord Salisbury, but the Liberal sponsor of public expenditure cuts and 'payment by results', Robert Lowe, the Norman Tebbit of the nineteenth century. But Thatcherite 'radicalism' has been highly selective, of course, and here any real alignment with Victorian Liberalism becomes quite misleading. In the nineteenth century there was an intelligible, if not strictly necessary, connection between, on the one hand, invoking the virtues of self-respect and hard work, and, on the other, proposing to abolish the House of Lords, dispossess large landowners, and disestablish the Church of England, causes which seem mysteriously absent from our neo-liberals' reforming agenda. And the more we dwell on the political as well as moral distance between the two periods, the more the invocation, at once manipulative and sincere, of 'Victorian values' comes to seem a topic requiring investigation by a whole team of cultural pathologists.

The politicians' phrase-making is parasitic upon, as well as a stimulus to, a more general interest in the world of our great-grandparents, but the connections do not all tell in the same direc-tion. One correlation the psephologists may not have investigated in recent elections is that between, on the one hand, restoring rather than replacing Victorian fireplaces and banisters, and, on the other, voting Alliance or Liberal Democrat rather than Conservative or Labour. I suspect it would be quite high, as might be the correlation between voting Tory and thinking of the Victorian era as a time when life was harder than it is now. There may be some rather complex social and psychological processes at work here. But among the reflections such findings might stimulate surely ought to be the modest conclusion that the part which professional historians can play in helping to explain, let alone in successfully contesting, the appeal of 'Victorian values' in contem-porary Britain is necessarily a limited one. None the less, hogwash is still hogwash; perhaps the man in the pub should be told that they're using it to water his beer.

III

By a curious twist that is characteristic of propaganda, the Victorians have also figured in recent years as the villains rather than the heroes, as contributors to 'national decline' rather than as models for 'national revival'. In the 1970s and 1980s, right-wing think-tanks and their academic lapdogs put about the idea that the ills of contemporary Britain were fundamentally due to its genteel aversion to industrialism and its sentimental attachment to collectivism. The selective and often tendentious accounts of the past that were intended to support this diagnosis traced the aetiology of these ailments back to the late nineteenth century, and particularly to the influence on social and economic policy of that cultivated elite of the well-connected and the well-intentioned who laid the foundations of the welfare state. Central to the would-be 'cultural revolution' of the Thatcher years was an aggressive populism which attempted to dislodge the descendants of this elite and the values they represented from their long-standing centrality in British culture, while characteristically feeble echoes of this assault were evident in John Major's later sneering at 'progressive theorists'.

There is, as I remarked above, always something rather quaint about seeing Tories complaining of 'elitism', but on closer inspection it usually turns out to be a certain kind of 'elite' who are being denounced in remarks of this kind. It is not the financial and business elite of managers, bankers, directors, and accountants who actually control so much political as well as economic power in modern Britain, but a cultural elite—stereotyped as paternalist, highbrow, mandarin, and (confusingly) 'progressive'. These were the people who for decades, it is alleged, had arrogantly presumed to prescribe what other people should have and what they should spend, what they should read and what they should watch. Latter-day members of this elite may have been being true to their Victorian forebears in exacting duty from themselves and deference from others, but both of these attitudes now stuck in the gullet of Essex Man. The policies of the 1980s were intended to strip these traditional elites of their cultural authority, and put power in the pockets of the people to enable them, through the market, to decide these things for themselves.

Interestingly, the Left, priding itself on being 'democratic' rather than 'populist', frequently attacked some very similar targets in *its* denunciations of 'elitism' (though these attacks, it must be said, were for the most part conducted in a more sophisticated theoretical idiom). Those who had inspired the welfare state were revealed to have had paternalist attitudes; those who shaped public broadcasting had transmitted mandarin tastes; those who instituted a national system of secondary education had inculcated class-bound

values, and so on. Although some individuals among 'the Great
and the Good' may have played admirable parts in furthering
particular radical causes, collectively these worthies were
condemned for their complicity with governing-class attitudes,
their assumption of intellectual superiority, and their patronizing
treatment of those working-class leaders who were, it is claimed,
speaking with the authentic voice of the victims of exploitation and
injustice.

In the demonology of both sides, a very large part was played by
a very small number: rarely in human history have so many blamed
so much on so few. The same people were to be found at the bulls-
eye of both targets: that thin layer of well-heeled, well-educated,
upper-middle or professional class men and, scarcely less prominently, women who continued both to endorse an ideal of the
public provision of social and cultural goods and to exemplify the
belief that those from cultivated and comfortable backgrounds
have an obligation to try to improve the lot of the less fortunate.
Their instincts were high-minded, high-handed, and high-taxing.
They had a vital hand in almost every measure which in the twentieth century had, until the 1980s, made Britain a less horrible
country to be poor in. They also supported things like public
libraries, taxing the ratepayer to provide the kind of improving
literature that was not always a popular taste; they supported
highly selective universities, taxing the entire working population
to provide a high-quality, culturally conservative education for a
meritocracy; they supported the BBC, taxing the licence-holder to
provide programmes that upheld high, and again not always vastly
popular, standards of instruction, information, and entertainment;
and so on. The combination of tireless philanthropy with unshake-
able cultural self-assurance was not always endearing, but both the
altruism and the confidence indicated the nineteenth-century roots
of these attitudes. Clearly, members of this elite were, metaphorically but also sometimes literally, the descendants of the Victorian
'intellectual aristocracy'.

IV

Much of the cultural history of twentieth-century Britain (and
some of its political history, too) can be told in terms of the long,

slow retreat of this stratum from the high places of political and
intellectual authority. The fact that we may now be able to begin to
get some kind of historical perspective on this development
suggests, as so often, that this extended historical episode is essentially over. A useful starting-point for trying to get to grips with this
complex development is the collection of essays edited by Susan
Pedersen and Peter Mandler under the title *After the Victorians*. As
the editors emphasize in their introductory essay on 'The British
Intelligentsia after the Victorians', the volume is intended to challenge the once-conventional assumption that the early decades of
the twentieth century saw a decisive break with the values of the
Victorian era, the assumption symbolized by Virginia Woolf's celebrated hyperbole that 'in or about December 1910, human character changed'. Those intellectuals whom we still find it convenient
to refer to as 'Bloomsbury' had their own reasons for parading
their revolt against Victorian parents and grandparents, and they
particularly emphasized the need to turn away from the coercive
moralism of public life to cultivate the more authentic satisfactions
of personal relations. Against an historiographical tradition which
has tended to take this self-description at face value, Pedersen and
Mandler argue that most British intellectuals in the first half of the
twentieth century maintained 'a quintessentially "Victorian"
tendency to link private behaviour to public morality', and that it
is 'the continuity of their activism . . . that is striking'.

Although this claim is hardly original, the combination of richly
documented detailed studies and a certain distance provided by the
overwhelmingly North American perspective of the volume
produces a particularly persuasive case which future historians of
the period will have to reckon with. The book is a fitting posthumous *Festschrift* for the Harvard historian John Clive (here fondly
recalled by Simon Schama). Clive's fascination with England and
its history went back to the period in the late 1930s when, as a
young German Jewish refugee (he arrived as Hans Kleyff), he was
exposed to the rigours of a minor public school. For the rest of his
life he remained drawn to, ambivalently admiring of, yet almost
anthropologically distant from, the mores of the English social and
intellectual elite. As an historian, Clive distinguished himself above
all as the biographer of Macaulay, and the trajectory described by
the essays in this volume could well be seen as that in which the
Clapham sect gives way to the Clapham omnibus.

As stages along this route, consider the following selection from
the ranks of the well-placed and high-minded who here receive
sympathetic discussion. There is Henrietta Barnett, patron of the
East End Settlement movement and founder of Hampstead Garden
Suburb; Raymond Unwin, architect to both Letchworth, the first
Garden City, and to the Hampstead project, a Socialist who drew
much of the inspiration for his democratic housing design from an
idealization of the cottages of medieval England; Eleanor
Rathbone, member of Liverpool's leading philanthropic dynasty,
local councillor and MP, and the ultimately successful sponsor of
family allowances; John Reith, sternly translating private
conscience into public broadcasting, and then failing to find
another pulpit of comparable reach; G. A. Lefroy, a bishop in
search of a church whose missionary spirit took him to the East
rather than the East End, and who became Bishop of Calcutta;
John Summerson, ambivalent champion of architectural
Modernism, disillusioned by the British public's unwillingness to
act as patron of this particular art.

If there was less obvious do-gooding about Leonard Woolf or
J. M. Keynes, it is none the less illuminating to consider them in
this company, and emphasizing their high conceptions of public
duty usefully complicates the easy stereotypes of Bloomsbury's
revolt against Victorianism. In some ways J. B. Priestley fits less
well, partly because of a quite different class background and
correspondingly less mandarin manner, but even so there are
numerous links between his pipe-smoking-and-good-fellowship
vision of England and the social attitudes displayed by those I have
just listed.

It is important, however, not to fall into the political historians'
trap of concentrating too narrowly on matters of *policy*, even
social policy or cultural policy. Doing so risks producing an unduly
narrow conception of 'the British intelligentsia' in this period, and
may thereby discourage a wider exploration of the sources and
forms of cultural authority. One might, after all, get a somewhat
different sense of how the relation between private conscience and
public duty had been negotiated by that intelligentsia if one
concentrated on, say, Russell, Trevelyan, Tawney, Lindsay, Ayer,
and similar figures. The danger in taking a too predominantly
policy-centred approach is that one risks perpetuating the familiar
philistinism of political historians for whom intellectuals only

'matter' when they directly affect political outcomes. Pedersen and Mandler are not altogether immune to this failing, and their frequent judgements about the 'effectiveness' or otherwise of these intellectuals in a 'democracy' imply a rather limited standard of assessment. Summerson, for example, the most recent of the figures I mentioned (he died in 1992 aged 88), might be thought to have exercised a widespread influence in Britain in the middle decades of the century on the understanding of architecture and its history. But although Mandler alludes to the general educative impact of Summerson's writings, his essay on him prefers to emphasize how the operative agents in the 're-building of Britain' in the 1950s and 1960s were government departments, local authorities, and speculative developers, among whom there was precious little trace of Summerson's ideal of an informed conversation between architects and public.

One benchmark against which the role of these figures can be measured is that provided by those mid- and late Victorian public moralists whose cultural leadership rested on, among other things, an appeal to a widely shared set of moral values. Here, private conscience and public duty could coincide, and, in the socially restricted political and cultural life of the mid-nineteenth century, they could be effective in shaping both policy and wider attitudes. This was partly because although Victorian Liberalism hymned the self-development of the individual, in practice only a rather narrow range of forms of such self-development proved to be acceptable. This in turn meant that an invitation to join the political nation was only extended to those who had already demonstrated their possession of the requisite virtues of sobriety, thrift, and 'character'. In other words, in the political, domestic, and cultural spheres the authority of the educated Victorian elite rested on a good deal of deference from those below.

One way to plot the fate of the subsequent generations of this elite is in terms of the slow uneven crumbling of this deference. For one thing, the eventual arrival of full democracy and a powerful Labour Party changed the terms on which political effectiveness could be achieved. The spread of more egalitarian social attitudes, including towards relations between the sexes, further eroded the sphere of action accorded to the well-connected Victorian moralist. The licence derived from deferential attitudes survived best, perhaps, in the cultural sphere, though even here there were signs

by the time of the Festival of Britain in 1951 that the Reithian writ
would no longer run.

As with all forms of cultural authority, there are clearly interesting two-way relationships to be explored between the confidence of
the elite and the deference of their public. Clearly, the combination
of personal privilege and moral certainty could produce a dauntingly robust self-assurance: a neighbour once remarked of
Henrietta Barnett that 'she was the only person I've ever known
who could recite the Ten Commandments as if she had just made
them up'. Eleanor Rathbone displayed a similar assurance when,
concerned to protect Indian women from Indian men, she appealed
to comfortably situated British women as 'the natural custodians of
that portion of the Imperial burden'. And Raymond Unwin spoke
from a deep moral self-confidence when, in comparing the architect
to the doctor, he spoke of building such homes as would develop
their occupants' 'higher natures' and 'better selves'.

This confidence was further nourished by the attention
bestowed on these individuals by the major cultural institutions of
the country: *The Times* reported Reith's speeches in full, Keynes
could place his articles where he wished, Summerson had almost
unrestricted access to the airwaves. Such confidence can more
easily coexist with occasional bouts of self-doubt than with the
acid of self-irony, and the terms of the contract between Privilege
and Duty rarely seem to have been questioned. 'The English system
of government', wrote Henrietta Barnett, 'is based on the belief
that there is in every district a leisured and cultivated class able to
give time and thought to municipal and other public duties, and
when such a class is absent the whole suffers both financially and
ethically.'

Nous avons changé tout cela! No doubt most of us would now
bridle at being told what to do by the likes of the formidable Mrs
Barnett or the no less formidable Miss Rathbone, and the tones in
which Lord Reith or Sir John Summerson attempted to instruct
their audiences might well grate on our touchily egalitarian sensibilities. But having been supplanted by the aggressive bottom-
lining of the gutter individualism of the 1980s and 1990s, the
figures discussed in *After The Victorians* are recovering the dignity
of which a couple of generations of post-Stracheyan debunking
had deprived them. They have proved easy to mock but difficult
to replace. Recognizing this, future historians may come to agree

that real 'Victorian values' of the kind exhibited by this 'cultural elite' persisted far deeper into the twentieth century than has commonly been acknowledged. Who knows, perhaps they will even conclude that in or about May 1979, human character changed.

II
MINDS

6

High Mind: John Stuart Mill

I

As I indicated in the Introduction, all the essays in Part II focus on individual biography in an attempt to explore the relations between ideas, sensibility, and personality in several leading English writers and thinkers. A secondary part of my purpose here, as I acknowledged, is to show how some of the most substantial or forbidding forms of modern scholarly publication—a comprehensive 'Collected Works', a thoroughly researched biography, an annotated edition of correspondence—can yield interest and insight to non-specialist readers beyond the austerer purposes that such learned publications are intended to serve. Of these three scholarly forms, the complete and fully annotated edition of an author's works may, at first sight, appear the most forbidding, useful only to the dedicated researcher trying to track down an obscure article or a textual variant. But such an edition can in some circumstances lead us to revise and extend our sense of an author's range and interest, as well as making available minor works which might otherwise be thought not to merit a modern edition. A striking

John Stuart Mill, *The Collected Works of John Stuart Mill* (University of Toronto Press and Routledge and Kegan Paul), vol. i: *Autobiography and Literary Essays*, ed. John M. Robson and Jack Stillinger; vols. xxvi and xxvii: *Journals and Debating Speeches*, ed. John M. Robson; vol. xx: *Essays on French History and Historians*, ed. John M. Robson, with introd. by John C. Cairns; vols. xxii–xxv: *Newspaper Writings*, ed. Ann P. Robson and John M. Robson, with introd. by Ann P. Robson; vols. xxviii–xxix: *Public and Parliamentary Speeches*, ed. John M. Robson and Bruce Kinzer, with introd. by Bruce Kinzer (1982–9).

example of how interpretation can be transformed by such careful and comprehensive editing is provided by the massive *Collected Works of John Stuart Mill*, which, between 1963 and 1991, deposited 33 forbiddingly large volumes on the shelves of the better libraries (and of a few wealthy or imprudently zealous academics). The stated aim of the edition has been 'to present fully collated texts of those works which exist in a number of versions, both printed and manuscript, and to provide accurate texts of works previously unpublished or which have become relatively inaccessible'. Since general readers often know little more about Mill than his name, this essay is an attempt to make some of the most recent fruits of this new edition accessible to a wider public by drawing attention to what it tells us about some of the more engaging aspects of his life and work.

II

A passage from *Middlemarch* provides the opening theme. Challenged to explain what he means by calling Lydgate a prig, Fred Vincey declares that by a prig he means 'a fellow who wants to show that he has opinions'. 'Why, my dear, doctors must have opinions,' soothes Mrs Vincey, adding her rather minimalist view of the medical profession: 'What are they there for else?' 'Yes, mother, the opinions are paid for,' returns Fred, and then, immortally, 'But a prig is a fellow who is always making you a present of his opinions.' By this—or even, perhaps, any other—standard, John Stuart Mill was a prig.

There is in principle, likely to be something particularly disagreeable about a prig's autobiography. Apart from the self-importance inherent in the undertaking itself, the voice seems bound to be at once didactic and self-justifying. One who constantly parades the correctness or superiority of his own opinions and who habitually affects a lofty moral tone has more to lose than most of us by the record of inconsistency, evasiveness, and self-deception which any life must leave behind it. Given the intensity of feeling by which priggishness is fuelled, the requisite distance will be hard to attain: where everything is potentially a matter of principle, there can be no matters indifferent. Mill, as we are reminded by the editors of the volume containing his

Autobiography and Literary Essays, was far from being the 'chill
pedant of caricature'; on the contrary, he was, as the hostile *Times*
complained, 'intemperate and passionate' in public life, a man, as
his disciple John Morley later recalled, 'of extreme sensibility and
vital heat in things worth waxing hot about'. Such heat is
frequently fatal to that sense of irony, especially self-irony, which is
indispensable to the good autobiographer. Mill could sometimes
manage a kind of irony, particularly at the expense of political
opponents, though it tended to degenerate into sarcasm as the heat
did its work: but a reflective irony about himself did not come
easily if at all. This makes him an unpromising case since a pinch
of salt is usually regarded as an essential ingredient in any successful recipe for an autobiography, and as with other dishes it is better
if it is added by the cook rather than the consumer.

   None the less, despite these disqualifications, Mill's
Autobiography is undoubtedly a nineteenth-century classic, a work
which has fascinated, if not always charmed, generations of readers, and which has a secure place in the history of the genre. In
part, of course, this reflects Mill's own stature in so many fields of
thought, 'the only writer in the world', exaggerated Morley, 'whose
treatises on highly abstract subjects have been printed during his
lifetime in editions for the people, and sold at the price of railway
novels'. In part, too, it reflects the very extraordinary story he had
to tell about being the guinea-pig for a unique experiment in education, not just the well-known progression through Greek at 3,
Latin at 7, logic at 12, political economy at 13, and so on, but his
complete isolation from the usual influences of school and peers,
and the correspondingly pure impress of his father's views and
character. It was not Mill's precocity as such that was remarkable:
one can easily imagine him being beaten by owlish chess champi-
ons and Rubik's cube solvers younger than himself. It was, rather,
the forced, over-bred development of his powers of analysis and
argument in complex subjects like philosophy and political economy. He became, as contemporaries remarked, very much a 'made
or manufactured man', a high-speed, sharp-edged, turn-it-on-and-
off-it-goes 'reasoning machine'. Taken cold, the facts of this
upbringing have engendered in most people the response caught by
the lines from *The Prelude*, 'For this unnatural growth the trainer
blame, | Pity the tree'.

   And yet what constitutes the real fascination and achievement of

Mill's book is the way he manages, for all his occasional priggishness, to tell the story of this intellectual forced-feeding and his
partial, but only partial, recovery from it in that same calm,
comprehensive, judicious tone which distinguished almost all his
mature writing. The priggishness remains an obstacle: explaining,
self-justifyingly, his avoidance of 'society' during his years with
Harriet, he cannot resist asserting that such socializing has a
deplorable tendency to rub the edges off one's convictions ('not to
mention loss of time'), adding sententiously: 'A person of high
intellect should never go into unintellectual society unless he can
enter it as an apostle . . . Persons of even intellectual aspirations
had much better, if they can, make their habitual associates of at
least their equals, and as far as possible, their superiors, in knowledge, intellect, and elevation of sentiment.' But the force of his
account survives such disfigurements because on the whole that
immense evenness of tone is being deployed in the telling of a story
which it seems could not have issued in an author capable of telling
the story in that voice. The tree is twisted and knows it, but it is
straighter than it had any right to expect, and is recounting its
growth without resentment or special pleading.

    This balance is most fully exhibited in the portrait of his father,
never an easy subject for an autobiographer and one posing
uniquely troubling and uncomfortable problems for Mill. Yet the
account is even-handed without being bland, and full of perceptiveness even about, perhaps especially about, those traits of
character from which the young Mill had suffered most pain. His
father's harshness and irascibility receive full measure along with
his abilities and energy, and it does not hit a false or patronizing
note when Mill reflects 'it is impossible not to feel true pity for a
father who did, and who strove to do, so much for his children
who would have so valued their affection, yet who must have
been constantly feeling that fear of him was drying it up at its
source'. Again, there is empathy and an eye for detail in Mill's
comment on his struggles with Greek texts between the ages of 3
and 7.

What he was himself willing to undergo for the sake of my instruction may
be judged from the fact that I went through the whole process of preparing my Greek lessons in the same room and at the same table at which he
was writing: and as in those days Greek and English lexicons were not, and
I could make no more use of a Greek and Latin lexicon than could be made

without having yet begun to learn Latin, I was forced to have recourse to him for the meaning of every word which I did not know. This incessant interruption he, one of the most impatient of men, submitted to, and wrote under that interruption several volumes of his History, and all else that he had to write during those years.

And just occasionally, though perhaps too rarely, we get a glimpse of the vulnerable and almost pathetic attempts of the small boy to ape his father and win his love, as in this passage which he eventually omitted from the final draft: 'A voluntary exercise to which I was throughout my boyhood much addicted, was what I called writing histories: of course in imitation of my father—who used to give me the manuscript of part of his history of India to read. Almost as soon as I could hold a pen I must needs write a history of India too.'

Where the balance is notoriously absent is in his embarrassing eulogy of the other figure who dominates his account, Harriet Taylor, the married woman with whom he fell in love at the age of 24, with whom he maintained a long, intense, and apparently entirely chaste friendship for the next twenty years, and whom he married in 1851 after the death of her first husband. To stop the gossip about the unseemly intimacy had been one of Mill's main motives for leaving a record of his life, and when Harriet died in 1858, four years after the completion of the first version of his autobiography (now known as 'the early draft'), he made much of the revised version a memorial tribute to what he saw as her remarkable talents—more of a poet than Shelley, more of a philosopher than himself, and so on. The extravagance of the praise is self-defeating, and most subsequent readers have concurred in the saddened judgement of his friend, disciple, and first biographer, Alexander Bain, that these parts of the work reflect 'his extraordinary hallucination as to the personal qualities of his wife'.

In fact, the chapter of the *Autobiography* dealing with the second half of his life, in which Harriet is so prominent, is also where his priggishness almost entirely submerges the qualities which distinguish the account of his early life. In it he deals, for example, at disproportionate length with his three years as a Member of Parliament, and even then does not really manage to controvert Leslie Stephen's subsequent assessment that the philosopher who took 'many-sidedness' as his motto was a good party man in the Commons (I shall return to his years as an MP below). Self-justification seems bound to be the stuff of such an episode, and although Mill affected surprise at his election in the first place and indifference to his defeat in the following election, there is a hint of wounded pride, characteristically transmuted into righteous posturing, in his over-elaborate explanation of the reasons for his rejection by the enlarged electorate of 1868 (including 'an unscrupulous use of the usual pecuniary and other influences on the side of my Tory competitor while none were used on my side'). The title of this final chapter—'General view of the remainder of my life'—is fair warning of the flatness of its contents.

The dramatic focus of the earlier chapters is, of course, Mill's famous 'mental crisis', which gives to the plot an almost epic structure of growth, crisis, and recovery. One odd consequence of this structure has been that the nervous breakdown of this particular 20-year-old, that world-historical depression which his upbringing seemed to have had in store for him all along, has come to be one of the most widely used arguments against the moral and political theory of Utilitarianism as a whole, a consequence which Mill would most certainly not have welcomed. Romantic poetry famously provided him with the lifeline on which he pulled himself out of the pit, though opinions have differed ever since over how successful he was in integrating the insights gained from these new sources into what he continued to regard as a fundamentally Utilitarian theory. Many scholars have endorsed the hostile view of John Bowring, Bentham's editor and Mill's contemporary, that Mill 'was most emphatically a philosopher, but then he read Wordsworth and that muddled him, and he has been in a strange confusion ever since, endeavouring to unite poetry and philosophy'. But whatever the coherence or other merits of the moral view which Mill fashioned out of this experience, his encounter with Romantic poetry was a serious and fruitful one in its own right, as the juxtaposition of his early literary essays with the *Autobiography* in this magnificent edition (of which more below) enables us to see.

Not that Mill's views on poetry have hitherto gone entirely unremarked. It is now over forty years since M. H. Abrams, in his classic study of Romantic critical theory, *The Mirror and the Lamp*, identified Mill's essays on the subject as the purest statement of the 'expressive' theory of poetry which he took to have displaced in the course of the Romantic period the 'mimetic' and 'pragmatic' theories of the eighteenth century. Mill's views may be thought to owe more to the 'Preface' to the *Lyrical Ballads* than to examples of Romantic poetry itself: and one might add to his statement that before this encounter it was 'not that I disliked poetry, but that I was theoretically indifferent to it', the rider that after it had done its work he was no less 'theoretically' disposed in its favour.

Still, the encounter issued in some interesting reflections on poetry, including his now well-known definition that 'poetry is feeling, confessing itself to itself in moments of solitude, and embodying itself in symbols, which are the nearest possible representations of the feeling in the exact shape in which it exists in the poet's mind'. In distinguishing poetry and eloquence as types of expression of feeling, Mill relied heavily on the epigram that whereas 'eloquence is heard, poetry is overheard'. As Abrams pointed out, this necessarily resulted in the characteristic Romantic dethronement of epic or narrative by the short, intense lyric as the purest form of poetry, and Mill correspondingly elevated Shelley above even Wordsworth, though some of the former's creations were perhaps rather more didactic and extended than would be quite proper for a soliloquy. In fact, Mill quite soon modified his early view to the extent of making the union of thought and feeling the hallmark of the best poetry, a view which consorted better with the high educative role he assigned to it.

The liveliness of Mill's aesthetic interests at this stage of his life is also evident in his attempt to apply his distinction to music, to discriminate the 'poetry' and the 'oratory' of music. For example, in the earliest of these essays he concedes that the then fashionable music of Rossini is expressive, but he sees this as akin to eloquence rather than to poetry: as he nicely puts it, 'it is passion, but it is garrulous passion'. Mozart, on the other hand, though also adept at musical oratory, adopts 'in his most touching compositions' the style of poetry: 'Who can imagine *"Dove sono"* heard? We imagine it overheard.'

The literary essays also reveal a further unfamiliar side of Mill, his genuine and unusual ability not just to consider the merits of a point of view with which he strongly disagreed, but also to enter into the kinds of resonance or pathos characteristically associated with it (an ability which seemed, perhaps inevitably, to decline as he got older). It is particularly well illustrated here by his long review-article on the poems and romances of Alfred de Vigny, where he writes with sympathy about the sensibilities of a Catholic, royalist, aristocratic soldier who lived through the false glories of the Restoration to the humiliations of the July Monarchy. This essay is also a reminder of Mill's idealization of French cultural and intellectual life ('where both politics and poetry are taken completely *au sérieux*'), a taste which opened a gap between him and that large number of his contemporaries, and majority of his successors, who if they looked abroad at all looked to Germany rather than to France for their intellectual and aesthetic sustenance (I return to this theme below).

As a critic, as distinct from a theorist, of literature Mill would not earn a place in any nineteenth-century First XI, and the priggishness is part of the problem here, too. A remark about his attitude to poetry in his early unreconstructed Benthamite days points to an enduring feature of his responses: 'I disliked any sentiments in poetry which I should have disliked in prose: and that included a great deal'. And even when dealing with matters of style the schoolmasterly tone intrudes. He has received credit for being one of the first to give favourable notice to Tennyson's early poems, in a review reprinted in this volume, and certainly the piece is appreciative and generous. Still, he could not resist rebuking the poet for his lack of development in 'general spiritual culture', and his concluding paragraph almost falls into pastiche of the school report: 'In some of the most beautiful of Mr Tennyson's productions there are awkwardnesses and feeblenesses of expression, occasionally even absurdities, to be corrected . . . His powers of versification are not yet of the highest order . . . [These failings] need not have been mentioned except to indicate to Mr Tennyson the points on which some of his warmest admirers see most room and necessity for further efforts on his part.' That will be all, thank you, Mr Tennyson.

None the less, it was not a negligible achievement to have devoted a substantial and discriminating essay to Tennyson in 1835, and the fourteen essays and reviews included in this volume (eleven of which date from the 1830s) indicate Mill's extraordinary range. While spending the greater part of his days at his desk in India House, the young Mill (he was still only 24 in 1830) turned out an enormous number of articles on subjects ranging from parliamentary reform to moral philosophy, from French novels to

English political economy, and from Tennyson to Tocqueville, essays, moreover, which have earned a significant place in the history of the subjects with which they deal. James Mill had always insisted that questions be considered in the light of what he, alarmingly but probably not carelessly, referred to as 'the whole of the knowledge which we possess upon any subject'. In several obvious ways the son was a poor advertisement for the merits of the father's system of education, but there is no doubt that that education provided its victim with almost unmatchable equipment for carrying on the trade of man of letters.

The literary essays did not, on the whole, present the editors of the *Collected Works* with any major textual problems. The *Autobiography* most certainly did. There are, to begin with, three surviving manuscript copies: the first is of the early draft Mill wrote in 1853–4; the second is of the revised and extended draft which was largely written in 1861 and completed in 1869–70; and the third is the transcript from this draft made hurriedly by Mill's stepdaughter and other copyists after his death in 1873, from which the first edition was printed in the same year. Some indication of the differences between them is given by the calculation, first worked out by Professor Stillinger over thirty years ago, that Mill made some 2,600 changes, many of them very substantial, between the early and later drafts, and that there are then a further 2,650 variants, mostly minor, between that and the copy from which the first edition was printed, though some were corrected in printing.

All three manuscripts were sold by auction in 1922—Maggs paid five guineas for the lot. Mill's final draft went to Columbia University, whence a much improved but still, apparently, inadequate edition, by J. J. Coss, was published in 1924. The manuscript of the early draft was bought by a professor at Johns Hopkins, and after his death it languished with the rest of his papers in a Baltimore warehouse for almost twenty years before the collection was bought by the University of Illinois at Urbana in 1958. Thereafter the story belongs to Professor Stillinger, who produced the first published edition of the early draft in 1961, and then followed this up with his authoritative text of the final draft from the Columbia manuscript, published in 1969. These labours have now been *aufgehoben* in the present volume which contains, minor corrections apart, the texts of his two editions, their utility much enhanced by the printing of parallel passages from each draft on facing pages, supplemented by the kind of informative but discreet editorial material which one comes to take for granted in the Toronto edition of Mill's works (though this volume is billed as 'volume one' of the edition, it is in fact the eighteenth to appear). The Mill whom we encounter in these pages is not exactly new or unknown, but we are provided with such a wealth of detail and texture about the movement of his mind and his sensibility that it even becomes harder to regard him as a prig.

III

4 Decembre.
Je pris mes leçons ordinaires, je commençai avec M. Lentheric l'étude du Calcul Différentiel, j'arrangai mes plantes, j'achevai et j'envoyai une lettre à mon père.'

A day in the life of the future philosopher and sage? On the face of it, this is the sort of journal entry which any 14-year-old might make, practising his newly mastered French and diligently record-ing those doings of the day which would be most likely to earn adult commendation. But anyone who now turns to this particular adolescent record, newly available in the two volumes of *Journals and Debating Speeches*, is inevitably trying to extract from these flat, duty-driven entries some significant evidence about the devel-opment of the author of the many other works now gathered in the *Collected Works of John Stuart Mill*. Perhaps a footnote in some future study of Mill's resistance to marginalist economic theory fifty years later will refer to that early study of calculus, pursued under the private supervision of (so the unfailingly informative annotation tells us) the mathematics master at the *lycée* in Montpellier. For the rest, 'arranged my plants' could have appeared as part of the day's entry at any point in the next fifty-three years, had Mill continued to keep such a journal, so keen a botanizer did he become, though the reference to sending a letter to his father (never his mother) reminds us of the point of such scrupulous recording at this stage of his life.

There was only to be one other person in Mill's life to whom he would again wish to send such a daily account. When he and Harriet were separated in 1854 while Mill journeyed to Southern

Europe to try to recover his failing health, he set himself the daunting task of having one thought a day which would be worth recording, and the results offer the most complete contrast with the
characterless entry quoted above. It is true that Mill thought that
his death was imminent, which no doubt encouraged a certain lapi-
dariness of tone as well as the proverbial concentration of mind,
but there is a provocative crispness about many of these entries that
one does not always associate with Mill's prose.

March 9th
The characteristic of Germany is knowledge without thought: of France,
thought without knowledge: of England, neither knowledge nor thought.
The Germans, indeed, attempt thought; but their thought is worse than
none. The English, with rare exceptions, never attempt it. The French are
so familiar with it that those who cannot think at all throw the results of
their not-thinking into the forms of thought.

This comes dangerously close to blending, in almost equal measure,
a touch of the contrived Wildean epigram with a dash of post-
prandial pontificating, yet it (especially the last sentence) is an
observation not without interest in itself, quite apart from any
significance students of Mill's work might ascribe to it. Or again,
there is his longer entry for 28 February, in which he observes that
it is those thinkers who have a systematic theory of a whole department of thought who have enjoyed a permanent reputation: 'Yet
few of the systems of these systematic writers have any permanent
value as systems; their value is the value of some of their fragments.
But the fragments (the parts which are excellent in wholes which
are inadmissible) if published separately would probably have
attracted little notice.' A substantial collection of such nuggets
would constitute a very readable book with wide appeal; alas, the
1854 'Diary' occupies only 30 of the 760 spacious Toronto pages
that make up these two volumes. 'Je pris mes leçons ordinaires' is
no doubt a more faithful representation of time spent than are any
of the pondered and polished entries in the misleadingly named
'Diary', but as a result there are large tracts of these two volumes
which will probably only engage the attention of the most determined biographical researcher.
    The material falls into four unequal parts. First, there is the jour-
nal and notebook Mill kept during his year in France in 1820-1,
together with his notes on the logic he studied while attending

lectures at Montpellier University. Second, there are very full texts of twenty-five of the debating speeches he made between 1823 and 1829. Third, there are his journals of five of the summer walking tours he took in various parts of England between 1827 and 1832. And finally there is the 1854 'Diary'.

While the intellectual interest of much of the material assembled in these two volumes may be more limited than in any of their predecessors, the technical virtuosity required of the editor was in some ways greater than ever before. The items posed contrasting textual problems. The 1854 'Diary', for example, now only exists in the form in which it was published by Hugh Elliot as an appendix to his 1910 edition of Mill's correspondence; even the Toronto bloodhounds have failed to locate the original. By contrast, the story of the manuscripts of the speeches is immensely complex—indeed, the tracing of their fortunes, as summarized in the editor's introduction, has a fascination of its own for those interested in the vagaries of Mill's posthumous reputation. The central part in what Professor Robson mildly terms 'the regrettable history' of these documents was played by Harold Laski, who acquired the manuscripts in 1922, published some of them as an appendix to his (textually unreliable) edition of Mill's *Autobiography*, and sold or gave away others, sometimes without recording the fact. (Indeed, it is clear from Robson's scathingly restrained comments on Laski's editorial conduct—'Laski . . . appears never to have made a list of the manuscripts'—that that avid collector would never have been able to hold down a desk in the offices of the Mill Project.) As a result of the labours of the Toronto team, many of the speeches are here published for the first time, while the texts of those published by Laski are corrected in various ways.

The journal of Mill's French sojourn had been published thirty years ago by Anna J. Mill (no relation), to whom Professor Robson pays generous tribute, but of course this and all the related French materials have been re-edited according to the principles of this collected edition, and supplied with the appropriate explanatory annotations. The journals of the walking tours had, with a minor exception meticulously noted here, never previously been published. Editorial comment is in this case very usefully supplemented with extracts from the diary of Henry Cole, one of Mill's friends and occasional walking companions. In the case of both the French and the domestic tours, not only have the chronology and itinerary been checked and amended, but also the intelligibility of both accounts has been greatly facilitated by the provision of notably clear maps.

Different readers will doubtless value each of these sources differently. The speeches, for example, enable us to supplement or modify our accounts of Mill's intellectual development during the crucial period on either side of his 'mental crisis', providing further insight into his views on topics ranging from parliamentary reform to the respective merits of Wordsworth and Byron. On the other hand, I have to report that I found the prospect of reading another extremely detailed account of the scenery admired on one of the walking tours excited in me the sort of emotions normally associated with the invitation to come round and look at a neighbour's holiday snaps. That other responses to the walking-tour journals are not only possible but also more discerning is indicated by the very perceptive and well-informed discussion of Mill's conscious exploration of the aesthetic of the picturesque which is provided in the editorial introduction by John M. Robson, an unfailingly tactful cicerone for all visitors to Mill's mind.

IV

The role of the cultural critic who constantly appeals to the alleged virtues of another contemporary society as a way of correcting, or, less ambitiously, of condemning, the deficiencies of his native country offers peculiar opportunities and temptations. It is a role which seems to have been assumed with increasing frequency in modern English intellectual history, so frequently indeed that it is coming to seem a typical, and perhaps typically masochistic, form of Anglo-Saxon attitudinizing. Sharply drawn contrasts between the parochial, complacent, atheoretical nature of intellectual and political life in England and the more exciting alternatives supposedly offered elsewhere have not been in short supply for some time now, though the case for having one's political tradition primarily distinguished for its excitingness may only ever enjoy a brief if recurrent *succès fou*. Going native in the foreign culture involves, of course, a quite different response: a discontent with one's inherited cultural lot may obviously lie behind such a move, but the focus of attention thereafter becomes the effort to adapt to one's adopted milieu, to speak its language both literally and metaphorically. But for the writer who continues to be practically and (often despite himself) emotionally implicated in his own society, all the while nurturing a vivid sense of alienation, the scorned features of that society remain an obsessive preoccupation and his despised compatriots still constitute the relevant audience.

One obvious danger of this role, though by no means of this role alone, lies in the tendency (or perhaps it is really the necessity) to trade in stereotypes, and especially to homogenize one's own culture in order to produce a liberatingly uncomplicated target. Another, subtler, danger consists in the slide towards self-congratulation. For it is an essential part of the critic's case against the native culture that so few can escape its suffocating embrace, that so few are *au courant* with more significant developments elsewhere, that so few have the largeness of vision necessary to see its parish-pump doings in the wider cosmopolitan perspective. One's relation to one's culture thus becomes an irregular verb: I rise above it, you are constrained by it, he is its prisoner.

John Stuart Mill may be thought of as one of the first to occupy this role in its recognizably modern form. He was certainly marvellously adept at exploiting its opportunities for effective cultural criticism, though he was also, I would suggest, far from immune to its dangers. Mill saw himself as an outspoken, self-consciously 'extreme', radical critic of the whole established order of English politics and society; he was also, in important ways, a strong Francophile. As an example of a different aspect of the impact of the *Collected Works* on our understanding of Mill, we may consider some of the ways in which the appearance in one volume of his previously scattered *Essays on French History and Historians* enables us to explore the connection between these two parts of his intellectual identity.

The essays which make up this volume essentially fall into three categories, grouped by their decade of composition. There are those from his youthful 'Benthamite propagandist' phase of the 1820s, largely contesting Tory accounts of the French Revolution, among which his remorseless hatchet-job on Sir Walter Scott's *Life of Napoleon* is the most substantial; there are those from the 1830s, which marked a more eclectic phase in his intellectual life, the chief fruits here being his enthusiastic review of Carlyle's *French Revolution* and his unusually passionate memoir of the journalist and politician Armand Carrel; and there are those from the 1840s, written in his matured magisterial style, largely concerned with the philosophy of history, of which the fine essays on Michelet and on Guizot are the most significant. The stages are interestingly correlated with the changes in journal of first publication: the 1820s pieces all appeared in the frankly sectarian *Westminster Review*; those of the 1830s largely in the reconstituted *London and Westminster Review* which, under Mill's editorship and eventually proprietorship, was designedly more receptive to a variety of interests; and the two great essays of the 1840s first appeared in the pages of the more imposing *Edinburgh Review*, which indicated not only Mill's enhanced status as an author but also his concern to address a less partisan and more influential audience. It is indicative of Mill's pragmatic use of the crucial medium of the great periodicals, then in their heyday, that for the last of the pieces reprinted here, his brave and unpopular vindication of the 1848 revolution in France, he reverted to the shelter of the *Westminster*; since his article contained an unrestrained assault on the aged Lord Brougham it would anyway never have been carried by the staunchly Whig *Edinburgh* which Brougham had helped to found.

As these essays bear ample witness, Mill was drawn to France as both the home of democracy and the home of ideas. In paying homage to the French contribution on these matters, he was deliberately setting his face against the prevailing treatment of French history in England in the first half of the nineteenth century, where it was held up as a standing warning against the related dangers of revolutionary change and abstract doctrine. The notorious instability of post-1789 French politics provided one of the chief sources for self-congratulation among Whig celebrants of English political adaptiveness and constitutional continuity. Mill, enraged by the smugness that was prone to accompany this interpretation and all too aware of the part played by this reading of events in sustaining the aristocratic grip on English political life, passionately hoped that France would yet teach Europe a more encouraging lesson about the possibilities of popular government. He hurried to Paris in 1830, eager for the kind of political spectacle that was unthinkable in England, just as in 1848–9 he keenly and sympathetically followed the fluctuating fortunes of the constitutional and economic experiments of the new Republic. In each case, of course, as with the parent upheaval of 1789, revolution soon engendered reaction, and Mill had sorrowfully to acknowledge that unfortunate circumstances—or, more suggestively for the purposes of comparative sociological analysis, defects of the French national character—had once again diverted political improvement from its natural course. The long night of the autocratic Second Empire depressed his hopes still further, and it is surely revealing that after his vindication of 1848 he never again, in the extremely productive last twenty-five years of his life, wrote anything of substance on French history or politics. This may also have been because some of Mill's hopes had by then been transferred to the United States, the fate of whose 'Great Experiment' came to seem more consequential for human progress even than the barricade-erecting traditions of Parisian popular unrest.

However, it was the 'French Mind', in its larger utterances, that engaged Mill's sympathies most unreservedly, especially in the 1830s and early 1840s when he was brooding upon the philosophy of history or what, following Comte, he came to call 'sociology'. Here he identified a new 'school' of French thinkers who shared an original and distinctive approach to the great issues of social philosophy, but, as a closer scrutiny of the essays in this volume reveals, this conception of a 'school' was essentially a projection of his own theoretical preoccupations at the time. He insisted particularly on their vision of history as a progressive development and on their analysis of 'states of society' as profoundly explanatory of changes in forms of government. That these were in fact significantly original contentions is highly disputable, and it is far from obvious that any but the blandest similarities united figures as diverse as Michelet, Comte, and Tocqueville. Of course, what counts as similarity depends upon one's angle of vision (and even more, possibly, on one's distance from the object), and here again we have to recognize that the energizing centre of Mill's concern in these essays is provided by his exasperated antagonism to what he regarded as the 'merely empirical' character of English political reflection. This impulse, evident throughout, is best caught by the way he gleefully (but also, it has to be said, self-servingly) seized upon Guizot's remark from his *History of Civilisation in Europe*: 'If we open an English book of history, jurisprudence, or any similar subject, we seldom find in it the real foundation, the ultimate reason of things. In all matters, and especially in politics, pure doctrine and philosophy . . . have prospered far more on the Continent than in England.'

Mill, not unnaturally, found a congenial justification for his own chosen role in such remarks, but in these essays we can, I think, trace how certain limitations of his sensibilities and interests combined with the occupational hazards of this kind of cultural criticism to produce subtle distortions both of French history and thought and of their English counterparts. Here, as in so much else, we must begin by returning to the very young Mill.

V

In the 1820s Mill several times referred to his intention to write a history of the French Revolution, largely to correct the hostile misrepresentations of it still prevailing in post-Napoleonic England, and his early reviews of other works on the subject, which are reprinted in *Essays on French History and Historians*, constituted exercises in ground-clearing and claim-staking. As with all his writing of this early period, such a history, had he written it, would have no doubt been a pretty unvarnished piece of Philosophic Radical polemicizing. Though he continued to gather materials for some years, it was clear by the mid-1830s that he had definitely abandoned the project; the fact of his maid's burning the entire manuscript of Carlyle's *French Revolution* was an innocent accident, not the suspicious good fortune of a rival. In fact, as the confident simplicities of his early creed yielded to deeper understandings following his 'mental crisis' of the late 1820s, and as his heady enthusiasm for the 1830 revolution cooled in the face of the grubby realities of the self-interested politicking that marked the Citizen King's reign, the subject lost much of its appeal.

Of course, not writing a book, we may sympathetically reflect, is a fact less in need of explanation than most, but, as the majestic march of the stout volumes in the Toronto edition attests, there weren't many books Mill didn't write. A work of history, however, is a conspicuous absentee, and this is surely revealing of a deep feature of Mill's cast of mind. The truth is that he was not so much interested in history as in views *about* history: his was the social scientist's concern with the principles of explanation, not the historian's fascination with the obstinate idiosyncrasy of the particular, and this was both a strength and a weakness in thinking about the respective courses followed by English and French political development.

For although he could with some justice object to the combination of hysterical Francophobia and cosy self-congratulation that frequently characterized the English governing class's attitude towards the French Revolution in the half-century after 1789, there remained a subtler case—mounted first and most influentially by Burke, of course—against the kind of politics practised by the National Assembly. Mill did not, needless to say, wish to endorse the Terror or the decline into Bonapartism; he tended instead to stress the evils of the *Ancien Régime* and to defend the reformism of the Girondins. On this view, the Revolution was essentially complete by 1791. Individual ambition and other defects of the French national character accounted for the unfortunate turn of events thereafter.

But the deeper Burkean point, elaborated in different ways by the leading Whig historians in the succeeding century, was that such a violent disruption of the established order inevitably led to anarchy followed by despotism, especially when the disruption was carried out in the name of a schematic programme of absurdly abstract goals. No doubt the ritual citation in this historical literature of the virtues of 1688 and, eventually, of 1832 involved a certain amount of pious self-deception, but the case to be answered was, in essence, that a continuous tradition of political adaptability, even a tradition largely carried and given practical expression by a paternalistic oligarchy, provided a better guarantee of liberty than did dramatic attempts to institute popular power directly. 1789 did, after all, produce 1793, just as 1848 was, to Mill's immense chagrin, to be followed by 1851. There were, to be sure, rival historical stories to be told about each particular case, but Mill never really attempted to tell them, partly because his intellectual inclinations did not lie in the direction of detailed historical narrative, but partly also, it seems to me, because his unrelenting, self-defining, antagonism to a stereotype of English complacency obscured any more appreciative view of the cogency of the Whig case in particular or of the intellectual strengths of this style of thought in general.

Something similar may have been at work in his tendentious celebration of the original theoretical contribution of the new 'school' of French historians and social philosophers. What stimulated such exaggeration both of their homogeneity and their originality was, as I have already suggested, his urge to reproach his fellow-countrymen for the 'merely empirical' character of their reflections on history, or what he called the 'vulgar mode' of using history, which consisted in treating it as a storehouse of debating-chamber maxims. Mill, by contrast, was eager to emphasize the possibilities of a science of historical development, one in which it was recognized that 'changes in political institutions are the effects of previous changes in the conditions of society and of the human mind'. Whoever grasped this, he announced emphatically in 1840, 'possesses more of the science of politics than was known even to eminent thinkers fifty years ago'.

Now, it is true that this remark was expressive of his involvement in what he called 'the reaction of the nineteenth century against the eighteenth'; 1840 was, after all, the year of his famous essay on Coleridge. But what, in this context, seems so striking is the very considerable over-simplification involved in this and similar remarks of the kinds of reflection upon historical development that were, in the most general sense, available in Britain (here more accurate than 'England') in the first half of the nineteenth century. One has only to think of the late eighteenth-century Scottish 'historians of civil society', such as Adam Smith or John Millar, of whose work Mill was by no means ignorant, to see that the Copernican revolution he was celebrating in 1840 would have seemed rather trite to some of the 'eminent thinkers' of 1790. Carping at an author's omissions, or even at his degree of selectivity, is, of course, an easy sport: Mill was certainly under no obligation in such periodical writing to produce a systematic survey of recent political thought, and there were anyway some important differences between the Scots and the more recent French writers to which he could profitably have drawn attention. The point, however, is that his characterizations of the intellectual achievements of both the society he admired and the society he scorned were squeezed out of shape by the pressure of his need to justify his adversarial relation to what he took to be the dominant strains in English culture.

Of all the essays in this volume, the one which is most revealing of the deeper springs of Mill's attraction to French intellectual and political life is that memorializing the radical journalist Armand Carrel, which was first published in 1837. While figures such as

Guizot no less than events such as 1848 may seem understandable subjects for Mill's pen, the modern reader may wonder why a comparatively insignificant figure such as Carrel merited such extended treatment. Again, the answer is to be found in Mill's own longing, particularly acute in the 1830s, to be at the centre of dramatic and effective radical political activity. The flushed, swelling cadences of this eulogy, so untypical of Mill's prose, suggest a strong and only partly conscious fantasy-identification with Carrel. The genre of the extended tribute naturally called out the taste for classical parallels which Mill and his readers shared. 'It is now beginning to be felt', wrote Mill, somewhat wistfully, 'that journalism is to Modern Europe what political oratory was to Athens and Rome, and that, to become what it ought, it should be wielded by the same sort of men.' This last phrase signals the almost heated reverence which Mill felt for Carrel, the Journalist-as-Hero, and as his essay moves towards its rhetorical climax the elevated register Mill strives for is intended both to express the dramatic significance of the causes Carrel (and, by implication, Mill himself) fought for, and to do homage to the qualities of a man whom Mill had a desperate urge to admire. These themes came together in his resounding conclusion: 'He died a martyr to the morality and dignity of public discussion.' In fact, Carrel was killed in a duel with a fellow-journalist, the cause of which seems in part to have rested on a misunderstanding.

Mill's passionate engagement with French history and thought has a larger interest beyond even what it reveals about the interdependence of temperament and role. It is significant that the *Collected Works* could contain no volume of his writings on 'German History and Historians', and in his comparative neglect of Germany he stands out among the leading intellectual figures of Victorian England. In part, this was a consequence of his political radicalism, but it was also in part a consequence of his extraordinary precociousness: the main lines of his development were laid down before the fashion of looking to Germany for cultural nourishment had become at all widespread, though of course Coleridge and Carlyle among his subsequent mentors were two of the earliest and most influential *Geist*-importers. Much of nineteenth-century intellectual history can be seen as a coming to terms with the legacy of German Romanticism, especially in philosophy and historical scholarship, and it is arguable that Mill, who in so many ways remained a man of the Enlightenment, never really took the measure of this cultural sea-change.

It is true that he was, as Morley observed, one of the best-informed men of his day, but there are limits to the range of intel-lectual developments the cultural critic can keep up with. Moreover, his sensitivity to more local currents may also be impaired by the effort, as Mill himself seemed to recognize later in his life: 'I sometimes think', he confided to his diary in 1854, 'that those who, like us, keep up with the European movement, are by that very circumstance thrown out of the stream of English opinion and have some chance of misjudging and mistaking it.' The self-knowledge is, as ever, attractive, but Mill employed this modest confessional voice only rarely; in the pieces brought together in this volume a more hectoring note is dominant. A later assessment by one of the shrewdest of his friends and followers, Alexander Bain, seems particularly apposite here. Mill, he reflected, 'always dealt gently with [France's] faults, and liberally with her virtues', whereas 'his habitual way of speaking of England, the English people, English society, as compared with other nations was posi-tively unjust and served no good end'. Gladstone famously dubbed Mill 'the Saint of Rationalism': on some views of the matter both saints and rationalism have been judged a little 'un-English', but that may, on reflection, only make the epithet the more appropri-ate. Certainly, the appearance of this volume should help to make it harder to get away with the slipshod assimilation of Mill to any stereotype of Victorian parochialism and complacency. It may also make it seem quite fitting that he is buried just outside Avignon.

VI

Anyone still inclined to think of Mill as an unworldly and disin-terested philosopher, addressing a few fellow-thinkers through large tomes composed at an appropriately unhurried pace, should simply try lifting the four hefty volumes of his collected *Newspaper Writings* (after having first completed the necessary warm-up exercises). They are a reminder—in fact a revelation, even to those moderately familiar with Mill—of just how closely and practically engaged he was in many of the political and social disputes of his time. The pieces gathered together in these volumes are quite different from the expansive, reflective essays which Mill contributed to the great quarterly and monthly periodicals of general culture: they are pieces of pragmatic political journalism— short, hard-hitting, topical, and repetitive ('an article in a news- paper', he observed in 1833, 'is to the public mind no more than a drop of water on a stone; and like that it produces its effect by *repetition*'). They are frequently intended to support particular proposals currently under discussion, and here his policy was 'to make no compromise of *opinions* . . . but to negotiate the most advantageous compromises possible in actual *measures*'. He contributed to a great variety of radical causes in this way throughout his writing life, but especially in the 1830s and 1840s; thereafter he did indeed tend to stand back from the fray a little, publishing only 58 items in the newspapers in the last 25 years of his life compared to 368 in the preceding 25 years. Perhaps his most impressive and sustained campaign came in the winter of 1846–7 when he tried to persuade the British government of the need to act decisively to mitigate the appalling effects of the Irish famine and to reform the underlying evils of 'landlordism': in the space of 94 days he wrote no fewer than 43 anonymous leading articles in the *Morning Chronicle*.

By their nature such contributions, littered with allusions to never-realized proposals and the names of long-forgotten individu- als, are ephemeral, and pose particular problems for even the most learned readers a century later. One's gratitude to the resourceful- ness and tact of the editors of these volumes is correspondingly great. While always preserving a clean page of original text, they unobtrusively provide, in headnotes, introductions, and appen- dices, all that the scholar or browser could require by way of expla- nation and identification. Almost none of the 427 items in them has been reprinted before, and they could otherwise only be found in the practically inaccessible files of now defunct nineteenth- century newspapers, while the 220-page appendix identifying persons and works cited in these writings is at once a symbol and embodiment of the services to scholarship rendered by this edition. In addition, the 80-page Introduction by Ann P. Robson is unfail- ingly helpful in locating Mill's journalistic activity in the often violent and abrasive political life of the period (and itself contains some peppery, trenchant judgements as well as touches of sharp wit). Appropriately, she draws particular attention to the largely neglected series of 'joint productions' upon which Mill and Harriet Taylor collaborated in the late 1840s and early 1850s. Mill emerges from her account as a very pragmatic idealist, whose 'career as a journalist ensured that he kept his feet firmly on the ground while he urged mankind forward towards his hoped-for heaven'.

The tendency to think of Mill as regarding the affairs of his society from some position of Olympian detachment will henceforth also have to come to terms with the existence in two volumes of his *Public and Parliamentary Speeches*. Mill was the Member of Parliament for Westminster from 1865 to 1868, and as these volumes demonstrate, he was a more active and in some ways more effective parliamentarian than he is usually given credit for. Moreover, in the years between leaving parliament and his death in 1873, he was much in demand as a public speaker in favour of a variety of radical causes, and the material assembled in the second of these volumes makes clear that by the end of his life Mill had become an accomplished platform orator. Appropriately, the final words in the report of his last speech with which this volume concludes were '(*Loud Cheers*)'.

Speeches, of course, present editors with special problems. What survives is often only the published form of a reporter's transcript; the relation of this document to what was actually said may be complex, yet it is not altogether clear how far 'what was actually said' constitutes a posited ur-text which editorial labour should try to reconstruct. What can one say about the success of the Toronto team in coping with these problems? Well, pastiche being a form of homage, one might, perhaps, say this:

Of the manifold merits of this remarkable edition, to which it may be thought proper in this place gratefully to advert, I have already spoken elsewhere (*cries of Order!*). My belief that there is no text that may not, given due regard for general principles moderated by the practical exigencies of each case, be justly and economically edited, has long since been admirably demonstrated by the achievements of this noble undertaking in dealing with works the continual revision of which by the author we shall not describe as confusing, for there never was an author whose concern to be lucid was so equally matched by his talent for that quality, but which, to put it no more strongly, occasioned difficulties of judgement and presentation before which lesser editions have stumbled and fallen (*Hear, hear!*). But whatever may be said of the complications thus arising with respect to materials which began life in written form, the same may be multiplied a hundredfold in the question of those utterances originally given the form of speech. That my honourable and learned friend the Member for Toronto [Professor Robson] has not only disposed of these difficulties in practice with an abundance of those felicitous touches of which he is an acknowledged master, but has, furthermore, raised their resolution to the status of a minor science, there is more than sufficient demonstration in the pamphlet not long published under his own name [John M. Robson, *What Did He Say?*]. In the present undertaking, in addition to the labours of that council which sits in permanent session in the first city of the province of Ontario, my honourable and learned friend has been assisted by one whose growing reputation among those gentlemen—and, I may add, ladies—who have made a special study of the political life of this epoch is attested by those admirable works we have elsewhere had cause to cite [Professor Kinzer]. His Introduction to the present volumes maintains a standard which I shall not say has never suffered a blemish (*cries of Name!*), and of which modesty forbids me to give too extended or too favourable a consideration (*laughter*); but for command of information concerning the doings of the public men of the time, combined with sympathetic familiarity with the principles governing our great author's thought on all germane subjects, his discussion could be equalled by few and bettered by none (*applause*). In company with all future historians of the public life of our nation, no less than of all students of the writings of that illustrious and selfless mind to whose earnest endeavours this ample edition is so worthy a monument, we can only acknowledge our debt and gratitude both to Mr Kinzer, and to my honourable and learned friend whose prodigious and universally admired labours have now drawn to a triumphant close (*loud cheering and prolonged applause*).

There are some cases where the publication of a 'Collected Works' seems pointless and depressing, especially where the edition inches its way through a statesman's career like a scholarly infantry offensive, and with corresponding loss of life. And even where the edition is of a writer whose works are worth reading, these works are sometimes so besieged by scholarly apparatus, pressing distracting references upon us and clarifying what was never unclear, that we start to long for a clean page of print be the text never so 'corrupt'. Not only is the Toronto edition of Mill's works entirely free from such reproaches, but it has already wrought a substantial and wholly beneficial change in the face of Mill scholarship, and thus of much else besides. At one point Professor Robson observes of Mill's strenuous efforts at self-improvement: 'The highest standards he set were for himself.' The same can most

certainly be said for the man who has self-effacingly produced one
of the most distinguished editions in modern scholarship.

Mill is sometimes singled out as a quintessentially English
thinker. In its crudest form this judgement is made up of equal parts
of ignorance and prejudice, often laced with a dash of hostility. In
fact, he was the least parochial of writers, and, with due allowance
for the simplification inherent in such epitomes, one could as well
say of him what Engels said of Marx, that the development of his
thought combined English political economy, French Socialism,
and (via Carlyle and Coleridge) German philosophy, as well as
many other things. Still, he is undoubtedly one of the most central
figures in modern English intellectual history, and the fact that this
fine edition has been conceived, funded, and executed in Canada
may prompt some wry reflections about the handing on of imperial burdens.

7

Literary Minds: Anthony Trollope and George Eliot

I

'Thus you will perceive, it is impossible for me to give any encouragement to you to proceed in novel writing.' The publisher no doubt thought this was the kindest thing to say. He was writing, in 1848, to a 33-year-old minor official at the Post Office, reporting that half of the edition of 375 copies of the young man's second novel would probably have to be remaindered; it had already lost the comparatively large sum of £63 10s. 1½d.

Apart from the rebuff to literary ambition, the letter was dispiriting because its recipient, like most budding authors, needed the money. Seven years earlier he had been going nowhere as a copying clerk in the Post Office in London, on the barely respectable income of £140 a year. He had been well educated up to a point: he had initially been sent to Winchester, but he had to be removed when the financial affairs of his unlucky father, an unsuccessful barrister who lost money in a modest farming venture, took a particularly bad turn. He completed his education at Harrow, while living at home, but there was no question of his being able to afford to reside at a university; indeed, he retained vivid memories of his father narrowly escaping imprisonment for debt when the duns came. So when, in 1841, the opportunity offered to transfer

R. H. Super, *The Chronicler of Barsetshire: A Life of Anthony Trollope* (University of Michigan Press, 1989).

Frederick Karl, *George Eliot: A Biography* (HarperCollins, 1995).

to Ireland, where his income would be somewhat higher and the cost of living somewhat lower, he accepted. He made a success of his duties there, visiting sub-post offices and improving the rural deliveries, but not until his appointment to a district of his own back in England in 1854 was his salary to rise to the relatively comfortable middle-class level of £700 a year. Meanwhile, he had married and become the father of two expense-provoking sons. Stirred by the example of his novel-writing mother, driven by social as much as literary ambition, perhaps sensing that the market for fiction was growing in the 1840s, he began to send packages to publishers. His fourth novel at last brought him some success. Forced to accept the risky arrangement of 'half profits' (the author received half the profits, if any, once all the publisher's costs had been covered), he none the less found that after six months his latest effort had done well enough for him to receive his first cheque from a publisher, for £9 1s. 2d. The year was 1855; the novel was *The Warden*. Anthony Trollope was on his way.

But why do we want to know these facts? Would it matter to the many admirers of Trollope's novels (discussed in Chapter 2 above) if the cheque had been for £9 1s. 3d.? Even to raise such a question may suggest a captious resistance to the whole enterprise of literary biography, and a peculiarly pointless resistance, too, given that the genre is at present the one indisputably booming sector of the publishing trade. There could be no better indication of the appeal of the genre itself than the fact that two such dissimilar Victorian novelists as Trollope and George Eliot should each have received the almost simultaneous attention of several serious biographers in recent years. It may help us to understand this appeal, therefore, to see what different kinds of biography can tell us about these two almost exact contemporaries.

II

After his unpromising beginnings, Trollope's career took him far towards, if not quite up to, the peak of Victorian society. One of the many services rendered by R. H. Super's awesomely thorough and authoritative *The Chronicler of Barsetshire: A Life of Anthony Trollope* is to provide far fuller evidence than was ever available before for placing Trollope within the delicately graduated layers of that society. Such an exercise may have greater literary as well as historical interest in his case than in that of many novelists, not only because his tales present themselves as closely observed chronicles of the doings of the comfortable classes, but also because the almost obsessive concern of his characters with the status of being a 'gentleman' has recently attracted extended critical discussion.

Trollope may have cherished the traditional conception of that status the more fiercely because he was in reality a representative of a new professional middle class. His writings refer frequently to that condition which has since been inelegantly dubbed 'ruling-class egalitarianism'. To cite only the most obvious instances, there is his well-known discussion in his *Autobiography* of the terms on which one should live with those of superior 'rank', and his insistent conclusion that 'intimate friendship admits of no standing but that of equality'. Or one might turn to the passage in *The Last Chronicle of Barset* in which he has Archdeacon Grantly reply to Josiah Crawley's wish that they stood on more equal terms financially: 'We stand on the only perfect level which such men can meet each other. We are both gentlemen.' It is no less suggestive of the importance Trollope attached to this precarious condition that his chief justification of fox-hunting should lie in the way in which, once all are in the saddle, 'a community is formed in which equality prevails'.

But this equality presupposed fifteen hundred a year and a roof of one's own. It was really only once his literary earnings outstripped his salary that Trollope was able to join clubs, sit on committees, and be invited to dinners alongside men (women, even Trollope's wife, figure very little in this book) whose wealth and standing were more secure and more ancient than his own. Trollope's membership of this indefinable freemasonry was not in doubt all the while he could maintain a good table, ride his own hunters, and smoke the best Havanas. Even then, of course, there were limits to his social success: he was elected to the Garrick and the Athenaeum, not Brooks's or White's, and dukes were more common in his novels than in his life (as in less distinguished examples of romantic fiction, snobbery may form part of the fantasy for the author as well as for the reader).

The facts which Professor Super provides in such abundance enable us to chart in detail the working-out of Trollope's social ambitions and anxieties. One result is to induce a deeper appreciation of that often-cited passage in his *Autobiography* in which he recalls the humiliation of his visibly underfunded school days and his sense that where his contemporaries 'would go into Parliament, or become rectors and deans, or squires of parishes, or advocates thundering at the Bar', his lack of means would prevent him from living among them in later years. 'Nevertheless', he adds with palpable triumph, 'I have lived with them.'

He owed his position to his writing, or at least without his writing he would always have had an anxious struggle to maintain even the appearances required by his sense of his desired station. His *Autobiography*, published posthumously, notoriously boasted of his literary earnings, all meticulously recorded, and of the worldly pleasures they had brought him. Trollope, of course, produced— there is no other word for it—at a rate that makes even Iris Murdoch or Anthony Burgess look like fitful Werthers unable to settle to anything. Previous biographers have leaned heavily on Trollope's own (apparently somewhat exaggerated) account of his writing habits, but Professor Super's researches now enable us not only to take the full measure of the prodigious labours of this Stakhanovite of the writing-table, but also to imagine with great concreteness a day in the life of the author of *Barchester Towers*.

That day, as we know from the *Autobiography*, usually began at 5.30, or even 4 according to one account (characteristically Trollope records that the servant whose duty it was to wake him at this hour received extra payment of £5 per year for the task). He then wrote for several hours, having determined at the beginning of each novel exactly how much he had to write each day to meet his deadline. The greater part of the day's stint done before breakfast— a late and sociable event by today's standards—he then went about his Post Office duties, which were never so onerous as to be allowed to interfere with his great passion, riding to hounds. There might then be a noisy and far from abstemious dinner, perhaps preceded by a few hands of whist at one of his clubs, often a late-night cigar, and then, not early, bed. But whatever the state of his digestion, his head, or his soul (if one can imagine that un-Trollopian appurtenance), the pen had to flow as freely as ever next morning.

And flow it certainly did. Consider, if you are at all susceptible to facts of this sort, the twenty-four months between November 1866 and November 1868, admittedly the period Trollope described as 'the busiest in my life'. For the first half of this period he was still a Surveyor in the Post Office (a regional superintendent, in his case for Essex and adjoining counties); he retired, early, at the end of October 1867. Overlapping with the end of that employment, and extending through the subsequent twelve months, he was editor of the new monthly magazine *St Pauls*. He hunted three times a week in the season, he dined about a good deal, he played a lot of whist, and took holidays with as much gusto as ever (a month in Europe one year, five weeks the next, with lesser holidays in England as well). In early April 1868 he sailed for America as the representative of the British Post Office, charged with the task of renegotiating details of the postal convention between the two countries. He returned at the end of July, took a holiday in Scotland, and then decided to make his one bid for Parliament, delivering his first address to the electors of Beverley before the end of October 1868.

A full life? Not so full as to prevent the odd bit of writing. On 15 September 1866 he had completed *The Last Chronicle of Barset*, one of his longer novels at almost 350,000 words. On 15 May 1867 he finished *Phineas Phinn* (almost 270,000 words); in five weeks that summer he wrote *Linda Tressel* (a mere 70,000 words). The demands of launching the new magazine meant that it took him seven weeks to complete *The Golden Lion of Granpere* (66,000 words). However, flagging was not a Trollopian activity. On 13 November 1867 he began *He Knew He Was Right*, and brought it to its conclusion, 340,000 words later, on 12 June 1868, while he was in Washington (he didn't allow travelling to slow his production).

So, there was the relatively affluent 53-year-old Trollope, who had just completed a 340,000-word novel in seven months, stuck in the heat of a Washington summer, making no progress in his ultimately fruitless negotiations with the US Post Office. There was clearly nothing else for it: three days after writing the last word of *He Knew He Was Right*, he wrote the first of *The Vicar of Bullhampton*, and by 1 November 1868, the day after his first election speech at Beverley, he came to the end of its 205,000 words. Thus, in twenty-four far from otherwise empty months, and quite apart from several articles for periodicals, pieces for *St Pauls*, and a great volume of letters, both business and personal, Trollope seems to have sustained his imaginative concentration across almost a million words at an average rate of 40,000 words a month.

III

All of this, it will be evident, is to deal with Trollope's life only under its public and, as it were, quantitative aspect. It is very much the sort of story he told of himself: matter of fact, full on financial detail, reticent about his emotional history, an exemplum to the aspiring author who needed to learn how much could be achieved by perseverance and sheer application. But there is, of course, a different biographical story which might be attempted, one which probed the experience of the man in search of the imagination of the novelist. Trollope himself, it hardly needs to be said, did not exactly invite this sort of inquiry; a celebrated passage in his *Autobiography* in effect tells any future biographer where to get off.

It will not, I trust, be supposed by any reader that I have intended in this so-called autobiography to give a record of my inner life. . . . If the rustle of a woman's petticoats has ever stirred my blood; if a cup of wine has been a joy to me; if I have thought tobacco at midnight in pleasant company to be one of the elements of an earthly Paradise; if now and again I have somewhat recklessly fluttered a £5 note over a card table;—of what matter is that to any reader? I have betrayed no woman. Wine has brought me no sorrow. It has been the companionship of smoking that I have loved, rather than the habit. I have never desired to win money, and I have lost none. . . . I will not say that I have never scorched a finger,—but I carry no ugly wounds.

Yet this is, of course, a very teasing kind of 'Keep Out' notice, since it simultaneously hints at discoveries that could be made, and almost coquettishly delights in withholding the charms it half displays. The biography which allowed itself to be seduced down this dangerous path might have to speculate on many matters where the historical record is unforthcoming, where in the nature of the case the evidence could only be indirect and its interpretation disputable. Such a biography might make much of the youthful Trollope's habit of building elaborate castles in Spain; it might speculate about his desire to obtain the love and approval of his novelist mother; it might ponder his intense identification, at once snobbish and imaginative, with the settled patterns of English county life; it might want to know more about why 'enforced idleness' was his greatest fear, greater even than the fear of death; and it might at least wonder about the possible complexities of relation between the many love stories in the novels and their author's own romantic and sexual longings.

Professor Super has not attempted to write such a biography. In his preface he tells us that his book is intended to be 'a source of accurate information', and accuracy, he forbiddingly reminds us, 'implies detail and precision'. Taken on such terms, the book is beyond reproach: it is a magnificent distillation of the most thorough kind of scholarly research. His economical footnotes suggest a story of quite remarkable care and resourcefulness; any one paragraph of the text may rest on untold hours of patient, often unrewarded, labour. The range of sources mined is itself extraordinary, stretching chronologically from late eighteenth-century parish records to Quaritch's 1987 sale catalogues, and taking in the shipping lists in the *Sydney Morning Herald* for 1873 along the way.

Quite simply, *The Chronicler of Barsetshire* supersedes all earlier biographies; it is in a class of its own as a source of information about Trollope's life. In nothing is this more marked than in its exceptionally full and thorough account of Trollope's work at the Post Office (Super has already published a small monograph on the subject). In the unlikely event of any of this research needing to be done again, the path is clearly signposted by such footnote references as 'Post Office Records, "Substitution of bags for iron boxes in transmission of mails to Australia", Post 29/126, packet 256R/1866'. (What such packets have to record is not necessarily trivial: we must remember that Trollope was responsible for introducing pillar boxes in England.) Super is similarly meticulous in itemizing Trollope's business arrangements with his publishers, and indeed his financial affairs generally. In these and other ways, the book provides much grist for social as well as literary historians, its usefulness enhanced (and its thoroughness exemplified) by its vastly detailed, helpfully divided, 29-page index.

Henry James spoke of the 'density, blockishness, and general thickness and soddenness' of Trollope's *Autobiography*, and the accumulated detail and lack of large interpretative themes in what is now clearly the definitive biography may seem to invite a similar characterization. But James also recognized that one of Trollope's great virtues was 'a complete appreciation of the usual', and Super's attentiveness to the mundane circumstances of his hero's life (and there is deep admiration at the heart of this biography, though it is never allowed any fulsome expression) could earn a similar commendation, though one might also be reminded of Carlyle's far less generous description of Trollope as 'irredeemably imbedded in commonplace, and grown fat on it'. This is not the book everyone will want to read about Trollope, but it is the book every serious scholar who wants information about Trollope's life will henceforth turn to.

Trollope's life was itself one of his major achievements: far from sacrificing his life to his art, it is arguable that he sacrificed his art to his life. He knew what he was good at and what made him enough money to live the kind of life he wanted to live. He enjoyed his pleasures, and they included the satisfaction he obtained from contemplating his own productivity. In admiring certain portions of *The Way We Live Now*, the young Robert Louis Stevenson perceptively observed that 'the man who could do that, if he had had courage, might have written a fine book; he has preferred to write many readable ones'. Trollope had some kinds of courage, and took many a five-barred gate at full gallop, literally as well as metaphorically. But his courage was not of the kind that might have forced him to deeper intellectual or literary explorations; he was content to leave the limits pretty much where he found them, and to get on with the puppet-show. Professor Super evidently has considerable sympathy with this attitude, and he has given us an appropriately Trollopian biography, even down to its refusal to inquire too closely about what a gentleman does before breakfast. But I can't help wanting, ungratefully, to know more about the rustle of those petticoats.

IV

George Eliot was, of course, a very different kind of writer from Trollope, and she requires a more imaginative and, so to say, less businesslike biography. But, from the start, she has posed some troubling problems for her biographers. 'If it is true that the most interesting of George Eliot's characters is her own, it may be said also that the most interesting of her books is her Life.' Thus Lord

Acton, in recognizable book-review mode, launching himself on
the delicate task of writing about *George Eliot's Life as Related in
Her Letters and Journals*, 'Arranged and Edited by her Husband
J. W. Cross'. The significance, or irony, of the title-page's insistence
on the marital relation would not have been lost on contemporary
readers. Marian Evans had lived for twenty-four years with
another woman's husband—Charles Kingsley referred to her as
George Henry Lewes's 'concubine'—and the respectability she had
craved had only been accorded her in the final year of her life
when, eighteen months after Lewes's death, she finally became a
married woman. But even this was hardly a conventional union,
for Johnny Cross was twenty years her junior and had been her
financial adviser.

When Cross's compilation appeared in 1885, five years after his
wife's death, the contemporary response was polite but unenthusi-
astic, especially among those who had known her (a category
which by then included a substantial proportion of the metropolitan literary and intellectual elite). Certainly, George Eliot was
allowed to speak for herself in Cross's three volumes, but his selec-
tions and suppressions meant that she was only allowed to speak
in grave and considered tones ('It is not a Life at all', Gladstone
complained, 'It is a Reticence in three volumes'). The picture
presented was too reverential, and those who had loved the books
were reluctant to accept that they could have been written by such
a bloodless paragon. Henry James was not alone in feeling that
Eliot's letters, at least as presented by a husband protective of her
memory, 'do not explain her novels; they reflect in a singularly
limited degree the process of growth of those great works'.

None the less, Cross's *Life* was to remain the indispensable
biographical account for three-quarters of a century. The first part
of the twentieth century saw the trough of George Eliot's reputation, and (Virginia Woolf's much-quoted centenary tribute in 1919
notwithstanding) there was little interest in rescuing her life from
the standard categories of 'the sybil', 'the Victorian moralist', and
so on. Then, in 1933, a young American scholar, Gordon Haight,
came across a collection of Eliot's letters in the Yale library, and
realized how much had been omitted from Cross's *Life*. This was
the beginning of one of the more notable of those lifetimes of scholarly labours devoted to a single author (Haight died in 1985). In
1954–5 he published George Eliot's letters in a fully annotated

seven-volume edition (two more volumes of subsequently discovered material were added in 1978). And finally, after many other incidental publications, Haight brought out his *George Eliot: A Biography* in 1968.

To say that Haight's biography was a 'landmark' would be a feebly inadequate metaphor; it was the land. His many years of research had uncovered a wealth of new material, and, of course, he drew upon the passages Cross had excised or omitted. Haight, needless to say, was a great admirer, but his biography, while sympathetic, displays commendable restraint and fair-mindedness. One particularly notable aspect of this restraint was the tactful way in which he did not over-zealously pursue the identification of real-life models for characters and episodes in Eliot's fiction. Leaving the imaginative achievements of 'George Eliot' intact, he gave us the first full life of Marian Evans.

That life was remarkable enough in itself. Born in 1819, the daughter of the agent or manager of an aristocratic estate in Warwickshire, Mary Ann Evans ('Marian' was the form she later adopted in the course of self-fashioning) grew up in a milieu that was rural, religious, and reactionary. In her late teens, she took over the running of her widowed father's household, but her bookish and introspective nature was nurturing a serious spiritual crisis. The eventual break from her inherited Evangelicalism, together with her increasing intellectual attainments, opened never-to-be-healed gulfs with her family that were to cause her great distress in later life. The displacement was physical as well as emotional: first she travelled with some like-minded free-thinking friends; then, following her father's death, spent a period living on her own in Geneva (she was a more than capable linguist: her German was good enough for her to undertake the translation of difficult works by Strauss and Feuerbach); and finally, like so many escapees from the constraints of provincial life, she moved to London.

Here she worked as assistant to the publisher John Chapman who was also editor of *The Westminster Review*; she soon became the virtual deputy editor of the journal as well as a regular contributor. This period, the early 1850s, also saw her involvement, or extended period of mutual misunderstanding (it was, as so often, not easy to make the distinction), with Herbert Spencer, who eventually made clear his preference for undistracted fidelity to his 'Synthetic Philosophy'. Then, in 1854, she took the bold decision to go on an extended European tour with Lewes, already quite well known as a polymath man of letters, and on their return they set up house together as man and wife. Lewes had for some time been estranged from his wife, who had several children by his friend and colleague Thornton Leigh Hunt, but the new union was still largely greeted with moral condemnation and social ostracism.

The de facto marriage to Lewes seems to have brought Marian Evans great happiness; certainly, the appearance in the world of 'George Eliot' could be seen as its fruit. Encouraged by Lewes, she turned from articles to stories, cautiously beginning with anonymous publication, then adopting the soon-to-be-famous nom de plume. In 1859 Blackwoods published her first full-length novel, *Adam Bede*, which immediately enjoyed a huge critical and commercial success. Marian Evans was just 40; George Eliot was launched.

Two decades of fame and considerable fortune followed (the ever-practical Lewes made sure that she got the most advantageous terms from her publishers). The Leweses—she always insisted on being referred to as Mrs Lewes—began to be received more widely, especially after the great acclaim attendant upon the publication of *Middlemarch* in 1871–2. They in turn held their regular Sunday afternoon receptions, to which many of the great and famous came to pay homage (worship of George Eliot was mockingly referred to as the unbelievers' Sunday service). The construction of the image of the all-wise sybil got under way, a process that found its apotheosis in Cross's literary tombstone.

V

Given such a highly biographable life, it is hardly surprising that there have been several modern retellings of it, though nothing has matched the scale or scholarship of Haight's work. But now we have a massive new biography by Frederick Karl: *George Eliot: A Biography* runs to around 300,000 words. This book, Karl tells us, took four years to research and write, though it is not clear whether he regards this as culpably slow, commendably quick, or simply an indication of the magnitude of the task. To most scholars, it will surely seem a rate of production worthy of the most prolific of Victorian novelists.

The immediate question to ask is whether Karl's biography will, on the basis of new material, fresh interpretations, or literary and imaginative excellence, supersede Haight's (which is still available in the popular 'Penguin Lives' series). The blurb claims that this biography 'draws heavily upon previously unpublished letters', though this must be a special sense of 'heavily' meaning 'very slightly'. Karl cites as the most important such 'new material' Eliot's letters to Herbert Spencer, but these were published by Haight in his supplementary volumes of letters in 1978. While it is, therefore, strictly true that this and some other items (chiefly the correspondence of the phrenologist George Combe, who belonged to the circle around Eliot's Coventry friends, the Brays, plus some letters received by Cross when he was compiling the *Life*) were not available when Haight wrote his biography, they have already been quarried by other scholars, and they anyway only inform a tiny part of Karl's narrative. The endnotes identifying the sources of quotations are, passages from the novels aside, almost entirely to material published by Haight in his edition of the correspondence or elsewhere, though Karl's system of citation suggests he has checked all the manuscript originals as well. In any event, whatever claim to novelty this biography may have, it cannot be said to rest on the incorporation of significant amounts of new evidence.

What about new interpretation? Part of the merit of Haight's biography is that, although it is tightly organized and informed by a consistent view of his subject, it does not attempt to force everything into a single interpretative frame. It is true, none the less, that Haight made 'the need to be loved' a central element in Marian Evans's life, especially as it shaped her relationships with a series of older or more established men before she met Lewes. Karl explicitly rejects this line, arguing that 'we now possess more diverse ways of observing her role as a strong woman' and her place in 'the gender war and its various battlefields'. In his view, 'her relationship to each man was a form of absorption into herself of their place in the masculine world denied to her directly', and in this way she 'assimilated their power'. Actually, this claim, set out in the Introduction, does not inform the subsequent treatment of the relevant episodes of her life in any very noticeable ways—the quotations from her letters inevitably make her familiar emotional needs and doubts seem overriding—but Karl's declared emphasis certainly sits well with some of the most powerful trends in recent criticism of her fiction.

In practice, Karl's biography differs from Haight's in three main ways: first, he attempts to establish a much closer correspondence between characters and episodes in the novels and figures and events in the life; secondly, he allows himself much more speculation where the evidence is silent or only yields a gnomic murmur; and third, he makes larger claims for Eliot as 'the voice of the century', the figure who was most 'emblematic' of 'the Victorian era', and so on.

The first of these characteristics raises some delicate questions. To say, in general terms, that those experiences of the individual's life of which we have some record (as well, of course, as the vastly greater number of which we don't) may, in some way or other, have nourished and prompted the writer's imagination, is not to say much, though it is a justification of sorts for literary biography. But the attempt to go beyond this and establish direct correspondences between events in a writer's life and episodes in the fiction is a notoriously hazardous enterprise, almost bound to oscillate between the banal and the reductive. Undeterred, Karl sees sources and parallels at every turn in Eliot's life.

This is such a constant feature of the book that it is hard to illustrate adequately, but the following passage gives some indication of Karl's handling of this tricky matter. Speaking of John Chapman, with whom the young Marian worked closely and towards whom she at one period felt a more than merely colleagual attachment, he writes: 'George Eliot never tried to catch him directly, but spread him out among several egoists: Grandcourt in *Daniel Deronda*, Tito Melema in *Romola*, Harold Transome in *Felix Holt*, and Arthur Donnithorne in *Adam Bede*. While none is Chapman . . . they have some of his movement, his energy for intrigue . . .' and so on. In this case, the alleged resemblances seem too slight and general to be illuminating, and in any case, George Eliot's social experience, like most people's, presumably provided ample stimulus to reflecting on the varieties of egoism. More generally, the cumulative effect of this intemperate exegesis can be the opposite of what initially drives the admirer to want information about the author: the novels simply become so much coded information, grist to the biographer's mill rather than imaginative creations in their own right.

The second distinctive feature is the freedom with which Karl allows himself to speculate: for him, 'possibly', 'was surely', 'could have been', and so on are key components in the biographer's lexicon. Predictably this trait, which is becoming increasingly common in modern biography, is most marked in relation to sex, and, no less predictably, the greatest temptation occurs in narrating the episode during the honeymoon in Venice when Cross jumped out of the hotel window into the Grand Canal. Haight sticks close to the sources here, simply recording the, rather slight, evidence that Cross may have previously been subject to fits of insanity, but Karl tries to get his nose round the bedroom door. One factor which 'may' have contributed to Cross's aberrant behaviour 'could have been a sudden sexual demand made on him by Eliot'. 'What we have, in any event, is a response to something in his relationship to Eliot, to Venice, to his honeymoon and to marriage, possibly to his dead mother, possibly to his cohabitation with a woman of maternal age, possibly to demands made on him he could not fulfil, possibly to his recognition of impotence or even disgust.' The slide here from plausible general truths to unsubstantiated specific suggestions is characteristic.

Nor is he content to leave it there. In the subsequent pages he recurs to the situation 'in that hotel room—possibly a sexual situation Cross could not deal with', and soon he is confidently depicting Cross as 'a younger man on his honeymoon, finding himself in the footsteps of his predecessor, with a fixation on a woman he worships as a divine presence, [who] is confronted by this woman perhaps in a state of undress, or naked, and all his inhibitions, anxieties, confusions come to haunt him in a sudden expression of impotence'. Karl adduces no evidence whatsoever to support this fantasy; the sexual demand, the nakedness, the impotence are pure invention, about as well-judged as speculation that Cross was frustrated because he couldn't make his camcorder work.

The constant claims about how 'her life and fiction, together, speak of the entire century' comprise the third way in which Karl's biography differs from Haight's. In themselves, these claims may seem unexceptionable, though exaggeration and repetition erode rather than increase their plausibility. But Karl's treatment of the larger historical setting does not encourage confidence. For example: 'The fact that England had a popular queen did not change its assumptions about what women could do. Sexist notions were still mediaeval . . .'. The fact that at this time England had a largely *un*popular queen is not the greatest defect of this statement. Or

again, when Marian makes some remarks about the power of
certain words to stir 'the long-winding fibres of your memory',
Karl steps in: 'The foreshadowing of certain elements in Proust
which bind past and present is uncanny . . .' and so on.

The book would seem to be addressed primarily to an American
readership, and some of its glosses and explanations are bound to
grate on the British reader. The early nineteenth-century Utopian
Socialist Robert Owen is described as a 'British social planner',
which is a bit like calling Karl Marx a 'German investment
analyst'. We are told, in a curious phrase, that the young Marian
was attracted to 'alternate lifestyles', and the Leweses are later said
to be wealthy enough 'to take a vacation in the Scilly Isles, twenty-
eight miles southwest of Land's End, Cornwall, of King Arthur
fame'. Or what about the following priceless farrago of misinfor-
mation: 'Nuneaton is 10 miles north of Coventry, 20 miles east of
Birmingham, and 107 miles Northeast [*sic*] of London, just south
of the Midlands and not far from Shakespeare and Robin Hood
country'. That should keep the travel agents busy.

VI

Oppressed by Karl's relentlessness, I turned to F. R. Leavis's notorious essay on the defects of professional Lawrence scholarship, a
polemic written over thirty years ago, but one which, for all its
excesses, has only gained in pertinence. In his opening sentences,
Leavis registered 'the provocation . . . to an ungracious and appre-
hensive stiffening' that he encountered in the first few pages of the
scholarly edition he was writing about. A burden shared is not
always a burden lifted, but I did immediately feel better for this
acute diagnosis. One *is* bound to seem 'ungracious', at the very
least, yet Leavis's characteristically trenchant (shall we graciously
call it?) judgements still seem so apposite, particularly where he
begins to itemize 'the accumulating impertinences—anti-critical
identification of *personae* and fictive episodes with actual persons
and collected facts, gratuitous annotations, useless and betraying
vulgarities of insensitiveness and unintelligence . . .'.

Professor Karl may not deserve to have the full force of Leavis's
critical vocabulary deployed against him, for he is surely only exem-
plifying a general tendency, and his is by no means an exceptionally

bad book. But this biography is obviously more a symptom of current publishing trends than it is an expression of any significant new developments in the appreciation or study of George Eliot (the *TLS* of 18 August 1995 reported that no fewer than *seven* biographies of George Eliot have been commissioned by various publishers). Biographies sell, and big biographies sell big. There have been some recent complaints about 'bibliobesity', but biography seems to be one area of contemporary life resistant to the ubiquitous aesthetic, or ethic, of the 'lean' and 'slimmed-down'. A lot of careful marketing calculations will have gone into the decision by one of the biggest transatlantic publishing houses to offer the public 300,000 words at a relatively modest price. It would be surprising if the popularity of the BBC's adaptation of *Middlemarch* had not come into those calculations.

No doubt, there is a misplaced purism in maintaining that the only justification for writing the life of an author is the light the biography can shed on the work. Inevitably, we have come to have a semi-autonomous interest in the trajectory of the life itself, in how that particular individual negotiated the common cycle. We may also have an interest in the cultural and intellectual life of the period and biographies of writers, especially such learned and well-connected writers as George Eliot, can incidentally provide much valuable information. But the current taste for the biographical equivalent of the Whopper or Big Mac seems to be fuelled by a quite other appetite, perhaps not unlike that which is gratified by visits to the kitchens of country houses or reconstituted rooms in 'living museums'. It is a taste for the concrete details of everyday life, the minutiae of the mundane, arranged into the simplest and least troubling form of order, the chronological. Biography in this vein, a biography so big that you can live in it for quite some time and come to feel familiar with its characters' quotidian doings, surely serves some of the same needs as soap operas do. Seen in this light, Karl's enterprise may be more shrewdly pitched than is at first obvious to the scholarly eye.

Dazed by Karl's garrulousness, but drawing back from Leavis's vehemence, I returned to the deceptive *politesse* of Henry James's review of Cross's *Life*. In fact, in this essay James was really taking the occasion to propose a criticism of what he saw as a limitation of Eliot's fiction, especially the later work, which was, roughly, that it rested too much on reflection and not enough on perception. Her 'deep, strenuous, much-considering mind, of which the leading mark is the capacity for a sort of luminous brooding' was too much in evidence, while there was, by contrast, not enough 'breath of the streets'. Needless to say, this is a critical judgement which may be disputed, and has been, but it is precisely a *critical* judgement, arising from an exceptionally interested and attentive reading of Eliot's work. It is the intensity of James's engagement with the novels which gives him the air, not of one who is confessing defeat or frustration, but of one who, quietly triumphant, has seen something precious elude the blunt instruments of the labellers and explainers when he concludes that, for all the interesting information in Cross's three volumes, how 'this quiet, anxious, sedentary, serious, invalidical English lady' came to write *those* novels 'remains inscrutable and mysterious'.

8

Young Minds: Charles Darwin and Bertrand Russell

I

'You care for nothing but shooting, dogs, and rat-catching, and you will be a disgrace to yourself and all your family.' Such parental admonitions are not, of course, intended as purely predictive statements, and the words of a prosperous Shrewsbury doctor to his younger son in 1825 no doubt served various less scientific functions. Still, considered merely as a piece of crystal-gazing this almost ranks with those unfortunate affirmations of the stability of the French monarchy made in 1788 or prophecies of perpetual peace made in 1913. Few fathers—Vicenzio Galilei, Isaac Newton, Hermann Einstein may be candidates—have produced offspring who have so fundamentally changed mankind's view of the natural world as Dr Robert Waring Darwin's son was to do. Darwin *fils* was still to get in a few scrapes, to be sure, but his achievements have given the paternal name a greater currency than could be boasted of by any fathers, Heinrich Marx and God excepted.

The relationship to nature implied in this early rebuke—intimate, predatory, traditional—provides something of a keynote for the letters of the young Charles Darwin. Such letters fill the first volume of what will ultimately be a huge multi-volume edition of

Frederick Burkhardt and Sydney Smith (eds.), *The Correspondence of Charles Darwin*, vol. i: *1821–1836* (Cambridge University Press, 1985).

Nicholas Griffin (ed.), *The Selected Letters of Bertrand Russell*, vol. i: *The Private Years (1884-1914)* (Allen Lane, 1992).

his correspondence, but perhaps such efforts at comprehensiveness should give us pause. Inevitably, the first volume of such large-scale editions is likely, the freakishly precocious aside, to concern the subject's life before he or she had completed any of those achievements which are held to merit such lavish posthumous attention. The shelves of university libraries are filling up with volumes of letters by prospective writers who had yet to do more than confess large ambitions, rising politicians who had yet to find a seat, and a host of square pegs chafing at the frustrations of round holes. Is there really any need for this scholarly labour? What value does such early correspondence have when it is their subjects' mature ideas we are interested in? The contrasting first volumes of the correspondence of the young Charles Darwin and the young Bertrand Russell suggest some positive answers to these nagging questions.

II

One interest of such early letters lies less in intimations of the subject's future greatness than in the unusually rich picture they provide of the lives of certain historical categories of people. And so it is with the 338 letters to and from Darwin in the first volume of his correspondence, spanning the period from his Shrewsbury schooldays to his return from the *Beagle* voyage at the age of 27. These letters are grist for the historian of the mores of the Shropshire gentry in the early nineteenth century at least as much as they are for the historian of science narrowly conceived, and they have a less austerely professional appeal for many other readers besides.

Partly, perhaps, because many of the letters are to or from Darwin's marriageable sisters, much of their substance concerns speculation about the romantic intentions and tactics of the respectable young gentlemen of the neighbourhood. One almost expects Mr Darcy or Mr Knightley to put in an appearance. Indeed, there are interesting signs of the sensibilities of several of the principals having been partly formed by immersion in that fictional world. Darwin's future wife, Emma Wedgwood, is described by her sister as refraining from attending upon a group of young officers for fear of appearing 'too Lydiaish', and his sisters imagine the captain of the *Beagle* to be, so perfect does he seem from their brother's description, 'quite a Captain Wentworth'. Darwin well knew how gratified his sisters would be by his report that Jane Austen's novels were on all the best tables in Rio de Janeiro.

It is a world dominated by the traditional pursuits of the English country gentry: 'we are going on in much our usual hum-drum style', writes Squire Owen, father of some of Darwin's closest childhood friends, in 1832, 'a little hunting, a little shooting, and now and then a little argument about the Reform Bill'. The young Darwin grew up in a world where huntin', shootin', and reformin' provided the recipe for a respectable life. He certainly seems to have been almost as eager to bring partridges to earth as to add beetles to his specimen tray. His botanizing, of which his beetle-mania was the most highly developed expression, here appears as a natural outgrowth of his pragmatic familiarity with the ways of the countryside. It was a relation to nature that could have religious and intellectual as well as social dimensions. Like so many younger sons of his station, Darwin went to Cambridge in order to become a parson; a taste for natural history would be considered a positive adornment in a country vicar. Since the gentry and the clergy were often separated only by a few months or years in the order of their birth, the rural pursuits common to the class were as much a foundation for the intellectual edifice of natural theology as they were for the more practical deliberations of the magistrates' bench. The evidence of the Creator's benign intentions and endlessly ingenious devisings was, after all, more obvious in Shropshire than in, say, Shoreditch. Reading Paley was the part of the undemanding Cambridge syllabus Darwin most enjoyed: they shared a sense of delighted wonder at the intricate arrangement of the order of nature. *The Origin of Species* is not unlike a version of Paley without God, and in the case of Paley's enlightened eighteenth-century rational Christianity the omission would not have made as much difference as might at first be supposed.

By the time Darwin went up to Cambridge in January 1828, he was already on his way to becoming an unusually ardent and methodical entomologist, and his studies there and for two years previously at Edinburgh, unsystematic as they were, gave him an acquaintance with a range of cognate sciences not possessed by most of Gilbert White's imitators. Still, when he graduated in 1831 (he never showed any aptitude for Mathematics and did not take Honours, a very common and not at all discreditable course in the early nineteenth century), it was to life in a country vicarage surrounded by children and beetles that he looked forward. And even during the voyage whose results were, from one point of view, to cast doubts on the whole enterprise of natural theology, he continued to anticipate, even to yearn for, such an image of future contentment: 'Although I like this knocking about', he reported to one of his sisters from South America in 1832, 'I find I steadily have a distant prospect of a very quiet parsonage, and I can see it even through a grove of Palms.'

By then, of course, the formative opportunity of Darwin's life had offered itself and been accepted. A close sequence of letters written at the time when the question of the *Beagle* voyage first arose brings out, with the immediacy of day-to-day reporting, the extent to which the decision hung in the balance. Darwin's father at first objected to the proposal, anxious that a long absence on such a voyage might be prejudicial to his son's prospects as a clergyman. In a sense, his fear was to prove well-grounded; indeed, a little more firmness by Darwin senior at this point might eventually have swollen the ranks of the Victorian clergy with more than one recruit. But after a short period of resignation on Darwin's part ('Charles has quite given up the idea of the voyage'), his father, persuaded by his Wedgwood cousin, relented, and what Darwin referred to at the time as his 'second life' began.

His correspondence during the five-year *Beagle* voyage, when he was more written to than writing, occupies pride of place in the first volume, and will, presumably, be the part of most interest to historians of science. As he himself confesses, he was not at this age a particularly gifted or prolific letter-writer, though naturally stirred to greater efforts by isolation and homesickness. His chief virtues as a correspondent, from the point of view of disinterested eavesdroppers on his epistolary conversations, are a certain freshness of observation—the impact of the tropics is rendered very vividly—and that direct simplicity of emotion which seemed to characterize him throughout his life. When not writing about the natural history of the regions he visits, his reflections are of a fairly predictable kind: he looks forward to shooting some cannibals, worries that upon his return he will be too old to look for a wife, discusses the charms of their common female acquaintances and relatives with his cousin and Cambridge contemporary W. D. Fox, and constantly reassures his father and sisters about the state of his health. Though not a particularly revealing letter-writer, he does occasionally allow his swings of mood to make their way onto the page. His enthusiasm for the whole business, engaging in its boyishness at the outset, declines into a slightly willed Pollyannaism as life's little drawbacks make themselves felt ('I am sure, as soon as sea-sickness is over I shall soon fall into sea-habits and like them'), so much so, in fact, that one is rather relieved when yet another delay in the homeward voyage prompts him to a rare moment of undisguised rage ('I loathe, I abhor the sea, and all ships which sail on it').

There is a sense, of course, in which this volume is not only all overture and no play, but is also practically Hamlet without the prince, or certainly without the murder. These letters do, after all, only provide an incidental commentary: the main intellectual action is meanwhile taking place in the notebooks and records which were to form the basis for Darwin's later publications. Moreover, throughout the period covered by this volume, Darwin was still a believer in the fixity of species. Only when arranging his materials in the course of the homeward journey in the late summer and autumn of 1836 did he begin seriously to ruminate on the possibility of the mutability of species, and it was not until the following spring that his ruminations led him to become a convinced transmutationist. This volume ends with the initial stages of the reception of the promising young geologist and ento-mologist by the London scientific community: at this point, even the hero had no idea of the drama that was now afoot. But he was soon to realize the nature of the piece; as he put it when revealing to one or two close friends in 1844 that he had definitely aban-doned belief in the fixity of species: 'It is like confessing a murder'.

III

With forty-six years of Darwin's life still to come, years when his domestic seclusion, his illnesses, and the nature of his work all made him peculiarly dependent on letters, the Cambridge edition of his correspondence has clearly been conceived along ample lines. Whether one welcomes such a prospect will depend in part on one's attitude to the whole current academic preoccupation with the monumentally complete, exhaustively annotated, variant-recording collected edition. Certainly, modern editorial principles have established formidably exacting criteria for such enterprises, and the names of Frederick Burkhardt and Sydney Smith as the two chief editors are themselves guarantees that in the application of these principles no less than in the intimacy with Darwin's life and work the standards of this edition will be beyond dispute. There is an odd kind of grandeur about such projects, and in this case the combination of immensity of scale with tireless attention to detail seems a particularly appropriate form of homage to the author of *The Origin of Species*. The conduct of military campaigns or the building of Gothic cathedrals suggest themselves as apposite comparisons or metaphors, such is the orchestration of diversely skilled and largely anonymous labour involved. Merely to praise the judicious editing, the agreeable layout, the helpful biographical appendices, and the very usable index seems somehow clumsy or presumptuous, like commending the creators of Notre Dame for having got the doors in the right place.

Although many of Darwin's letters from this period had been published before in various forms, sixty-six now appear in print for the first time, as do almost all the letters to him. Even those historians of science deeply versed in Darwiniana will doubtless find suggestive novelties here. But, more generally, an edition of this kind also constitutes a rich resource for social and intellectual historians of the period, and one of the telling justifications of such completeness is that no one can predict just which detail may be relevant to some future historical inquiry. The pattern of expenditure by fashionable doctors, the religious tone of a particular generation of undergraduates, the literary tastes of the daughters of the gentry, the hours of dining, styles of mating, and forms of address of one section of the idle classes (indeed, the immense idleness of the idle classes), all are themes for which the future historian may find apt illustration in these accessible pages.

Laundry lists? Well, it may not merely be wilful professional loyalty which says that even they can prove to be revealing witnesses in the hands of a skilful cross-examiner, but in fact the contents of this volume are not of that fragmentary, impersonal kind. Rather, they are complete letters, letters expressive of an always interesting, if narrow, range of familiar human interests and emotions. Darwin, as more than one of his correspondents noted, had an enviable gift for inspiring affection in those who knew him at all well, and generations of readers of his later writings, especially of his disarming autobiography, have felt something of this pull in his eager, frank, apparently artless style. There may, arguably, be signs of his future scientific powers in these early letters, but the dominant impression is of an enthusiastic, sincere, amiable, even lovable, young man; even had he stuck to his shooting and his dogs, it is hard to believe that he would ever have been a disgrace to himself or his family. Some parish lost a good vicar off the Galapagos Islands.

IV

'One does not like him. Yet he is brilliant of course.' Thus Virginia Woolf, after meeting Bertrand Russell at a party. She went on to itemize his failings ('he has not much body of character . . . and he has no chin & he is dapper'), but concluded: 'Nevertheless, I should like the run of his headpiece'. In the two decades before 1914, that headpiece generated a remarkable quantity of original thinking in works that helped to determine the course of twentieth-century philosophy. However, most of this writing was dauntingly technical, and only a few learned historians of philosophy would be able to trace direct connections between Russell's correspondence of this period and the forests of symbols that fill the pages of works such as *The Philosophy of Mathematics*. But with the appearance of the first volume of *The Selected Letters of Bertrand Russell* the non-specialist reader is given the run of that extraordinary headpiece as it applied itself to more accessible (if in some ways even more intractable) topics like sex, love, and marriage. Perhaps by the close one still does not *like* him: the young Russell fascinates and repels in almost equal measure, but the drama of seeing that headpiece struggling to come to terms with needs and emotions that could not be subjugated by algebraic notation does finally compel a certain admiration.

The provenance of this volume attests its scholarly credentials. For some years now, the Russell archives at McMaster University in Ontario have been home to one of the academic industry's big manufacturing projects, *The Collected Papers of Bertrand Russell*;

several of the projected thirty volumes have already appeared, and
the faithful are kept informed of shop-floor developments through
their own newsletter. This edition does not plan to publish Russell's
letters: this is a relief, since there are a huge number of them—in
fact so many that not even the archivists seem quite sure of the total
(which new discoveries are still augmenting), though they confidently place it somewhere between 40,000 and 50,000. But
although the present volume is not, strictly, part of this edition, it
is clearly a spin-off from it. Nicholas Griffin is one of the editors of
the Russell project and has written authoritatively on Russell's
early philosophy, though this selection (a mere 240 letters, all but
one previously unpublished) is evidently aimed at a more general
audience.

Indeed, this volume may be a little frustrating for the student of
Russell's thought: not only does the selection focus overwhelmingly
on the ups and, even more, the downs of Russell's relations with
two women, but some of the more technical passages have been
omitted from those rare letters which deal with his philosophy.
Moreover, there are disappointingly few glimpses of other aspects
of his public life: there are only three letters from the event-filled
year of 1910, for example, and no mention at all of his failure to
be selected as Liberal candidate for Bedford, even then still something of a family fief. By far the largest number of letters in this
volume are written either to his first wife or to his first (it seems)
mistress, clustering heavily around his marriage to the American
Quaker Alys Pearsall Smith in 1894 and his affair with the English
aristocrat Ottoline Morrell in 1911.

Russell was a very young 22-year-old when he married: his love
comprised, therefore, especially large elements of blind need and
unconscious egotism. The pattern is set early: even before his
marriage, a considerable number of his 'love letters' to Alys consist
of his apologies for some fresh instance of insensitivity (though it
was one of the tiresome things about Alys that she was so easy to
offend). As one might expect of two inhibited and high-minded
people, sex was primarily a matter for earnest discussion. Alys
seemed to think they might on the whole manage not to have much
of it; Russell, by contrast, regarded it as A Good Idea ('I have never
been able to see any harm in moderate intercourse, where it is
perfectly mutual and *quite* subordinate, which in people so unsen-
sual as ourselves it will be very easy to make it'), though he

prospectively referred to the experience in the kind of it-would-be-good-to-do-it-once-to-know-what-it-felt-like terms most people would reserve for experimenting with a new drug or making a parachute jump. He didn't really begin to discover the force and requirements of his sexuality until he was almost 40 (and of course some of his subsequent behaviour had the unmistakable stamp of someone trying to make up for lost time).

The numerous letters from the weeks leading up to his wedding are, in truth, a bit tedious (and all too frequent: they sometimes wrote to each other several times a day). This phase of the correspondence is dominated by the need to persuade, conciliate, and deceive 'Granny', Russell's paternal grandmother, the dowager Countess Russell (both Russell's parents had died before he was 4 years old). A sequence of the Index entries for Lady Russell gives the flavour of her role: 'further attempts to prevent marriage', 'sues for peace', 'objects to wedding arrangements', 'absent from BR's wedding'. She may, as things turned out, have had a point, and Russell later managed to write charitably about her character, but in this volume Granny largely comes across as a joyless and obstinate old bitch.

Even once he and Alys are safely married and Russell professes to regard himself as blissfully happy, there remains something more than a little stilted about their expressions of their love, something not simply to be accounted for as a matter of the contrast between a late Victorian and a late twentieth-century idiom. Their adoption of the Quaker 'thee' plus third-person verb added to the awkwardness. 'If thee would like to do me a real kindness, and give me some pleasant hours, thee would mention some special points in the Bradley on which thee wants elucidation, and I would write notes on them for thee.' (This was not an isolated offer: the previous year he had courted Alys by writing her an essay on T. H. Green's *Prolegomena to Ethics*.) The egotism of the very clever is all too frequent at this stage of Russell's life. He points out to Alys the disparity in their intellectual firepower, and then attempts to resolve the problem with the following piece of crisp insensitivity: 'Of course, one doesn't imagine thee would do any brilliant original thinking, but thee might form part of the indispensable intelligent audience.' It is hard to know whether to feel sorrier for the writer or the recipient of a sentence in which the offhand hurtfulness of the 'of course' is matched by the brutal functionalism of the 'indispensable'.

As Russell's life unrolls over the next twenty years, we have further confirmation of the bleak truth that other people's distress is easier to engage with than their happiness, since the most arresting parts of the volume are those glimpses of the strain of his managing the long-drawn-out failure of his marriage. One day in 1901 when he was out cycling, as he famously recorded in his *Autobiography*, Russell realized, with that mixture of flat clarity and brisk decisiveness that marks so much of his reflection on his emotional life, that he no longer loved Alys. For the next ten years, he appears to have thought he was doing the honourable thing in not actually leaving her, but intermittently he becomes aware of how she experienced his reserved correctness as cruelty, and the few glimpses which the editor gives us of Alys's side of the story are heart-rending. Her depression manifested itself as illness as she tried to avoid recognizing the fact of Bertie's having fallen out of love with her. In 1906 she confided her despair to her diary:

I do so long to leave Bertie free to live with a woman who . . . does not bore him desperately and get on his nerves as I do. . . . Little duties keep me going from day to day. But they don't satisfy the awful craving hunger for Bertie's love. . . . If only I could die—it's such a simple solution.

In some moods Bertie hated himself for his behaviour—'when she is not present I am sorry for her; but when I see and hear her, I become all nerves and think of nothing but the wish to escape'— but was caught in a kind of passivity which it would eventually take an outside force to overcome.

Viewed from another angle, his letters of these years read like a Teach Yourself Sublimation success-story of epic proportions. It was during this period that he finished *The Philosophy of Mathematics*, and then embarked on what proved to be the huge labour of his three-volume collaboration with A. N. Whitehead, *Principia Mathematica*. (It was huge in every respect: when they had finally finished, the manuscript was so unmanageably large that they had to hire 'an old four-wheeler' to deliver it to the Cambridge University Press.) For much of this period he worked ten or twelve hours a day, a man on the run from unhappiness: reporting his projected movements to one correspondent in 1905, he concludes 'and then I shall get back to work, which for a time will solve all my problems for me'. As so often in these letters, it is Russell's intermittent flashes of self-knowledge that redeem the picture. 'I have made a mess of my private life—I have not lived up to my ideals, and I have failed to get or give happiness. . . . So all my idealism has become concentrated on my work, which is the one thing in which I have not disappointed myself, and in which I have made none of the compromises that destroy faith.' But here, too, we see the destructive power of Russell's purism as well as something of the variety of forms taken by his habitual egotism.

In fact, the workings of his egotism may have been more widely ramifying still, since the chronology suggests that only when he had finished his great work did he really allow himself to risk that satisfaction of his sexual and emotional hunger which, indulged earlier, would have distracted him from his writing. Only a matter of months after completing *Principia*, he began his liaison with Ottoline Morrell, which must already rank as one of the most thoroughly footnoted affairs in history. It was not, in fact, the earth-moving expression of mutual desire that readers of Russell's *Autobiography* might assume: he was by some way keener on her than she on him; she was not really drawn to his body; his bad breath was a further barrier; and anyway Ottoline seems to have preferred more spirituality than animality in her lovers. But for Russell the experience involved the more common mixture of, in turn, rapture, release, and regret. It also provided the external impulsion he had, without acknowledgement, been waiting for to make him leave Alys.

His letters to Ottoline certainly exhibit more excitement and vitality than his somewhat duty-driven correspondence with the high-principled Alys. At first, they do seem to suggest a variant of Tolstoy's adage: every happy love-letter is the same, but every unhappy one is different in its own way. Certainly, some of his declarations could have been culled from a Handbook for Ardent Lovers: 'After I had stopped writing to you this afternoon, I went out to see the sunset and hear the birds—everything seemed a thousand times more beautiful than other springs—the daffodils and young lime leaves and thrushes and the sky and the meadows—it all seemed transfigured.' But in the inevitable bust-ups, too, he could sound almost equally formulaic; 'I am *utterly* and absolutely miserable—I feel I *cannot* face life without you' and so on. Still, Russell was undeniably *alive* during this affair, in a way that he had not been for years, and despite their differences he and Ottoline were sufficiently compatible for the relationship to have given him an enticing glimpse of a life in which his erotic and intellectual energies might stimulate rather than obstruct each other.

What this volume gives, therefore, is a kind of epistolary *Bildungsroman* in which the interest centres on the young hero's character. At one point in his helpful linking commentary, Nicholas Griffin quotes from the shrewdly perceptive character-sketch of Russell which Beatrice Webb recorded in her diary in 1902. It was his 'subtle absoluteness' that she chiefly remarked: 'Compromise, mitigation, mixed motive, phases of health of body and mind, qualified statements, uncertain feelings, all seem unknown to him. A proposition must be either true or false; a character good or bad, a person loving or unloving, truth-speaking or lying.' Quite a few clever young philosophers conform to this type, of course, but in these letters we see the almost limitless emotional damage he could inflict by his ill-judged insistence on squeezing experience into these narrow boxes. (In passing we may note that Russell was not without his insight into the Webbs: having visited Normandy with them, he complained of how 'they have a competent way of sizing up a Cathedral, and pronouncing on it with an air of authority and an evident feeling that the LCC would have done it better'.)

He signed many of his letters to Alys 'thine in every thought': one is tempted to see even his unguarded choice of a conventional form of salutation as a symptom of the priority Russell accorded to 'thought'. It was part of his egotism that he believed he could think his way out of his unhappiness, when in fact it was something that could only be resolved by action, or rather by that pattern of actions that becomes a new habit. The fact that this basically reserved man was so quickly drawn to those he regarded as uncompromising truth-tellers, such as Joseph Conrad or Ludwig Wittgenstein, was all of a piece with this loyalty to the empire of thought. As he reported after an early meeting with Wittgenstein: 'I have the most perfect intellectual sympathy with him—the same passion and vehemence, the same feeling that one must understand or die.'

As he came to recognize, he also had the puritan's fear of his own appetites. During a visit to Paris in 1894 (admittedly, at a time just before his marriage when his desire was most troublesome to him) he reacts violently against the evident eroticism and easy acceptance of pleasure in the city: 'I get to loathe the prettiness of everything, the pleasure-seeking air of the whole town. I should almost love to plunge into some ancient monastery and take any number of vows, to get away from the oppressive sinning of this place.' Once again, it is the effort after self-knowledge that is redeeming: eight years later he is reflecting that 'austerity is not needed by those who do not have to struggle with all but over-whelming passions'.

His absoluteness extended to his judgements on how well he played the parts he had scripted for himself. One reason why he could experience those sudden, clear-cut reversals of thought or feeling which he recounts, with such chilling abruptness, in his *Autobiography* is that, committed to living within a coherent description, he was highly vulnerable to its falsification and the imperative need to replace it with an equally coherent one. Arguably, those who struggle on within much untidier and less tightly integrated views of themselves have a bit more elasticity: things can give without the whole edifice needing to be scrapped and replaced.

V

We can see the power of these self-descriptions at work in some of his more confessional essays of this period in which he declared his belief in 'the supreme virtue of candour, of fearless acknowledge-ment of what is'. His choice of 'fearless' here indicates a character-istic kind of self-dramatization, giving himself full marks for courage in face of the unpleasant. In these essays Russell may seem to display a somewhat surprising continuity with the stern beliefs and highly-coloured rhetoric of late Victorian 'free thinkers' such as Leslie Stephen and W. K. Clifford, striding with a rugged, manly resolution into the icy winds of a godless universe. But the letters published in the first volume of his correspondence also suggest another way to read his best-known excursions into this genre such as his 1903 essay 'The Free Man's Worship'. Russell had more than a dash of that pride which says 'if I can't win I shan't play'. Reread alongside these letters, 'The Free Man's Worship' suggests a man striving to cope with deep unhappiness by deliberately limiting his expectations of life. The sub-text of this much-anthologized essay is that if the universe was going to be so miserly in the allowance of happiness it gave to Russell, then *tant pis pour l'univers*! The conscious adoption of stoicism is always in part an expression of disappointment (without some notion of unsatisfied or unsatisfiable wishes, the renunciatory element in stoicism has no point), and the essay's teeth-gritted acceptance of scientific naturalism does look like yet another of Russell's attempts to extend the range of intellectual control. It would be too simplistic to say that Russell was in danger of reproaching the cosmos because he wasn't having a good time in bed, but the wilful tone of the essay calls out for comment, and this is one of the few points where these letters bear upon the interpretation of his published writings.

But by the end of this fat volume, Russell's ceaseless effort after understanding, though it took some pretty unappealing forms and was clearly hard to live with, ultimately compels our admiration. One of the many ways in which at this stage of his life he resembled his godless godfather, John Stuart Mill, is that we are left feeling that his occasional accounts of himself as a priggish, logic-chopping machine couldn't have been written by someone who was *only* that. As I suggested in Chapter 6, part of the poignancy of Mill's *Autobiography* comes from the fact that the voice in which it is written is all too clearly continuous with the character whose early life it is used to describe, but it is also a voice which hints at more than that character. So with the best of Russell's letters: the over-development of his intelligence is represented as the source of much of his early ineptness and unhappiness, and yet that intelligence also appears as the beak with which the young Russell is struggling to break out of the shell.

The editor shrewdly remarks at one point that 'like many lonely people, he cultivated a rather self-conscious sensitivity to the troubles of others', and it is true that his replies to his female correspondents have rather too much of the I-do-sympathize-but-you-must-pull-yourself-together tone of the agony aunt. As a result, the letters selected here contain disappointingly little about his relations with his friends or about social life more generally. There are one or two camped-up vignettes of the philosophizing life—'I saw Moore in the evening, and discussed whether there was any difference between knowing Arithmetic and knowing one's grandmother; he thinks not'—and the editorial notes keep up a nicely sardonic commentary, as, for example, when, in identifying a reference to the mathematician G. H. Hardy, Griffin adds: 'At the height of his powers Hardy was (by his own no doubt accurate evaluation) the fifth best pure mathematician in the world'. But for the most part we remain in the hothouse world of the emotions shared, or more usually not, by Bertie and his female correspondents.

Although the first volume of his correspondence throws little direct light on Russell's political development, a few of the letters do give some insight into the source of that unhesitating confidence with which he later addressed presidents and populace alike. He grew up with a strong sense of his family's part in shaping the nation's history and of the expectation that he would extend the tradition: 'I was brought up in the instinctive and unquestioned belief that politics was the only possible career'. He carried this confidence, this sense of an unquestioned right to be at the heart of things, over into everything he did. Perhaps partly for this reason, Russell was in every sense lordly about reputation. His letters indicate that he could be admirably uncompetitive, as, for example, when he discovered that Frege had anticipated so much of *The Philosophy of Mathematics* or when Wittgenstein later caused him to abandon a large manuscript on the theory of knowledge, and he found it easy to keep his distance from professional squabbling.

His financial independence, as well as his consciousness of caste, obviously contributed to this detachment. He had a private income, and until 1910 (when he was 38) he never held any kind of post which brought with it regular duties. These letters contain many instances of his easy generosity with money, yet it is the generosity of someone who takes for granted that his needs will be supplied somehow. They also bring home just how entirely his time was his own, as indeed was his choice of a part of the country in which to live (he and Alys rented a succession of houses to be unhappy in). But his freedom surely compounded his personal difficulties: denied the alibi of necessity and the balm of routine, he took entire responsibility for the direction of his considerable energies, and, not surprisingly, he frequently let himself down.

The last letter reproduced in this volume was written on 3 August 1914, with Russell distraught at the 'utter madness' that was about to begin: 'I try to fix my thought on the future—the present is too unbearable'. From first to last, Russell instinctively turned to 'thought'—and time and again it failed him. The period to be covered by the second volume of letters will see Russell the public figure preoccupied with realities outside

himself, above all war and children, and one cannot help feeling
that for both the patience of its readers and the development of
Russell's personality this will be a good thing. The chief lesson
of this volume seems to be that humankind cannot stand too
little reality.

9

Moral Mind: R. H. Tawney

❧

I

The name of R. H. Tawney still evokes the heroic phase of social-ism. His work is associated with the belief in equality and fellow-ship, with the commitment to strive for the creation of a just social order to replace capitalism, and with the obligation of the educated and the privileged to put their talents at the service of the working class. (It is, of course, one sign that the heroic phase of socialism is over that few of the terms in this sentence can now be used confi-dently and without qualification.) Within the international history of socialism, and still more within the history of 'the labour move-ment' in Britain, Tawney has a secure place in the pantheon of influential thinkers—and he was definitely a 'thinker', not a 'theo-rist'. Moreover, he was revered for his personality and example as much as for his writings, above all for his unaffected manner, his unworldly asceticism, and his deep sympathy with the efforts of working people to improve their lot, especially through adult education to which he devoted a great deal of his own time and energy. He remained a cherished figure in English radical and working-class circles long after his death in 1962 at the age of 82, and mention of him still sends writers to their thesaurus to find variants on the stock of adjectives that are constantly applied to him—strenuous, sincere, committed, admirable. He is one of the

R. H. Tawney, *The Acquisitive Society* (Allen and Unwin, 1921). An earlier version of this essay was written in 1998 as a 'reconsideration' of Tawney's book for the journal *Dissent*.

few secular figures to whom the label 'saint' gets applied unironically.

This makes any kind of reappraisal difficult. Where a saint is concerned, anything short of hagiography is bound to seem debunking or merely negative, even to be taking pleasure in toppling an icon from his pedestal. I feel no such inclination in reconsidering Tawney, in part, perhaps, because I am not old enough, or perhaps just not politically responsive enough, ever to have come under his spell in the first place. In my case, the experience of reading *The Acquisitive Society* (first published in 1921) at the end of the twentieth century is chiefly governed by my formation as an intellectual historian, especially of modern British social and political thought. No modern reader, I imagine, can fail to be struck by the period flavour the book now gives off, but I find myself instinctively moving on to 'place' the work in historical and political context, to identify its informing intellectual traditions and its distinguishing cultural affinities. There is, of course, nothing original in remarking Tawney's datedness: even during his lifetime he was recognized as having a somewhat archaic quality, part Victorian moralist, part Old Testament prophet. But, from this distance, *The Acquisitive Society* seems remote at least as much on account of the conditions its writing presupposed as for any outdatedness in its proposals, and in this 'reconsideration' I primarily want to focus on why that might be so.

II

The book has long been regarded as one of the classics of socialist political thinking. Richard Crossman, Left intellectual turned Labour Cabinet minister, may stand in for many others with his declaration that 'Tawney's *The Acquisitive Society* is my socialist bible', while a whole generation of historians have concurred with Margaret Cole's judgement of it as 'perhaps the most powerful of all post-war [sc. First World War] appeals for socialism'. And yet the book is not in any obvious sense a general manifesto for socialism, nor an outright condemnation of private property and the market—indeed, he dismisses 'the idea of some socialists that private property in land or capital is necessarily mischievous' as 'a piece of scholastic pedantry'. It is not even—as those who know

nothing of it other than its title and reputation tend to suppose—
primarily an indictment of the advertising and consumerism inte-
gral to a mass-market economy. It deals almost entirely with
production rather than consumption; it can still come as something
of a surprise to find that a book with such a title makes no reference to shopping. For the book offers something that is more
general, and yet also more limited, than any of these descriptions
might suggest.

The Acquisitive Society operates at two levels. At the more
general, it is a plea that the goals of economic gain, increased
productivity, and individual self-interest should be subordinated to
some 'higher' set of values. At the more specific level, Tawney
concentrates on the organization of industry: he argues that with
the growth of capitalism has come a divorce between ownership
and the actual running of businesses, that the greater part of the
income derived from ownership in such circumstances is 'functionless wealth', and that society could be beneficially reorganized on
the basis of rewarding 'functions' rather than of allowing the
largely passive owners of capital to accumulate wealth created by
others. Until the final chapter, the more general case is only pass-
ingly alluded to; it is implicit in Tawney's idiom and moral passion,
but it is not argued for in any extended way. Much the greater part
of the book is devoted to an analysis of the different forms of relationship between ownership and control in industry, focusing on
the need for incomes to be restricted to rewarding the performance
of socially necessary functions.

However, this bald summary of the book's central argument
needs to be supplemented by an account of several of its less-
noticed features. First of all, there is the extent to which Tawney
depicts the situation he criticizes as a recent and contingent development, brought about by erroneous or inappropriate ideas. The
book rests on markedly intellectualist assumptions about the motor
of social change. It is the individualist idea of property, developed
from the late seventeenth century onwards, that is at the root of
present ills. Enlightenment rationalism prepared the ground for the
individualism unleashed by the Industrial Revolution; as so often in
this vein of criticism, the Utilitarians and early political economists
are singled out for particular opprobrium. The notion of absolute
property rights, valuable in the struggle against the relics of feudal-
ism and the impositions of absolutism, has become a curse in the

very different conditions of large-scale industry. The opening
sentence of the book accurately signals this concern with changing
prevailing *ideas*: 'It is a commonplace that the characteristic virtue
of Englishmen is their power of sustained practical activity, and
their characteristic vice a reluctance to test the quality of that activity by reference to principles.' In the body of the book, Tawney
explores several means of bringing function and reward into some
more direct relation, not all of them involving nationalization, still
less expropriation of the owners of capital. For example, he is willing to grant that capital may be allowed to earn a certain return,
but suggests that this could take the form of a fixed rate, in the
manner of a debenture or mortgage, rather than an open-ended
claim on the profits of an enterprise. Similarly, he would sever the
automatic link between ownership and control, depriving the mere
providers of capital of any say in policy or management. But
throughout these apparently practical discussions, the *idea* of
absolute, puchasable property rights is the target.

'The acquisitive society' is, therefore, seen as an extremely recent
and, he implies, temporary aberration in a longer history of societies that have subordinated the production of wealth to larger
social purposes. Indeed, although the Industrial Revolution of the
late eighteenth and early nineteenth centuries is seen as the vital
transition to an historically unprecedented form of society, Tawney
is at pains to stress how very recent several of the key features of
the acquisitive society actually are. The establishment of shares and
dividends as the standard form of financial property was only
achieved 'less than two generations ago'; the impact of the mid-
century legislation on joint-stock and limited liability companies
had only been fully felt 'within the last twenty years', and so on.
Tawney can sound surprisingly indulgent to the much pilloried
owner-managers of the early days of industrialism, because they
were at least actively involved in running their businesses; his
sharpest barbs are reserved for absentee shareholders in public
companies, the undeserving financial beneficiaries of the notion of
unlimited property rights.

This historical account is tacitly underpinned by a considerable
idealization of the economic system that preceded the Industrial
Revolution: like the Hammonds, whose 'catastrophist' interpretation of the rise of industrialism he endorsed, he is for the most part
silent about the forms of oppression and exploitation inherent in

the economic relationships of early modern England. Instead, the yeoman and the craftsman of a vaguely specified past are lauded at the expense of the all-too-visible rentier in the present. 'The past has shown no more excellent order than that in which the mass of the people were the masters of the holdings which they ploughed and the tools with which they worked.' And the virtues of this direct engagement in productive activity were complemented by the acknowledgement of a larger moral framework. Revealingly, he uses the term 'industrialism' to refer not to a socio-economic system itself, but to a question of attitude, 'a particular estimate of the importance of industry', which results in all other goals becoming secondary to the pursuit of material gain. For Tawney, industrialism signifies 'the confusion of one minor department of life with the whole of life'. But this characterization implies that if the prevailing ideas could be changed, the problem would be solved— hence his confident conclusion that this 'obsession by economic issues is as local and transitory as it is repulsive and disturbing'.

This is where the more general moral argument of the book and its interpretation of English history intersect most interestingly. References to the need 'to admit that there is a principle superior to the mechanical play of economic forces' and to recognize that society must be based on 'some moral principles which command general acceptance' accompany his more substantial discussion like a figured bass repeatedly making itself heard through the main melody. But only when we reach the final chapter is it suddenly revealed that the propagation of such principles was formerly the function of the Church, and that it is the 'abdication' of this role by the Church in England from the late seventeenth century onwards that allowed economic activity to appear to be an end in itself (Tawney was to develop this theme on a broader canvas in *Religion and the Rise of Capitalism*, published five years later). In the course of the eighteenth century the Anglican clergy became 'the servile clients of a half-pagan aristocracy'; in the nineteenth 'they acquiesced in the popular assumption that the acquisition of riches was the main end of man, and confined themselves to preaching such personal virtues as did not conflict with its achievement'. This final chapter of the book is entitled 'Porro unum necessarium', a phrase (generally translated as 'but one thing is needful') from the Latin Vulgate version of St Luke's gospel that had also been used as a chapter heading by Matthew Arnold in *Culture and*

Anarchy. But whereas Arnold had gently mocked the modern puritan's conviction of finding in the Bible the one necessary truth—'so fatal is the notion of possessing, even in the most precious words or standards, the one thing needful, of having in them, once and for all, a full and sufficient measure of light to guide us'—Tawney's use of the phrase is quite without ironic intent: the one thing needful is that 'society must rearrange its scale of values' and for this to happen the Church must resue its historic task.

It is difficult, on closer inspection, to say quite what part an active form of Christianity would play in moving to 'the functional society', since Tawney does not identify any relevant *content* in Christian teaching. Structurally (and, one cannot help suspecting, psychologically), the overriding importance of Christianity for Tawney at this point is simply that it out-trumps economic criteria. It is the organized assertion of an alternative standard of values that he seeks, values to which the calculations of economic reasoning would be subordinate, and in the light of which proximate goals and purposes could be identified in moral, non-economic terms. The biographical evidence leaves the nature of Tawney's own religious beliefs opaque: he appears to have participated in Anglican social organizations and economic discussion-groups with more commitment and regularity than he showed in his devotions. (His biographer observed of the latter that 'he would frequently but not regularly go to church, often taking his dog, less frequently his wife'.) But one is left feeling that for Tawney as for many other proponents of 'social Christianity' in the late nineteenth and early twentieth centuries it was the *idea* of the moral glory of the Sermon on the Mount that mattered. The accompanying assumption was that once the authority of this selfless ethic was properly acknowledged, it would not be difficult for men of goodwill to reach agreement on otherwise divisive matters like the distribution of wealth. Or as the final paragraph of *The Acquisitive Society* confidently has it, once society has 'learned to see industry itself in the right perspective' it will be able to 'persuade its members to renounce the opportunity of gains which accrue without any corresponding service'.

This is recognizably the idiom of the Christian Social Union which Tawney joined while an undergraduate at Balliol in the late 1890s, and its leaders, such as Canon Scott Holland, Bishop

Charles Gore, and Archbishop William Temple, were prominent among the influences and associates that shaped Tawney's thinking. But it is hard not to feel that he was drawn to 'social Christianity' because it provided a language with which to censure the unfettered pursuit of material gain rather than that it was his belief in Christian principles which led him to become such a severe critic of economic self-interest. Perhaps quite a lot of English 'socialism' has been like this: sometimes the appeal has been to the overriding values represented by 'culture' or 'art', sometimes to the ideals incarnated in Ancient Greece, sometimes to the standards of Christian ethics, but the common element has been the desire to be able to invoke some cherished and powerful realm of value to set over against the world of commercial and financial activity that is thereby condemned as much for its vulgarity as for its injustice.

III

While placing the book in this general cultural milieu, there are two more particular affiliations or debts that need to be remarked. The first is to point out how the tone and general argument of the book signal the extent of Tawney's allegiance to Ruskin, even though explicit mention of him in the text is rare. Again, there is nothing even mildly revisionist in placing Tawney in a tradition that includes Ruskin, and there is ample biographical evidence to confirm Tawney's recognition of the affinity. Even so, the pervasively Ruskinian nature of *The Acquisitive Society* has perhaps not been fully recognized. For anyone familiar with Ruskin's social writings there are a few tell-tale signs, such as sardonic coinages like 'the production of futilities' or the contrast between 'property' and 'improperty' which recall Ruskin's attempt to contrast 'wealth' with 'illth' and similar ill-fated neologisms. The rather surprising appearance of the army as a model form of social organization on the grounds that its members act for some motive other than profit or personal gain directly echoes a celebrated passage in Ruskin's *Unto This Last* (as well, perhaps, as reflecting Tawney's own experience as a soldier during the First World War).

But the pervasive, if unobvious, Ruskinian properties of Tawney's book can be most economically illustrated by means of the following brief textual comparison. The first chapter of the book contains several paragraphs setting out, in general and assertive terms, 'the principles on which industry should be based', 'the conditions of a right organisation of industry', and so on. These are Tawney's premises the elaboration of which is to follow in the succeeding chapters. But if one turns to an article Tawney published on John Ruskin in 1919 in the *Observer* on the centenary of the latter's birth, two years before the publication of *The Acquisitive Society*, one finds *exactly* the same paragraphs, but in this case offered as paraphrases of Ruskin's thought (the article is reprinted in a posthumous collection of Tawney's essays entitled *The Radical Tradition*, edited by Rita Hinden). For example, a paragraph in the book begins: 'Yet all the time the principles upon which industry should be based are simple, however difficult it may be to apply them; and if they are overlooked it is not because they are difficult, but because they are elementary. They are simple because industry is simple.' The reader's sense of direct contact with the author's fundamental convictions is strong here. Yet *exactly* the same wording appears in the earlier *Observer* article, with the small (but huge) difference that the phrase 'Ruskin tells us' appears after the opening 'Yet all the time'. So complete was the identification between Ruskin's ideas (at least as summarized by Tawney) and Tawney's own that no other change needed to be introduced in using these paragraphs for what would seem, on the face of things, to be a very different purpose.

Moreover, this identity extends to the idea which is generally thought to constitute the defining distinctiveness of *The Acquisitive Society*: 'The first principle is that industry should be subordinated to the community in such a way as to render the best service technically possible, that those who render that service faithfully, should be honourably paid, and that those who render no service should not be paid at all, because it is of the essence of a function that it should find its meaning in the satisfaction, not of itself, but of the end which it serves.' Thus Tawney, expounding his central argument in the book's opening chapter. But two years earlier the passage had already appeared, word for word, in the *Observer* article as a summary of the informing idea of Ruskin's social thought. When *Unto This Last* first appeared in the early 1860s, it was widely condemned for its ignorance and misrepresentation of political economy. But in the 1920s Ruskin's ideas were clearly having their revenge on what Tawney stigmatized as 'the bloodless abstractions of experts'. And this underlines Tawney's long-standing hostility to the very discipline of economics. Before the war, he had expressed himself very forthrightly on the subject in the privacy of his diary: 'There is no such thing as a science of economics, nor ever will be. It is just cant and Marshall's talk as to the need for social problems to be studied by "the same order of mind which tests the stability of a battleship in bad weather" is twaddle'.

One of the chief conduits through which Ruskin's social thought came down to 'progressives' of the next generation was J. A. Hobson's *John Ruskin, Social Reformer* (1898), and this signals the second intellectual affiliation to be mentioned here. There is no acknowledgement in *The Acquisitive Society* itself of the extent to which its central conception of 'functionless wealth' rests upon the notions of 'rent' or 'the surplus' which the early Fabians and, most influentially, Hobson developed out of a modified form of marginalist economics. This theory, as elaborated by Hobson and drawn upon by fellow 'New Liberals' like L. T. Hobhouse, provided one of the foundations for the radical critique during the Edwardian period of the individualist conception of society, and it was drawn upon directly to justify the beginnings of a system of progressive taxation through death duties and a graduated income tax. The central postulate of this theory was that the prospect of a certain return or reward was needed to draw each 'factor of production' into play, whether it was the exercise of talent or the application of labour or the investment of capital. The return which any of these factors of production received over and above what was functionally necessary for their full productive operation was, for the purposes of economic theory, seen as a 'rent'. It was Hobson, above all, who claimed to have demonstrated by means of this kind of reasoning that the greater part of the wealth accruing to the rich was part of the 'unproductive surplus', which could thus be redistributed for social use without stunting any productive capacities. It is in precisely these terms that Tawney identifies what he calls 'functionless wealth'. (Interestingly, Ruskin, for all his denunciation of 'parasites', had not developed any such theory, and Tawney's summary of Ruskin's social thought quoted earlier has clearly been infected by Hobsonian formulations. In so far as the critical theory of rent traced itself back to one of the great Victorian sages it was rather to one of the more radical features of the political economy of J. S. Mill, namely his criticism of urban ground rents as an economically indefensible form of absolute property rights.)

It was from within this theoretical framework that Tawney was able to be so dismissive of the 'scholastic pedantry' of the generalized hostility to private property shown by 'some socialists'. The crucial distinction is between property which is a legitimate return for the performance of a socially desirable 'function' and property which is not; only 'functionless' property is to be abolished. Urban ground rents and mining royalties are instanced as pure cases of income which is strictly functionless; that is, are not needed to bring a relevant factor of production into play. But Tawney also suggests that a large part of the return on capital and indeed of high salaries should come under the same indictment, and here he runs up against the problem which even the greater theoretical and economic sophistication of writers like Hobson and Hobhouse had failed to solve: how to determine what return was 'necessary' to call into play a factor of production, be it capital or labour. If the market mechanism is rejected—and of course its (partial) rejection was the starting-point for all these 'progressive' theorists—then there was no theoretically satisfactory stopping place short of using political authority to set 'desirable' levels of return. What presents itself in this strain of New Liberal theorizing as the conclusion of purely economic reasoning is revealed, upon closer analysis, to depend upon a prior social judgement. This would presumably not in itself have been an objection in Tawney's eyes, but it is indicative of his absorption of this body of thinking that he can present the process of determining the rewards 'necessary' to stimulate the performance of 'functions' as having the same impersonal, self-regulating properties as the market mechanism it is designed to replace.

Recognizing this intellectual affiliation also raises, from an unusual angle, the question of the extent to which Tawney's position is properly characterized as 'socialist' as that term has generally been used in the twentieth century. Consider the following passage: 'The central point of Socialist economics, then, is the equation of social service and reward. This is the principle that every function of social value requires such remuneration as serves to stimulate and maintain its effective performance; that everyone who performs such a function has the right, in the strict ethical sense of that term, to such remuneration and no more; that the

residue of existing wealth should be at the disposal of the community for social purposes.' This is recognizably the informing idea
behind what Tawney calls 'the Functional Society'. But in fact the
quotation is taken not from *The Acquisitive Society*, but from L. T.
Hobhouse's *Liberalism*, first published in 1911. And the term
'Socialist' in the first phrase is my substitution; in Hobhouse's text
this is offered as 'the central point of Liberal economics'. Of
course, the line between 'progressive' Liberalism and 'moderate'
Socialism was hard to draw in British politics and public debate
before 1914, but the point is not a merely verbal one since it serves
to bring out the location of Tawney's central ideas in the very
particular political and intellectual milieu of late Victorian and
Edwardian 'social reform'.

   There is, however, one very specific feature of *The Acquisitive
Society* that clearly indicates its post-First World War provenance.
Tawney (along with Sidney Webb) had been a member of the royal
commission set up in 1919 to consider the future of the coal-
mining industry, and this experience is reflected throughout the
book. Coal was a chronically inefficient industry in Britain in the
first half of the twentieth century, and the coal owners, who were
far more often absentee capitalists than active proprietors, were
notoriously obstructive of all attempts to rationalize its operations
in the public interest (Tawney's picture of how private enterprise
typically operated may have been distorted by his concentration on
this atypical industry, as he later tacitly acknowledged). The
commission, chaired by a prominent judge, Sir John Sankey,
included representatives of both the miners and the owners;
perhaps inevitably, it failed to arrive at a unanimous recommenda-
tion, though Sankey himself came down in favour of a form of
modified nationalization. (As it turned out, of course, no government before 1945 was willing to take this drastic step.) But the
commission's report not only made a series of practical suggestions
about more collaborative, and more efficient, forms of management; it also raised the larger question of the legitimacy of the unrestricted private ownership of essential natural resources. Tawney's
frequent favourable references to the Sankey Commission in *The
Acquisitive Society* are, therefore, unsurprising if slightly disingen-
uous, given his substantial contribution to its proceedings. That
such an impeccably respectable figure as 'Mr Justice Sankey' could
be cited (and cited often) as willing to entertain proposals which

only a generation before would have been howled down as dangerous and revolutionary nonsense clearly encouraged Tawney to
hope that the ground under 'the acquisitive society' was already
shifting. He is perhaps the only writer in the history of socialism
who has pictured capitalism's gravedigger as wearing the robes of
a High Court judge.

Although Anthony Wright, in the most recent book-length
assessment of Tawney, argues for his continuing political relevance,
he at one point, speaking of the trajectory of Tawney's intellectual
development, recognizes that the First World War 'produces no real
dent in the structure of fundamental beliefs about man and society
which he had put together before 1914, and his God had also
survived intact'. This seems to me true; that 'archaic' quality in
Tawney which, as I mentioned earlier, has long been noted partly
stems from the fact that he remained a late Victorian or Edwardian
moralist all his life. *The Acquisitive Society* does concern itself with
what were then some of the more recent forms of the organization
of capitalism, and it is clearly addressed to the tense and antagonistic state of industrial relations in Britain in the years immediately
following the First World War. But it does this with ideas and
assumptions that belonged within an essentially Victorian debate.

IV

Any 'reconsideration' of *The Acquisitive Society* must, at the
outset, acknowledge the kind of book it is. It is not a work of
philosophy, nor even, in the strict sense, of political theory; it is
historical without being genuinely scholarly and it is topical without being merely journalistic. It is nearer in spirit to that kind of
essay in social criticism which surrounds certain practical proposals with an appeal to a general moral vision. The writing is marked
more by a kind of biblical eloquence than by analytical finesse, and
the book's origins in an article and a pamphlet that Tawney
published in 1919 remain visible. It does not, therefore, really
belong in the company of such works as, say, Lukács's *History and
Class Consciousness* or Rawls's *A Theory of Justice*. Its closest
kinship seems to me rather with works like Ruskin's *Unto This
Last* or Eliot's *Idea of a Christian Society*.

It has to be said, however, that the book does not really seem to recognize its own identity in these terms, above all because it claims to offer a serious and feasible view of how a sophisticated modern economy might be organized in terms of the rewards necessary to the fulfilment of 'functions'. But this is precisely, in my view, the weakest feature of the book. Indeed, the central conception of 'the Functional Society' strikes me as not just unpersuasive, but also as potentially coercive. Tawney simply ducks the hard questions about the authoritarianism involved in deciding which activities constitute desirable 'functions' and which do not, and he deludes himself that there could be any kind of modified market mechanism, short of decision by central authority, by which the appropriate level of 'reward' for such functions could be determined. He assumes that others would share his (rather puritan) convictions about what is 'worth' doing and what level of 'reward' one should legitimately expect: my scepticism about the likelihood of such agreement being reached is only exceeded by my alarm at the consequences if it were.

Another notable, though perhaps more forgivable and certainly more limited, lacuna in Tawney's argument is any consideration of how far the international nature of capitalism sets limits to what could be done within any single national economy. Quite apart from technical problems concerning a potential 'flight of capital'— where Tawney and his contemporaries obviously took for granted a degree of legislative control over relatively self-contained national economies far in excess of anything available to governments in the internationalized markets of the 1990s—there is the larger issue of historical and, as it were, cognitive insularity. He is calling for a national change of heart, yet the book's central category of industrialism or 'the acquisitive society' is not a national unit. This is the problem of what might be called 'moralism in one country'.

But to my mind the most damning of the criticisms that can be levelled against Tawney's writings in general, and against *The Acquisitive Society* in particular, is that they are all too likely to encourage high-mindedness for its own sake. Setting up a binary polarity between 'self-interest' and 'morality' is in itself an unhelpful over-simplification, and one particularly likely to lead to self-deception. Such a starting-point also tends to require people to act out of unrealistically strenuous or heroic motives, and involves an unwarranted disdain for simple, common wants such as the desire for ease spiced with excitement. One of Tawney's warmest admirers was perhaps indirectly acknowledging this tendency when, with fond irony, he remarked that 'the severest criticism' to be made of Tawney's social theory 'is that it would be easier to realise in practice if all men were Tawneys'. Moreover, high-mindedness is constantly vulnerable to being rendered inconsistent by shifts in circumstance. Various figures on the British Left in the middle of the century testified to the way Tawney's arguments had permanently inoculated them against the temptation of personally owning shares and receiving dividends. But now, given the intricate interdependence of the elements in the financial structure of contemporary capitalism, there looks to be something slightly foolish in deliberately avoiding share-ownership while happily accepting the benefits of a pension-fund.

But at the risk of seeming wilfully to court paradox, I would even suggest that it is the general attitude or tone of the book that has dated more than its concrete proposals. It is not just that Tawney is too sanguine about the possibility of arriving at some agreed sense of 'social purpose' from which more specific 'goals' and 'functions' could be deduced. It is, rather, that his writing constantly seems to suggest that the invocation of the *idea* of 'higher principles' is a good in itself. Even if these principles are not given much content, as for the most part they are not in this book, the suggestion is that we range ourselves on the side of the angels by repeating, frequently and with feeling, that moral principle must override unbridled self-interest. But this issues in a tone and a stance that are always in danger of becoming merely moralistic. This in turn tends to encourage a certain self-righteousness and ultimately brings discredit on the critical case against unfettered capitalism, a case which, in more measured and realistic terms, needs to be made as pressingly as ever.

It may be said that this is to misunderstand the function of utopian thinking, which is precisely to jolt us out of what we think 'realistic' by painting a beguiling picture of life within an utterly different social order. I recognize that I am not the most responsive reader of such utopian critiques. But, more immediately, I would also point out that *The Acquisitive Society* was not offered as such. Tawney clearly intended the book to be severely practical, with concrete proposals for the better as well as fairer management of specific industries, such as coal and building, in 1920s Britain. Indeed, some of its practical suggestions seem to me among the more persuasive parts of the book. But I persist in thinking that the tone of generalized moral uplift with which he surrounded these proposals is bad for the mind. We certainly still need—perhaps we need more than ever before—a publicly effective language with which to combat the relentless pseudo-realism of 'the return upon capital' and, more generally, invocations of the priority of 'the bottom line'. I would like to think that a book by someone so transparently serious and warm-hearted as Tawney would be one place to look for help in developing such a language. I fear, however, it is more likely to encourage certain bad habits all too common on the Left, above all that of finding consolation for constant defeat in the comforting assurance of one's own greater moral seriousness.

Two years after Tawney's death, Alasdair MacIntyre lodged a memorable dissenting judgement along somewhat similar lines, complaining of his 'cliché-ridden high-mindedness', and concluding that in a political theorist 'goodness alone is not enough'. (The essay is reprinted in MacIntyre's *Against the Self-Images of the Age.*) Though needlessly dismissive, MacIntyre's judgement was in some ways a healthy corrective. None the less, simply to leave the matter there may seem to display a certain intellectual laziness as well as a rather cheap kind of self-congratulation—it is not difficult, after all, to establish oneself as being more hard-headed than Tawney. The more demanding question to ask is why, if his work now seems to invite such damaging criticism, he exercised such influence and achieved such standing—and why, for that matter, various prominent political and intellectual figures in Britain and elsewhere still profess to draw inspiration from his writings.

Part of the explanation may be structural as much as personal. The Left needs intellectuals in the way sports fans need heroes. Tawney seemed to correspond to one idealized notion of the intellectual, the figure who achieves distinction in some scholarly or creative field while at the same time 'applying' his ideas in active political engagement. Tawney was an economic and social historian of standing, and he wrote widely admired works of social criticism; at the same time, he was tirelessly active in various left-wing or, more accurately, working-class, causes, and he was directly influential in the shaping and expression of Labour Party policy (he played a large part in drafting the Party's manifesto for the 1929 election, for example). He was notable for his consistent advocacy of and counsel to working-class groups of all kinds during a period when the organized working class was a major player in British political and economic life. And at a time when print journalism was the undisputedly dominant medium for shaping opinion, Tawney had ready access to some influential publications, and he had what it takes to make a mark: he was not afraid to repeat himself, he wrote forcefully, and he wrote a lot.

Tawney's impact was also bound up with the kind of social authority he could draw upon, and this, too, is something that makes us feel our distance from him today. For all his genuine sympathy and engagement with ordinary working people, it must not be forgotten that Tawney was Rugby and Balliol at a time when this mattered. Two anecdotes catch something of his position. On the outbreak of the First World War, Tawney deliberately refused the possibility of a commission in the army and enlisted as a private, but when in 1916 he was lying in the 'other ranks' section of the military hospital recovering from his wounds, he was, to the surprise of the nursing staff, visited by his friend, Bishop Gore. After the bishop had left, the matron scolded Tawney: 'Why ever didn't you tell us you were a *gentleman*?' For all his hostility to the historical privileges of the English upper class, Tawney was, by upbringing and connection, emphatically a 'gentleman'. His Balliol contemporaries included several of the future Great and Good, including William Beveridge, whose sister he married. On another occasion, Tawney was visited in his London flat by William Temple, soon to be Archbishop of Canterbury. After they had improvised a meal and talked late into the night, Temple slept in his clothes on Tawney's living-room floor. Recounting this episode, his biographer simply comments: 'Thus the informality of the tie between these two quite different Rugby old boys'. For all his personal sincerity and lack of affectation, there was an ineliminable element of *noblesse oblige* in the class relations which structured Tawney's career and which, arguably, informed his social thinking.

But more than all this, he gave pointed and relevant expression in the inter-war period to attitudes that were deep-seated and of long standing in English culture. Perhaps the moral criticism of capitalism flourished in no other country as it did in England between the early nineteenth and the mid-twentieth centuries. The 'condition of England' question, that hotchpotch of concerns about the human consequences of the Industrial Revolution, remained a central and recurring theme in public debate, and Tawney was a 'condition of England' writer *par excellence.*

In the 1960s the Young Turks on the *New Left Review* complained that this tradition had not issued in any conceptually sophisticated analysis of the nature and functioning of society, economy, and the state in Britain: it had, they charged, contented itself with the untheoretical, even anti-theoretical, task of the *moral* criticism of capitalism. One does not have to be an enthusiast for the high Althusserian or Gramscian theorizing then offered as the alternative to recognize some truth in this account. But that being so, it is perhaps otiose to single out Tawney for special criticism. Rather, we should acknowledge that he owed much of his standing to the eloquent expression (and authoritative historical illustration) he gave to what were in effect the moral commonplaces of the 'progressive' educated class in Britain in the late nineteenth and early twentieth centuries.

In saying this, I do not at all mean to suggest that the ideals at the heart of those commonplaces were so purely a matter of that time and place that, appropriately reformulated, they can no longer move us. Attempting to reduce inequality, attempting to control rather than being controlled by global markets, attempting to make non-economic values tell in public debate—these aims seem to me admirable and urgent, and recognizably connected to the values cherished by Tawney and his peers. But the terms in which I have stated them deliberately suggest a much more modest and realistic (and thereby, perhaps, more liberal) political idiom than that used by Tawney, and this may help explain some of the ambivalence which I (but not, I think, I alone) cannot help feeling about *The Acquisitive Society*. What still seems to me so problematic in Tawney—and, I am suggesting, the milieu that enabled him to write with such untroubled confidence—is the combination of a sweeping conception of 'the functional society' with an assumption of a high degree of moral consensus. The shared commitment to selflessness that he takes for granted can seem not just unrealistic but even in some ways unattractive.

That one's response is ambivalent rather than merely critical is also in part due to the force of Tawney's style—the barbed ironies at the expense of the rich, the almost Miltonic cadences of his Latinate sentence structures, the fine preacherly fire. That eloquence can still, intermittently, do its work, and even the politically sceptical or agnostic modern reader can be seduced into a sense of belonging, if not quite of belief. With Tawney taking the service, the incense of earnestness stirs memories of unfulfilled good resolutions, the pleasing cadences of the liturgy offer reassurance that this is no vulgar evangelical sect, and the urge to go forward and take one's place at the communion rail starts to be felt. Such rituals of identification and solidarity, even if conducted in the privacy of one's mind, have a necessary part to play. Perhaps no purposeful large-scale changes in society are brought about unless preceded and accompanied by a considerable amount of what may properly be called moral emotion. Tawney was a virtuoso of moral emotion.

And yet as, the service being over, we return to the lower temperature of our daily lives, stubborn doubts and even antipathies start to creep back in. Underlying the arguments and proposals of *The Acquisitive Society* and Tawney's other political writings, there is a simple, massive assertion that the teaching of morality points towards the politics of socialism. Not only may the destination now look more uncertain and the logic of the connection more disputable, but few of those likely to read Tawney today can easily share his unargued conviction about the nature and force of something called 'morality'. For Tawney, and perhaps for the first couple of generations of his readers in Britain, 'morality' had talismanic power, warding off demons of all kinds. It can no longer be confidently expected to play this role, nor do we really feel we would want it to. Not the least of the ways in which we are conscious of inhabiting a different world from Tawney's may lie in our grudging recognition that the demons have most of the best tunes.

10

Liberal Mind: Isaiah Berlin

I

Probably no one in our time has come nearer to being regarded as the academic equivalent of a saint than Isaiah Berlin. Merely to list his principal honours is to lay oneself open to charges of exaggeration: while still in his forties he had been appointed to an Oxford chair, elected to the British Academy, and knighted; he was awarded the Order of Merit over twenty-five years ago and he is a past President of the British Academy; he is an honorary fellow of five Oxbridge colleges, holds honorary degrees from over twenty universities, and so on. An accolade of a quite different sort is represented by the appearance of a study of his work in the Fontana 'Modern Masters' series.

This academic recognition has been coupled with an apparently effortless entrée into the overlapping social worlds of Britain's upper class and governing elite. Born into a Jewish family in Riga in 1909, he witnessed the Russian Revolution in Petrograd (as it then was) as a child, arriving in England at the age of 11. As a young Oxford don in the 1930s and 1940s (apart from a spell at the British Embassy in Washington during the war), he soon became the dining companion of the great and the good; having his portrait taken by Cecil Beaton represented merely one of the more visible signs of consecration. Thereafter, public appointments came

Isaiah Berlin, *The Proper Study of Mankind: An Anthology of Essays*, ed. Henry Hardy and Roger Hausheer (Chatto, 1997). This essay was completed in the summer of 1997; Sir Isaiah Berlin died in November of that year.

steadily, including extended periods as a Director of Covent Garden and a Trustee of the National Gallery. Membership of the Athenaeum might seem almost obligatory for one of such academic eminence; membership of Brooks's, an institution not overflowing with philosophers and historians of ideas ('ideas, eh?'), bespeaks social acceptance of a quite other order. For years, it would seem, when the Establishment wanted legal advice it asked Arnold Goodman and when it wanted a cultural committee chaired it asked Noel Annan; similarly, when it wanted judgement about intellectual quality its reflex was to 'ask Isaiah'.

Despite these various forms of worldly success, those who know Berlin seem to be unanimous in reporting his unaffected human warmth, his curiosity about others' lives, and a winning absence of any tendency to stand upon status or trumpet achievement. Renowned as a talker, he was for long regarded as someone who had written comparatively little, but since his enthusiastic admirer and editor, Henry Hardy, began to assemble volumes of his occasional writings, the quantity as well as quality of Berlin's work has become readily apparent, and seven collections of his essays have appeared to date. Now 88 years old, he has lived to see his work start to become the focus of a small scholarly industry in itself. In addition to two *Festschriften*, there is already a longish list of essays and chapters devoted to analysing his contribution to moral and political philosophy and to the history of ideas, themes which have been explored with increasing thoroughness in full-scale monographs by Robert Kocis, Claude Galipeau, and, most rigorously, John Gray.

The Proper Study of Mankind is not, strictly speaking, an addition to Berlin's oeuvre, since it reprints seventeen of his most celebrated essays, all of which have already appeared in earlier collections of his work. The essays span the range of Berlin's career as well as representing the scope of his interests: one piece dates from the 1940s, five from the 1950s, five from the 1960s, four from the 1970s, and two from the 1980s. The secondary works mentioned earlier have initiated a fruitful discussion of Berlin's liberalism and pluralism, a discussion that will no doubt be long continued in the pages of the appropriate professional journals in moral and political philosophy. But for the historian of modern British culture there remain some teasing, unaddressed questions about the sources of his remarkable standing and the nature of his

role. The more one attempts to place him among comparable
figures, the more he starts to seem, in the strictest sense of the term,
peerless. The publication of this anthology inevitably prompts
some reflection on the properties that make his essays so distinctive
and that have contributed to the position, at once central and idiosyncratic, that he has occupied in British intellectual and academic
life during the past half-century.

II

Beginning with one of the most immediately apparent features of
these pages, one can speak of the characteristic 'cadence' of Berlin's
prose in a way that would seem inappropriate or merely inflated in
the case of most academic writing. It is in some sense the cadence
of the speaking voice, but not obviously that of conversation, since
there is something more high-toned and even oratorical about it
than that. There is great warmth and vivacity in the writing, but
not exactly intimacy: the prose has the character of a lecture that
has been subdued into an essay rather than that of a meditation
that has finally got up the courage to appear in public. And the
distinctive timbre of a Berlin essay comes through not so much in
the individual sentence, capacious and highly fashioned though
that often is, but in the rising and swelling of a succession of paragraphs.

What is most often going on in these paragraphs, and what
gives them a kind of stylistic momentum, is something that I can
only describe as 'historical ventriloquizing': Berlin states, restates,
and amplifies the views of the thinker under discussion in a
manner which is the scholarly equivalent of the novelist's free
indirect style. There is often surprisingly little direct quotation,
and, for all his deep love of Russian literature, an almost
complete absence of the kind of close critical engagement with the
details of the verbal texture of the works that one associates with
a certain style of literary-critical essay. Instead, the dominant
mode is more frankly expository, but it is exposition recollected
in familiarity, so that a given thinker's view of the world begins
to assemble itself before us without any of the usual parade of
evidence and sources.

This is one of the reasons why Berlin's work has always had a

slightly angular relation to established academic forms and procedures. No one could doubt the extraordinary erudition displayed in
his essays, yet it has not been immediately recognizable as 'scholarship'. For the most part, the pieces as originally published
contained relatively little reference to the work of other scholars,
and footnotes were usually conspicuous by their absence. (One of
the ways in which the present volume presents a slightly
bastardized state of his essays is that Henry Hardy has done his
diligent best to kit them out in full footnoted fig: this is no doubt
helpful for anyone wanting to trace one of Berlin's references, but
it does threaten to domesticate what had been personal and stylish
into appearing merely conventional and industrious.)

In addition, the genre at which Berlin has excelled falls between
several familiar academic stools: at least three of the pieces in this
volume weigh in at around 30,000 words, while several others
comfortably exceed 20,000—too long to be easily accommodated
as articles, too short to stand alone as books. Moreover, they do
not, for the most part, have the character of learned scholarly
communications, filling in cracks in the edifice of collaborative
knowledge, yet nor are they amply documented monographs or
surveys, laying out the evidence that supports a new interpretation
or map. They are more like one-breath arguments, amplified with
digression and wide reference to the classics of European thought,
but not in any conventional way dependent on the presentation of
'the evidence'. As a result, they are pieces of writing that manage,
not altogether paradoxically, to be at once voluble and distilled.

For this and other reasons, it cannot be said that Berlin has
commanded an area of 'research' in the way some of the great
barons of scholarship have done. There have been many students,
but they have not been allotted roles in extending and defending a
territory, in the way in which (to take representatives of two quite
different scholarly fields not wholly dissimilar to each other in
temperament and effect) the pupils of Karl Popper or Geoffrey
Elton were apparently commanded to do. He has probably had
more admirers than any figure in recent British academic life, yet
there has not been a widely established style of work that could
lead followers to be labelled as 'Berlinians' in the way in which, to
take two other figures graced with distinctive and far from conventionally academic voices, it was common in post-war university
circles to speak of 'Leavisites' or 'Oakeshottians'. Berlin's manner

of speech has attracted countless affectionate imitators; one has to wonder whether his manner of writing is likely to die without issue.

Then there is the question of academic field or discipline itself. It is well known that Berlin began his career as a philosopher, at the very heart of the origins of Oxford 'ordinary language' philosophy in the late 1930s and 1940s, but that he became personally dissatisfied with this enterprise and moved on to issues of political theory. Also on record is his decision to resign the Chichele chair of social and political theory after ten years, in part because, in addition to his willingness to become the founding president of Wolfson College in Oxford, he felt he had no 'doctrine' to teach. His writing in recent decades has tended to concentrate instead on the overlapping topics of the rise and influence of European, especially German, Romanticism and on the intellectual origins of nationalism. In this latter part of his career his own preferred description of his chosen field appears to be 'the history of ideas'.

The history of ideas, in this sense, is inevitably in large part the history of exaggeration. 'Ideas' here refers to those large-scale intellectual constructions that offer a systematic redescription of part of human understanding or experience. Those writers whose characteristic mode has, by contrast, been to enter mild, piecemeal caveats about the excesses of any such prevailing paradigm tend to attract little attention either at the time or from subsequent thinkers. This goes instead to those who propose theories elaborated at the same level of abstraction and generality as the one they are attempting to displace, even though in so doing they inevitably overreach themselves, and introduce a whole new set of exaggerations and oversimplifications, and so on. Berlin has always been an acute critic of the makers of Procrustean beds—indeed, such criticism has become part of his stock-in-trade—yet those who dealt in such large ideas have none the less remained his chosen historical company. He has declared more than once that 'an intellectual is someone who wants ideas to be as interesting as possible'. This seems to me to be discussable on several counts, but it surely expresses a truth about Berlin himself; indeed, his skill at sympathetic exposition is such that the ideas can sometimes seem more interesting in his account than in the original. Be that as it may, temperament and cultural formation seem to have conspired to lead Berlin to constant engagement with 'ideas' in their largest, most imperial, forms.

There is an interesting question here about how one best

contests the exaggerated claims inherent in certain sorts of system and abstraction. In Berlin's lifetime, there have perhaps been three notable particularist idioms that have attempted to *embody* a persuasive alternative rather than merely *stating* a contrary case, each of which has enjoyed considerable support and approval in English academic culture. The first is that of Wittgensteinian philosophy (or anti-philosophy), the second that of close literary criticism, and the third that of densely detailed historical reconstruction. It is striking that Berlin has cultivated none of these idioms. He has consistently mounted the case against dangerous forms of monism and scientism in general conceptual terms. And although in his later work, in particular, he has championed those figures who have been notable critics of the Enlightenment's tendency to over-indulge the *esprit de système*—figures such as Vico, Hamann, and Herder—his own writing about them has still tended to expound their defence of complexity in general terms rather than to exhibit the complexity inherent in that accumulation of local insights and culturally specific characterizations that make up any good piece of critical or historical work.

Moreover, throughout his later work he has retained the philosopher's primary concern to distinguish the good argument from the bad: in the most recent piece reprinted in this volume he remarks almost in passing on the need, in discussing the goals human beings have set themselves, to consider their force 'and above all their validity'. (It is perhaps in this spirit that we find him, a few pages later, confidently asserting 'Voltaire . . . was mistaken'.) In an earlier piece, also included here, he asserts that the 'inadequate' ideas in the history of political thought have 'perished' while the 'great illuminating models' still stir us either to adherence or to criticism. The latter, as he revealingly puts it, 'all survive and contend with each other today'. Despite his vividly conveyed sense of the development and historical specificity of European thought from the seventeenth century onwards, Berlin's writing can at the same time seem to suggest that all really important ideas are in some sense contemporaneous.

In so far as the characteristic voice in these essays has a recognizable cultural location, it is surely in the confident tones of 'Oxford philosophy' in its heyday, albeit enriched, chastened, and warmed by wider reading and yet wider human sympathies than naturally seemed to inform that sometimes chilly idiom. 'It is plainly the case that . . .', 'it clearly follows that . . .', and similar phrases provide the scaffolding of his prose, which is also laced with brisk judgements that certain 'propositions' are 'demonstrably false' or, worse, 'nonsense'. There is an admirable commitment in all this to reason and to argument, and Berlin has no truck with that kind of scepticism about general concepts that can degenerate into another form of irrationalism. None the less, giving the past this kind of brisk tutorial can make for a slightly impatient style of history, one in which the weaker students, as it were, find it difficult to get their share of attention.

In other, more autobiographical pieces (not republished here) Berlin has often indicated in passing his habitual discrimination between the best and the rest. For example, in describing the impact of first reading an essay by Lewis Namier on Zionism, he writes: 'In reading it one had the sensation—for which there is no substitute—of suddenly sailing in first-class waters.' It is similarly revealing when, in quite a different context, he recalls his difficulty, having agreed to give a lecture on an Italian topic, in finding a subject: 'The Italians are not rich in first-class thinkers'. Berlin has several times disavowed the identity of 'an historian', and it is surely true that an historian would tend to have a different reflex here.

As all this suggests, Berlin's is an aristocratic mode of intellectual conduct, moving easily in the company of the leading thinkers of all ages, a kind of All Souls of the mind. There are vast benefits to this manner of leading one's intellectual life, including a liberating distance from the common academic vices of fashion-following and stamp-collecting. But just occasionally it can lead one to wonder quite what the status is of some of Berlin's historical roll-calls. At one point when talking of the different forms through which the need to belong to a group has been fulfilled, he observes that 'various theories [have been] offered to account for the historical progression of these forms, from Plato and Polybius to Machiavelli, Bossuet, Vico, Turgot, Herder, Saint-Simon, Hegel, Comte, Marx and their modern successors'. Such a sentence should perhaps be regarded as no more than the kind of little cadenza in which the soloist hints at his virtuosity, or as the dealer's elegant show of the cards between hands. The danger, of course, is that the list starts to become pseudo-history: it contains enough names to suggest that it is more than a piece of shorthand (in the way that, say, 'from Plato to the present' would have been), and so it cannot avoid seeming to suggest that *these* eleven proper names, rather than any of a score of others, are the main loci (or perhaps just the most 'interesting' exponents) of ideas of the progression of forms of human association, although as soon as one runs one's mind over such names as Smith, Sismondi, Tocqueville, Spencer, Tönnies, and so on (to stay with the same period), the selectiveness of Berlin's list becomes obvious. My point is not that other names could have been included, something of which Berlin would of course be better aware than anyone, but that the status of such a list itself is not clear: one begins to wonder whether the 'historian of ideas', when reaching for illustrative names, doesn't tend to recall those who have provided him with the most stimulating company.

The history of ideas as thus practised also has some of the characteristics of high-altitude aerial photography. Broad patterns that would otherwise be hard to discern stand out clearly, while there tends to be a corresponding loss of local detail. To take an ex-ample almost at random, when speaking of the origins of nationalism Berlin has a phrase about the 'florid and emotive prose . . . used by Herder, Burke, Fichte, Michelet' and others after them, and then on the next page he speaks of the critique of science and enlightenment 'which begins in the pages of Hamann and Burke, reaches a climax in Fichte and his romantic followers, is systematised by Maistre and Bonald' and so on again. In both cases, the almost casual sweep of the observations is genuinely illuminating, and readers who already know something of, say, Burke's *Reflections* can be jolted into a new phase of understanding by seeing him placed in this company. At the same time, such passages are also reminders of why we do not come to Berlin to learn about Burke as one among several kinds of English Whig, engaged in dispute with a particular style of English radical Unitarianism, as part of the political debate in England of the late 1780s, carried on in certain journals and pamphlets, and so on. In these ways, the focus and texture of a Berlin essay differ strikingly from one by, say, John Pocock, who has placed Burke in illuminating company in an utterly different way. Perhaps the more general contrast involved here can be brought out by saying that in Berlin's practice of 'the history of ideas' the emphasis is on the *ideas* whereas in the most recent forms of 'intellectual history' the emphasis tends to fall on the *history*.

Reflecting on the origin of so much of his work in commissions and invitations to lecture, Berlin has nicely compared himself to a cab which only moves when it is summoned. And yet despite the fact that almost all his writing can, for this reason, be called 'occasional', it is striking how consistent the tone and substance of the pieces are, and how *little* they are marked by the circumstances of their first appearance or delivery. Moreover, although they address a variety of figures and issues, there is a sense in which they are variations on a central theme, namely his repudiation of what he at one point calls the 'naive craving for unity and symmetry at the expense of experience'. In this respect (to play once again with the most famous of his own playful typologies), he should perhaps be understood as a hedgehog who has chosen to publish as a fox.

Rereading this large selection of Berlin's essays one becomes aware of the presence in his writing of what might be called 'the pathos of stoicism': we are constantly exhorted to forswear much that may at first sight seem intellectually beguiling or satisfying, and instead to endure the frustrations and disappointments of finding only partial answers. Realism has its own rhetoric, of course, and it can be flattering to feel oneself in the company of those unillusioned spirits who can live with ambivalence and uncertainty. For this note not to turn into a self-indulgent pseudo-stoicism, however, what we are being urged to abjure must be a real and attractive option. I am sure it is so for Berlin himself, partly because he is personally drawn to large ideas and can exercise a wonderful imaginative capacity to feel the power of alien styles of thought, partly because he is so acutely aware of the horrifying consequences in twentieth-century history of others' susceptibility to utopian simplicities. But how far is it so for his contemporary readers? This raises the deep, and at best only partially answerable, question about the audience for Berlin's essays, as well as the slightly different question about what some literary theorists would call their 'implied reader'. These essays, I have suggested, are nearly all, explicitly or implicitly, arguments, above all arguments against various forms of monism and reductionism. But has the function of reading them changed in the four decades since the earliest of them were first written?

Of course, important truths can bear restatement, and it remains a wicked world. But the danger is perhaps that the phenomenology of the experience of reading Berlin now is likely to take the form of a kind of collective self-congratulation. *We* like once again to hear these comforting abjurations of positions by which *we* are not tempted in the first place. Consider the most recent piece reprinted here, 'The Pursuit of the Ideal', which dates from 1988. In the course of his familiar (but in my view admirable and wholly right-minded) rejection of ideas of a perfect state and similarly utopian 'final solutions', and his also familiar (but in my view also admirable and wholly right-minded) insistence upon the ineradic-able conflicts between deeply prized values, he declares that the idea that, once the classless society (or whatever) is established, all such conflicts will resolve themselves is 'a piece of metaphysical optimism for which there is no evidence in historical experience'. Now, had such an argument about the lack of 'evidence in histori-cal experience' been addressed to, say, Christopher Hill or Eric Hobsbawm as part of a public debate in the early 1950s (as it may have been privately, for all I know), it would be easier to see that it was genuinely cutting wood. But I wonder whether, when addressed to, say, the subscribers to the *New York Review of Books* (where the most recent as well as several of the earlier pieces included here were first published), such arguments do not tend instead to have some of the reassuringness of a bedtime story.

In so far as this is so, Berlin himself is clearly not responsible for the possible complacency of his later readers, and it is arguable that the tendency to draw such easy comfort from these essays is only to be had by overlooking the still-challenging nature of his insis-tence that liberty is not to be confused with other desirable social goals—a message which, if genuinely understood, might be as unwelcome to some of those currently committed to trying to erad-icate injustice grounded in differences of race or sex as it appar-ently was even to some liberal-democratic proponents of Socialism in the 1950s.

It is obviously very important, therefore, to recall the different force and resonance some of the earlier essays had when they were first published. Not only were unilinear theories of history still flourishing, vulgar Marxism among them, but ideas of the super-session of the traditional moral framework for understanding human action by a deterministic, 'value-free' social science seemed to have the upper hand in much academic debate in ways that are no longer true. And recovering a sense of the timeliness of some of Berlin's classic essays can also take us back, by another route, to the question of the sources of the success of his career.

III

The 1950s was the decade that saw the making of Berlin's fame, and this involved a conjunction of personal and public developments. In 1950, at the age of 41, Berlin resigned his Tutorship in philosophy at New College and was elected to a Senior Research Fellowship at All Souls. From this point on, he was not only released from the repetitive grind of tutorial teaching, but he no longer had to conform to the expectations laid upon a professional philosopher, and this change inaugurated what still seems to me his most fertile period. An early version of 'The Hedgehog and the Fox' appeared in 1951, the full version in 1953; the first version of 'The Originality of Machiavelli' was delivered as a paper in 1953 (though the expanded text was not published until 1972); 'Historical Inevitability' was published in 1954 and in the same year he gave the Northcliffe Lectures on Russian thinkers of the 1840s. With the appearance in 1958 of 'Two Concepts of Liberty', his inaugural lecture on taking up his Oxford chair (surely one of the most widely reprinted and referred-to inaugurals in history), the main lines of the position with which he has been associated ever since were laid down.

These writings appeared at a time when the Cold War was the dominant political concern in the West, and when, not coincidentally, there was widespread preoccupation, which took both popular and more analytical forms, with the nature of 'totalitarianism' in general and with the horror of Nazi genocide in particular. At the same time, in the more purely academic sphere, a reductive positivism threatened to carry all before it, leading one commentator to declare in 1956 that 'political theory is dead'. It wasn't, of course, though in Britain it had possibly been taking a long afternoon nap, but Berlin replied directly to the challenge with his essay 'Does Political Theory Still Exist?' (reprinted here), with its ringing affirmation of the ineliminability of questions about values and the conflicts between them from any consideration of collective human action. More broadly, Berlin's criticisms of various forms of scientism or of single-explanation theories of history linked up with a more general resistance in the higher reaches of English academic life, then headquartered in Oxford philosophy, to what were perceived as the imperial claims of (largely American) social science. His discussions of these and other topics reached a wider audience through the talks (notably the series on 'Freedom and Its Betrayal') he regularly gave on the Third Programme in the first decade or two of its existence, when it was still seriously committed to the Reithian ideal that public broadcasting should instruct as well as entertain.

Part of the importance and appeal of Berlin's writings at this time was that they made it seem that there were necessary and not merely contingent connections between these different levels of inquiry and areas of concern. During these years there was no shortage of Cold War liberals in the West ready to denounce (certain kinds of) oppressive political systems, but there were few, if any, who could make such a position seem the natural outcome of a properly reflective, properly sensitive engagement with the great minds of the Western intellectual tradition (Leo Strauss may seem to some people to be a possible candidate, though he was less easily recognizable as a liberal). In fact, Berlin extended the canon of relevant thinkers by bringing the leading nineteenth-century Russian writers into the fold, and, more generally, his familiarity with things Russian was perceived as a further asset during the Cold War years. Above all, among those who did attempt to explore the intellectual roots of totalitarianism (the names of Hannah Arendt and Jacob Talmon come to mind), there were none, it would seem, who could offer the combination of the cultural range, the intellectual power, the moral passion, the institutional authority, and the personal charm that cultivated readers on both sides of the Atlantic found in the author of the early essays included in this anthology.

While these remarks may suggest at least the beginnings of an account of the broader political appeal of Berlin's work, his academic and institutional standing remains harder to characterize. For example, the journal to which he, as a professor of political and social theory, might have been thought to have the closest professional affinities would have been something like *Political Studies*, yet its staple fare hardly consisted of essays on, to take just two of the many subjects he has illumined, the novels of Turgenev or the operas of Verdi. In these respects, one could be tempted to describe Berlin's work as 'maverick' did that not connote a kind of outsiderish non-conformity quite at odds with both the facts of his career and the habitual tone of his authorial persona. Still, writing on such a range of topics, moving easily among those classics of

Western thought and literature that have now become the property
of several academic disciplines, linking one's work to forthright
moral and political convictions—this is not the obvious route to
the highest scholarly and institutional honours. That it has been so
for Isaiah Berlin we have come almost to take for granted, but to
help us think of this as an issue requiring some mildly explanatory
redescription we have only to ponder the likelihood of, say, Ernest
Gellner having been awarded the OM or of George Steiner being
made President of the British Academy.

Although Berlin has tended to write essays rather than treatises
or monographs (apart from his early but constantly reprinted study
of Marx), the thorough bibliography of his writings compiled by
Henry Hardy (most easily available in *Against the Current*, an
earlier volume of his essays in the history of ideas) suggests that he
has done comparatively little journalism. He seems to have been a
rare and reluctant reviewer: certainly, his has never been a regular
byline in the Sunday broadsheets in the way that those of, say,
Frank Kermode or Hugh Trevor-Roper have been, nor (apart from
his radio talks mentioned earlier) has he been a media-friendly don
with ready and quotable opinions in the way that, say, A. J. Ayer
or A. J. P. Taylor were. And this brings out how little he has played
the role of the public intellectual in other ways, too. He has by and
large avoided taking public stands over the political and moral
issues of the day, apart from a few cases of intellectual freedom and
his consistent support for a tolerant Zionism. Nor has he set up
shop as a cultural critic, appraising and arraigning the attitudes
and values manifested in contemporary social mores, in the manner
of an Anglicized Adorno or a Europeanized Hoggart.

All this draws us back to the tricky question, alluded to earlier,
of who exactly should be regarded as Berlin's 'peers'. In terms of
what might be considered the 'ideological effect' of his writing in
the 1950s and 1960s, the most apposite comparison is probably
with Karl Popper, while his idiosyncratic influence across the field
of the history of political thought was probably only matched by
that of Michael Oakeshott (little as it seems this oft-made comparison was welcome to either of them). I suspect the affinities have
actually been closest with a group of rather younger Oxford-
connected philosophers, drawn to considering technical issues in
ethics or the philosophy of action in the light of wider interests in
politics, literature, and the arts—figures such as Stuart Hampshire,

Richard Wollheim, Bernard Williams, and Charles Taylor. If it is
harder to think of leading intellectual historians with whom he
may be legitimately compared—though there are clearly points of
resemblance to figures such as Ernst Gombrich in art history or
Arnaldo Momigliano in ancient history—that may just be another
way of pointing up the extent to which Berlin's work has been
animated more vitally and productively by the concerns of the
philosopher and political theorist than by those of the historian.

Much of what he wrote in his fine eloge of his colleague, and
successor in the Chichele chair, John Plamenatz (reprinted in
Personal Impressions, an earlier collection of such portraits, but
not in this volume), seems to ask to be applied to Berlin himself,
above all the observation that although he spent his entire adult life
in Oxford 'and his work and his influence are part of the intellectual history of Britain and that university', there was a sense in
which 'he remained in exile all his life' (Plamenatz was
Montenegrin by origin). In pointing to Plamenatz's intellectual
roots in 'that sober, pre-positivist, pre-linguistic, realist tradition in
moral philosophy' that was so strong in Oxford in the 1920s and
early 1930s, Berlin gives a helpful clue to his own formation, and
there are clearly further similarities if not exact resemblances when
he speaks of the combination in Plamenatz of an 'acceptance of
British empiricism, together with a deeply un-British, romantic
vision of the human predicament'.

Something rather like this combination of sensibilities informs
the deft, engaging sketches of friends and contemporaries collected
in *Personal Impressions*, a genre of his writing best represented in
the present volume by his reports of meetings with Akhmatova and
Pasternak in Russia in 1945. These are some of the most vivid and
moving things he has ever written, in part because of his humble
sense of merely leaving a record of figures much greater than
himself. In another essay in that same volume, he describes how, as
young Fellows of All Souls, he and J. L. Austin would habitually
start to have a philosophical conversation at breakfast and then
find that it had continued uninterrupted until lunch, but even that
is eclipsed by his second meeting with Anna Akhmatova. He
arrived at her apartment at nine in the evening: 'Our conversation,
which touched on intimate details of both her life and my own,
wandered from literature and art, and lasted until late in the morning of the following day.' This is talk on an heroic scale. As he

himself says of Herzen (with whom there has surely been at least a tinge of identification): though a wonderful talker, 'he had no Boswell and no Eckermann to record his conversations, nor was he a man who would have suffered such a relationship'. A pity in each case, perhaps, though as far as Berlin is concerned much of the testimony of friends and pupils has, presumably, still to find its way into print.

For many readers only encountering Berlin through the essays represented in this volume, I suspect that his most important contribution will remain his exploration of the various forms of connection between theoretical monism and political illiberalism, especially as undertaken in his three or four major essays from the 1950s mentioned earlier. In addition, the recent academic discussion of his insistence on the irreducible plurality of moral values has in effect been a form of belated tribute to his early, and perhaps sometimes rather lonely, opposition to the intellectual hubris he detected at the heart of both Kantianism and Utilitarianism, variants of which two positions have dominated Anglo-American moral philosophy for a generation or more. His voice in these matters has always been a sane and salutary one, certainly, but what seems to me to have been the most consistently admirable and distinctive thing about his writing has been its engaging and resourceful campaign to prevent intellectuality from conquering and laying waste lands that are properly the territory of emotional or aesthetic or other human needs. He has been such an inspiriting representative of the intellectual life above all because he has constantly reminded us that there is so much more to experience than even the most comprehensive theories tend to allow for—even though it has been those theories that have most engaged him.

11

Critical Minds: Raymond Williams and Richard Hoggart

I

When Raymond Williams died suddenly, at age 66, in January 1988 the tributes were generous and admiring to the point of being fulsome, and he was hailed as, among other things, the greatest Socialist thinker of his time in Britain. Yet as obituary piety has started to give way to more measured assessment, even sympathetic critics cannot help compiling long lists of defects, and the basis of his very considerable standing becomes more and more to seem puzzling or at least in need of some fuller explanation. He wrote too much; he often wrote badly; much of what he wrote has been subjected to damning and justified criticism; his political judgement could be poor; and so on and so on. And yet the tributes accumulate: for many he remains a model of what a Left intellectual should be, and there is already a considerable body of secondary literature whose very existence testifies to a widespread sense that he is a culturally significant figure whose work repays extended investigation. But it is not easy to account for this standing. What is it about Williams and his work that attracted so much admiration and that continues to underwrite his claim to an important niche in recent intellectual history? Since part of the answer (to which I shall return) seems to be bound up with the authority conferred by the

Fred Inglis, *Raymond Williams* (Routledge, 1995).
Richard Hoggart, *Townscape with Figures. Farnham: Portrait of an English Town* (Chatto, 1994).

exceptionally close fit between his personality, his life, and his work, a biography seems likely to throw an unusual amount of light on this question. Fred Inglis's *Raymond Williams* is so far the only extended account of the life to have appeared, but although it is an affectionate and perceptive portrait, in some ways it does more to deepen than to resolve the puzzle.

Among his contemporaries, the figure with whom Williams has constantly been compared is Richard Hoggart. For a decade or more after their almost simultaneous rise to prominence in the late 1950s, their common working-class origins and abundant contributions to the analysis of cultural change in modern Britain ensured that they were often spoken of in the same breath. But for some time now it has been clear that Hoggart has not attracted anything like the degree of attention, still less reverence, accorded to Williams. In Hoggart's case there is no biography we can turn to for illumination: he is, after all, still alive and well, and writing. But he has been a much more personal and self-revealing writer than Williams, and in addition to his three-volume *Life and Times*, his idiosyncratic account, in *Townscape with Figures*, of Farnham, the town in which he now lives, offers an inviting avenue for the exploration of some rather different connections between life and work. This essay examines some of the contrasts between these two dissimilar men who seem fated to be bracketed together.

II

In its outward aspect, Raymond Williams's life was not particularly unusual or exciting. He was born in 1921, only child of a railway signalman and his wife. He grew up in a semi-rural working-class community just inside the Welsh border; following the pattern of the clever boy from such a background, he won a scholarship to the local grammar school and then, in 1939, entered Trinity College Cambridge to begin a degree in English. Both his studies and a brief membership of the Communist Party were interrupted by the war, and he saw active service commanding an armoured anti-tank unit in the Normandy invasion and subsequent campaigns. In 1945 he returned to Cambridge to complete his degree, during which period he fell under the spell of F. R.

Leavis, and in 1946 began a fifteen-year career as an Adult
Education Tutor in English for the Oxford Extra-Mural Delegacy.
   The appearance of his first two books in 1950 and 1952
signalled the start of what was to be an exceptionally prolific writ-
ing career, but it was the publication of his fourth book in 1958,
Culture and Society, that first brought him widespread recognition.
He returned to a teaching post at Cambridge in 1961, where he
stayed until his early retirement in 1983; at his death he had
published some thirty books, including five novels, and a scarcely
credible abundance of journalism and other occasional writing.
Among the best known of his widely selling works were
Communications (1962), *The Country and the City* (1973),
Keywords (1976), and *Marxism and Literature* (1977). He was
intermittently prominent in various left-wing causes, though
frequently and increasingly disillusioned with the Labour Party. By
the time of his death, he had for some years been emphasizing his
distance both from the criticism and teaching of English literature
as conventionally understood, and from the chief institutional
expressions of British politics and culture. In opposition to
'English' and to England, two determining preoccupations of his
earlier career, he now described himself as a 'cultural materialist'
and a 'Welsh European'.
   Inglis's book is much less of a conventional biography than it
first appears. He has not pursued archival material and correspondence to any great extent; large expanses of the prose are unfoot-
noted; much of the writing is by turns personal, lyrical, and
evocative; and large slabs of quotation are taken, oral-history fashion, from the transcripts of interviews or letters to Inglis from
people who knew Williams in various capacities. The book is above
all an evocation—an evocation of a man Inglis knew (not well) and
admired (a lot), but also an evocation of a world, a milieu, a mood.
Inglis is responsive to the loyalties and commitments informing
Williams's work, rather less good as an analyst of their theoretical
ambitions and shortcomings. But the book is distinguished above
all by Inglis's writerly energy, here essaying a novelistic sketch,
there interjecting a remembered vignette; it is a prose not afraid of
trying the high leap and pirouette (not always quite landing on its
feet), while at the same time willing to let a demotic gruffness do
the work of moral commentary.
   The book, it will be clear, has its faults, but it is never boring,

and that is a remarkable achievement given Williams's capacity to be a relentlessly boring writer and, it would seem, in some ways a boring man. And by the end its faults come to seem a necessary and not always unreasonable price to pay for some marvellous cadenzas on unlikely themes—on the culture of the railway signal-box, or on the finger-numbing chill in the bleak, drafty halls in which adult education classes took place immediately after 1945, or on the 'espresso-and-Existentialism' atmosphere of the early New Left. By turns, this biography metamorphoses into a prose-poem to English Socialism's best self, an anguished keening for the intellectual Left's idealized lost leader, and a meditation on solidarity and its discontents. Other biographers are already at work, and no doubt there will be more thorough, more scholarly, and in some ways more usable lives to come. But it is hard to imagine that any of these future studies will contain as many passages of inspired, moving portraiture as this one does. Inglis's writing asks for, and needs, the reader's indulgence: once get out of sorts with it, and a catalogue of failings will irresistibly start to compile itself. But grant it its own tune, and it will carry you along with rare buoyancy.

It is part of Inglis's achievement that this portrait of a man he greatly admired and wanted to like leaves even the sympathetic reader with a strong sense of the ways in which Williams was neither wholly admirable nor easily likeable. It is, as perhaps the life of any prolific author must be, a portrait of egotism, of the ceaseless, all-subordinating egotism of the writer who gives priority to turning out his daily quota of words. This was the *telos* around which domestic life was arranged, around which his marriage shaped itself, and around which he neglected his students, was only half-available for his friends, kept his distance from the world. (There is much evidence in this book of what an unresponsive companion Williams could be—his star pupil Terry Eagleton speaks of his 'clenched withdrawal'.) And to a quite extraordinary extent his writing depended not on receiving and rearranging impressions from outside himself, whether in the form of books, people, or the public world, but on reaching inside himself, and drawing up, as from some inexhaustible but little-varying well, the convictions that he elaborated, restated, and then restated again, undeterred by criticism ('several people report occasions on which he simply didn't read or didn't heed central objections made to some part of his work'). He wrote his immensely influential little book on analysing the popular media, *Communications* (1962), without owning a television; he was a professor of drama who practically never went to the theatre; he was an organizer of the Left who could rarely be reached by telephone; he was the great evangelist for the values of 'community' who unflinchingly ignored all claims that might interfere with his solitude—the solitude necessary for the daily indulgence of his habit, his private vice, his only partly socialized addiction to the typewriter.

Yet the sense of purpose this suggests, that centred conviction about who he was and about (in the title phrase of a collection of his essays) 'what I came to say', is one clue to his remarkable impact. In person as well as on the page he clearly gave off a strong sense of wholeness, of someone whose beliefs and experiences and ambitions were all of a piece. This, rather than any claim based on his expertise or his research or even the acuteness of his analysis of the contemporary scene, was the basis of his authority. And it was essentially a kind of *moral* authority, expressed in serious, unshowy prose, an authority which came from the sense that he had connected, reconnected, a given topic to the great verities of human need and social relationship. Often, there is not much 'information' in his writing, not much close analysis of other people's work, not a carefully elaborated conceptual scheme: there is just that determined, massively confident, assertion that he spoke out of a grounded, elemental hold on the imperatives of the ethical enterprise of collective living.

His own working-class background was the professional diploma that licensed him to practise this peculiar trade, and Williams was not slow to display his credentials in this respect. He made much of being the son of a railway worker (characteristically, the pre-feminist Williams—and he remained pretty unreconstructedly pre-feminist to the end—presented himself as only having one relevant parent); his fiction and a good deal of his cultural criticism revolve around the clash between the human values embodied in working-class family life and the pretensions and coldnesses that disfigure social relations in the worlds in which the successful scholarship boy later finds himself. The tendentiousness evident in this contrast seems the more culpable when we learn from Inglis of the tensions that dominated the actual Williams home. (It is interesting to note in passing how unlike the model of the warm, expressive,

noisy two-parents-and-several-children home were the family situations of both Williams and Hoggart, the two most notable spokes-
men for working-class culture in their generation: the orphaned
Hoggart grew up in an almost entirely female household of grandmother and aunts, while the only child Williams observed from an
early age the distance between his increasingly silent parents.)

III

In trying to understand Williams's impact, it is partly true, but
partly too easy, to say that the timing was right. Certainly, the question of 'authentic' working-class voices acquired a sudden prominence in metropolitan literary and intellectual circles in the late
1950s in Britain; certainly, the early 1960s was *the* time to be a
rising star of the intellectual Left; certainly, the 1960s and 1970s
created a hugely expanded audience in higher education for anyone
able to address 'academic' issues in an accessible way. There were
several figures who benefited from one or more of these developments, but practically no one other than Williams who turned their
conjunction into the preconditions for sustained intellectual
celebrity. Hoggart was his nearest rival in the late 1950s and early
1960s, E. P. Thompson in the 1960s and 1970s (and into the 1980s
as an anti-nuclear campaigner), perhaps Stuart Hall in the late
1970s and 1980s, and of these only Thompson comes close to shar-
ing Williams's stature as a Socialist theorist (or, in his case, anti-
theorist).

Exposure and celebrity—the dynamics of what the advertisers
call 'brand-recognition'—are a vital part of the mechanism by
which intellectuals, including Left intellectuals (who tend to
disdain such matters), come to perform their distinctive role. If,
after the great success of *Culture and Society* in 1958, Williams had
then fallen silent while devoting six or eight years to the research
for his next book, this life would most probably not now have been
written about him. The kind of turning-point represented by that
book's success can be crudely indicated by the following figures
from the bibliography of Williams's work prepared by Alan
O'Connor. In 1955 he published one review essay, in 1956 one article and two pieces in the adult education house journal, in 1957
one article and three reviews. But in 1959 alone he published 17

essays and reviews of various kinds; in the same year he also published a further six reviews in the *Guardian*, followed by 15 for the paper the next year and almost three hundred in total during the rest of his career. O'Connor's extraordinary bibliography also reveals that in total Williams published 91 chapters, introductions, and similar contributions to books; *all* of them date from after the publication of *Culture and Society*. And the listings of his other categories of publication tell much the same story.

As with so many successful publicists, the sheer quantity of his writing was important. As Inglis reports, he practically never turned down a commission or a request. As a result, he frequently repeated himself, he published a good deal of slack, sub-standard writing, he gave hostages with a lavish generosity. Inglis again has to shake his head sadly: 'He wrote too much, the colossal discipline wasn't worth all of it'. But it was all part of the mechanism of reputation, all part of becoming 'Raymond Williams'. After a certain point, his opinions were printed because he had become the sort of person whose opinions were printed.

This is not to suggest that it is of no account what those opinions were or how persuasively they helped make sense of parts of his readers' experience. And this relates to the question of range. If the intellectual is 'the specialist in the general', then there can be no staying within the narrow confines of expertise. Part of Williams's appeal lay in the way in which he calmly disregarded the border guards who patrol the boundaries between disciplines and, still more, between academic endeavour and political and social activism. His writing, at whatever level of theoretical sophistication, embodied the conviction that literature, politics, society, the media, everyday life were all part of a connected and mutually determining whole whose elements we were bound to distort if we studied them in isolation from each other. But in his occasional pieces, in particular, he perhaps too often confined himself to asserting this truth in a programmatic way. He handled these abstractions with the decisiveness of a Grandmaster moving the pieces in a simultaneous exhibition, yet curiously, given his endlessly reiterated use of terms like 'concrete' and 'particular', it could sometimes seem as though his very familiarity with the terms had worn them smooth, so that they no longer snagged any actual detail of experience.

Williams's career also raises interesting questions about the tensions between reaching local and international audiences. *Culture and Society* is now venerated, in the United States and other English-speaking countries as well as in Britain, as one of the founding texts of the 'cultural studies' movement (an appropriation I return to in Chapter 13 below), though its frame of reference, informing perspective, and initial impact were all highly, almost aggressively, local. More generally, and especially in the United States, Williams's name is associated above all with 'cultural materialism', though very few of his books were explicitly written under the aegis of that late-formulated label.

In practice, his international reputation really only took off once he began to engage with the work of the leading Western Marxist theorists in the early 1970s. Inglis sadly remarks 'a certain unthinkingness in some of his theoretic labours in the 1970s', and flatly describes *Marxism and Literature*, now probably his most widely known work, as 'his unreadable book', though there can be no doubt that 'cultural materialism' was the strike force that earned Williams a place at the negotiating table of international high theorists. Yet by inclination and talent he was not primarily a theorist, and in some deep ways he always remained parochial rather than international in his outlook: perhaps no one whose intellectual life had been born under the star of Leavis could ever shake off that obsessively local focus (consider by contrast how widely and naturally international someone like, say, Eric Hobsbawm has been).

Inglis's book may well strike some non-British readers as too readily collusive with that parochialism, too little appreciative of what Williams, like any theorist, has to say to those who grew up in utterly different national circumstances. But the emphasis and inwardness seem to me right and illuminating. Inglis makes no pretence at writing like a visiting anthropologist: this is his own tribe, and he understands, loves, and is exasperated by the same sentiments and rituals that bore Williams's career along. There are many vantage-points from which much of Williams's writing is now in danger of seeming overblown and overrated, but part of the achievement of this unusual, flawed, and impressive book is to make us understand, make us feel, that if one were struggling to give expression to one's socialist convictions by teaching the imaginatively liberating power of literature to children in a state school within the still deeply class-structured society of 1960s Britain, then Williams's writings would fall as Scripture, manna, and textbook rolled into one.

And the book helps us generalize this particular, informing case, and thus to come closer to understanding how Williams did something for hundreds of thousands of readers. Having quoted an autobiographical tribute by Eagleton, Inglis glosses:

That's what he [Williams] most characteristically did: he broke with the established, calmly superior assumptions and way of talking in England, but did so with a manner, an idiom and diction themselves so unassailably assured that those on the wrong side of the break couldn't see how to stop him. And then, into the space made by the break, he dropped his own calm commonplaces about human connection, about solidarity and equality, about those things we had been most fired by as young idealists, and that he—and Leavis before him, in his queer, fierce, intimidating, contradictory way—had best given voice to as an academic, as an educational project.

Elsewhere, more simply, he praises him for 'keeping alive a speakable moral idiom of the old Left'.

Inglis brings out well just how seriously Williams took the task of addressing a wide readership, and just how much journalism and occasional writing he did. Although in his books Williams, it has to be said, could be an exceptionally dreary writer, 'conjuring weight out of abstraction' as Eagleton accurately and unkindly put it, he could be, and often was, a notably effective journalist and reviewer—direct, engaged, instructive. And the mark of his most successful writing in this vein, as of comparable figures one might think of, was that he didn't patronize his readers. His contract with them was to explain as clearly and persuasively as he could what he thought mattered about a given issue or book. He wrote as though there were readers who wanted to be made to think harder than usual. And as a result, there were.

For all the misgivings one may have about both his writing and his ideas, there is no doubt that Williams had—to use one of the cant words of our time, though not his—an 'enabling' effect on many of the thousands and thousands of readers who read his journalism and went on to buy cheap paperback editions of his works or to read them in university, school, and public libraries. This owed something to the circumstances of Britain from the late 1950s to the early 1970s, certainly, but it also reflected his willingness to try to connect the austerer realms of intellectual inquiry to the often puzzling realities of thoughtful people's everyday lives. However well or badly we now judge that Williams carried out this task, his life is a reminder of the need for those who can put recent events or new books in a wider historical and intellectual context, or coin phrases that disturb or corrode unreflectively held assumptions, or give people tools to think with, or—above all—just write in a serious, engaged but analytical way about things which are either treated superficially elsewhere or not treated at all.

Williams first became a father when he was 23, and he went on to become a father-figure to many on the Left with no less precocity. Reading the literature about Williams, written before as well as since his death, one has to recognize that he had many admirers who *wanted* to idealize him, wanted to overlook the failings, because they wanted there to be in the world a stirring example of that cherished category, the 'general intellectual of the Left'. Williams represented a possibility, a space that many people felt needed to be kept open—a space for the figure who combines academic standing with passionate commitment, who is a leading theorist but also easily accessible, who has reshaped scholarly fields but is far from being a specialist, and who, above all, experiences no inhibiting tension between his intellectual projects and his human needs, between his 'work' and his 'life'. This remains a seductive and perhaps necessary ideal, and perhaps Raymond Williams came as close as anyone in recent years to embodying it.

IV

One afternoon, walking along the main street of Farnham, Richard Hoggart was accosted by a drunk. No ordinary drunk, it turned out. The man didn't ask for money or spit ill-focused abuse. 'I know who you are', he slurred, 'and I've got one question for you. Who's the better writer, you or Raymond Williams?'

On reading this, I found I was disappointed that the level of literary criticism among Farnham's drunks was so low. Even an unrelieved diet of British Sherry surely cannot obscure the fact that Hoggart is a far better *writer* than Williams. Hoggart's prose— colloquial, concrete, structured rather than merely adorned by metaphor and simile—constantly suggests a craftsman who appreciates the natural properties of the materials he works with and respects their resistance to his will. His oeuvre contains remarkably little writing that is merely dutiful, though in the 1960s fame perhaps gave him too many opportunities to sound off in a

programmatic way, and some of his lectures and essays of that
period lack the wryness and specificity generally characteristic of
his prose. His best writing has nearly always been his most autobiographical, whether in the thinly disguised form of the first part
of *The Uses of Literacy* (1957) or the full-dress three-volume *Life
and Times* published between 1988 and 1992. As an apt image or
surprising pairing of words shoulders its way past the expected
description and plants itself unerringly at the sweet spot of a
sentence, we again and again sense the presence of a strong writerly
urge that has only found partial fulfilment in conventional academic genres.

Williams, it is true, wrote novels (Hoggart only speaks of once
having started one), but in so much of his writing, even in some of
the fiction, a leaden pall of abstraction and position-taking settles
over the page like low cloud cover. There are certainly passages in
Williams, sometimes whole essays (his memoir of Leavis is a good
example), which suggest some of the literary resources he could
draw upon when he was willing to take a few hours off from being
the Great British Socialist Cultural Theorist. But reading Williams's
later work is so often a slog, a forced march across a swampy
terrain of generalizations in the company of a self-important
commander with his eye fixed on the far horizons of strategy.
Williams, it is already clear, will be regarded as the more important
figure, intellectually and politically, and Hoggart has never written
anything that could match the historical and analytical reach of
Culture and Society or *The Country and the City*. But the better
writer? No contest.

The tone of the Farnham drunk's question conjures up a background of learned disputation with his park-bench colleagues, as
though their seminar had settled several issues in recent cultural
history, but had left this earnest seeker after truth with one nagging
uncertainty. Of course, Hoggart and Williams are a natural
comparison, though Williams and E. P. Thompson, the third side of
the now familiar triangle, are the more discussed, partly because of
their greater prominence as Left intellectuals. Since Williams's
death in 1988 there has already been, as I remarked above, a small
industry of writing about him, both in Britain and elsewhere;
Thompson died in 1993, and the commemorative conferences and
volumes are well under way. But what of Hoggart? Though he has
been a lifelong Socialist, of that English kind that owes more to

Tawney than to Marx, neither his career nor his opinions have qualified him to be exalted as an exemplary intellectual of the Left, at least as that category is usually interpreted. Though constantly invoked as the celebrant of the virtues of 'community', he has in fact been something of a loner: he has not always been willing to toe the party line on test issues of the day (the Falklands War, the Miners' Strike), while on the other hand he has been willing to take on practical tasks which the purists tend to regard as inherently corrupting. He has not pretended to be a theorist, but nor has he, like Thompson, set himself up as an anti-theorist either. He exercised great institutional influence through his founding of the Centre for Contemporary Cultural Studies at Birmingham in 1963, but his own work has been idiosyncratic and not readily imitable.

In this respect, the contrast between Hoggart and Williams illustrates a familiar general point. The writer can be admired, enjoyed, criticized, but not exactly 'applied', whereas the theorist offers tools which others can use, and a blueprint for future work, often complete with model problems. Theorists are always likely to win the academic equivalent of the Queen's Award for Exports; isms are the machine-tools of the academic industry, and Williams patented one, with the result that there are now cultural materialists from Kansas to Kalgoorlie. But in struggling to advance an academic career in the internationalized world of the late twentieth century, there is little mileage for the globe's assistant professors in trying to write as though one had grown up in working-class Leeds between the wars. Hoggart is a one-off.

Although Hoggart is now the only one of this distinguished trio still alive, many readers may have the vague impression that he is past his sell-by date. The peak of his fame came in the late 1950s and early 1960s, and his later writing has never achieved the same impact. One minor indication of his relative neglect in academic literary circles today (he is, of course, still prominent in the wider culture) is provided by the MLA bibliography: it records 72 items dealing with Williams since 1981, whereas for Hoggart it lists two, both in articles primarily devoted to other matters. By writing an autobiography, the last volume of which appeared when he was in his 75th year, Hoggart himself may have contributed to the sense that the finishing touches could be put to the draft obituaries of him. But in 1994 he published *Townscape with Figures*, which was both sufficiently like and sufficiently unlike his earlier writing that

222 MINDS

it makes it easier to see the shape of his still unfinished career (it
was followed a year later by *The Way We Live Now*, and he is still
writing).

V

Townscape with Figures is a difficult book to classify, and in this as
well as much else it is representative of Hoggart's writing. It is at
once a piece of impressionistic empirical sociology, an essay on
social change, a meditation on the everydayness of life, a report
from the frontier of the Third Age. But although in these ways it is
an unclassifiable and intensely personal book, it clearly belongs in
a particular tradition of unclassifiable and personal writing: it is a
Condition-of-England book. Among the properties of Hoggart's
writing that announce its affinities with this tradition are its
winning and distinctively personal voice, its direct appeal to its
readers' experiences and emotions, its deft touch with representative anecdotes, its unembarrassed moral passion, and that mix of
fondness and exasperation that comes from a deep sense of familiarity with the long-sedimented characteristics of English life.

But it is a more informal, chatty book than placing it in this
rather earnest company may suggest. Take one of the central topics
of his discussion. Unusually for someone who has been a professor,
an assistant director-general of UNESCO, and a member or chairman of several nationally important committees, Richard Hoggart
loves shopping. It is not just the fact that, being retired, he can now
potter off at hours when others are chained to their desks; even in
The Uses of Literacy there were signs that we were talking serious
shopping. The Yorkshireman's love of a bargain is one thing at
work here (he reports with some pride that even now most of the
books he buys are second-hand or remaindered, including extra
copies of his own works), and his responsiveness to the charms of
family life and the rhythms of domesticity is another. But beyond
this, shopping is Hoggart's preferred form of fieldwork.

Indeed, to judge by this book he must be the chief economic
support of Farnham's supermarkets. The check-out queue is his
laboratory for social observation. One suspects him of deliberately
only buying a few items at a time in order the sooner to justify
another jaunt with the trolley, an activity he seems to regard as

children do fairground rides. Shopping, of course, has become a fashionable academic subject or metaphor (the movement between those terms being one sign of the fashionableness). But Hoggart is not interested in any clever-clogs stuff about the commodity as signifier: he's interested in peering into his fellow-shoppers' trolleys and inferring whole ways of life from their contents. Hoggart can see life in a handful of dusters.

He is not, of course, simply a disinterested ethnographer. He is ultimately a moralist, brooding on the human condition as manifested in the mundane and the habitual. When Hoggart pops down to the shops (he surely never 'goes marketing'), he is always on the look-out for little packets of significance. At one point, he remarks with satisfaction that he has been able to live in Farnham practically anonymously, none of his fellow inhabitants (the representative of the park-bench cultural studies seminar apart) giving any sign that they know who he is. But he has blown his cover now: the days when he could collect nuggets by standing unrecognized in the check-out queue are surely over. Will outraged housewives complain to the manager about That Man in cakes and biscuits who is persistently appraising their class background? If so, the park-bench seminar might get a new recruit.

Townscape with Figures is a very writerly book, dotted with the small triumphs of one who habitually engages in the intolerable wrestle with words and meanings, and this is one of the ways in which it helps us to see Hoggart's earlier career in its proper perspective. Observing the abstracted, day-dreaming secretaries waiting for the morning train to London, he describes them as 'stroking or turning their engagement rings like one-bead rosaries'. Or again, in contrasting the styles in which young middle-class and working-class women walk, he says of the latter that they 'tend to walk from the knees, trottily'. The observation may not allow enough for changing styles of skirts and shoes, but 'trottily' is perfect.

His prose is marbled with phrases from the spoken language, old and new: he speaks of a machine that has 'packed in' (not the now more common 'packed up'), but also of a tradesman who will 'rip you off' and of 'double-breasted conmen'. Seeing a bumper-sticker—in the supermarket car-park, of course—which says 'The horse was on our roads before the car', he comments laconically: 'a bit wonky, that, historically; the car brought the roads' (the precision of punctuation

here confirms how carefully wrought the effect is). Another sign of his
vocation is his penchant for some quite ambitious prose effects. He
closes his reflection on family life in the second volume of his autobiography with the cautious judgement that the pleasures seem to
have outweighed the pains in his own children's relation to their
parents, and then adds a syntactically incomplete final sentence: 'As
we, characteristically inhibited by nature and by Englishness, just
manage at last to say.' The self-characterizing clause introduces one
arrest into the sentence, and the almost Jamesian placing of the 'at
last' enforces another, so that the effect of the whole is to enact (to use
one of his own favoured critical terms) the hesitations and indirect-
nesses it describes.

Nothing is more revealing of the centrality of writing to
Hoggart's identity than his tendency to see the world as populated
by so many topics for essays. He begins his rumination on the
language of advertisements for local private schools by saying
'what a revealing, sad, hilarious essay could be written on those
repetitive, gesturing, imprisoned themes; or threnodies'. The
sentence is in one respect untypical of Hoggart: the six adjectives
make up just over a third of the words used (as he says himself elsewhere: 'Piling up adjectives is a second best'). But their presence
here surely suggests that he is already sketching that essay in his
mind; the adjectives are *aides-mémoire*, shorthand symbols for
what he would want to go on to say, and in the fuller saying they
would disappear as adjectives to reappear as paragraphs. There is
a comparably revealing moment in his autobiography when he
speaks of trying to set down his impressions of England in 1945
after being away for several years: 'I wrote a short essay about it
but was out of practice and it was portentous'. Whether the criticism was merited or not, this is the reflection of a writer who
knows the importance of 'practice'.

Similarly, the Farnham book reminds us that Hoggart's cultural
reference-points have always been overwhelmingly literary. Arnold
Bennett, Virginia Woolf, and Robert Louis Stevenson appear in its
first, short, paragraph (which assumes its readers are familiar with
Woolf's Bennett and Brown essay, here unnamed), and Auden,
James, and Flaubert have all made their appearance before the end
of the second page. This is in fact untypical of the book, perhaps a
sign of the nervousness of beginning, letting the bigger boys go
first. But rereading *The Uses of Literacy* now, one notices that a

work usually recalled for its intimate portrait of working-class culture is studded with references to the hallowed names not just of English literature but of European culture more generally—Tocqueville, Freud, and Kafka are there alongside Arnold, Eliot, and James. There has always been much more to Hoggart than hostile allegations of professional eebygummery have allowed.

In *Townscape with Figures* the two literary presences who are repeatedly acknowledged are William Cobbett and George Sturt. Hoggart tells us he came to live in Farnham largely by accident, but one could be forgiven for thinking that Cobbett and Sturt, both sons of Farnham who wrote memorably about the place, had already fingered him as their most likely successor in the mixed mode of writing about the moral life of the local community, and that they had exercised some pull with the great Literary Agent in the sky to attract Hoggart to set up his typewriter in the town. Hoggart recognizes (self-knowledge is, of course, his strong suit, often played in this book) that he shares with Cobbett 'a touch of driven puritanism and a special hatred of . . . the incivilities of presumed status', but the greater warmth of fellow-feeling is reserved for Sturt, 'a quieter, more solitary and ingrown man'. In so far as Sturt has had any kind of presence in recent literary-cultural discussion, it has largely been on account of Leavis's high regard for his depiction of a world we have lost. Hoggart, characteristically prone to be a bit counter-suggestible where a party line might seem to be involved and, like Orwell, tending to take pride in the stubborn honesty of his own achieved identity, confesses that he had 'always been a little uneasy with the didactic way Leavis and some of those most influenced by him seemed to use Sturt'. Hoggart may not seem to be terribly well placed to tick others off for their didacticism, but the resistance to 'using' someone, dead author or contemporary acquaintance, lies deep in the Hoggartian ethic.

VI

The reference to Leavis suggests one helpful way of placing Hoggart in English cultural history. He shares some of Leavis's deep belief in the power of literature, and has similarly worried over the morally damaging effects of a commercially driven 'mass'

culture (*The Uses of Literacy* was immediately recognized as a kind
of successor to Queenie Leavis's *Fiction and the Reading Public*).
But he has always firmly distanced himself from the Leavises'
intransigent elitism and their 'barbarians-at-the-gate' cultural
pessimism, and he has taken a far more positive view of the potential of new media such as television, though latterly his optimism
has taken some hard knocks. Leavis could never have written such
a mild and indulgent (including occasionally self-indulgent) book
as this, and not just because in his untravelled case Cambridge
would have to have taken the place of Farnham. One of the things
that makes this forgiving book such agreeable reading is the way
Hoggart largely accepts the weaknesses and fallings-short of his
fellow-citizens without requiring of them implausibly strenuous
feats of self-transcendence.

In going back to Hoggart's earlier work, I had expected to find
it sentimental, my own memory of first reading it now being over-
laid with later academic charges against it of too fondly evoking a
world of scrubbed doorsteps, bread and dripping, and a ha'p'orth
of wine-gums from the corner shop. But it is the literary confidence
and stylishness of *The Uses of Literacy* that now seems so striking:
its reputation for cosiness and nostalgia does not do justice to its
experiments in form and its allusive, learned, manner. Its assurance
also indicates that Hoggart was able implicitly to take for granted
the existence of an educated, non-specialist audience that was not
confined to an academic discipline. The book has none of the
defensiveness about transgressing academic norms that one might
now expect to find in a comparably ambitious work by an
unknown lecturer in his late thirties.

Of course, this kind of rereading risks something similar to the
pitfalls of hindsight: I now read the book for what it tells me about
Hoggart, whereas, like, presumably, most of its first readers, I
initially read it for what it told me about my own society. In that
respect, its central concern can now be seen to have formed part of
a quite general but historically specific theme: it was the 'entry into
society' of the old urban working class. A certain effort of historical reconstruction is now required to recall just how separate and
self-contained the world of the industrial working class had been
between the period of its formation in the first half of the nineteenth century and the Second World War. The first part of *The
Uses of Literacy*, written in the mid-1950s but set in the inter-war

period, was widely seen as something of an elegy for the passing of this separate world, while much of Hoggart's later writing has been preoccupied with the consequent democratization of culture and 'communications', as well as with the pressures encountered by individual members of the working class displaced by social and educational mobility.

These were fashionable concerns in Britain in the late 1950s and early 1960s, although it is arguable that Hoggart did not just benefit from this fashionability but that he also did something to help create it. This was, for example, the period that saw the 'discovery' of the so-called working-class novelists (Alan Sillitoe, John Braine, Stan Barstow, *et al.*), the discussions surrounding the work of Jackson and Marsden on education and the working class, the beginnings of 'labour history', even Dennis Potter's early television plays. A special premium attached to those who embodied as well as analysed this social change, and Hoggart, an articulate and engaging speaker who was never afraid to commit himself and who was what editors and producers regard as 'good value', achieved a national reputation.

Two more specific episodes completed the transition from being a university lecturer who had written a little-noticed book on Auden's poetry to being a 'public figure' (an experience that he has written about with his now customary wryness). One was the unforeseeable turn of events which led him to appear as a star witness for the defence in the *Lady Chatterley* trial in 1960, where he memorably trumped all the po-faced moralism appealed to by the prosecuting counsel by describing Lawrence's treatment of sex as 'highly virtuous, even puritanical'. The other was his membership of the Pilkington Commission on Broadcasting, which reported in 1962, especially the rumour that he was largely responsible for its principled defence of the ideal of public service broadcasting. In both cases, the relation between culture and class was a central issue.

In the 1960s Hoggart had a programme: the imaginative understanding of social change in contemporary Britain and the maintenance of serious moral assessment of it in public debate. The first part of this fathered what has become known as 'cultural studies', although, as I remark in Chapter 13 below, the place Hoggart assigned to literature in fostering that 'imaginative understanding' has changed out of all recognition. But the second half of the programme has fared less well, as it was perhaps bound to do: moral appraisal of the Hoggartian kind has struggled to get a hearing in political debates increasingly conducted in the idiom of double-entry book-keeping. None the less, this insistence on moral judgement has been the cornerstone of his career, both its foundation and its distinctive note.

Hoggart casually classifies *Townscape with Figures* as belonging to the genre of 'discursive non-specialist writing', and one of the interesting things about his career is how little his cultural authority has rested upon his presumed command of a body of specialized knowledge. In the wake of *The Uses of Literacy* he was invited to hold forth as an expert on 'working-class culture', it is true, but it soon became clear that his public standing, like Williams's, rested at least as much on the moral force of his own personality. This, to use Bourdieu's idiom, has been his 'cultural capital'. The frequently rehearsed story of his background and upbringing has functioned almost as a professional qualification. In the Britain of the 1960s it could seem hard to challenge the moral authority of someone who had grown up in a back-to-back. But Hoggart has never been simply reducible to this stereotype, partly because the intelligence at work has been more creative and wide-ranging than this suggests, and partly because he has cultivated a writing voice ('out of Leavis by Orwell' would be one characterization, though that perhaps suggests too dramatic a register) which constantly implies that freedom from cant is the chief prerequisite of serious ethical appraisal.

The chief danger of this voice is not so much that of falling into priggishness and preachiness—his earthiness saves him from being priggish and he almost gives preaching a good name—but rather a kind of self-congratulatory complacency, an excessive pride in one's own integrity. Hoggart has surely been guilty of this earlier in his career, and it is not altogether absent even from the milder tones of the Farnham book. But perhaps it is impossible to use one's own character as a touchstone in public debate, as he has done, without a bit of moral stiffness setting in.

Townscape with Figures is a kind of *Uses of Literacy* for the garden-centre age. As far as Hoggart is concerned, a lot of things haven't changed much. Class remains the dominant social fact of British life, and you can still, he thinks, spot someone's class a mile off. And what has always most bothered him about class still does so: not so much the inequality or unfairness or exploitation, though he deeply abhors all those things. It is the arrogance and condescension he can't stand. Both here and in his autobiography, but also in *The Uses of Literacy* in muted form, the anecdotes of class are nearly always about this. Again and again one meets his sensitivity to slights, to being patronized or put down. And this suggests from another angle how individual, almost private, his focus really is. Though he talks a lot about class, he does not in fact deal in social structures and their systematic injustices: he deals in individual instances, frequently instances where he is both actor and witness. In his autobiography he recalls an anecdote in which a buffet-car waiter, expertly appraising details of Hoggart's appearance and manner, challenged his right to occupy a seat in the First-Class buffet. In reflecting on the episode, he tartly labels the man 'a sniffer-dog of class', but the cap fits, for Hoggart himself is as ready as the fiercest enforcer of 'political correctness' (which he deplores) to denounce language that prejudges or diminishes people on account of their social origins.

Townscape with Figures is also a minor Domesday Book of English moral possessions. Hoggart returns, as he has done throughout his writing life, to certain prized qualities which he sees as quintessentially if not uniquely English. 'Decency' must lead the field, and a cluster of related terms come close behind: 'neighbourliness', 'fairmindedness', 'considerateness', and so on. Like Sturt, he celebrates 'the settled phlegmatic decency' he finds in so many of his Surrey neighbours, a 'strain of reasonably fair-minded, laconic considerateness'. Although he tries to end his book by dwelling on the concreteness of Farnham, tries to resist taking it as a text for a wider moral, he can't in the end manage it: the book concludes with an appropriately muted little cadenza on the historical good fortune that has allowed 'fair play' to flourish in England. It's hard to imagine Williams, determined unmasker of official pieties as well as a self-described 'Welsh European', doing that.

Continuities, both national and personal, continually strike Hoggart now, and reflecting on the brute, purposeless fact of personal existence he has more than once been drawn to the bleakly Beckettian: 'One goes on going on'. But the manner of Hoggart's going-on compels admiration, and the terms of praise that most readily come to mind to describe his public voice point, for all the distinctiveness of that voice, towards one typically

English way of being an intellectual: unpretentious, morally serious, reflective, and (the word is inevitable) decent—unshowily but
bottomlessly decent. Above all, he has had the priceless gift, apparently from quite an early age, of knowing who he is. Some may not
like who he is, some may think it doesn't amount to much; but he
has shown an enviable conviction not just that it'll have to do, but
that, in the end, nothing else will do as well.

Townscape with Figures confirms what should have been clear
for a long time, that Hoggart's natural home is not with that international company of cultural analysts, literary theorists, and
assorted academic superstars who are today's most familiar intellectuals. He belongs, rather, to an older family, one with strong
local roots and some pride in ancestry; his forebears include Ruskin
and Lawrence on one side, Cobbett and Orwell on the other.
Richard Hoggart is an English moralist. More than ever, we need
him to be in good voice.

III
ARGUMENTS

12

Against Prodspeak: 'Research' in the Humanities

I

This essay falls into two distinct though clearly related parts, and, by contrast to most of the other chapters in this book, I have deliberately left each part pretty much in the form in which it was originally published. I have done so for two reasons. The first is that both parts take issue with ways of misconceiving the nature of scholarly research that were, as a result of government policy, particularly threatening in the mid- and late-1980s, and it would be misleading to try to disguise this very specific chronological reference. This applies particularly to the second part which dates from the years when official moves seemed to be favouring the use of 'bibliometric methods' (i.e. measuring the quantity of publications) to determine the funding of research in higher education. The other reason is perhaps a rather more sentimental consideration. The fact that a larger number of people seem to have been stirred to write to me by reading these two articles as originally published than by reading anything else I have ever written, and that their letters expressed not only support but what I can only call delight— delight that someone had expressed publicly convictions which they deeply shared but which seemed to be having a hard time of it in their own academic institutions—persuades me to leave them as

Current Research in Britain: The Humanities (The British Libary, 1987).
University Management Statistics and Performance Indicators in the UK (CVCP, 1988).

minor records of that unhappy period in British universities. Of course, it would be nice to think that there is less need to say such things now…

II

Between them, Nietzsche and Morris Zapp provide much sound guidance through life, but it has to be said that there is one problem, at least, which finds them both a little wanting. They would neither of them wish me to affect the mask of impersonality, so let me state the problem in its frankly subjective form. I believe passionately in the value of those activities we call 'the Humanities', yet when I see a compilation like the British Library's *Current Research in Britain: The Humanities*, I feel sick. I don't think this is just a matter of being hard to please or having a weak stomach. After all, when I hear the usual phrases in the annual addresses of vice-chancellors and college presidents the world over—'deepening our understanding of ourselves and our history', 'exploring the dimensions of human creativity', 'the unflinching pursuit of truth, the cultivation of humane judgement'—I find myself only mildly uneasy at the hyperbole, and indeed sometimes, if the provision of cheap white wine at the reception has been unusually abundant, something like a tear of regimental pride wells up in the corner of my eye.

And yet when I go into the New Periodicals room of my university library I feel renewed reverence for that last librarian at Alexandria against whom the charge of arson is still pending. I know that this reaction, in particular, is ungracious to the point of bad faith. Over the years, I have been much instructed by what I have read in this room; I have sometimes come out with new respect for the way disciplined scholarship demands a range of human capacities, and at times I have even been abashed at the sheer quality of other people's work. Worse still, I have actually written the odd scholarly article myself, and I can't say I altogether regret it. Yet still the sight of those unstoppably multiplying learned journals arouses in me some mixture of despair, shame, and pyromania. At the very least I want to give a false name at the desk, and write rude words across the cover of the *Journal of English and Germanic Philology*.

Now, Nietzsche and Morris Zapp do let one down a bit at this point. Not that the young Professor of Classical Philology at Basle didn't come to feel what was obviously a rather similar unease. It surely underlay his tirades against the industrious *Gelehrten* of his day: they had lost sight of the point of their activity, but 'the habit of scholarliness continues without it, and rotates in egoistic self-satisfaction around its own axis'. The omnivorous scholar 'often sinks so low that in the end he is content to gobble down any food whatever, even the dust of bibliographical minutiae'. That's possibly a bit frank; perhaps there's something more judicious in his later work? 'The proficiency of our finest scholars, their heedless industry'—yes, this sounds more like it—'their heads smoking day and night, their very craftsmanship: how often the real meaning of all this lies in the desire to keep something hidden from oneself! . . . scholarship today is a hiding place for every kind of discontent, disbelief, gnawing worm, *despectio sui*, bad conscience'. Oh dear! Probably best to leave that last bit out of the department's submission to the Research Assessment Exercise.

David Lodge's Morris Zapp, even before he took up jogging, was rather more deeply implicated in the trends of his time, and he had not become a full Professor at Euphoria State on account of a squeamish aversion to increasing the printers' work-load. His heart, of course, was in the right place, and he always had a proper concern for the positioning of other, more importunate, organs; yet even I find his proposed resolution of the existential dilemma we both share a little drastic. He planned, you will recall, a series of commentaries on the works of Jane Austen, and eventually upon every author in the canon, which would be 'utterly exhaustive', leaving 'simply nothing further to say'. 'The object of the exercise, as he had often to explain with as much patience as he could muster, was not to enhance others' enjoyment and understanding of Jane Austen, still less to honour the novelist herself, but to put a definitive stop to the production of any further garbage on the subject . . . After Zapp, the rest would be silence.'

In both these responses, the baby/bathwater ratio seems a touch high. And yet there surely is a real issue here which is not just to be dissolved by references to an over-fastidious sensibility about the inevitable gap between ideal and reality or to the complacent ladder-kicking-away behaviour of the middle-aged and tenured. There is something wrong with our present practice of 'Research in the Humanities'. Or rather—since there is not just one form of that practice and 'we' are a diverse lot—much of what is done under this rubric, and perhaps even more of what is said *about* what is or should be done, sends the mind reaching for terms like 'incongruous' and 'misconceived'. Since this may not be a popular thing to say, or, far worse, may risk being popular in the wrong quarter, let me try first to dispel some possible misunderstandings.

First of all, I am not suggesting that people engaged in the cultivation of the humanities (who are for the most part supported by institutions of higher education) shouldn't write things. Writing is an essential part of their activity, though more writing and less publishing may be a quite intelligible, even possibly healthy, state of affairs. Secondly, I do not think 'more means worse'. More means more, and I would have thought that it was undeniable that there was more good stuff as well as bad stuff written in these fields now than there was thirty years ago or even, in so far as the comparison can be made at all, 130 years ago. My response is not, I think, that of the late Roman patrician surveying the barbarians within the gates, which is so often disguised as the 'more means worse' or 'back to standards' argument (if it can be called an argument).

Nor, thirdly, are most of the topics written about in themselves trivial or pointless. Attempts to define in advance what is going to prove to be important or to have 'point' nearly always end up being made to look silly by the unpredictable winds of intellectual change. An interest in Hegel would have seemed like an ostensive definition of a dead end in English-speaking philosophy forty years ago, and now look! Intellectual history is full of examples of how pronouncements that a certain topic was exhausted were shortly followed by a period of unprecedentedly creative work on it. It is true that a special version of the general problem of diminishing returns applies to intellectual inquiry, but in practice (for reasons I'll try to spell out in a moment) this so often seems to come down to the quality of the work being done, not the quantity of previous work in the area. It is true that second-rate work on a new topic (especially if it requires a good deal of empirical legwork) may seem easier to justify than second-rate work on an old topic, but first-rate work on either embodies its own justification, and in effect changes the topic as well.

None the less, some disquiet may be a legitimate response to the conception of 'Research in the Humanities' underlying the British Library's compilation. The main reason for this, surely, is that the sense of 'research' that is implied may not be altogether appropriate here. That sense is the one borrowed from the natural sciences, where research is usually thought of (wrongly, according to many philosophers and historians of science, and, indeed, to many practising scientists as well) as a matter of 'pushing back the frontiers of knowledge'. (This sense of the term brings stowaways with it: each 'research project' in the British Library listing is given under the name of 'the principal investigator'.) But however far that description may be appropriate to the life of the lab, the not entirely dead metaphor it contains looks very unhappy in its new surroundings. 'Frontiers' here suggests that 'knowledge' is to be seen in geopolitical terms as an expanding imperial state; what is inside the 'frontiers' is a secure possession, and the direction of advance is simply given by the lie of the land. 'State-of-the-Art research' is just the West Coast version of the old policy of *Drang nach Wahrheit*: knowledge takes no prisoners, the compass provides all the justification needed, and there's no doubt where the front line is.

Moreover, 'knowledge' itself is surely less than ideal as a description of what we're after. The contrast with 'understanding' indicates a lot of what it leaves out or misrepresents, and even a term like 'cultivation' has a claim here, or would do had it not come to be so closely associated with images of affected connoisseurship and simple snobbery. 'Knowledge' is too easily thought of as accumulated stock, as something that doesn't need to be discovered again and is simply there for anyone who wants to use it. But 'understanding' underlines that it's a *human* activity, and so is inseparable from the people who do it. Notoriously, the possibilities of extending our understanding depend not just on what we already understand, but also on what sorts of people we have become.

Now, I don't pretend that it's easy to see what follows from this thought for the question of 'Research in the Humanities', but giving it more salience in our reflections could at least make it harder for the language of Productivity-Speak to carry all before it. It can alert us, for example, to the overvaluation of a particularly narrow conception of 'novelty' that is commonly involved. In Prodspeak, the publication of one's 'new findings' is the only acceptable outcome of 'research'. It is true, of course, that there are large areas of the humanities where reporting on 'new findings' may seem a perfectly proper description for part of the activity— the unearthing of new sources is an obvious form of this. But for the most part, something more like 'nurturing, animating, revising, and extending our understanding' would seem nearer the mark, and here it is harder to isolate the 'new findings'.

The truth is that there is often work by our predecessors which it may be right neither simply to repeat (even were that strictly possible) nor to repudiate and replace with something else. The proper response may be to acknowledge it, possess it, learn from it, and allow it to inform our understanding. One trouble with this way of putting it is that it may seem vulnerable to the charges of rigidity and passivity: any suggestion of merely handing on our cultural inheritance makes us seem like rather indolent museum curators—and socially and culturally conservative ones, too, who are sure that everything worth preserving is already in the collection. But this is a misconception of what this kind of understanding involves. For each generation to repossess a cultural inheritance, in the fullest and not merely the bailiff's sense of that verb, is to modify and extend it. Apart from anything else, our understanding has to be different from that of previous generations just because it is ours: we fit it into the framework of other things we understand, we articulate it with our other concerns (which are far from purely intellectual), and we restate it in our idiom and for our audience. The humanities, it has been well said, are inherently 'conversational' subjects (which is one reason why the close connection with teaching is not simply a historical contingency), and conversing, unlike activities as different as haranguing or cataloguing, requires a constant, flexible, responsiveness.

Moreover, it can take a great deal of time and effort for any one individual just to get to the point where a genuine and imaginatively effective understanding of, say, Kant's philosophy of the legal arrangements of medieval England is possible. But during that time, and indeed even once there, our 'principal investigator' may not have any 'new findings' to publish, though a prolonged meditation on such topics, combined with wide reading in other fields and reflection on a variety of experience, may eventually issue in something that Prodspeak would call new. This may take quite some time, but meanwhile there are, as we know, very strong economic and existential pressures on 'researchers' in the humanities to come up with something new fast. This gives an important role to what can properly be called intellectual fashion, which speeds up the business of slaying the fathers (and mothers) no end. New sausage-machines turn out different-looking sausages and plenty of 'em. Fashion and Prodspeak are mutually supportive.

III

The general point I am trying to make here is a very old one, and not in the least original to me. But, of course, it is part of the point itself that we do need to repossess such old truths and understand and state them anew in new circumstances. Some of those circumstances are very obvious, like the enormous expansion of higher education in this and many other countries in recent decades which, for Malthusian reasons, may have forced later arrivals to attempt to extract fresh yields from marginal or unfertile plots. But there are also less tangible circumstances, like the way in which public debate in modern liberal democracies has come to combine utilitarian valuations with a distrust of procedures that are not mechanically universalizable. It is a curious feature of such debate that where 'understanding', and still more 'cultivation', can be pilloried as 'elitist', 'research' retains an open and ostensibly democratic character: the stock of 'knowledge', it suggests, is accessible to all, and anyone can replicate the experiment (give or take a few IQ points and several years' 'training'). 'Results' are seen as something objective, and so the role of the exercise of judgement is usurped by the kind of totting-up of 'items published' that can be made intelligible to the average accountant-in-the-street.

Any suggestion of resisting this slide into an inappropriately utilitarian vocabulary is likely to look quixotic, and at times downright suicidal. But in fact, simply colluding with Prodspeak may be more fatal still, because our contribution to the GNP is, as Morris Zapp would remind us, 'zilch'. We don't best defend our activities by dressing them up as something they're not: the humanities, as those vice-chancellors' addresses imply, are essential to our society's understanding of itself, but degrees of success in furthering an aim of this kind can only be measured qualitatively.

And this general point is connected, albeit rather deviously, with

the unsteadiness of my response to the Sorcerer's Apprentice night-
mare of the New Periodicals room. The more we talk the language
of Prodspeak the more we have to live by it. Moreover, and more
insidiously, the more we let it become the only acceptable justifica-
tory language, the more it shapes and partly constitutes our own
individual senses of identity. Shall we, for example, become unable
to accommodate the thought that there may be more admirable
qualities displayed in the decision *not* to publish the outcome of
some extended rumination than to turn it into another 'item' for
the annual listing?

Meanwhile, those sodding forms keep coming round asking us
'principal investigators' what our current 'research projects' are,
and forms have a way of imposing their own categories. I suppose
it is, alas, unlikely that next year's list will contain entries like
'Brooding on Wittgenstein' or 'Trying to Get the French Revolution
Straight'. And here again neither Nietzsche nor Morris Zapp
provides a very helpful model. I don't imagine Nietzsche was much
of a one for filling in such forms, though if he had I would have
liked to have seen the British Library's computer trying to decide
how to classify 'Self-Overcoming'. I suppose Zapp, more of an
adept at the jargon, might try to get away with 'Towards a General
Theory of Gender Interaction: Some Comparative Findings'. And
me? Well, one year, in Mittyish protest, I'm going to put down
'Rereading the Complete Works of Henry James with Special
Reference to Getting to the End of *The Golden Bowl* This Time'.

IV

Not everything that counts can be counted. It's true that where the
catchphrase of late nineteenth-century politics was 'We are all
socialists now', the motto (epitaph?) of our age seems rather to be
'We are all accountants now'. Yet, perverse as it may seem, there
are issues where the most important among the things that cannot
be counted are the costs. The question of 'performance indicators'
in universities is one such issue. But perhaps, sensing what is to
follow, you are already starting to feel impatient: 'Doesn't he realize that this is the way the world is run these days, and we either
work within their categories or we pay the cost'. *Their* categories?
The cost? Now read on.

Under the joint auspices of the Committee of Vice-Chancellors and Principals and the University Grants Committee [shortly hereafter to be superseded by the University Funding Council which in turn was quickly replaced by the Higher Education Funding Council], a subcommittee has been set up to carry out a 'pilot scheme' preparatory to developing 'a methodology for counting and classifying publications'. The membership of this subcommittee is published in the 1988 edition of *University Management Statistics and Performance Indicators in the UK*. It comprises two vice-chancellors and one registrar, two specialists in science policy, a professor each of Physics, Chemistry, and Financial Management (good to see the Arts have not been forgotten), and eight administrators from the DES, UGC, and other such bodies. In the 'Introduction' to its 'Pilot Survey of Research Publications', the subcommittee tells us that 'those consulted so far accept that one thing is crucial—the need to establish a database of research output . . . on which appropriate bibliometric methods can be demonstrated'. Perhaps, in that case, a little more 'consulting' might not come amiss.

The four subjects selected for the pilot survey are Physics, Chemistry, Economics, and History. Forms and notes on their completion have been sent out, asking for a full list of staff, a full list of publications, and a 'statistical summary' (glossed as: 'A numerical summary of the full bibliography on the form provided. For each specified subject a single row of figures should appear in each half of the table.'). The object, we are told, is 'to seek suggestions on matters of principle and practice to ensure that the eventual format is as satisfactory as possible'. The eventual use to which the 'appropriate bibliometric methods' will be put is not explained. The accompanying letter speaks of 'promot[ing] studies of ways in which bibliometric methods can be used to assist judgements of research'. Just 'assist', you understand; nothing drastic.

Perhaps a little more light is cast—well, all right, not exactly 'light'—by the minute of the CVCP meeting noting the proposal to conduct the pilot scheme. 'The ultimate objective', it explains is 'for there to be quantitative data on publications in every university department, but this would only be an adjunct to the traditional quantitative forms of peer group assessment of research'. I'm sorry, I'll read that again. No, it doesn't matter which way up you hold it, it still seems to be saying that we used to do it by counting publications, but now we've had this super new wheeze and we're going to do it by . . . counting publications (counting better? more systematically? differently?). Not quite what I had imagined 'traditional peer group assessment of research' to be like. Ah, but perhaps all is explained by the hypothesis that 'traditional quantitative forms' in the latter part of that sentence is a slip of the CVCP pen for 'traditional qualitative forms'? Slips of the pen, are of course, like slips of the tongue, simply accidental and reveal nothing; certainly nothing to worry about in the fact that the administrators of the CVCP write 'quantitative' when they mean 'quantitative'.

'All right, smart-arse, you've had your fun; but what's the alternative? We know that the Cabinet Office has demanded that we come up with measures of "productivity" in universities [sorry about the quotation-marks, I know it's like throwing a handful of flowers at an advancing tank]. How else are we going to measure it?'

Well, let's start there. We don't *measure* it; we *judge* it. Understanding that distinction, really understanding it, is the first step of wisdom in these matters. And what is 'it'? 'Research Productivity'? Just think about that phrase for a moment—and then we can agree to start somewhere else.

The impulse behind the UGC/CVCP pilot scheme is financial and managerial. The amount of time spent on 'research', so we are told, has to be distinguished from the amount of time spent on 'teaching' (these are apparently the only two activities conducted in universities), so that 'resources' can be assigned to each. 'Research selectivity' involves finding out which 'cost centres' are good at 'research', or at least do a lot of it, or at least publish a lot of it, so that the amount of money which other institutions receive for the 'research' they're not very good at, or at least not doing enough of, or at least not publishing enough of, can be reduced. An exercise like this innocuous-seeming pilot scheme is, therefore, highly consequential. More generally, what is fundamentally at issue is the adequacy of the categories in terms of which we are being asked to represent our activities to ourselves and others. How appropriate are the categories proposed in this pilot scheme, and what do they suggest about the assumptions and purposes of those who have framed them?

I'm afraid we have to start with the very category of 'research' itself—'afraid' because many may think it obstructive or quixotic even to express any reservations about this fundamental category. But while we are no doubt committed to using the word, we have to be careful not to let it bring in its train assumptions and expectations which are damagingly inappropriate. It has to be said—and has to be said now more emphatically than ever—that in many areas of the humanities 'research' can be a misleading term. It is difficult to state briefly how work in these areas should be characterized, but, as I suggested in the first part of this essay, we are at least pointed in the right direction by phrases like 'cultivating understanding', 'nurturing and extending a cultural heritage', 'thinking critically about the profoundest questions of human life', and so on. Both publication and teaching are in a sense dependent on this more fundamental activity, however we characterize it, and are natural and inseparable expressions of it; but the activity itself is not reducible without remainder to those two categories. Publication in the humanities is, therefore, not always a matter of communicating 'new findings' or proposing a 'new theory'. It is often the expression of the deepened understanding which some individual has acquired, through much reading, discussion, and reflection, on a topic which has been in some sense 'known' for many generations.

The difficulties involved in expressing this truth were brought home to me when, at my previous university, a new vice-chancellor arrived, and it was decided that he should make a series of visits to different parts of the university to see representative figures at work in the various activities carried on there. He hovered over practicals, sat in on lectures, wandered round laboratories and so forth, but it was suggested that he should also visit one or two selected members of the Arts departments in their offices (he was a scientist). I was selected to be one of these, and told that the expectation was that he would find me 'carrying on with my research'. Naturally, I brooded a good deal over just what sort of *tableau vivant* best represented this activity: should I be correcting the proofs of my latest publication, or be discussing my exciting new 'findings' with one of my colleagues, or be on the point of filling in a large grant application? Finally, I realized that if I was supposed to represent 'research in the humanities' it was clear what I ought to be doing: I ought to be sitting alone reading a book. The emblematic figure of humane scholarship is not the professor at the lectern or the would-be author at the word processor, still less the white-coated member of a research team collecting 'data' and publishing 'results'. It is the person sitting alone reading a book.

Things are, I am quite willing to believe, different in the sciences, and even to some extent in the social sciences. (For this reason it is unfortunate that the two 'Arts' subjects chosen for this exercise should be Economics and History; the limits of its appropriateness might be even more sharply defined if it was addressed to, say, Philosophy or one of the literature-based disciplines.) Even so, it is revealing of the difficulties any uniform scheme will encounter that one very senior scientist whom I spoke to about it immediately replied: 'Well, the main problem is that the categories are obviously designed to reflect research in the Arts', remarking, for example, the way the category of 'review' or 'review-article' really has no standing in his field, where it suggests, if it suggests anything, an appraisal of a research-team or grant application. The head of another large scientific research-group complained that: 'The authors of the questionnaire have not thought it out properly in advance', urging that it was misleading in certain areas of team and collaborative research to try to list publications by individuals. What all this suggests, surely, is that we need to be alert to the differences *among* the various activities carried on in universities, and to ensure that we judge excellence in their conduct accordingly. This pilot scheme does just the opposite.

The premiss of the exercise is that the categories must be uniform. For the purposes of developing 'bibliometric methods' it is no good whingeing that editing early medieval Latin texts is a touch different from conducting research in particle physics; just make sure we have a number in each box, will you? Even leaving aside for the moment the question of the point of such an exercise and the uses to which the 'data' will be put, and even leaving aside the whole question of judgements of quality and significance to be made between publications, it should still be obvious that even for the task of simply *recording* the publications of those working in universities, a far more variegated and nuanced set of categories would be required. Where are we to place activities, crucial to others' scholarship, such as compiling dictionaries or editing texts? In which box do we report the creative role of the editor of a collaborative volume or the critical role of the editor of a literary journal? How do we record that seminal review-essay in the *New*

York Review of Books or that letter to the *Times Literary Supplement* definitively demolishing a purported new edition of some classic text? What sense does it make in the humanities to propose classifying journals as either 'academic', 'professional', or 'popular'? What does it mean to limit entries under 'other media' to 'work which represents a contribution to research'? Is it irrelevant that our literary critics write poems and novels, that our historians develop TV documentaries, that our economists challenge official statistics in the weeklies, and so on? Many more objections of this kind might be made, and I can only hope that some of the departments involved in this pilot scheme have had sufficient self-respect to make them.

But again the Voice of Realism pipes up: 'Surely it is not unreasonable to ask those employed at public expense to provide some record of their activities? Or is it only those with something to hide who object to proper records being kept?' For the moment we may ignore the innuendoes and question-begging aspects of this all-too-familiar refrain, but it does invite us to probe a little more deeply the purpose of this exercise.

No one would suggest that we should not collectively keep records of our publications. That we do already. The question is, what difference will the development of 'bibliometric methods' make? If the answer is: 'Don't worry, it won't make any difference at all—it just means keeping records of our publications', then there would be no need for pilot schemes and the rest of it. Plainly, it is intended to enable us (let's keep the polite fiction of 'us' for the moment) to do something we don't already do. Like what? Judge which departments are doing good research? I don't believe that anyone has ever suggested that those conducting peer review exercises should be *denied* material which would be helpful to arriving at an informed judgement. Ah, but now the 'data' will be more precise; for example, an assessing committee will be able to tell at a glance how many publications *in each category* various comparable departments have. Oh yes, we agree that the categories are never going to be perfect, but only if we have a uniform system of classification can comparative assessments of departments be made.

But wait a minute, the point about *peer* review is that they are just the people who understand about publications in the field in question: they are the people who know what weight to attach to

various kinds of publications in that discipline, they are the ones
who know which are the good journals, and so on. 'Bibliometric
methods' will not provide any 'objective' criteria here; they will
simply iron out differences in category appropriate to each discipline. There is, in other words, *no point* in trying to devise a set of
categories of publication appropriate to all disciplines unless you
intend to *reduce* the extent to which decisions rest on judgement by
peers and *increase* the extent to which they rest on measurement by
administrators. It is not just that someone still has to discriminate
a good piece of work from a mediocre one, or that there might be
other considerations altogether to take into account in making the
decision. It is that a uniform set of categories will be an obstacle
and not an adjunct to making peer-group assessments. Those qualified to make such an assessment will have in effect to ignore the
categories the 'database' presents, and recognize what a review-
essay or a letter to *Nature* or whatever means in their own field.

So, the clear implication is that this information will be used to
make decisions, primarily about funding, by those who are not
qualified to judge (if they are qualified to judge, then casting the
information into inappropriate uniform categories will only be a
hindrance). 'Bibliometric methods' will provide a spurious sense of
judging by objective criteria. This is borne out by the 'research
selectivity' exercise now under way. The UGC lists four criteria by
which the 'ratings' of the various 'cost centres' will be determined.
The second and third of these are the predictable 'market-forces'
indicators: success in obtaining research grants and students, and
success in obtaining research contracts (a great way to sort out
departments of, say, Philosophy or Classics). The fourth criterion—
not the first, note—is 'professional knowledge and judgement of
advisory group and panel members, supplemented where appropriate by advice from outside experts'. This, I take it, is what most
of us understand, roughly speaking, by 'peer review'. So what is the
first criterion? 'Publication and other publicly identifiable output.'
The fact that this is given as a quite separate criterion from that of
'professional knowledge and judgement' gives the whole game
away.

Further down the line, of course, stands the spectre of the
'Citation Index', which is what most people understand by 'bibliometric methods' (if they understand anything by it at all). The CVCP
have not made clear whether they regard the present 'initiative' (a

word fallen on hard times if ever there was one) as an alternative to counting citation-frequency or as a step towards it. The latter seems the more plausible answer, alas, so for those of you who have led sheltered lives up till now it may be worth explaining that it involves, roughly (oh, so roughly) speaking, establishing the significance of a piece of work by totting up how often it appears in the footnotes in other people's work. I agree, I didn't believe it when I first heard about it. Apparently, there are one or two areas in the sciences where this produces a fairly reasonable guide to the importance of the 'new findings' in a given publication. The idiocy involved in using this as an indicator of anything of importance in most fields is too obvious to need rehearsing.

However, since in these dark days we need things to cheer us up, let me just report that the whole business can be sabotaged with ridiculous ease. All you do, of course, is simply fill your publications with more references to the work of your friends or of other members of your department or of other members of your citation co-operative or of people you know are in danger of losing their jobs because a crack-brained scheme has determined they should unless their citation-rate goes up. In the United States there are now said to be 'citation-rings' in those fields where any weight is placed upon this pottiness. One can even imagine the kinds of advertisements one would find in the samizdat publications giving the names of those in need of citations: 'You could prevent a child going hungry this Christmas. Just one reference to a publication by its parent ...'.

Yet even if we are not led down the cul-de-sac of citation-counting, the introduction of 'bibliometric methods' will, in indirect and perhaps less obvious ways, have more generally damaging consequences on the quality of the intellectual activity carried on in British universities. There can be no doubt that if 'bibliometric methods' are pursued (and it is still not too late for the UGC/CVCP to acknowledge that the whole idea is misconceived), then this will very significantly increase pressure on those in universities to increase the quantity of their publications. This will be demonstrably harmful to the 'excellence' which, in other of its pronouncements, the UGC declares itself to be committed to fostering. Again, one would have thought this was too obvious to need spelling out. Scholarly activity in the humanities requires time; making everyone so jittery that they suffer from *publicatio praecox* will no more improve the quality of our intellectual life than a faster 'rate of production' of ejaculations would necessarily improve our sexual lives. It will, for example, make it more difficult, especially for younger scholars, to think of undertaking a major project which might not yield any entries for the annual return for several years to come, but which might when completed be worth far more than a whole CVful of slight articles and premature 'syntheses'. Moreover, the ethos encouraged by the overvaluing of quantity in publication will have a pernicious effect upon the other judgements which we are continually called upon to make in academic life. This ethos would, for instance, put considerable pressure on a head of department to appoint to a new post that candidate who is most likely to increase the volume of the department's publications in the shortest time, and so on.

Since it is said, both by those who would welcome as well as those who would regret such an outcome, that developments of this kind will make academic life in Britain more closely resemble that in the United States, it may be as well to address directly the preconceptions and prejudices called up by this prediction. I have no wish to encourage that kind of condescending snobbishness still sometimes found in British universities (and not just in universities) towards what is dismissed as American 'vulgarity' and 'earnestness'. In many fields the fact is that far more of the really significant work is done in the US than in Britain; the current 'brain-drain' is testimony to this, among other things. But an even larger proportion of the bad work is done there too, and there is no doubt that a greater emphasis in various forms of career assessment upon quantity of publication encourages this. We are all familiar with the inflexibility with which some American college deans (administrators, incidentally, and not genuinely 'peers') apply quantitative measures of publication; when 'no book' means 'no tenure', you get a book published whether it's ready or not. Inevitably, this leads to a great many unnecessary and inadequate publications. This does nobody any good; it does the people who write it some harm; it wastes the time of other scholars and students; it costs libraries and other institutions a lot of money.

The motor for the whole misconceived business is the market ethos of US academic life, where quantity of publication (what the UGC so delicately terms 'publicly identifiable output') has come to be allowed excessively to determine 'market value'. It is revealing

that it is only the very best American universities which are
prepared to be flexible and to back informed judgement against
bibliography-measuring ('this young philosopher has only
published two articles, but he/she is so good we are going to give
him/her tenure anyway'), and that is because they are the only ones
which can afford the self-confidence needed to do so. In pursuing
'bibliometric methods' we shall not be adopting the practices of the
most admirable and distinguished universities in the United States,
but rather we shall be inadvertently importing some of those
aspects of American academic life which are least worth emulating.

<h1 style="text-align:center">V</h1>

When a body notionally responsible for promoting and fostering
the purposes for which universities exist engages in a course of
action manifestly likely to misrepresent and ultimately harm those
activities, we are bound to wonder why. Three possible explanations suggest themselves.

The first is that they genuinely do not understand the nature of
much of what goes on in the institutions for which they are responsible, and so do not realize that they are misrepresenting it. This is
certainly possible. Quite what scholarship in the humanities is
'about' is, as I have already acknowledged, notoriously hard to
define, and it is very difficult to justify in terms of economic growth
or technological development, which now seem to be the only
terms offered by some of the hard-faced accountants sitting round
the relevant tables. But if this is the case, then obviously we only
make things worse by sending in our returns in the categories asked
for, since this will simply confirm the administrators in their misunderstanding.

The second possible explanation is that the members of the UGC
and the CVCP understand very well that this and related exercises—no one pretends that this scheme can be considered in isolation from other government-prompted 'rationalization
exercises'—are likely in the long run to restrict the intellectual independence of universities, to reduce support for scholarship in the
humanities, and to damage the ethos of British academic life.
(Indeed, the run may seem uncomfortably short if you happen to
be, say, a Lecturer in Philosophy at Hull.) But it may be their

genuine conviction that this is what should be done. They may, for example, believe that the humanities are not 'real subjects', or that public funds should not be spent on activities which bring no demonstrable economic benefits. In which case we must oblige them to make these convictions manifest. We may at least find some small solace in the international chorus of contempt which will then greet this expression of narrow-minded philistinism.

The third, less drastic, explanation is that some members of these two bodies recognize well enough that these and other recent measures are harmful to many of our activities, but feel that it would be imprudent or pointless to say so. Before rushing off to mount our moral high horses, I think we must extend a limited measure of sympathy to this position. Those in positions of such responsibility have an obligation to be realistic, and those of us not in the hot seats should not be in too much of a hurry to distinguish realism from cowardice. None the less, part of the reason why individuals in these exposed positions may be reluctant to speak out is that they fear they would get little support from the majority of colleagues in less exposed positions, where responses seem, on present showing, to reflect some mixture of fear, apathy, and narrow self-interest. If this is the most nearly correct explanation, it is clear what our response should be. If this genuinely *is* a 'pilot' project, then the CVCP has to be told to find the ejector seat before it's too late. We have to start from the recognition that the nature of the activities carried on in universities is not such as to issue in something describable as 'productivity'; we have to go on to point out that that activity can be judged but not measured; and we have to insist that 'bibliometric methods' will be a hindrance rather than a help to those who are properly capable of making such judgements.

It is no secret that the present Government is hostile to universities and is determined to reduce their real autonomy. Reflecting on the achievements of the Government's second term of office, Mr Norman Tebbit, then Chairman of the Tory Party, was well satisfied with the progress made in taming institutions like the trade unions and local authorities, but the universities, he observed, had been allowed to be foot-draggingly obstructive: the third term would see to that. The language used by Mr Robert Jackson, the ironically titled 'Minister *for* Higher Education', in his recent Chevening discussion paper on ' "Manpower planning" in higher education' indicates chillingly enough what's now coming over the loudspeakers. Having observed that it was infuriatingly difficult to get universities to change their 'hallowed academic practices', he went on: 'Instead, if we are to reduce unit costs to the public purse, we must find ways of obliging the higher education suppliers themselves to address the problem more realistically.' Elsewhere, Mr Jackson has spoken of 'the process of national renovation which is now under way', of which these changes in the position of universities, we are to understand, are an essential part. Perhaps one should not see too much significance in these phrases, which are just the sound of busy politicians reaching for the nearest cliché, but one cannot help recalling that the twentieth century's experience of the consequences of such language has not been a happy one.

It was said in occupied France during the Second World War that one way to tell *collaborateurs* from *résistants* was that the former used the bureaucratic terminology of the occupying power without grimacing. The language of many of the documents issuing from the UGC these days sends the mind reaching for such historical illumination. At one point, the letter accompanying the UGC/CVCP pilot survey speaks of 'the need to establish a database of research output which has the confidence of the academic community'. The plain fact is that the recent behaviour of the UGC has gone a long way towards forfeiting that confidence. One way in which it might start to regain it would be to return to using categories and concepts which suggest an adequate understanding of the activities which an academic community exists to promote in the first place. Until the UGC shows some sign of recognizing this truth, the charge of *Pétainisme* will remain to be answered.

13

Grievance Studies: How Not to Do Cultural Criticism

I

With an increasing and depressing frequency, newspaper reviews of books on contemporary culture treat 'unreadable' and 'academic' as more or less synonymous descriptions. Sometimes the particular judgement is obviously merited, but at least as often the more general complaint simply indicates a resistance to having the familiar described in the unfamiliar language of systematic analysis. And this is not, as is sometimes alleged, a passing or contingent phenomenon, a consequence of the taste for particularly ungainly prose among the most fashionable contemporary theorists: the belligerence with which this resistance tends to be expressed is a symptom of a deeper cultural tension.

When academic scholarship was thought to confine itself to things like the emending of classical texts or the deciphering of medieval charters, the level of technicality involved was accepted, partly recognized as the price of disciplinary rigour, partly regarded as properly removed from the concerns of daily life. But as universities have increasingly laid claim to study all areas of

Lawrence Grossberg, Cary Nelson, Paula A. Treichler (eds.), *Cultural Studies* (Routledge, 1992).

Fred Inglis, *Cultural Studies* (Blackwell, 1994).

Andrew Milner, *Contemporary Cultural Theory: An Introduction* (UCL Press, 1994).

David Morley and Kuan-Hsing Chen (eds.), *Stuart Hall: Critical Dialogues in Cultural Studies* (Routledge, 1996).

contemporary culture, as everything from teen-talk to tourism comes to be analysed in textbooks and monographs, so the boundary between the academic and the non-academic comes under greater pressure, which in turn increases both the allure of, and the resistance to, day trips in each direction. In this context, 'unreadable' and 'jargon-ridden' are often just sounds made by the small-arms fire of the border-guards of journalism, potting at academics suspected of colonizing the ancestral lands of the common reader.

One strip of the border that is particularly prone to flare up in this way is that adjacent to the burgeoning field of 'Cultural Studies'. The fact that this field is not just a particularly delicate point of intersection between academic and non-academic readers but also presents itself as heir to disciplines in which I have an interest (in both senses of the word) has several times prompted me to jump over the fence and explore a bit of it. It is on this basis that I attempt in this essay to answer a question than can be asked in several sharply contrasting tones: 'So, what *is* "Cultural Studies"?'

II

Here are three recipes for doing 'Cultural Studies':

First recipe. Begin a career as a scholar of English Literature. Become dissatisfied: seek to study wider range of contemporary and 'relevant' texts, and extend notion of 'text' to cover media, performance, ritual. Campaign to get this activity accepted as a recognized academic subject. Set up unit to study the tabloid press or soap operas or discourse analysis. Describe resulting work as 'Cultural Studies'.

Second recipe. Begin a career as an academic social scientist. Become dissatisfied; reject misguided scientism, and pursue more phenomenological study of relations between public meanings and private experience. Campaign to get this accepted as a recognized academic subject. Set up unit to study football crowds or house music parties or tupperware mornings. Describe resulting work as 'Cultural Studies'.

Third recipe. Identify your major grievance. Campaign to get the study of this grievance accepted as a recognized academic subject.

Theorize the resistance to this campaign as part of the larger analysis of the repressive operation of power in society. Set up a unit to study the (mis)representation of gays in the media or the imbrication of literary criticism in colonialist discourse or the prevalence of masculinist assumptions in assessments of career success. Describe resulting work as 'Cultural Studies'.

It may seem that the obvious way to answer the question 'What is "Cultural Studies"?' is to look for a definition of its subject-matter and methods that will distinguish it from other forms of inquiry. But the term is used so variously at present that this approach seems to me doomed to fail. As the above conceit is intended to suggest, we get more illumination by reflecting on the shifting relations among disciplines and on the trajectories of those who have been led to claim the label of 'Cultural Studies' for their very various activities. Although the proponents of 'Cultural Studies' sometimes make large claims about their engagement with the forces at work in contemporary society, and although the label occasionally crops up in self-descriptions by critics and journalists outside academia, the current prominence of the term can best be understood as a function of disciplinary decomposition and re-formation. In its programmatic form, 'Cultural Studies' is part of the noise made by the great academic ice-floes of Literature, Sociology, Anthropology, and so on as their mass shifts and breaks apart.

One ingredient that is common to all three of the above recipes is discontent with what are perceived to be the limitations and obstructiveness of the institutionally well-established academic disciplines. Indeed, it sometimes seems that 'Cultural Studies' needs the idea of powerful and repressive disciplines in the same way that national liberation movements need the idea of an alien oppressor. In neither case is the enemy entirely invented, of course, but the logic of self-promotion and self-justification also has a part to play.

It may be, however, that this self-consciously insurgent identity is in danger of becoming a bit dated. It spoke to the situation of those who wished to extend or dissolve the frontiers of the academic disciplines in which they themselves had been educated. But there is now a whole generation of teachers whose own education was in departments of 'Media and Communication Studies', 'Women's Studies', 'Cultural Studies', and so on. In Britain in the 1970s and 1980s, non-university institutions of higher education initially proved the most receptive to these new developments, and these courses met a market need by offering a more accessible and more applicable form of the training in skills of textual and cultural analysis supposedly fostered by traditional English departments. For similar reasons, 'Cultural Studies' is now an established element in school (and examination board) curricula. None the less, the label still retains a radical edge: most of those who make it part of their self-description regard the demystifying or unmasking of the essentially ideological operation of various forms of (primarily verbal) representation as the core and purpose of what they do, and this no doubt accounts for some of the strong feelings, for and against, aroused by this recent claimant to disciplinary respectability.

Another way to try to understand the confusing variety of things now pursued under the label of 'Cultural Studies' is to tell an historical story about its origins. The present boom in popularity of 'Cultural Studies' is primarily a North American phenomenon, and that has profoundly shaped its concerns and its style. But, like any intellectual endeavour which hankers after institutional respectability, it gives itself a history, even a foundation myth. And in the case of 'Cultural Studies' the roots to which it again and again returns are British. The sacred trinity of founding texts are taken to be Richard Hoggart's *The Uses of Literacy*, Raymond Williams's *Culture and Society*, and E. P. Thompson's *The Making of the English Working Class*, and the Golden Age is traced back to the setting up of the Birmingham Centre for Contemporary Cultural Studies in the early 1960s (see the discussion of Williams and Hoggart in Chapter 11 above). The whiggish genre to which such origin-narratives belong always leaves room for 'precursors', and in the present case this role is now most often assigned to two groups who, in the inter-war period, attempted the serious critical study of various forms of popular culture: the Frankfurt School around Max Horkheimer and Theodor Adorno, and the *Scrutiny* group around F. R. Leavis (a formative influence, as I indicated, on the early work of both Hoggart and Williams). As Leavis's name suggests, the disciplinary roots of the enterprise in Britain were primarily in literary criticism, and the enabling circumstances owed much to the conjunction of the idealism of post-war adult education and the optimism of the early New Left. In retrospect, much of the early impetus to what became 'Cultural Studies' derived from the attempt by writers and teachers from this background to introduce working-class experience into the mainstream of academic concerns.

It would take another essay to explore why the rather few similarities between the three works mentioned in the previous paragraph have come to be emphasized at the expense of the far more telling differences between them, but it is obvious that they grew out of a similar ethos and spoke to a particular historical situation in Britain in the 1950s and early 1960s. It is (or at least it should be) no less obvious that the activities pursued under the label 'Cultural Studies' in universities in the United States in the 1990s address a quite different agenda and bear a very different significance. As one small emblem of the differences, one may recall how Hoggart described the animating inspiration of his work as the attempt 'to apply the skills of the literary critic' to the study of popular culture. That confident, imperial identity now seems worlds away; the contemporary practitioners of 'Cultural Studies' express instead a theoretically informed suspicion of the value of 'textualist strategies'.

The work of both Williams and Thompson has left its mark on a wide range of work in the fields of social and cultural history (that of Hoggart much less so). I would certainly not claim that it has been an entirely desirable mark: it has, for example, surely played a major part in perpetuating a stereotyped picture of British nineteenth-century intellectual history which represents it as divided between, on the one hand, the unfeeling rigidities of atomistic liberalism and political economy, and, on the other, the more generous but also more nostalgic responses of an essentially Romantic cultural criticism (I single this out simply because part of my own work has involved helping to attempt to replace that picture with a more adequate one). Such references to nineteenth-century Britain as one encounters in the literature of 'Cultural Studies' suggest that these stereotypes, which originally served legitimate polemical purposes, are still being allowed to stand in for any more probing or attentive intellectual history. None the less, it cannot be denied that the impulse these early exemplars gave to 'Cultural Studies' as it developed in Britain was in the direction of an inescapable engagement with the concrete details of the experience of earlier generations (as opposed to pious but referentially empty invocations of the category of 'History'). Speaking broadly, that impulse does not seem to have survived into the practice of 'Cultural Studies' in the universities of the contemporary United States, and it is the lack of imaginative sympathy with those who lived and died before us (especially if they lived comfortably) that I find chilling and distancing. The past is 'interrogated' but not listened to. Whatever else might be said against the work of Hoggart, Williams, and, especially, Thompson, it is not this.

Although this trinity of authors is still accorded official hero status, developments in the last three decades have transformed the enterprise almost out of recognition. From the 1960s onwards, successive waves of European theory were selectively assimilated, beginning with Marxism, in both its Gramscian and Althusserian as well as its Frankfurt forms, and going on to include elements of structuralism, psychoanalysis, and post-structuralism. During the 1970s and 1980s, feminism effected major changes in both the scope and the style of 'Cultural Studies'. And the last ten or fifteen years have seen an extraordinary boom in the popularity of the term in the United States, where it has come to seem the most enabling disciplinary label under which to pursue theoretical and practical inquiries into gender and sexuality, race and ethnicity, colonialism and post-colonialism, mass media and popular culture, and much else besides.

In this more than in most academic fields, it has become important to specify whether one is talking about British or American styles of doing 'Cultural Studies', despite the appearance of a common transatlantic conversation. Although it has in many ways left the work of its founding generation far behind, 'Cultural Studies' in Britain still tends to be more historical, more empirical, and perhaps more nostalgic, than is generally true in the United States. The dramatic recent expansion of 'Cultural Studies' in North America has been shaped above all by the marriage between literary theory and what has been called 'the politics of identity', both of which have been comparatively weaker in Britain.

One way to characterize this brief history is to see it as the story of how 'culture' has replaced 'society' as the preferred object of study in a range of academic fields. In the frequently incanted quartet of race, class, gender, and sexual orientation, there is no doubt that class has been the least fashionable in recent years. This is certainly true in the United States, perhaps for some of the same reasons that class has so often been an underexplored topic when

talking about American society. But in Britain, too, it is the preoccupations, often of a directly personal kind, of academics and their
students with the other three topics which have largely determined
the agenda of even the most self-consciously radical forms of
'Cultural Studies' in recent years, despite the fact that all the
evidence suggests that class remains the single most powerful determinant of life-chances. Nor can it be said that the truth of this last
claim has really been challenged by the experience of a period in
which a marked dilution of the traditional cultural styles and
patterns through which class identity was expressed has been
accompanied by a significant increase in economic inequality.

III

In asking 'What is "Cultural Studies"?', it is, I suppose, still possible that the innocent general reader (or any academic in the
humanities who has spent the last few decades on sabbatical on
Mars) may be misled by the term 'cultural'. We are emphatically
not dealing here with the traditional notion of 'culture', which
would now usually be stigmatized in 'Cultural Studies' circles as
'high culture'. Indeed, we are not dealing with 'culture' in the
singular at all, but with that plurality of symbolic systems and
practices that enable different groups to make various kinds of
sense of their lives. This usage clearly owes more to anthropology
than to Arnold, but at the same time it has not altogether disowned
the connotations of value surviving from the older usage, and this
has no doubt contributed to the polemical heat of discussions of
the topic.

Inherent in the traditional notion of culture, and hence an
element in the justification for university studies as well as for
museums, galleries, and concert halls, was the idea that culture
allowed people to have important kinds of experience not available
in their ordinary lives. This was part of why it was exciting—exciting to encounter, say, the architectonic grandeur of *Paradise Lost*
or the insatiable reasoning of Kant's critiques or the heightened
passion of a Verdi opera. On this view, culture was the repository
of what the sifting of time had established as the most fruitful
prompts to a kind of experience that was at once valuable, enjoy-
able, and uncommon. Moreover, it was part of the appeal of

culture, and of the prestige of the 'cultured', that these masterpieces were in many respects distant and difficult. They were in other languages, literally or metaphorically; they were full of allusions to things not now commonly referred to; and to enter and possess them required learning, concentration, discipline. On this view, culture, like the notion of scholarship that it supported, was cumulative, impersonal, and severe.

Where once these characteristics were part of the appeal of this notion of culture, they have now become precisely the failings with which it is commonly reproached. 'Cultural Studies' looks at the alleged remoteness and narrowness of traditional university curricula and says 'Get real.' The ensemble of texts, objects, and activities that had, at least since the first half of the nineteenth century, been picked out by the term 'culture' should rather, it is argued, be seen as the tastes of a dominant class at a particular historical moment. On this view, the traditional notion of 'culture' is the pack of tricks that we let the dead play on us. And, the objection moves a stage further, they are not even 'our' dead; they are other people's dead. On his election, President Clinton promised to form an administration that looked like the American people. In the United States, 'Cultural Studies' sometimes seems like an attempt to do the same for the university syllabus. Many of the American people are not white, the majority are not male, and by definition none of them is European or dead. 'Cultural Studies' is one of the names given to the organized breakout from DWEMsville.

However, it is noticeable, as mentioned above, that 'Cultural Studies' has not altogether abandoned the idea that the study of certain things rather than others might have a fructifying effect on people's lives (aspirations inherited from English department origins may be discernible here). What has obviously changed is the idea that it is not those things which are unfamiliar and difficult which are likely to be most fructifying, but rather those things which recognizably connect with one's present identity. At the same time, this shift of focus has been accompanied by the widespread diffusion of an intellectual idiom (whose pedigree is out of Foucault by literary theory) which is part of what has been termed 'the hermeneutics of suspicion'. Texts are interrogated (a favourite term) to demonstrate how they distort, occlude (another favourite), or in other ways inadvertently reveal the ideological pressure which shaped them. These pressures are in turn taken to be symptomatic of the way in which power operates in society to the systematic disadvantage of certain marginalized or oppressed groups. One effect of these combined developments is that 'Cultural Studies', particularly as practised in the United States, is in constant danger of turning into 'Grievance Studies'.

The move towards studying things that are familiar from, or directly connected to, the lives of teachers and their students has also meant that the subject-matter of 'Cultural Studies' has been drawn almost exclusively from the present and the immediate past. In defining the field of his Birmingham centre as '*contemporary* cultural studies', Hoggart was making a polemical point against the scepticism or stuffiness of his more traditional colleagues. Now, thirty years later, the phrase sounds almost pleonastic, whereas there would be something faintly comic or embarrassing about the idea of, say, 'Carolingian Cultural Studies' (but should there be?). Indeed, one of the most interesting things about the way in which 'Cultural Studies' has grown up as a self-consciously interdisciplinary enterprise is how little nourishment it has taken from, or been offered by, History departments. It may just be that historians are less given to cuckoo-rearing than are literary scholars, but 'Cultural Studies' ' near-exclusive focus on the present has surely tended to underplay the obvious overlap of substantive concerns.

Of course, 'Cultural Studies' is such a diverse and fast-moving field that any general statement about it is vulnerable to counter-examples. Perhaps the nearest there has yet been to an authoritative *summa* is a great door-stopper of a book called *Cultural Studies*, edited by Lawrence Grossberg and others, which issued from an all-star international conference held in Urbana, Illinois. Perhaps, I thought as I first hefted it, this impressive-looking compendium would help resolve some of my confusions and doubts about the field. Or perhaps not.

IV

In the course of the two weeks over which I read (most of) the 780 pages of *Cultural Studies* I also happened to have three experiences which are, alas, still all too typical of academic life in Britain, though I suspect they are now less common in the United States. The first was to sit through a lecture by a prominent political historian about a topic in the history of 'high politics' (the details are best omitted here), a lecture pervaded by an intellectual complacency and cultural narrowness which, though hardly unfamiliar, I found deeply depressing. The audience, largely made up (or so it seemed to my increasingly jaundiced eye) of plumply comfortable and smoothly satisfied late-middle-aged male historians, evidently shared the speaker's unspoken assumption that he was dealing with what 'really mattered'; ideas and cultural activities generally were mentioned only to be dismissed as 'ideological smokescreens'. I came away raging, resolving to write an essay called 'Why I hate political historians'. The second experience involved being a dissenting member of a committee to make a junior appointment in English. After considerable disagreement, a talented woman was passed over in favour of a more conventional young man on the grounds that her work (anonymity requires I withhold details here, too) was 'not really literary'; it later emerged that some members of the committee saw her interest in the connections between the history of ideas and the history of criticism as a Trojan Horse out of which would spring the murderous hordes of 'literary theory'. The third experience was the arrival in the mail of an invitation to contribute to an encyclopaedia of philosophy. What had I ever done to deserve this? The philosopher-editor who wrote to me made some flattering references to work I had published on figures like J. S. Mill and Henry Sidgwick, but as I stared at the list of inappropriate topics I had been asked to write about, I felt again the dismal incapacity of those at the heart of the conventional disciplines to grasp that figures traditionally regarded as their intellectual property might be written about from quite other perspectives.

I realize that dispiriting experiences like these are a frequent occurrence in the turf-conscious world of academic disciplines and departments, but I recount these anecdotes from daily life in university committee-rooms and lecture-halls because, as the practitioners of 'Cultural Studies' would be the first to insist, it is there (though by no means only there) that the politics of disciplinary conflict and development are worked out. And reflecting on this particular conjunction of experiences I thought I ought to make a natural recruit to 'Cultural Studies', especially when one recognizes that the single most important thing to say about the current 'Cultural Studies movement' is that its proponents are trying to escape from something else. As I suggested earlier, the old empires of History, Literature, and Philosophy may be creaking and losing control of some of their more distant territories, but they still possess more than enough professional power to frustrate the aspirations of those diverse groups who would like to inaugurate a new academic world order. Yet although I, too, have squirmed under the condescension and hostility (real or imagined) of those securely placed at the heart of the traditional centres of disciplinary power, I became increasingly certain as I read on that this was not the right displaced persons' camp for me.

The refugee origins of the 'movement' are evident in the quite numbingly compendious way in which the editors of this huge volume attempt to characterize the 'field'. Consider the following vote-catching list of 'the major categories of current work in Cultural Studies': 'the history of cultural studies, gender and sexuality, nationhood and national identity, colonialism and post-colonialism, race and ethnicity, popular culture and its audiences, science and ecology, identity politics, pedagogy, the politics of aesthetics, cultural institutions, the politics of disciplinarity, discourse and textuality, history and global culture in a postmodern age' (after which breathless attempt to encompass the globe the editors warn that 'Cultural Studies' can only be 'partially' identified even by this list, 'since no list can constrain the topics cultural studies may address in the future'). A similar anxiety not to exclude appears in the remarks on 'methodology': 'no methodology can be privileged or even temporarily employed with total security and confidence, yet none can be eliminated out of hand. Textual analysis, semiotics, deconstruction, ethnography, interviews, phonemic analysis, psychoanalysis, rhizomatics, content analysis, survey research—all can provide important insights and knowledge.'

As I suggested earlier, all this seems to indicate that it is a mistake to regard 'Cultural Studies' as a discipline or even a single 'field' of inquiry: it is the name, rather, of a protest movement. Behind the many calls in this volume for new approaches and new programmes echoes a recurring cry of rage and resentment that the contributors' preferred objects of inquiry and methods of study have not traditionally had the institutional power and prestige of longer-established practices which have managed to get themselves recognized as 'disciplines'. In other words, we are dealing here less with a new intellectual development and more with the academic form taken by what has been called 'the politics of recognition'.

For this reason, it can at times seem, especially in the United States, as though one is observing the academic equivalent of the Rainbow Coalition: in this form, 'Cultural Studies' increasingly looks like Affirmative Action carried on by other means.

What unites so many of the contributors here is less a common body of theory or shared corpus of material, and more a suspicion, an idiom, and an anxiety. The suspicion is that most forms of cultural activity are essentially a disguise for the fact that Somebody is Trying to Screw Somebody Else (or, more formally, 'a commitment to examining cultural practices from the point of view of their imbrication with, and within, relations of power'). The idiom is the expression of the suspicion: hardly a page of this fat volume goes by without our being told that somebody who possesses some kind of power (political, economic, or cultural) is trying to 'dominate', 'suppress', 'occlude', 'mystify', 'exploit', 'marginalize' ... someone else, and in response it is the duty of those engaged in 'Cultural Studies' to 'subvert', 'unmask', 'contest', 'de-legitimize', 'intervene', 'struggle against' . . . And the anxiety, so palpable in these pages, is that one may be vulnerable to the charge of having endorsed or colluded with or simply failed to detect the ways in which one's own way of putting things may assist, encourage, or fail to protest against some form or other of 'oppression'. The motto of the movement appears to be *pas d'ennemi à gauche*.

In my view, these characteristics are at the root of one of the chief substantive weaknesses of 'Cultural Studies', as illustrated here and elsewhere: namely, its insensitivity to the rich texture of those cultural strands it regards as 'dominant'. Part of the self-dramatization that appears to be so necessary to those who see themselves as making 'radical interventions' is to represent themselves as going forth to battle against a dragon called, variously, 'the Establishment', 'the dominant culture', 'the centre', 'the elite', 'the metropolis', and so on (the choice of terms reflecting, of course, different theoretical traditions). But these are all unhelpfully objectifying labels. The 'centre' is a night in which all cows are black, virtue exclusively inhabiting peripheries. 'The dominant elite' denominates a featureless landscape of sameness, populated by privileged robots who unreflectively carry on their daily round of perpetuating dominant images, excluding marginal groups, and reproducing exploitative practices. The complexity of a culture can never be adequately depicted using such clumsy instruments.

Proponents of 'Cultural Studies' urge us to be more alert to difference, but they too readily assume that the business of a 'dominant culture'/'hegemonic power'/'ruling elite' or whatever is to suppress difference in an ideological construction which normalizes 'the centre' and demonizes or exoticizes the 'marginal'. This exaggerates both the agency and the singleness of purpose of such groups. Moreover, cultural difference is both more and less pervasive than this: more because these so-called dominant groups or cultures are themselves far from monolithic; less because the different groups and 'discourses' in a culture are never self-contained or purely oppositional, but share concepts and values and engage in constant commerce, often intelligible and profitable commerce, with their cultural neighbours, including the most powerful ones.

There is always a danger that successful freedom-fighters will end up imposing a more grimly coercive regime than that of the slab-faced old men in dark suits whom they have overthrown. Certainly, I should be sorry if the study of literary and intellectual history were to be given over entirely to the kind of work represented in this volume. For one thing, too many of the contributors automatically stigmatize an interest in the writings of the most articulate and influential intellectuals of a society as 'elitist'. And for another, there is a disabling deference to the idea of 'theory' which does not seem to me necessarily to lead those who write in its idiolect to any greater subtlety or richness of perception. The coercive power of the deference is illustrated by the nervousness which hedges even Stuart Hall's attempts at self-clarification: 'I'm extremely anxious that you should not decode what I'm saying as anti-theoretical discourse'. There is something paralysing in having to be constantly looking over one's shoulder lest any tough-minded criticism or detailed individual study be fatally branded as 'anti-theoretical discourse'.

So, although I am interested in the history of culture in general and in the history of ideas of culture in particular, and although I am almost a professional intellectual refugee, I do not feel at home in the company of the theory-toting 'Cultural Studies' militia. Perhaps unsurprisingly, I found Carolyn Steedman's 'Culture, Cultural Studies, and the Historians' the most congenial piece in the whole collection. This no doubt has something to do with her presentation of herself as a historian, peering with somewhat quizzical goodwill at the excitable throng around her, and also something to do with her very welcome wryness and self-irony. But above all I warm to her modestly expressed reservations about the practical consequences of the doctrine of 'the connectedness of everything'. Those dauntingly inclusive lists I quoted earlier suggest to me that the proponents of 'Cultural Studies' are for the most part unwilling to accept the responsibility for making *exclusions*. (The 'discussions' which follow each contribution are an almost comical parody of the 'I didn't mean to exclude/I should have mentioned/You are quite right to remind me . . .' form of conference-speak.) At present, anyone who can claim refugee status is allowed in with no questions asked. But until hard choices are made about some connections being more persuasive and interesting than others, and until the aggressive programmatic manifestos are matched by illuminating and thickly textured particular studies, it seems prudent to suspend judgement on the likely long-term fruitfulness of the approaches recommended here. Agnosticism is not the same as 'lacking all conviction', but Yeats's lines should remind us that when 'things fall apart' there may be something to be said for a response other than that of 'passionate intensity'.

V

Thus far, I have mainly been discussing 'Cultural Studies' as an academic enterprise, which in the United States it overwhelmingly is. But shifting the focus back to Britain has the merit of also returning me to my starting-point about that fraught borderland populated by representatives of both the academic and the non-academic worlds. For while the subject no doubt needs to have its journals and its conferences like any other academic specialism, it can never be, or want to be, entirely confined to these relatively cloistered settings. 'Cultural Studies' in Britain also needs a toney kind of street cred as it engages with the full range of contemporary popular culture, from film to football, from rock to retro, from sabbing to snorting. Accordingly, its exponents are as likely to be found in radical film-makers' collectives or at round tables at the ICA or in the features section of the *Guardian* as in the lecture-hall or the classroom.

No figure better represents this hybrid world, and probably no figure is held in higher regard within it, than Stuart Hall. Hall's trajectory has given him an iconic but distinctively individual status. He came to Britain from his native Jamaica in 1951, having excelled in the classic public-school-aping education offered to the sons of a small fraction of the middle class of colonized peoples throughout the empire. This meant that he came not to take up a menial job in the labour-hungry post-war economy, but to become a student at Oxford—the institution he later recalled as 'the hub, the motor, that creates Englishness'. On graduating three years later, he deferred the expected return to an oppositional political career in the West Indies, and instead stayed in Oxford to do a thesis on the decidedly metropolitan subject of the novels of Henry James.

By the late 1950s, he was already a leading figure on the young intellectual Left: he was one of the founding editors of *Universities and Left Review*, and then of its successor, the *New Left Review*. By then Hall was school-teaching in South London, but a decisive turn in his career came when Richard Hoggart set up the Centre for Contemporary Cultural Studies at Birmingham. Hall became its deputy director (in 1964), and later, after Hoggart's departure to UNESCO, its director, where he stayed until 1979 when he moved to become Professor of Sociology at the Open University.

The Birmingham centre was, as I remarked above, the Bethlehem stable from which the later world-wide movement of 'Cultural Studies' traces its origins, and in the late 1960s and 1970s Hall was very much its animating figure. 'Gramsci meets Coronation Street' might be one flip description of CCCS's preoccupations in its early years, and certainly Hall has played an influential part in domesticating the notion of 'hegemony' as a tool for critical social analysis. As this suggests, his frame of reference was broadly Marxist, but he was attempting in various ways to replace the 'base/superstructure' model of explanation with an emphasis on the semi-autonomous ideological power of 'culture' in the broad sense.

He gave this form of social analysis a more immediate political relevance in the early and mid-1980s as he sought to characterize the phenomenon of 'Thatcherism' as something more significant and more insidious than the personal style of one particularly forceful and dogmatic politician. But increasingly (belatedly, say one or two of his severer critics) the issues of race and ethnicity have been pushing their way to the forefront of Hall's concerns, and his recent writing exemplifies in new ways his characteristic mixture of engagement with a specific political conjuncture, alertness to new cultural and intellectual trends, and determination to furnish theorist and activist alike with a more adequate conceptual grid than that offered by the old war-cries of the Left and the new marketing pap of the Right (or is it now the other way round?).

One source of Hall's success has been the skill with which he has negotiated the ineliminable tension between the exigencies of systematic theorizing and the aspiration to help non-specialist readers make better sense of their lives. One of the notable features of his self-assessment in this respect is his recognition of the locatedness and particularity of the role he has played. While claiming a certain outsiderness—'I'm not and never will be "English" '—he rejects any fashionably postmodern 'nomadic' identity: 'cultural identity is not fixed, it's always hybrid; [but] it comes out of a very specific historical formation, out of very specific histories . . . it's not just anything'. Some of Hall's work is now read and translated around the world, but, partly prompted by his own autobiographical reflections, it seems most illuminating to see it in relation to particular features of the political and intellectual culture of radical circles in Britain, and more especially London, in the years between the rise of the New Left and the fall of Clause Four. Seeking to characterize his role, two of his admirers recently declared: 'For us, Hall's major intellectual contribution does not lie in making definitive statements on theoretical and political issues, but rather in his involvement with a wide range of collective projects, and in his capacity and willingness to take on new issues and to constantly move on, beyond his own previous limits.' An attractive modesty can be read into that way of putting it that contrasts sharply with some of the position-statements I quote earlier from the *Cultural Studies* volume, and Hall's current activities, including helping to set up and edit a new radical magazine, suggest that Hall—the thoroughbred hybrid, the rooted cosmopolite, the globalist next door—is still on the move.

But many of those who would follow him lack the requisite lightness of foot. In reading recent examples of work in 'Cultural Studies', it is noticeable how often one encounters that Lefter-than-thou note which seems almost a ritualized requirement in this literature. 'A democratic common culture', concludes Andrew Milner's *Cultural Theory* (books on 'Cultural Studies' often conclude like

this), 'cannot be made from within the intellectual class itself, but
only from within those exploited and oppressed classes and groups
the cultural lives of which have proved, by turn, the objects of realist neglect, modernist disdain, and postmodernist pastiche.'
However sympathetic one may be to the convictions which surface
here, one cannot help feeling that this sort of declaration makes
much of what is done in the name of 'Cultural Studies' seem more
than ever a kind of displacement activity. If this (or some even more
explicitly political version) really *is* the goal, there is the old, but
still pertinent, question of whether writing books about cultural
theory is the most useful thing to be doing. In asking this I am far
from denying the mutually enabling connections between reflection
and activity, and I intend no distancing sneer at anyone who really
does care what happens outside the walls—quite the contrary. But
the most that books of this kind can do is to help those, including
students at any level, who are minded to think about these things
to do so more clearly. This, when really pulled off, is no small
contribution. We delude ourselves, and patronize the really
'exploited and oppressed', by pretending that we are doing more
than this.

'Cultural Studies', for the reasons touched on earlier, has inherited the dual burdens of academic subject and social therapy. Once
upon a time, English promised to appease both gods, and once
upon another time so did Sociology, the new trade's two step-
parents. The history of those two disciplines suggests that while a
refusal of arid academicism animated some of the most interesting
work done in their names, a too insistent parading of uplift was
intellectually stultifying. Moreover, no discipline has a monopoly
on serious human concern. What Fred Inglis calls 'the moral imagination' is in fact at work in all humanities subjects done at their
best. But the route from such intellectual work to changes in the
world is neither short nor direct, and we betray our own disciplined understanding if we pretend it is. So let us not hurry to close
down the old departments of History, Literature, Philosophy, and
so on. However 'culture' is defined, it is too important to be left
entirely to the proponents of 'Cultural Studies'.

14

Company Histories: CamU PLC and SocAnth Ltd.

I

If you are reading this sentence, it's very likely that you are a graduate of an institution of higher education. If you had been reading such a sentence in such a book fifty years ago, it's most likely that you would not have been a graduate. There has been a huge expansion of higher education across the developed world in the past half-century, not least in Britain. In 1939 there were approximately 50,000 university students in this country; 98 per cent of the population did not go to university. By the year 2000 there will be somewhere near one million students, at which point a little over one-third of the age cohort will be entering higher education. This transformation affects many aspects of British society and culture, some of which I have already referred to (and I return to its significance in another context in Chapter 16 below). One of the less-remarked consequences is that understanding what goes on within universities has already assumed and will surely continue to assume a greater cultural significance than ever before, and that in turn will entail a greater need for non-specialists to be able to obtain some grasp on the historical development of those activities.

However, both universities and their constituent disciplines have

Christopher N. L. Brooke, *A History of the University of Cambridge*, vol. iv: *1870–1990* (Cambridge University Press, 1993).

George W. Stocking, *After Tylor: British Social Anthropology 1888–1951* (The Athlone Press, 1996).

a strong tendency to be inward-looking, and this is reflected in the kinds of historical accounts usually written about them. In this essay, I want to suggest some of the ways in which such histories could be encouraged to take a wider perspective, to situate themselves within a broader social and intellectual history, and to make their goings-on more intelligible to outsiders. I take the histories of one university and one discipline as my examples. Both Cambridge University and 'British social anthropology' are seen as what the competition-conscious idiom of the day calls 'success stories': in the course of the twentieth century, the first has become a major world university—currently rated 'the best university in Britain' by various meretricious rating systems—while the second was for long regarded as one of Britain's surest bets to win the academic equivalent of an Olympic gold medal (though its disciplinary confidence has taken some hard knocks in recent years). But what factors have determined this success, if 'success' it be, and what follows about how their histories should be written?

II

Company histories are, inevitably, chronicles of growth. In 1992 CamU PLC, the rowing-to-radio-astronomy group, had a turnover of £190 million; production had risen again, to 3,500 graduates a year; and it had just taken the revolutionary step of appointing its first full-time Chief Executive (for the sake of continuity, a cherished value within the company, he is still called 'Vice-Chancellor'). Nationally, the company has maintained a secure market niche: name recognition scores are high, and analysts employed at the broking firm of HEFCE have again awarded it the top credit rating. Internationally, it is continuing to expand: it had customers in 104 countries last year, and its European counterparts in particular continue to regard it as a model of low-waste, high-quality production. None the less, the Chairman's annual report to shareholders struck a note of caution: the Government holds much the largest stake (£62 million in 1992), and is showing signs of wanting to use its financial muscle to redirect the company's focus.

All this represents a dramatic change of fortune since the mid-nineteenth century. 'Cambridge University' was then the name of a federation of seventeen small private corporations which provided agreeable hotels for the sons of the landed classes, whilst offering to those from less prosperous, but still largely genteel, backgrounds an appropriate preparation for a career in the Church. Leaving aside the three largest colleges (Trinity, St John's, and King's), the average size of the Fellowships of these institutions in 1870 was 12, and many, in some cases the majority, of the Fellows would not have been involved in any serious educational work. Their two chief preoccupations were likely to have been the size of the dividend and the occurrence of vacancies in college livings. Indeed, the Cambridge of the first half of the nineteenth century cannot be understood without an indulgent imaginative grasp on the concept of the sinecure.

The story of how this federation of conservative, inward-looking, and for the most part intellectually undistinguished colleges evolved into the media-attracting multiversity of today is a remarkable one, but it is not easy to see how it should best be told. This is partly because the task of encompassing the different dimensions of the story seems likely to be beyond the reach of a single historian: who could deal adequately with topics as disparate as college finances and religious sensibility, with details of academic administration and the broad sweep of social change, with developments in the study of Sanskrit as well as in theoretical physics, and so on? But, beyond this, the task is daunting because historians of education have alerted us to the variety of relations between universities and their parent societies, and once one looks beyond merely endogenous forces of change (never very powerful agents in Cambridge's case), one is faced with having to assess the relative impact of several of the major strands of modern social, cultural, and economic history.

Oxford's response to this challenge has taken the form of a large-scale collective enterprise: nine big volumes, with numerous specialist contributors to each, based on detailed original research. On the basis of the volumes that have appeared so far, it is clear that the Oxford history will constitute an impressive scholarly achievement which historians of all kinds, not just historians of universities, will find a valuable resource. The volume on the twentieth century, for example, which runs to almost 900 pages, including 32 maps and figures and 55 tables, is the work of twenty-four authoritative scholars. Cambridge has opted (at least for the present) for four briefer single-author volumes. Christopher

Brooke, the General Editor of the project, has nobly assigned himself the most difficult task, that of covering the period from 1870 to 1990. Professor Brooke's engagingly written survey contains a great deal of interesting information, but it cannot really be seen as a contribution to scholarly research at the same level as its Oxford counterpart (one cannot, for example, imagine a chapter of it holding its own in a learned journal). Brooke is presumably aiming at something which one would actually read all the way through, rather than consult or pillage; and the level of anecdote about eccentric or striking personalities suggests that he hopes to interest a more general audience (and, as with so many of Cambridge's activities, a pretty well-heeled audience, to judge by the price).

A medieval ecclesiastical historian by trade, Professor Brooke has here to apply his skills to unfamiliar material. The sources for twentieth-century history are disconcertingly abundant and not for the most part technically difficult to decipher; but the complexity of the forces at work in a modern industrial society makes it teasingly difficult to assess relative causal weights in explaining institutional change. Perhaps one reason why Brooke has not been more daunted by his translation to this sea of troubles is that he writes not only as a professional historian, but also as a lover, placing this colourful bouquet at the feet of a mistress who has clearly meant much to him. For this is emphatically insider's history. It is so not just in the sense of being written by somebody who is deeply familiar with the arcane mysteries of college life and who has a sure touch with the peculiar argot of the place. Brooke is also an insider in a more unusual way: he is a Professor of History and Fellow of Caius whose father was a Professor of History and Fellow of Caius before him. He grew up only a couple of rugby pitches away from the colleges in which so much of his story is set; many of the footnotes refer to what the *DNB* would call 'personal knowledge'.

Brooke writes best about what he loves most: religion bulks disproportionately large in these pages, and although with so much to cover it may seem self-indulgent to devote whole chapters to individual theologians and church historians, the portraits of figures like C. H. Dodd or Dom David Knowles are deft and unfailingly sympathetic. Similarly, the few pages on Maitland sing, and mention of the name of Caius College—mentioned amazingly often, as it turns out—always quickens the prose (the diary of

Maisie Anderson, daughter of the Master of Caius in the 1920s, provides some particularly charming touches). In other words, the strengths of this history derive from its inwardness with what it describes.

It would be only a little unkind to say that its limitations derive from the same source, but the modern historian is bound to hanker after rather more analysis of the larger social, economic, and political forces that have brought about the changes Brooke so lovingly chronicles. Taking a more distant view, two developments in particular look to have done most to shape Cambridge's destiny in this period. We now tend to take them for granted, but neither was inevitable. The first is the way in which the university became, and has in some ways remained, a finishing school for the sons (and latterly the daughters) of the social and professional elite, and the second is how it became a centre of international scholarly and, above all, scientific research. (Arguably, these two functions are still today somewhat awkwardly married within the one institution.) Although Brooke does not emphasize developments of this kind, his book provides much fascinating information which is germane to their analysis.

III

Taking the long view, certain key episodes in the making of modern Cambridge stand out. The first is the period of 'reform' in the 1860s and 1870s, when external pressures were deftly translated into deliberate internal efforts at change. The forces at work here were essentially cultural and political. The newly professionalizing Victorian intelligentsia were scandalized by the unjustified privilege and Establishment bigotry of the ancient universities, and an ad hoc alliance of radicals, Dissenters, and agnostics strove to drag them out of the long eighteenth century and turn them into properly 'national' institutions. The Royal Commissions of the 1850s and 1870s wielded real power, and the reformers within Cambridge (figures such as Henry Sidgwick and Henry Jackson) benefited from the awareness that if Cambridge did not take steps to put its own house in order, an altogether less congenial reorganization might be imposed from without. This all has an eerie familiarity for the contemporary academic, who may warm to the sentiments of Dr Corrie, diehard Master of Jesus throughout the great reforming period, who told the Royal Commission of 1877 that 'the present chief want of the University is exemption from the disturbing power of Royal or Parliamentary Commissioners'—but then it was also Corrie who memorably observed of the proposal to run trains to Cambridge on Sundays that 'it is equally displeasing to God and to myself'.

This extended spasm of reform was followed by a long period of expanding student numbers up to 1914, the golden age of the college teaching ideal. It would seem, although Brooke does not really comment on this, that this process was largely demand-driven: student numbers went up much faster than the numbers of college fellows (the financial constraints of the agricultural depression would have discouraged expansion of the fellowship in the first part of this period). It is also significant that the proportion of these students who came from the public schools increased faster than the overall expansion. In the late nineteenth century, parents in the gentry, professional, and cultivated business classes increasingly saw a sojourn at Oxford or Cambridge as an invaluable step towards one of those careers which would guarantee gentlemanly status in life, not the least of which was imperial administration. For many, especially those from already prosperous families, the consequent connections and social cachet were more important than any particular intellectual training. As late as 1914, at least a third of the undergraduates either took no degree or took the undemanding 'Pass' degree, which is to say that they were licensed to spend more time riding or rowing than reading or writing. (It is a salutary reminder of the colleges' complicity with this class that as late as the 1950s 10 per cent of the male undergraduates were still 'Pass men'.) In any event, by the opening decades of this century, Cambridge and Oxford had become central to national life in a way that they had not been even fifty years earlier.

But the very success of the college ideal in this period created new worries or new forms of old worries. In particular, the college tutor's devotion to the pastoral and pedagogic care of his pupils was seen by many inside and outside the university, uneasily aware of the achievements of German laboratories and American graduate schools, as a barrier to the pursuit of scholarship and research. There was also the criticism that it had become much harder for boys from poorer background to get into Cambridge, and that scholarship funds which had been established for this purpose were in fact being used to subsidize the comfortably-off. These and other problems were to be addressed by a further Royal Commission, under the fitful chairmanship of the ageing Asquith, which reported in 1922 (Brooke has a good account here of the important part played by Sir Hugh Anderson, Master of Caius and chief university fixer). The report initiated the second great episode of change, codified by the new statutes of 1926. This introduced essentially the present arrangement of Faculties, of the two-part Tripos, and the beginnings of the modern academic career pattern, including a retiring-age and pensions. But the most consequential of its changes was the establishment of university, as opposed to college, lectureships as the standard teaching appointment. The Commissioners assumed that university lecturers would normally also hold fellowships, but that faculty-based posts made for a more rational organization of teaching effort and would enable the lecturer to spend some time pursuing research rather than having to eke out an exiguous college income with extra teaching and other work.

This has proved a more consequential change than the Commissioners could have foreseen, and it has institutionalized a marked difference from Oxford. In Oxford throughout the nineteenth century, the College Tutor had had a more continuous and important teaching role than his Cambridge counterpart. Following the mid-nineteenth-century reforms, the association of Tutors became the real power in Oxford, strong enough, as Arthur Engel showed in his *From Clergyman to Don*, to see off any challenge to their power by the professors representing the claims of research. The Oxford tutors also proved strong enough to resist some of the proposals of the 1922 Commission, leading to the present arrangement whereby the standard Oxford post is a Tutorial Fellowship which, though jointly funded by the university and the college, in effect makes the college identity primary. Brooke, a college man at heart despite his professorial eminence, clearly prefers the Oxford system, and deplores the divide which the 1926 reforms opened up in Cambridge between university lecturers and those college fellows without university posts. But it is arguable that the patterns of both teaching and research benefit when a department or faculty is able to define the scope of new appointments in terms of the needs of the discipline, and as research ratings assume an ever more consequential place in determining a university's future, the relatively greater flexibility of the Cambridge posts may prove an added boon.

In any event, as government funding to the universities increased in the wake of the establishment of the University Grants Committee in 1919, the Cambridge system gave the university rather than the colleges the real say in determining expenditure and the pattern of growth. But perhaps the most striking unforeseen effect was that by the 1950s 50 per cent of these new university appointments were without college fellowships, and steps had to be taken to heal this breach, including the foundation in the 1960s of the graduate colleges, of which Brooke gives a good account.

It was the expansion of numbers, and above all of government funding, in the decades after 1945, the third key episode, that finally killed the Victorian university. This is the kind of unannounced, cumulative change that can have a more transforming effect than even the most dramatic policy decisions but which is hard to catch in the net of historical narrative. Moreover, it is important to remember that change takes place at an irregular pace. In many ways, the Cambridge of the 1880s more closely resembled the Cambridge of the 1940s than of the 1840s, but the growth of the last forty years has effected a yet more dramatic transformation, even without the intervention of Royal Commissions. The numbers of both students and 'staff' (always a tricky concept to apply to Oxbridge) roughly doubled between 1939 and 1969. In the same period, the UGC grant to Cambridge increased from £120,000 to £7 million. Within the framework established in 1926, this flow of funds increasingly strengthened the hand of the university against the colleges. But the most powerful agent of change has surely been the growth of research in the sciences since 1945, and especially since 1970. This has generated a financial requirement, a managerial structure, and a career pattern which could not easily be contained in the old collegiate system. If the emblematic buildings of pre-reform Cambridge were the college chapels, and if the symbols of the role it acquired in the late nineteenth century were the boathouses and cricket pavilions, then the monuments of the modern university are the science labs.

Brooke has least to say about the most recent decades (he may feel out of sympathy with many of the changes of these years, and he certainly treats the student unrest of 1968–9 as an entirely catastrophic watershed). In the late nineteenth century, student numbers expanded much faster than did the number of teachers, whereas in the last two decades, the opposite has been true: between 1970 and 1990 undergraduate numbers increased by 23 per cent, but academic staff numbers increased by 63 per cent (with the responsibilities of many of the new posts heavily weighted towards research rather than teaching). And it is particularly important to grasp how the preponderance of the sciences within this expanded system has grown in recent years (although this is not something Brooke discusses). One small but revealing indicator is the increase in the number of professors paid wholly from university funds (i.e. excluding others on 'soft money', which would further increase the numbers on the science side). Following the university's own pragmatic grouping of the disciplines, the totals for 1963 were 50 professors in the 'Arts' and 45 in the 'Sciences'; 30 years later the numbers were 74 in the 'Arts' and 133 in the 'Sciences', and the disparity has increased even further in recent years (an increasing dependence on external fund-raising will presumably only sharpen this contrast). Moreover, it should be recognized as a general law that wherever the drive to institute new procedures or arrangements in universities comes from the pressure to make them more 'accountable' (that is, analysable by accountants), then the resulting institutional arrangements will more closely correspond to the patterns of work in the sciences than in the humanities. The disproportion between the sums involved is simply too great for this not to happen.

There are also other, related, ways in which Cambridge is moving further in the direction of becoming a centralized university concentrating upon advanced scientific research. In 1993 a fifth school was established to stand alongside the existing schools in Humanities, Social Sciences, Physical Sciences, and Biological Sciences: it is called the School of Technology, and is dominated by the huge Engineering Department in union with expanding Computer and Management Studies programmes. (Dr Corrie, thou shouldst be living at this hour!) In 1995 engineering became a four- rather than a three-year course, further increasing its weight in the university; there are now three times as many university posts in Engineering as in English. At the same time, further steps have been taken to replace the old democratic 'republic of teachers' with a new slimmed-down 'line-management' structure. And in 1991 the university appointed its first ever pro-vice-chancellor: his remit was 'research' in the university and he was head of the Cavendish physics laboratory.

These changes have been accompanied by the 'proletarianization' of the academic profession in Britain, as recently documented in A. H. Halsey's *The Decline of Donnish Dominion*. Brooke seems oddly reluctant to acknowledge the facts of decline in both the economic and social position of academics. Reflecting on the detailed accounts kept by his parents in the inter-war period, he concludes that 'the first lesson such an account book teaches us is that there is no answer to the question, were the dons of the 1930s better or worse off' than their successors. But if the question is phrased a little more precisely, there are some pretty clear pointers. Brooke mentions various modern household amenities his parents did not enjoy, and contrasts these with other 'expenses which they took for granted [that] have not been within my grasp at all', and despairs of a meaningful comparison. But surely we need first of all to distinguish the *general* rise in living standards since the 1920s: the gains for nearly all social classes in comfort, security, diet, freedom from some sorts of drudgery and so on are beyond dispute, and the academic of the 1990s shares this general prosperity. But the *relative* position of academics has seen a significant decline which can be clearly measured. The familiar comparisons with higher salaries in the financial and commercial world make the point in one way, and it is tellingly emphasized by Halsey's calculation that in 1929 academic salaries were 3.7 times greater than average earnings in manufacturing industries whereas in 1989 they were only 1.5 times greater.

Establishing this relative decline, which of course involves matters other than salaries (public esteem above all), helps to bring out one of the constants of Cambridge history during the period covered by this volume: namely, that the undergraduate body has generally been drawn from a higher social class than its teachers. The average social background of both groups has fallen since the late nineteenth century, but Cambridge still functions as, among other things, a long coming-out party for some of the more exam-adept among the children of the professional and upper middle classes of, predominantly, South-East England (including London). And this is a reminder of how it has also maintained its intimate links with the governing elites. One of the things which will seem to the historians of a hundred years hence most to need explaining is how it was that even through the cost-cutting, privilege-stripping 1980s, the state continued in effect to subsidize the existence of colleges, a few of which are seriously rich in their own right, through a system of college fees which some regard as peculiarly indulgent (and others defend as essential to the maintenance of quality in a collegiate university). Not the least of the services now rendered to the university by its increasingly subordinate colleges may be to create networks of sentiment and loyalty among the political class that help secure more favourable treatment than ever the faculties' primary intellectual activities could do.

Still, nothing is immutable, even in Cambridge. We have become used to new colleges being founded and we take for granted they will prosper, but we also need to remember that they can fail: the fate of Cavendish College, which went bankrupt in 1892 after only fifteen years, is an appropriate reminder of what can happen to free enterprise in a competitive market during recessionary times. Perhaps more shocking to current sensibilities is the fact that the Commissioners of the 1870s were empowered to suppress or amalgamate colleges, and, as Brooke reminds us more than once, a plan was floated to combine Christ's and Emmanuel into one college. Were the Department for Employment and Education to propose this idea now, the Great and the Good would probably be tripping over each other in the correspondence columns of *The Times* trying to stave off the end of civilization as we know it. Familiarity with the university's history should remind us how it can survive what at the time appeared to be life-threatening changes. The story Professor Brooke has to tell is essentially one of adaptation, albeit often sluggish and unwilling, and of change-disguised-as-continuity. It thus gives us some reason to hope that the volume covering the history of Cambridge in the twenty-first century will not have to be written by the equivalent of Macaulay's New Zealander, meditating on the transience of grandeur as she contemplates the ruins of a once-proud university.

IV

Within universities, collegiate or otherwise, the chief locus of intellectual labour remains 'the discipline'. Academic subjects tell themselves various stories of how, through the heroic labours of the intellectual titans of the past, this respected status was finally 'achieved', but the accounts are often strikingly parochial and only partly intelligible to outsiders. Here are two versions of a relatively familiar story of how a methodological 'revolution' in an expanding but previously diffuse intellectual enterprise led to its finally establishing disciplinary identity and professional autonomy.

The first version begins with the arrival of a young Pole to study at the LSE before the First World War. Pursuing his own researches in relative isolation, he rebels against the inherited Victorian story of evolutionary progress, and instead, in works of great technical virtuosity, cuts synchronic rather than diachronic slices through the workings of his chosen micro-society, producing detailed accounts of the functioning of a 'system', an approach which is then imitated by an aggressive band of disciples. In this way, the naturalized Pole becomes the father of a quintessentially English academic style.

In the second version, the 'revolution' is brought about by the innovative work of several figures, with 1922 as the retrospectively significant symbolic date. Again, the shift involves displacing the eclectic and promiscuous inclusiveness of their Edwardian predecessors with the rigorously close analysis of a relatively restricted body of material. A small group of graduate students and young researchers, conscious of their 'outsider' status, gather round an acknowledged leader of charismatic power and legendary difficulty, and after 1945 this generation moves into a position of intellectual hegemony within an expanding discipline marked by fierce doctrinal and personal disputes.

Those who are familiar with the history of anthropology in twentieth-century Britain may be forgiven for thinking that these are easily recognizable versions of the decisive episodes in the establishment of that discipline. In the first, they will see Malinowski's displacement of grand evolutionary and diffusionist narratives with functionalist analysis based on detailed participant-observer fieldwork, while in the second the credit for the inter-war 'revolution in anthropology' is shared with Radcliffe-Brown and his students, and is seen to issue in the concentration on patterns of kinship and social structure that became the distinguishing feature of 'British social anthropology'. (The crucial monographs by both Malinowski and Radcliffe-Brown were published in 1922: respectively *Argonauts of the Western Pacific* and *The Andaman Islanders*.)

Seen in this way, both these episodes form part of a history that is usually told in markedly internalist and self-contained terms, and while all disciplinary communities have a tendency to understand their past as an endogenous development, anthropologists have perhaps been exceptionally prone to feel that their enterprise has developed in relative isolation from the general intellectual culture around it. The complete unfamiliarity of outsiders with the types of societies anthropologists have traditionally studied; the *Blutbrüderschaft* effect of having endured the solitary rigours of fieldwork; the small size of most university anthropology departments, perched uneasily between the big battalions of the 'Arts' and the 'Sciences'—for these and other reasons, practising anthropologists in Britain have frequently exhibited a strong *esprit de corps* allied to a sense of at least partial removal from the cultural and political debates in their own society, and histories of the subject, usually written by anthropologists, have tended to reinforce this self-sufficiency.

My two versions of episodes in disciplinary formation could, however, provoke some chastening reflection upon such narrowly internalist narratives, for the first is in fact one possible account of Sir Lewis Namier's impact on the profession of political history, replacing large-scale narratives of steady constitutional progress with the minute exploration of 'the structure of politics' at a particular moment (discussed in Chapter 3 above), while the second is an often-repeated description of the 'Cambridge revolution in literary criticism', inaugurated (following the appearance of Eliot's *The Waste Land* in 1922) by the work of I. A. Richards and William Empson, and vigorously embodied by F. R. Leavis and the *Scrutiny* group. The point of the device is not, of course, to suggest some common Polish quality to both Malinowski's and Namier's innovations, nor to propose detailed parallels between participant-observer fieldwork and 'practical criticism' (though the fact that several prominent post-war anthropologists began by studying English under Leavis could be made the starting-point for an interesting analysis of the historically changing forms taken by the urge to intellectual rigour and cultural significance).

The point of this conceit is, rather, to suggest, first, that a broader intellectual history could situate developments within anthropology as part of a much more general shift of focus and perspective in early twentieth-century British culture, and, secondly, that the establishment of anthropology could be seen as conforming to a common pattern of the dynamic of intellectual change within a given institutional framework. The broadest context would be provided by the long-drawn-out disintegration of the evolutionary and historicist paradigm that had furnished the guiding assumptions for so many intellectual enterprises in Victorian and Edwardian culture. Assumptions of socio-cultural evolution provided a common frame for topics as subsequently distant as the origins of religion or the nature of the human mind, while the canons of Germanic historicism governed scholarly practices across the study of the classics, of philology, of literature, of jurisprudence, and so on. The rejection of this common framework was, in different ways, a founding moment for the modern form of disciplines like philosophy, literary criticism, and anthropology.

The history of anthropology also exhibits some of the features common to the attempt to insinuate new and not wholly respectable subjects into the small and conservative world of British academic culture in the first half of the twentieth century. Such subjects were, for example, bound to have a complex relationship, at once antagonistic and deferential, to Oxford and Cambridge as the commanding heights of the academic economy. The relevant intellectual innovation often took place outside those snobbish and unadventurous institutions, but they none the less retained unrivalled capacity to confer the status of full scholarly respectability on both disciplines and individuals. Self-described 'outsiders' often expended a lot of energy trying to become insiders, as the different but comparably embittered careers of Namier and Leavis illustrate.

V

George Stocking's *After Tylor* does not dwell upon such general issues, but its dense and thickly textured account of the interplay of ideas, personalities, and institutions will provide abundant material for such comparative studies. Over the past three decades, Stocking has imposed himself as the dominant scholarly presence in the history of British social anthropology, with a rich stream of essays, articles, and edited volumes; *After Tylor* is explicitly intended as a sequel to his major monograph on *Victorian Anthropology* which appeared in 1987. Neither book has been prematurely rushed into print: Stocking confesses that 'the bulk of the primary research' for this volume was accomplished between 1969 and 1973. In other ways, too, the book is clearly the product of what the Victorians liked to term 'ripe scholarship': a painstaking attention to detail, an avoidance of glib judgement, and a remarkable command of the theories and disputes that animated British anthropologists in the period stretching from the peak of Tylor's authority in the 1880s to the dominance of Radcliffe-Brown and his pupils in the 1940s. Along the way, the reader will encounter some names which presumably still stir a flicker of recognition among non-specialists—William Robertson Smith, Sir James Frazer, A. C. Haddon, W. H. R. Rivers—but many more who stand in need of Stocking's meticulous and sympathetic historical recreation—Lorimer Fison, R. H. Codrington, W. Baldwin Spencer, R. R. Marett, A. M. Hocart, and several others.

At the beginning of the period covered by this book, 'anthropology' still indicated one category of inquiries which a cultivated gentleman with a taste for theorizing about the exotic and the remote might be drawn to pursue. Many a Casaubon was led to study the primitive peoples in pursuit of a pet idea about the origins of totem-worship or the evolution of language or the development of human cranial capacity, or one of the many other topics that were a legitimate part of the world of late Victorian learning. As a consequence, several of the figures who appear in the early pages of Stocking's book might have equal claim to a place in histories of classical scholarship or of comparative anatomy or some other discipline.

Perhaps none of them seems to have been quite so incidentally an anthropologist as the aesthete and essayist Andrew Lang. Lang was one of the those Victorian men of letters who seem to have been lifelong participants in some kind of non-stop writathon. What Lang did, Stocking observes wonderingly, was to produce books, whether 'alone, in collaboration, or by translation: biography, children's books, criticism, essays, fairy-tales, fiction, folk-lore, histories, parodies, poetry, renditions of and commentaries on Greek classics—until the total in the British Museum catalogue came to over 350'. His work habits account for much, of course:

he once composed a lengthy review during a short rail journey in the course of which he had engaged in continuous animated conversation, 'depositing the finished product in the post upon detraining'. And yet Stocking brings out that Lang was not a negligible contributor to what was for a while the hot issue of *fin de siècle* anthropology, the animist origins of religion.

This is also the period of 'armchair anthropology', before fieldwork became the defining rite of passage for the aspiring anthropologist, though not everyone took quite such a rigorous line on this as the Oxford Classic, R. R. Marett, whose 'fieldwork was limited to five hours with some pygmies in London . . . and an afternoon watching Aboriginal dances when the British Association met in Australia in 1914'. But already by 1927 the diffusionist Elliot Smith was professing himself unable to understand why 'the sole method of studying mankind is to sit on a Melanesian island for a couple of years and listen to the gossip of the villagers'. However, Stocking's is not one of those whiggish narratives in which a series of bumbling and confused 'forerunners' finally gives way to 'serious' practitioners of the new discipline, and the assumptions governing the work and careers of Marett, Elliot Smith, and their colleagues are treated with historical sympathy and respect.

The incidental detail in Stocking's account also brings out how the institutional respectability of anthropological work was initially dependent on its association with other activities of acknowledged standing and utility. Three such activities were particularly important: first, the curating of collections of archaeological and ethnographic material; second, the study of the origin and development of religion, including, eventually, Christianity; and third, the presumed benefit to future colonial administrators of some exposure to the study of the language and customs of native peoples. The majority of those who figure in this history of 'British social anthropology' never held established academic posts in the subject: Robertson Smith was Reader in Arabic at Cambridge (and University Librarian); A. C. Haddon was Professor of Zoology at the Royal College of Science in Dublin for much of his working life, providing unpaid teaching in anthropology at Cambridge; Sir James Frazer obtained the Trinity Fellowship he held for the rest of his life with a dissertation on Plato; Elliot Smith was a Professor of Anatomy; W. H. R. Rivers was a medically trained psychologist who dabbled in psychoanalysis; A. M. Hocart was Archaeological

Commissioner for Ceylon; Marett was an Oxford 'Greats' Tutor and eventually Rector of Exeter College; and so on. Although it was true that a special Readership had been set up for Tylor at Oxford, there was no established teaching programme for him to contribute to, and he was institutionally more important as Keeper of the University Museum. Even by 1945 there was only a handful of teaching posts in the subject in British universities.

Stocking's book also throws light on the question of the attraction of anthropology to 'outsiders'. There are two aspects to this question: the prominence of scholars from overseas in the history of anthropology in Britain, and the unconventional or marginal social position of many of those who were British by birth. Stocking observes with his customary gravity: 'From the time that anthropology first began to be systematically studied at British universities, it seems to have attracted students from beyond the British Isles.' Malinowski himself put it more pithily, wishing his seminar could attract someone 'not a Jew, Dago, Pole or any of these exotic products', someone who might become the 'future mainstay of British anthropology'. Even those of Malinowski's pupils who did successfully establish themselves in academic life in Britain were usually foreigners by origin, beginning with Raymond Firth, a New Zealander, and Meyer Fortes, a South African Jew. Alfred Reginald Brown embodied a differently oblique relation to the English social establishment of the day: of modest social origins, an alumnus of the Commercial Travellers' School, Pinner, he entered Cambridge at the late age of 21 after a year at Birmingham University, and only when he was 45 did he incorporate his mother's maiden name by deed poll and become A. R. Radcliffe-Brown. Audrey Richards and Lucy Mair, though socially well-connected, experienced exclusion of a different kind on account of their sex: Stocking recounts, without further comment, the appalling fact that when the Cambridge chair became vacant in 1950 Audrey Richards was 'discouraged from applying because the Disney Professor of Archaeology was a woman, and having two women in the same field was felt to be impossible'. Evans-Pritchard (Winchester and Exeter), son of an Anglican clergyman, had the most conventional social background, but Stocking thinks it may not be irrelevant that as a student, 'touched perhaps by the contemporary Romantic aura of T. E. Lawrence, he went to Oxford parties wearing an Arab

burnoose', though that might seem to be setting the qualifications
for 'outsiderness' a bit low.

VI

In his celebrated anatomizing of the defects of the national culture
in 1968, Perry Anderson claimed that the notion of 'totality',
which had given rise in other countries to Marxism and classical
sociological theory, had in Britain only manifested itself in
'displaced' form, finding its home in, surprisingly, literary criticism
and social anthropology. Cogent reservations have since been
expressed about almost every aspect of this brilliant, sweeping
hypothesis, not least by Anderson himself, but one thought that
suggests itself in the light of the much more detailed histories of
these disciplines that we now possess is how unequal was the position in the national culture in the middle of the century of
Anderson's two putative intellectual homes for the notion of
systematic critique. Literary criticism was at the very heart of the
culture and its controversies, and the study of English became one
of the largest and most flourishing subjects in post-war universities.
But anthropology remained a small-scale enterprise (many universities did not have anthropology departments; some still do not),
increasingly admired and respected, but oddly sequestered from the
wider intellectual life, a situation that was perhaps only partly
modified by the beginnings of the appeal of structuralism from the
early 1960s onwards.

It might also seem to have been an implication of Anderson's
account that those who were developing sophisticated analyses of
the general functioning of social institutions would from time to
time be tempted to deploy their expertise in debates about aspects
of their own society. But on the whole, the founding generations of
professional anthropologists seem to have shunned such public
engagement to a much greater extent than was true of their peers
among historians, political theorists, economists, or, indeed, literary critics.

The one notable exception to this pattern of reticence among the
early professors of the subject was Malinowski, who continued to
aspire to reach a broad non-specialist public. While in the
Trobriands in 1918, he dreamed of propagating a 'New

Humanism', which would acknowledge the place of instinct and desire in human society, and during the inter-war years he was in demand as a speaker on popular platforms about the subject of 'sexual reform', being bracketed with other perceived 'evangelists of sex' such as Havelock Ellis and Bertrand Russell. As usual, such activities did not meet with the approval of austerer colleagues: his one-time mentor at LSE, Charles Seligman, reproached him for his 'semi-popular propaganda work' written 'in the manner of the more strident kind of journalist'. But for Malinowski, such activities were not simply optional extras: he believed that the functional method revealed deep truths about the working of the human personality under different conditions. Without using the phrase, he continued in different terms to maintain Tylor's belief in anthropology as 'a reformer's science'.

Radcliffe-Brown, however, had a drier temperament and a mind that seems to have been naturally drawn to questions of method, classification, and system. He was also willing to devote considerable energy to the mundane tasks involved in building up academic departments, first at Cape Town in the early 1920s, followed by Sydney, and then from 1931 at Chicago. In 1937, when Oxford finally decided to convert the post that had been held by Tylor and Marett into an established chair, the 56-year-old Radcliffe-Brown assumed his institutional inheritance. Oxford was to be the power-base from which the science of social structure could be developed as the defining core of the discipline of 'social anthropology' (a narrower enterprise than that previously suggested by 'anthropology' *tout court*). The Heroic Age was over. Writing in 1951, a not uncritical American observer granted to what he saw as the 'school of Radcliffe-Brown' 'an average level of ethnographic competence and theoretical suggestiveness probably unequalled by any comparable group elsewhere in the world'.

Thereafter, the story becomes the familiar one of institutional growth and professorial succession. In 1944 Firth succeeded to Malinowski's chair at the LSE, in 1946 Evans-Pritchard followed Radcliffe-Brown at Oxford, while in 1949 Max Gluckman became professor at Manchester and in 1950 Fortes took up the chair at Cambridge. An obvious symbol of this newly professionalized world was the founding in 1946 of the Association of Social Anthropologists of Great Britain; membership, which was by invitation only, was confined to academic teachers of the subject. The implicit contrast was with the old Royal Anthropological Institute, which, in the manner of the Victorian learned society it still partly was, hospitably welcomed amateur and professional alike, and housed a motley collection of 'general anthropologists', including archaeologists, physical anthropologists, ethnologists, and so on. It is part of *After Tylor*'s achievement to make this development seem intelligible but not inevitable, and in the course of recounting the rise of this ostensibly narrower conception of the subject to a position of institutional dominance, it also helps us to see the discipline's past as part of a broader, and ultimately more interesting, social and intellectual history.

15

With Friends like These: John Carey and Noel Annan

I

England has a proud tradition of anti-intellectualism. It has deep roots, wide support, and enough sense on its side to make it an enemy to be taken seriously. Intellectual snobbery, pretentiousness, and sheer fraudulence deserve what they get, and the activity of taking these things down a peg or two (as the preferred idiom has it) is not without its merits. But 'enemy' it surely is for anyone who seriously wishes to see disinterested intellectual inquiry and unfettered aesthetic invention flourish in an unpromising climate. And what I find particularly enraging and depressing is the anti-intellectualism of the intellectual. The life of the mind meets enough indifference and downright hostility in England without some of its leading representatives joining in the sneering. I don't, needless to say (at least I *hope* it doesn't need saying), think that the doings of intellectuals should be beyond criticism, but that criticism in turn needs to be subject to critical scrutiny, and, if it doesn't pass the test, the encouragement it gives to forces that are already quite powerful enough makes it all the more culpable.

This essay is an unashamed polemic against *le trahison des clercs* that seems to me to disfigure two widely noticed books published

John Carey, *The Intellectuals and the Masses: Pride and Prejudice among the Literary Intelligentsia 1880–1939* (Faber, 1992).

Noel Annan, *Our Age: Portrait of a Generation* (Weidenfeld and Nicolson, 1990).

in recent years by two such leading cultural figures. Both John
Carey and Noel Annan are, without question, gifted and complex
individuals about whom more could be said, a great deal of it positive. But they have each written books which, in their different
ways, seem to me to exhibit related forms of betrayal. Carey's *The
Intellectuals and the Masses* is an exercise in Plainmanspeak, a
sweeping sub-Orwellian indictment of 'literary intellectuals';
Annan's *Our Age* is a more substantial as well as a more interesting book, but one which ultimately encourages a kind of adminis-
trative philistinism in attitudes towards higher education. My
discussion of them is written more in anger than in sorrow, but
stirred in each case by the thought that with friends like these ...

II

The noun 'intellectual' has two main senses in contemporary
English. In the first, and broadest, sense it picks out a socio-profes-
sional category within a comprehensive classification of occupations: in this sense, all writers, teachers, artists, and such like are
described as 'intellectuals'. The second sense concentrates on the
exercise of some kind of cultural authority or leadership. Here, it is
not enough simply to be employed in one of the above professions:
to be considered an 'intellectual', the individual must also be recognized as having acquired a certain cultural standing which is taken
to license and provide opportunities for addressing a wider public
on matters of common concern.

In both these senses, John Carey is an intellectual. He is Merton
Professor of English at Oxford, author of critical studies of Donne,
Dickens, and Thackeray. In other words, he is supported by public
funds to pursue a particular branch of learning. At the same time,
he is a well-known literary journalist, having been the chief book-
reviewer of the *Sunday Times* for the past twenty years, and in this
capacity he has offered instruction to his fellow-citizens on a wide
range of subjects, including the poor quality of election manifestos,
the naturalness of the nuclear family, and the right way to grow
parsnips.

To judge from his journalism (a selection of which was
published under the title *Original Copy* in 1987), Professor Carey
is a man of catholic and cultivated dislikes. He particularly dislikes

(other) intellectuals. Unfortunately, he does not use this term with the care it requires, but roughly he seems to have in mind any (other) highly educated person who succeeds in obtaining attention for general views about the nature of human existence, especially views (which Carey seems partly to share but hates to hear other people expressing) about the value of culture and the life of the mind. If one were to exercise on Carey's use of the term 'intellectual' the attentiveness to its verbal surroundings that he has himself exercised so fruitfully in the case of Dickens's imagery, I suspect one would find a cluster of qualities hovering in constant attendance: (other) intellectuals are pretentious, self-important, snobbish, inhumane, cut off from the necessities and decencies of 'ordinary' life.

More than most forms of writing, the essay (including the review-essay) depends for its success on communicating a strong sense of the author's voice and personality. This authorial persona is particularly strongly marked in Carey's case, and gives one a sense of knowing a lot about him. We know that wherever he lives, it is not in an ivory tower; however tall he is, his head is not in the clouds; whatever position he adopts, his feet are firmly on the ground; and whatever his taste in underwear, his knickers are decidedly not in a twist. There are no flies on him, no wool is pulled over his eyes, and no one ever takes him for a ride. He insistently (perhaps a bit too insistently) represents himself as, in words he has used of a writer he admires, 'a champion of ordinary existence against the whimsies of the over-educated'. He drinks Middlebrau, and doesn't reach parts everyone else can't reach.

His book *The Intellectuals and the Masses: Pride and Prejudice among the Literary Intelligentsia 1880–1939* is best seen as a piece of plain-mannish whistle-blowing on the giant cover-up that is twentieth-century literary culture. It argues (or at least asserts) that 'modernist literature and art can be seen as a hostile reaction to the unprecedentedly large reading public created by late nineteenth-century educational reforms', and, more polemically, that 'the purpose [*sic*] of modernist writing . . . was to exclude these newly educated (or "semi-educated") readers, and so to preserve the intellectual's seclusion from the "mass" '. The first four chapters assemble a large patchwork of quotations from a wide range of writers (not all of them British, not all of them obviously Modernist) on such themes as contempt for the masses, disdain of suburbia, and yearning for the rule of a 'natural aristocracy'. The remaining five chapters are 'case-studies', essays on the articulation of these themes by Gissing, Wells, and Wyndham Lewis, the repudiation of them by Arnold Bennett (the acknowledged 'hero' of the book), and their culmination in the 'intellectual programme' of Adolf Hitler.

Carey presumably does not think that the responses to mass culture which he indicts were shared by *all* writers, or even all Modernist writers, active during this period, but he does not attempt to define the scope of his case. Though its opening sentence declares that it is about 'the English literary intelligentsia', the book mentions or quotes from a wide cast of characters from T. W. Adorno to P. G. Wodehouse; its 'case-study' chapters apart, the names which occur most frequently are Eliot, Forster, Greene, Huxley, Joyce, Lawrence, Nietzsche, Ortega y Gasset, Orwell, Shaw, Waugh, Woolf, and Yeats. Carey does not suggest that this motley crew had something in common that distinguished them from their contemporaries during the sixty years in question other than their having committed to print some quotable and usually pretty unappealing remarks on their fellow human beings taken en masse and on the related phenomena of suburbia, popular newspapers, and tinned food. Still, the suggestion, conveyed with varying degrees of explicitness throughout the book, is that we should see the spirit of these remarks as characteristic of intellectuals in this period, perhaps of twentieth-century intellectuals generally.

It is, however, the discussion of Hitler that reveals the animus and excesses of the book most clearly. Its premiss is that Hitler was in many ways a typical European intellectual of the period, from which debatable starting-point Carey seems to think that two inferences should be drawn: first, that we should accord less respect for the views of other intellectuals on art and culture when we discover that they were shared by Hitler; and, second, that convictions about the valuelessness or disposability of whole sections of the population, which excite universal condemnation when associated with Hitler's name, ought to attract similar obloquy when found (admittedly in rather tamer form) in the writings of some of the most revered names of twentieth-century European culture.

The following sentences indicate the ways in which Carey tries to insinuate these connections. Hitler's 'own inclinations were undeviatingly highbrow'. 'Like other intellectuals, Hitler becomes rather muddled over his advocacy of individualism.' '[Hitler's] contempt for the vulgar materialism of America was, of course, shared by many European intellectuals, from Gissing to the Leavises and beyond.' 'Hitler also believed just as firmly as, say, T. S. Eliot or Wyndham Lewis in the permanence of aesthetic values.' 'Like Lewis, Steiner and many other intellectuals, Hitler believes that it is the presence of a divine spark that makes art great.' (Bracketing Hitler and George Steiner together in this way is characteristic of Carey's cheap shock tactics, though it perhaps marks a new low even for his deliberate offensiveness.) The conclusion which Carey wishes us to draw from all this is that 'the Holocaust may be seen as the ultimate indictment of the idea of the mass and its acceptance by twentieth-century intellectuals'. Thus, Virginia Woolf's tart remarks about shop girls or Eliot's sneers about typists are part of that disdain by intellectuals for ordinary people which reached its culmination in the death camps.

The breathtaking tendentiousness of this claim has presumably helped to draw attention to the book, but in other respects its laboured provocativeness falls a bit flat. It is, after all, hardly news that some early twentieth-century writers were alarmed and repelled by what they took to be the spread of 'mass culture'. It can only be because Carey thinks that this fact somehow discredits 'literary intellectuals' more generally that he can present it as a damning case with wide import (his Postscript tars contemporary literary theory with the same brush). His self-flattering sense that he is 'exposing' something is surely quite misplaced.

Similarly, Virginia Woolf's social snobbery or T. S. Eliot's studied aversions or Wyndham Lewis's appalling behaviour have hardly been secrets which some self-protective academic establishment has conspired to suppress lest they damage the standing of works of literature now taken to be constitutive of twentieth-century literary culture. Carey's tone, at once prickly and triumphant, assumes the existence of an 'official line' that he (and perhaps he alone) has seen through. In reading this book, one has a frequent sense of being backed up against a corner of the saloon bar by an obsessive monologuist who repeats, with finger-jabbing insistence, that he could tell you a thing or two about some of these famous writers.

On closer inspection, it would appear that Carey's righteousness is stirred more by manifestations of social snobbery than by anything that is intrinsic to the activity of being an intellectual. It is noticeable that many of the remarks that most excite his ire are either from the would-be upper-class Oxford aesthetes of the inter-war period or from Bloomsbury. In both cases, it is a patronizing, class-bound manner that Carey can't stand. In 1977 he wrote an amusingly savage review of a book on the former group, beginning: 'This book is richly stocked with people whom any person of decent instincts will find loathsome.' In it (the review is reprinted in *Original Copy*), he quoted an anecdote about Brian Howard responding to a policeman's request for his name and address with the words: 'I am Brian Howard and I live in Mayfair. No doubt you come from some dreary suburb.' Carey repeats the anecdote in his new book to illustrate intellectuals' use of 'suburban' as a term of disparagement, but I suspect that most readers will feel that it is Howard's social affectations (and Carey's entirely reasonable contempt for them) that is at issue here, and not something distinctive of intellectuals.

The frequent references to Bloomsbury betray a similar preoccupation with English class attitudes rather than with the characteristics of intellectuals as such. For example, in his energetic defence of Arnold Bennett against Woolf's reproaches in her classic essay 'Mr Bennett and Mrs Brown', Carey notes Woolf's reference to the manners of 'one's cook' and observes: 'This allusion to the servant problem is quite in keeping with the social tone of her piece, and of Bloomsbury and modernism as a whole.' More revealingly still, in his implausibly sweeping indictment of intellectuals' attitudes towards children, Carey declares: 'The intellectual code regards fondness for children as suburban and middle class.' Clearly, what Carey cannot abide are not really 'intellectuals', if the term is to be used in any reasonably rigorous way, but the kinds of affected or obtusely superior individuals who can condescendingly dismiss common human emotions as 'middle class'.

This observation may in turn help us to locate Carey's literary persona historically. His preferred voice is above all reminiscent of 'Movement' writers of the 1950s like Kingsley Amis and John Wain, not least because it is shaped by antagonism to some of the same social targets. (This also, I suspect, helps to account for his complex and ambivalent relation to Orwell, who cast a long shadow over Movement prose.) Carey is still in some ways fighting the old 1950s battle against the perceived legacy in British culture of a sinister alliance between High Modernism and High Society, but he tries to give it a more general form. The result is that the sympathy he attracts by his humane and unpretentious regard for the individuality of 'ordinary people' he then more than forfeits by his irritable and undiscriminating hostility to 'intellectuals'.

III

The Intellectuals and the Masses does not venture any explanations for the pattern of responses among intellectuals it claims to have identified, beyond the unsleeping pressure exercised by the qualities alluded to in its (typically donnish) subtitle: intellectuals (other intellectuals, that is) are exceptionally vain animals who construct elaborate theories and works of art in order to protect their own misplaced sense of superiority. Nor does it exhibit much sense of the ways in which the eddies and swirls of intellectual history produce and reproduce patterns of ideas which appear similar, but whose meanings are subtly altered in each new setting. At times, Carey tends to treat both books and theories simply as collections of discrete 'views', with no more organic relation to each other than a pile of bricks: this makes it easier to point to the presence of the same 'view' in writings by different authors, but one is left wanting to know more about how these ostensibly similar elements functioned in individual works (sometimes in different genres) in particular historical situations.

Moreover, for an established literary scholar Carey can be surprisingly insensitive to the literary properties of his sources. For the most part, his use of works of fiction in this book consists in quoting from those characters who appear to be favourably treated, and suggesting that this provides unambiguous evidence of their authors' 'opinions'. Thus, in the course of a paragraph intended to demonstrate H. G. Wells's low estimate of the nature of women, he quotes an observation by Masterman, a character in *Kipps*, that there is not a single woman 'who wouldn't lick the boots of a Jew or marry a nigger, rather than live decently on a hundred a year'. Carey then goes on: 'These were not precisely Wells's sentiments, but he seems to have shared Masterman's exasperation.' 'Not precisely' is culpable here: it suggests that these were *pretty much* Wells's sentiments, though on no stronger ground than that he wrote the novel in which a character says these words.

Carey frequently appears so eager to find damning quotations from canonical figures that he does not always seem to allow that there might be an element of irony or authorial distance involved. For example, he cites several hostile references by twentieth-century writers to tinned food as the epitome of 'mass' life, concluding with Orwell's comparison between the damaging effects of tinned food and of the First World War: 'We may find in the long run that tinned food is a deadlier weapon than the machine gun.' But if Carey wants to do more than observe that tinned food was referred to by several writers—if, that is, he wants us to see a pattern of sinister condescension or alarmism in these references— he might do well to indicate how close Orwell's tongue was to his cheek in writing that sentence, and indeed to invite us to ponder the role of ironic hyperbole more generally.

The larger point is that we clearly need a more precisely tuned sense of tone, as well as greater interpretative charity, than Carey displays in these cases if we are not to draw unwarranted conclusions about an author's 'views' from isolated quotations which the whole context of his writing gives us some reason for believing should not be taken quite so literally. Consider, for example, this passage: 'The degeneracy of the pampered masses, propped half-conscious before their telly screens, becomes, as you toil on your lonely plot, a profoundly satisfying subject of meditation.' Or again, this: 'Isn't it time we realized that, given our bulging populations, vegetables have now become more desirable inhabitants of the earth than people: less destructive, more peaceful, more service-able, for sustaining life? The day I see a row of houses being pulled down to make a vegetable plot, I shall feel that something sane and healthy has happened.' It may be that we *should* see these remarks as further illustrations of Carey's themes about the intellectual's disdain for the 'masses' and the consequent tendency to endorse utterly inhumane proposals. But in that case I imagine he would be the first to protest, since they are both taken from one of his own essays reprinted in *Original Copy*.

We might, finally, wonder why a man of Carey's acknowledged talents should have written such a poor book. It may be that those talents, though they have been winningly displayed in writing stud-ies of individual authors or in editing Renaissance texts or in writing regular book-reviews for the broadsheets, are not best adapted to sustaining a potentially complex argument across an interpretation of a long period of European cultural history. I suspect, however, that what has really gone wrong with this book is that Carey's desire *épater les intellectuels* has warped his judgement. He is so eager to make some moral mud stick to some of the great names of modern literature, so keen to show that the Emperor not only had no new clothes but had some pretty nasty habits as well, that the requisite grasp of the interplay of intellectual traditions and individual situation, and the corresponding sensitivity to tone and nuance, have been overridden by that kind of forensic brutality that does more to undermine one's confidence in the advocate than to persuade one of the merits of his case.

The Intellectuals and the Masses is, then, an unworthy example of the skills of the literary critic and an irreparably shoddy piece of cultural history. Instead, it is a knocking job, executed by an acknowledged master of that limited and disagreeable trade. Professor Carey appears to regard himself as bravely swimming against the prevailing tide, but in fact his reedy waspishness can hardly be heard above the swelling volume of philistinism that has sounded through the past decade or more. Anti-intellectualism has always been available on tap in the saloon bar, of course, but it is sad to find a Professor of English who is so desperately keen to buy his round.

IV

A new Royal Commission, indeed the Mother of All Commissions, has recently reported. Its report might well have been called '*The Great and the Good': How Great? How Good?* In fact, its title is *Our Age: Portrait of a Generation.* Its author, the chairman of all chairmen, is Noel Gilroy Annan, Baron Annan. As that catalogue entry rightly suggests, there are two Annans, and this important, unusual, provocative, depressing book cannot properly be understood without recourse to the Theory of the Two Annans: like Humpty Dumpty, he early in life fell off the fence on which he was sitting, and thereafter all the good causes and all the Kingsmen could not put Annan together again.

'Noel Annan' is a greatly gifted intellectual historian who has never really fulfilled his early promise. His first book, *Leslie Stephen: His Thought and Character in Relation to his Time* (1951;

reissued in 1984 in a greatly expanded and revised version as *Leslie Stephen: The Godless Victorian*), was an imaginative and subtle reconstruction of a sensibility and a milieu. In the early 1950s he also published an essay on 'The Intellectual Aristocracy' which must by now have broken all Citation Index records for an historical article. But in the next three decades his only substantial publication was a study of the first headmaster of his old school, *Roxburgh of Stowe* (1965). Along the way, he has been a frequent contributor to periodicals such as the *Times Literary Supplement* and the *New York Review of Books*, always writing with flair and sometimes with brilliance and courage.

'Lord Annan' is a well-known public figure. He has spent the greater part of his life running things. In 1956 he was elected (when only 39) Provost of King's College Cambridge, from where he moved to be Provost of University College London and subsequently the first full-time Vice-Chancellor of the University of London. He has been a member or, frequently, chairman of a large number of the committees of the great and the good over the last three decades, including Chairman of the Trustees of the National Gallery, Chairman of the Royal Commission on the future of broadcasting, a Director of the Royal Opera House, Covent Garden, and of course a member since 1965 of the Top Persons' club, the House of Lords.

Our Age, the book which these two figures have written together, is hard to classify, and all the better for that. It is partly their joint intellectual autobiography, from the heady days of aesthetic and political excitement at school and university before the Second World War to a world whose symbols are the long agenda papers and the always unstained blotters of the serious committee meeting. It is partly a collective biography of their friends and contemporaries: the Index contains literally hundreds of names between Sir Harold Acton and Sir Solly Zuckerman (more or less everybody mentioned in this book seems, curiously enough, to have a title). It is partly an intellectual history of Britain (or at least of a segment of the metropolitan educated class) in the period from the end of the First World War to the present. And it is partly an argument, or, more accurately, a polemic: the authors assert that their generation, reacting against the constricting manners and philistine prejudices which dominated upper-class England of the early twentieth century, were responsible for an immense liberalization and expansion of horizons, but that in their devotion to the pursuit of individual development and cultural excellence they neglected economic realities and were thus in large part responsible for Britain's 'decline'.

There is much to admire, and still more to enjoy, in this long book. The manner is dashing rather than merely vigorous, high-spirited rather than coercively jovial; it commands an enviable range of registers, from bar-room knockabout to high indignatory; it is serious but not earnest about sex and love; and it quotes a lot of quite good jokes. (John Sparrow appears in or behind several of the jokes, as in his prophecy that a proposed reform in Oxford would mean women Fellows of All Souls 'before you could say Joan Robinson'.)

The book is also a courageous rebuke to contemporary academic specialism, sailing to the four corners of modern intellectual endeavour, now rehearsing the arguments against Keynesian economics, now adjudicating between Utilitarian and Kantian moral philosophers, writing as confidently on the literary criticism of F. R Leavis as on the political theory of Michael Oakeshott. The ambitious intellectual historian has to be in some sense a polymath, though it may have been a problem for Lord Annan that he never really seemed to have the patience to become a specialist in the first place. (One could cite here the reply Tony Crosland made to the young Tony Benn who announced that as a Labour MP he needed to lose the stigma of being an intellectual: 'You'd better acquire the stigma before worrying about losing it.') What may seem on some occasions like enviable light-footedness can, however, ultimately have the effect of raising doubts in the reader's mind, doubts to which I shall return.

As a memoir of the tastes and sensibilities of a circle of friends, or as an anecdotal confession of faith, *Our Age* is a fetching, at times touching, performance. The Annans' zest for gossip and apparent memory for *bons mots* keep the narrative fruity and unstuffy—cherished values in themselves, we learn—and their reflective sense of what animated their generation of *intellectuels de salon* is embodied in the style itself, elegantly discursive and racily post-prandial, better than in the brisk, not to say schematic, summaries of the ideas and theories leading members of Our Age are associated with. Without labouring the point—such sweaty effortfulness is left to the Leonard Basts of this world—the Annans

nicely characterize the inseparability of wit and liberalism in their
circle as well as their genuine tolerance and curiosity and their spir-
ited refusal of that 'undeveloped heart' Forster saw as the curse of
the typical Englishman. Forster is a frequent reference-point in the
first half of the book (the part which seems largely to have been
drafted by 'Noel Annan'), and *Our Age* makes better sense than I
have come across elsewhere of the high esteem in which Forster
was held a generation or more ago. As it turns out, King's appears
to provide most of the major reference-points of modern British
intellectual history (but then, to paraphrase someone who was
contemporary with if not part of Our Age, it would, wouldn't it?).

As an historical sketch of the chief intellectual developments
within British culture of the last fifty years, the book is certainly not
marred by lack of range or confidence. But here 'Lord Annan' is
already beginning to make his weighty presence felt. For one thing,
he constantly injects the cadence of yet another kind of chairman,
the Chairman of Examiners. *The Nation Sits the Tripos* is another
might-have-been title, and this ever-assured chairman has no hesita-
tion in handing out Alphas and Gammas over a wide range of disciplines. In economics, for example, Sir John Hicks gets a starred first
('the outstanding theoretical economist of Our Age'), while Sir
Richard Stone and James Meade only get Nobel Prizes (and Lord
Kaldor 'should have won another'). A certain college always does
well in this Tripos—in fact 'the palm for originality' should really
have gone to Lord Kahn—and although Piero Sraffa somehow got
lost going down Trinity Street, the thing to remember is that he first
sketched his really important contribution in 'the dissertation which
won him his Fellowship at King's'. In other disciplines, Lord Young
(Michael not David) gets a starred first as 'the most original and
influential sociologist of Our Age', as does Sir Edmund Leach, 'the
most original anthropologist of Our Age' (and, it so happens,
Annan's successor as Provost of King's). Among Leftish historians,
solid firsts go to Sir Moses Finley and Christopher Hill, 'two of the
best historians of Our Age', but leading the list is 'the most impressive of all the marxist historians', Eric Hobsbawm ('my contemporary at King's', oddly enough). This obsession with ranking has
disfigured private discussion of individuals in England for too long,
but in Lord Annan it has clearly become an uncontrollable tic, and
hardly a name appears in these pages without its accompanying
global degree result (Carmen Calil was 'one of the most original

publishers', Richard Wollheim was 'the subtlest and most subversive philosopher' of Our Age, and so on).

As all this suggests, we get summary judgements of the work these people have achieved, rather than any extended analysis of it. Unavoidably, there is an unsettling sense of superficiality: the reports seem to have been written by someone who arrived at the seminar late and then did most of the talking himself. Perhaps references are a bit of a bore—more sweaty Bastliness—and other scholars mostly dull swots, but the many subjects about which the Annans write with such assurance have, after all, been debated in detail by large numbers of learned and surely not altogether unintelligent persons. Sometimes, 'Noel Annan' seems to have absorbed or drawn upon some of this writing with profit; at other times 'Lord Annan' booms on, handing out plaudits and reproaches with headmasterly finality. The startling simplification of complex ideas begins to shake the confidence of even the best-disposed reader. John Rawls's intricately balanced theory of justice is reduced to the claim that 'the freedom to exchange goods had to be limited to the point where the least advantaged were given most'. (Well that, as Bertie Wooster would say, was the gist.) Similarly the intellectual history gets a touch breathless here and there: 'Anthropology was not the only discipline affected by structuralism. In 1958 Yves Bonnefoy noticed the difference between literary studies in France and in England.' It is hard to say quite who is being most patronized by a passage like that; it may well be the reader. A shakiness over details further erodes the reader's trust. For example, Jim Prior's Employment Bill is misdated to 1975, and we are authoritatively, but wrongly, told that 'there are no posts in the history of ideas in British universities' (Sussex may be a long way from King's, but it's not far from Charleston or Tilton ...). To complain about the complete absence of references or other indication of sources could be a damning indication of over-professionalized Bastliness when discussing a memoir, but as one's doubts about the reliability of the book's historical statements begin to mount, this absence comes to seem at the very least a matter for regret.

V

It may be significant that these failings are much more noticeable in the second half of the book. The first half, which takes us from

the formative experience of rebellion against public-school hearti-
ness up to admirably large-minded discussions of the related topics
of homosexuality and the 'Cambridge spies', is on the whole a very
successful blend of autobiography and intellectual history.
However, as we enter the period when Our Age started to run
things, 'Lord Annan's' chairmanly briskness increasingly supplants
'Noel Annan's' nuanced historical characterizations. As we glide
into the corridors of power, the level of anecdotage rises (Roy
Jenkins 'once said to me that he would have liked . . .'; Lord
Robbins 'once told me how . . .'; and so on), though even when
faced with this much larger number of candidates the Chairman of
Examiners is still indefatigably classing away—Lord Eccles was
'the best minister of education since the war', indeed 'the ablest'
member of the Tory Cabinets of the fifties and sixties; no post-war
chancellor was the 'equal' of Roy Jenkins, 'not even Rab Butler',
and so on. This could be nothing more reprehensible than the
allowable self-satisfaction of one who has himself stepped onto the
stage at Prize-Giving Day more than most, except that by this point
the book has taken a serious turn for the worse as its polemical
purpose becomes more prominent.

The opening chapter in the last part of the book is entitled 'Was
Our Age Responsible for Britain's Decline?' Lord Annan shows
himself guilty of weak chairmanship from the start here, first by
allowing such factitious journalistic clichés to determine the
agenda, and then by letting Corelli Barnett get away with a series
of tendentious allegations. In these pages, 'Britain's decline' is the
tired columnist's tag that distracts attention from an immensely
complex set of issues to do with the changing shape of world politics, the balance of military power, secular changes in the British
economy and social structure, comparative economic performance,
the impact of welfare policies, and so on. But Lord Annan is not
going to put up with that sort of typically donnish cavilling from
lower down the table: were we responsible for it or weren't we?

Sometimes, the question appears to reduce itself to that of
whether 'we' might not have paid more attention to stimulating the
conditions for growth in manufacturing industry. At other times, it
expands to encompass the global self-doubt of whether Our Age
was 'to blame for choosing the wrong goals in life'. But as the
restatements of the question multiply, it becomes clear that a larger
cultural experience is in play here. The young Noel Annan was all

for cocking a snook at his elders, but by the time the really serious snook-cocking got under way in the 1960s, Lord Annan was well into his chairmanly phase and a little thrown by some of the new forms of 'permissiveness'. The aggressive flexing of trade union muscle in the 1970s found him almost purple-faced. There were 'communists, Trots, and anarchists' among the unions, and union behaviour 'destroyed social democracy for a decade and the political assumptions of Our Age'. (One cannot help wondering whether those assumptions were both so narrow and so fragile as to be so easily 'destroyed'.) By the end of the 1970s he clearly felt that things had all gone a bit far.

He was not alone in this view. It seems to have been quite widely shared by accountants in Finchley and small businessmen in Chingford, and, like them, Lord Annan was ready to admire anyone who had the power and the will to do something about it. The terms in which he praises Margaret Thatcher—'this remarkable woman, far less hollow than her predecessors'—suggests someone who is excited by the smack of a firm governess. It is true that he acknowledges that even she failed to change as much as had at one point seemed likely, but it is not altogether clear at the end of the book whether Lord Annan sees in this failure a welcome sign of the deep roots of certain established habits and decent attitudes or fresh evidence of an obtuse immobilism that would consign the country to yet further 'decline'.

Throughout the later stage of the proceedings, the tendentiousness increasingly evident in the chairman's directions reveals the way in which Lord Annan understands the place of education and intellectual activity in British society. Here is a vice-chancellor saying that dons needed to be told (not consulted or persuaded: told) that 'the top priority was now to train the workforce' (is that ever the 'top' priority for a university?). But he doesn't expect 'the dons' to listen: Charles Carter at the University of Lancaster, widely remembered for his insensitive management, was 'one of the few Vice-Chancellors with imagination about the future (and therefore regarded by right-minded professors as a dangerous man)'. Lord Annan even allows himself to endorse that most shop-soiled cliché of the resentful hack when he refers to 'dons in their ivory towers'. Similarly, Sir Peter Hall is not described as offering reasoned protest against cuts in the budgets of the national theatre companies; rather he 'mouthed abuse'. Those who concerned themselves with the question of aid to underdeveloped countries are patronized as 'another lobby among the intelligentsia'. The response of those who were dissatisfied with the official defence of the decision to sink the *Belgrano* during the Falklands War is said to reveal 'how fanatical some of Margaret Thatcher's opponents could be' (whereas her decision to ban union membership at GCHQ Cheltenham is described simply as 'maladroit').

The health of that national culture this book professes to be so concerned with is damaged by the easy sneers and slack writing evident in these examples. The blurb tells us that 'Lord Annan's career reflects a lifelong dedication to education and the arts', but with dedication like this who needs hostility? The root of the trouble, I suspect, is that somewhere along the way Lord Annan has lost touch with that constitutive experience of the intellectual life, the sustained, disciplined, effortful attempt to get beneath the surface appearance of things, to take a long time over something, to challenge the terms of the agenda. Instead, a sentence like the following suggests someone who has become the prisoner of the headline writers of the day: 'Some among Our Age recognized that although the entertainment industry might insist on total freedom to meet the material, erotic, and aesthetic appetites of the times, the spectre of AIDS, drugs, violence and alcohol stoked the fears of thoughtful people who saw children taking third place as the number of divorces mounted.' When 'thoughtful' comes to mean 'uncritically repeating the tabloid vision of society', it becomes less surprising to find an eminent vice-chancellor referring to 'dons in their ivory towers'.

This is why this book, for all the fun and perceptiveness it contains, leaves such a depressing aftertaste. It could have been so much better. There are precious few books willing to range intelligently across the various idioms that make up a national culture, precious few authors able to write with that mixture of vitality and cultivation evident in the work of Noel Annan at his best. Yet *Our Age* is not the triumphant embodiment of the values of the life of the mind and the life of the heart that the young Annan seems to have so engagingly represented; it is not even the roguishly seductive account of how the apostles of love and laughter came to occupy the high places of the land. The combination of complacency and tendentiousness evident in its closing pages suggests, rather, the chairman's summing-up at a meeting that has gone on too long.

16

Before Another Tribunal: The Idea of the 'Non-Specialist Public'

.

I

The anxiety that the learned may cease to communicate with anyone but the learned is probably as old as learning itself. Certainly, we can find examples in earlier periods of reflection upon the distance that separates the possessors of certain forms of knowledge from their uninformed or less informed or just differently informed brethren. But it may be a mistake, and a characteristically modern mistake, to think of this as always having been an 'anxiety', and there is surely a casualness bordering on error in referring to 'the' anxiety in the singular. It would be nearer the mark to say that what we find in different historical periods are various kinds of comment and reflection on various aspects of the relation between the learned and the not so learned, variously defined. I do not intend to try to map these responses here, or even to range back in time much further than the middle of the nineteenth century, since, as the subtitle of this essay should suggest, I am concerned with an issue which only acquired any prominence—which, indeed, could only be conceived as an *issue*—once institutions of higher education began to occupy a central place in the cultural life of modern societies.

That it *is* now a prominent issue hardly needs to be emphasized. In the last decade, in particular, we (and I shall return to the question of who 'we' might be) have been deluged with pronouncements about how academics in their ivory towers now only address other specialized academics and have lost all contact with 'the general public'. As I indicated in the previous essay, I think it is probably quite a good rule of thumb to presume that there is some pretty slack thinking in the vicinity whenever we encounter a sentence about academics in which the term 'ivory tower' occurs. Some of these pronouncements are nostalgic, some dismissive, some hortatory, some apocalyptic. But they generally have at least two things in common: the assumption that this is a very recent development and the implication that it is a very bad thing. As will, I hope, by now be obvious from the essays in this book, I do not believe that either the assumption or the implication are wholly wrong, but I do not believe they are wholly right, either, and the ways in which they are not right have a lot to do with the tendentious or foreshortened historical basis on which, explicitly or (more usually) implicitly, they rest. In this essay I want to look at this topic in a longer historical perspective, an exercise which will, I hope, not only help us to identify what, if anything, is distinctive about our present situation, but which may also help to fortify us against the seductions of alarmism, disdain, and nostalgia.

These emotions appear to have found a particularly welcoming home in the pages of the 'quality' press in Britain recently, but the rumblings and grumblings suggest that what is now at stake is not just an alleged gulf between worlds of academia and journalism, but also, and increasingly, a contrast between the academic cultures of Britain and the USA. Certainly, this is a topic where it is especially important to keep a weather eye on developments in the United States, since the divide discussed in this essay has in the late-twentieth century taken its most advanced or extreme forms there. If I were a confident Hegelian philosopher of history I would presumably have no trouble tracing *the* movement of history in this state of affairs. Being, in fact, a somewhat sceptical and decidedly un-Hegelian intellectual historian, I am normally much more inclined to emphasize how the precise manifestation of such concerns is highly culture-specific, appearing in an idiom and intellectual context peculiar to the cultural traditions of different societies. But in the present case there is some reason to think that the general pattern of the expansion of higher education from the mid-nineteenth century had some basic similarities in the major Western countries, and so some, at least, of what I have to say will describe developments that were broadly common to Europe and to North America, even if local conditions have affected the speed at which

they have manifested themselves. In any event, as far as the present
is concerned, those who work in British universities should hardly
need to be reminded how consequential for their own future experience developments in American academic life can be.

II

I do not, as I say, propose to range across the centuries, but I want
to begin with a familiar quotation from the eighteenth century,
since, the contrast it offers to more recent statements may help to
isolate the issue to be discussed here. In his *Lives of the English
Poets*, Dr Johnson famously declared: 'I rejoice to concur with the
common reader; for by the common sense of readers uncorrupted
with literary prejudices, after all the refinements of subtlety and the
dogmatism of learning, must be finally decided all claims to poetical honours.' This is a confident, even slightly truculent, assertion
of the way in which the enduring status of literary works depends
on the appetites and judgements of a broadly defined reading
public. Actually, the syntax of the sentence is not entirely clear: the
'after' and the 'finally' suggest a chronological process, something
akin to the judgement of posterity, though it could also be read as
suggesting that there is an underlying 'common sense' of readers
'after all the refinements of subtlety and the dogmatism of learning'
have been stripped away. But however this is construed, there is no
ground here for suggesting that what Johnson had in mind was the
gulf between the academic and non-academic worlds. No one in
eighteenth-century England would anyway have thought that the
opinions of the denizens of Oxford and Cambridge were of any
great significance in deciding 'poetical honours'. The 'learning'
Johnson was disparaging was not 'academic' in the institutional
sense, and it clearly mattered far more that his common reader
should escape the tyranny of metropolitan literary fashion than
that he should or should not be addressed by the monkish celibates
who studied the ancient languages on the banks of the Isis and the
Cam.
  The Johnson passage is, however, not only helpful as a defining
negative instance. It is noticeable how much of the theoretical and
polemical literature on the topic of 'the general public' takes the
eighteenth century, and especially eighteenth-century England, as

its benchmark for what Habermas has so influentially termed 'the public sphere'. As commentators on Habermas have pointed out, his original notion seemed to involve some idealization of the social conditions of Georgian England, where the 'public' in question essentially consisted of propertied gentlemen and the habitués of London coffee houses. And this, surely, is the world to which Johnson's celebrated remark belongs, a world which set a high value on the virtues of sociability and good sense as opposed to the private vice of pedantry or the solecism of one-eyed theorizing. It surely ought to be unnecessary to say that whatever charms such a world may now possess for us, neither its social structure nor these particular cultural assumptions provide a particularly useful model for the late twentieth century. Attractive though Johnson's robustness can be, it can provide only limited inspiration in our present situation.

For the development of something recognizably similar to the modern concern about reaching or failing to reach a 'non-specialist public', it needed a conjunction of cultural and institutional developments that only came together in the mid- and late-nineteenth century. These developments were complex, but in outline they included the following: the spread in the course of the middle decades of the nineteenth century of the German ideal of *Wissenschaft*, especially the historicization of knowledge in what we would now call the humanities; the reform and expansion of the ancient universities from the 1860s onwards, an expansion both in numbers and in the range of disciplines; the establishment of new universities in the large industrial cities from the 1870s; and the founding, from the 1880s, of specialized professional associations and of discipline-specific learned journals.

With these developments came a heightened sense that a wide range of intellectual, scientific, and literary topics were starting to become the preserve of people in a single occupational category whose authority was more than personal, deriving ultimately from the socially endorsed authority of the institutions of the 'higher learning' more generally. Actually, this states things a little too neatly: few topics were seen as wholly the preserve of university teachers, and all the early professional associations recognized the claims of bona fide scholars who had private incomes or were employed in other occupations. None the less, the central point here remains roughly true: from the late nineteenth century onwards, the existence of separate and increasingly specialized intellectual disciplines, more or less exclusively cultivated by those attached to institutions of higher education, was acknowledged. Some of the major preconditions for the recognizably modern anxiety about the loss of connection with a 'non-specialist public' were now in place.

The beginnings of this anxiety were thus distinct from an adjacent but actually quite separate concern, namely that characteristically nineteenth-century preoccupation with bringing the benefits of education to the uneducated classes. In its most basic form, this meant the inculcation of literacy and numeracy, but even in the somewhat more ambitious forms favoured by the Society for the Diffusion of Useful Knowledge in the first part of the century or the University Extension Movement later, the project was a fundamentally pedagogic one, quite distinct from the later preoccupation about the growth of barriers to communication *within* the educated class.

In the course of the twentieth century it became harder for commentators to speak of 'the educated class' with the kind of untroubled briskness evident in so many nineteenth-century pronouncements, and as a consequence of the democratization, albeit slow and uneven, of educational and cultural institutions, the very notion of a *single* general reading public itself began to come under strain. None the less, in the period from, roughly, the late nineteenth to the mid-twentieth century it became standard to invoke a relatively unproblematized notion of a general reading public and to lament that the newly specializing disciplines were increasingly withdrawing from its common conversation. And this verb—'withdraw'—catches the way these developments tended to be described, as if the national culture were a single cake whose existence is progressively diminished and threatened as newly established academic subjects carry off each successive slice. What seems so striking here is how each generation during this period appears to have thought it was witnessing the terminal stage in the decline of the general reading public, reports of whose death have therefore been greatly exaggerated. Even just identifying the recurrent and frequently alarmist nature of these diagnoses seems to me one helpful contribution an historical account can make, though, as will become evident, I do want to say that there are good structural reasons for believing that this concern has taken a new form in our own time.

That form focuses on the question of the (allegedly) increasing unintelligibility of work in the main fields of the humanities to any but the adepts of the relevant discipline. This question can be distinguished from those that may be raised about at least two other genres of writing that aim at (and, in these cases, largely succeed in reaching) a certain kind of 'non-specialist' audience. The first is popular science writing. This is clearly a flourishing genre, and in recent years individuals such as Stephen Jay Gould or Stephen Hawking have reached wide readerships without forfeiting any of their distinguished professional standing. But in such cases it is accepted that the scientist is working in two quite different modes, and that none but members of the relevant scientific sub-discipline could follow the primary research on which such popularization may be based. A book by, say, an historian or a literary scholar may simultaneously win its author academic promotion and honours and win a major national non-fiction book prize. No one disputes that the research scientist would have to write in two utterly different genres to achieve those two goals.

A second category consists of that writing, above all by social scientists, that is 'policy orientated'. There are certainly some interesting questions here about the routes by which the latest thinking by, say, economists or political theorists comes to affect the actions of those responsible for deciding and implementing policy, but the central relation here is that between the 'expert' and the politician or administrator, where the former is not necessarily an academic and the latter do not, of course, constitute a genuinely 'general' public. One could perhaps discriminate a third category, namely writing on topics such as health or the environment on which individuals as citizens may feel the need to acquaint themselves with some of the results of the most recent research. In practice, this tends to be something of a hybrid between my first two categories: there is undeniably a successful crossing of the academic/non-academic divide here, though the notion of 'popularization' is again clearly central, and the proliferation of 'how-to-do-it' books does not really speak to the larger cultural anxieties about the effects of increasing specialization.

I am dealing, therefore, with a question which finds its purest form in relation to those disciplines still referred to as 'the humanities'. Here, the specificity of the issue about the alleged loss of the 'non-specialist public' can be narrowed further by asking two apparently simple questions: first, for whom is this development supposed to be a problem?, and secondly, what standpoint or what idiom has been assumed to be available for discussing it if this fatally fragmenting process has been assumed to have already taken place?

So, first, for whom is it a problem? It would, after all, be perfectly intelligible, and up to a point persuasive, simply to say that specialization is one of the conditions of advances in knowledge, and as specialists develop more refined and exact ways of studying various phenomena, so their work is bound to become less and less intelligible to those not trained in these fields. We do not on the whole feel that the biological sciences have taken a wrong turn just because articles in the *Journal of Microbiology* would be pretty tough going for the average *Guardian* reader. Actually, I think there *are* some grounds for worrying about even this development more than we do—or, at least, more than most natural scientists are professionally encouraged to do—but that is an argument for another occasion (and I should say in self-exoneration here that I have tried to address that issue in my edition of C. P. Snow's *The Two Cultures*). That is, it has largely come to be accepted that there are many disciplines where a degree of technical complexity or of remoteness from central human concerns is inevitable and acceptable, but it is maintained that the core humanities disciplines, literature and history above all, are, or ought to be, intrinsically part of what is still revealingly referred to as 'general culture'. And on the whole, this claim is not propounded by those who bear the heat and burden of the day in the actual practice of those disciplines in the present, but rather by an assorted band among whom the most vocal tend to be either literary journalists or academics who have enjoyed considerable popular success (or who have retired). It might, however, help us all to keep a sense of proportion about these issues, were we to pin to the walls above our desks copies of the following passage from a recent report to the American Modern Language Association by a public relations firm who had been commissioned to survey the public perceptions of the humanities. 'Though the great majority of those interviewed claimed to have a favourable image of the humanities . . . a substantial number associated the term with "humanitarian" activities such as the prevention of cruelty to animals. Others who answered "yes" to the question of whether they themselves participated in the

humanities listed "singing in the shower" as an example of human-
istic activity.'

The second question—about the standpoint or idiom that
remains available for considering the issue itself—is more teasing.
Inevitably, those who raise the question about the damagingly fragmenting effects of the process of academic specialization seem to
represent themselves, if only for the moment in which they are raising the question, as occupying a privileged or transcendental position, above or outside the damaging process they are describing.
This is in part the logic of all metacritical inquiries, but in this case
it is also a reminder that specialization and unspecialized reflection
can coexist, even in the same individual. We each have many identities, not all of them reducible to a single professional label. Thus,
reflection on specialization does not have to be seen as another
specialism. In practice, those who have raised questions of this type
in anything like a systematic as opposed to a merely opportunist
way have always, of course, had some specific intellectual and
cultural identity, and it may be profitable to consider which have
been the most common of these identities.

On a wider view of the topic than I am taking here, one could
again go back to the eighteenth century when 'philosopher' would
have been the favoured description of those likely to raise such
general questions. This was perhaps most obviously true in the case
of Kant's critical philosophy, one of whose constitutive goals was
precisely to inquire into the conditions for the possibility of different types of knowledge. And this sort of inquiry was continued in
the German tradition in the nineteenth century, notably in Dilthey's
analysis of the logic of the *Geisteswissenschaften*. But this kind of
essentially epistemological inquiry is a far cry from the cultural
anxiety I am dealing with here, and in the nineteenth and twentieth
centuries, at least in the English-speaking world, it has not actually
been among philosophers that we have found the most influential
meditations on the issue of the relations between academic disciplines and a general or non-specialist audience. Instead, the most
common base from which to raise questions about the continuing
possibility of non-specialized discourse has been literary criticism,
broadly understood. (It continues, of course, to be raised by some
others as well, and I have referred to some of the specific features
of the case as currently mounted by historians in Part I above.)

In the nineteenth century the term which signalled this possibility was 'the man of letters', understood as a figure who might turn his (or sometimes her) hand to essays in history or criticism or philosophy as well as to poetry and, increasingly, to fiction. In the course of the century, more specialized identities were progressively hived off from this category, leaving it as something of a residual role. By the middle of the twentieth century the phrase 'a man of letters', by now most often used with a hint of irony, indicated someone whose concerns were primarily literary, while at the same time suggesting a deliberate or self-conscious amateurism in the face of a growing array of specialisms, as well, of course, as suggesting someone who lived by his writing rather than holding any kind of academic or salaried position. But if the *term* 'man of letters' came to have this archaic ring, the notion that there was something inherently generalist about the activity of the critic persisted. At the same time, of course, the study of literature became, in its turn, a professionalized academic discipline, and many of the recurrent and noisy controversies that have marked the history of literary studies right up to the present can in part be understood in terms of the unresolved, and perhaps unresolvable, tension between, on the one hand, being simply one specialized activity alongside other specialisms with its own distinctive subject-matter, techniques, and vocabulary, and, on the other hand, still carrying the burden of being a kind of residual cultural space within which general existential and ethical questions can be addressed.

Matthew Arnold's is probably still the name most readily associated with the idea of the critic as the general cultural legislator or judge. The nub of this position can, I think, best be illustrated not from one of his more famous essays, but from a less well-known piece entitled 'The Bishop and the Philosopher', which first appeared in *Macmillan's Magazine* in 1862. This essay was largely given over to a pretty damning assessment of a misguided and now forgotten work of popular theology and biblical scholarship. Arnold was aware, or affected to be, that he did not possess the scholarly credentials to set himself up as any kind of expert on these matters. His essay did not, therefore, presume to judge the work under review from any position of professional authority, Arnold indicating that he was content to leave such assessments to theologians and biblical scholars. But he insisted, in what I think is a particularly resonant phrase, that 'a work of this kind has to justify itself before another tribunal', and he went on to develop this point:

Literary criticism's most important function is to try books as to the influence which they are calculated to have upon the general culture . . . All
these works have a special professional criticism to undergo . . . theologi-
cal works that of theologians, historical works that of historians, philosophical works that of philosophers, and in this case each kind of work is
tried by a separate standard. . . . Not everyone is a theologian or a historian or a philosopher, but every one is interested in the advance of the
general culture. . . . A criticism therefore which, abandoning a thousand
special questions which may be raised about any book, tries it solely in
respect of its influence upon this culture, brings it thereby within the
sphere of everyone's interest.

Arnold, it may be worth pointing out, was not here equating
'specialized' with 'academic', though some, at least, of his readers
in the 1860s may have had the recent discussions of the German-
inspired ideal of the 'research' university in mind when they read
his words. But part of the interest of the passage precisely lies in
showing how a version of the now-familiar concern about specialization could be entertained without the issue having to be cast in
terms of the academic/non-academic divide, for Arnold is certainly
here articulating the recognizably modern anxiety that a society
suffers if it loses the sense that there can be in principle a space
within which shared reflection can take place on all the more
specialized inquiries.

Revealingly, he does not mention among the specialisms needing
to be brought before his 'other tribunal' any of the natural sciences.
By the 1860s a literary figure like Arnold no longer aspired to inte-
grate first-hand experience of the sciences into the shared cultural
conversation of the periodicals-reading classes. In his later celebrated exchange with T. H. Huxley on the nature of a liberal
education, Arnold could pay lip service to the contribution of the
sciences, but in practice he, and his successors in the role of cultural
critic, accepted that the findings of the natural sciences could only
enter into the common conversation in a diluted and second-hand
form. And this underlines how, by contrast, in that passage he
assumes that the members of his 'other tribunal' might actually
read the books on theology, history, and so on for themselves. In
other words, he recognizes the existence of two standards by which
such books may be judged—the specialist and the lay—but he does
still assume that they are sufficiently *within* the culture of the cultivated reader to be accessible to the latter judgement. In one sense,

you could say that Arnold's more famous essay on 'The Function of Criticism' is making the same point in relation to politics. Similarly, in his later writings on religion, he repeatedly insisted that matters too important to be left to the specialists, such as the interpretation of the Bible, needed to be handled with, as he characteristically put it, 'the tact which letters, surely, alone can give'. 'Letters', or, in Arnold's broad sense of the term, 'literary criticism', is here being looked to to supply the kind of general balanced assessment which was not to be expected from those immersed in arcane learning.

In voicing concerns about how the critical function was to be sustained in an increasingly fragmented or specialized culture, Arnold and his most notable successors such as T. S. Eliot looked to the non-academic man of letters, writing in the general literary or cultural periodical, as the best hope for maintaining the necessary wholeness of vision. One of the things that makes F. R. Leavis an insistent, but also teasing, presence in this discussion is that he looked to the *university* to counter the ills of which the current state of *academic* specialization was a major symptom. Of course, he looked to a highly idealized university, to a Cambridge of the mind that never quite assumed terrestrial form. And indeed, it was largely to one department of the university that Leavis looked: in his increasingly pessimistic and embattled view *only* English, as he conceived its study, could provide the necessary training in what he called 'general intelligence'. In an essay which appeared in 1932 in the first volume of *Scrutiny*, Leavis sketched his conception of the dual function of literary criticism, a conception which, with scarcely any modification, he was to uphold for nearly fifty years. In the course of defending the notion that criticism is simultaneously a matter of intelligence *and* sensibility, Leavis quoted Ezra Pound on the general social and political importance of maintaining exactness and vitality in the use of language. Leavis then went on:

This is well said. Literary criticism has a correspondingly high function, and literary study . . . should be the best possible training for intelligence—for free, unspecialized, general intelligence which there has never at any time been enough of, and which we are peculiarly in need of today. This is not to say that literary criticism should not be specialized, in the sense that its practice should be controlled by a strict conception of its special nature and methods. Indeed, the more one realizes its importance in the education of general intelligence, the more is one concerned for strictness of conception and practice.

This passage seems to me a particularly revealing symptom of the generalist/specialist tension within literary criticism: its first half states the generalist case, its second half the specialist case. It is as if, in the middle of the passage, Leavis realizes the danger that the limitless remit he is giving to literary criticism may deprive it of the status of a highly developed skill or discipline deserving of its place in the university, and so he swings the paragraph around to face in the opposite direction. Literary criticism *is* a specialism, but the proper cultivation of it produces the non-specialist intelligence.

Leavis frequently asserted that the social function of the literary critic was to bring to bear a non-specialist capaciousness of judgement, as in part a corrective to the distorting perspectives of any particular specialism. Thus, for example, when, in an early number of *Scrutiny*, he was responding to an anticipated complaint from Marxists that he did not have any concrete proposals for making the transition from capitalist society to something superior, he replied that 'one cannot reasonably pretend to lay down what are the right immediate steps without consulting specialists, and one of the functions of *Scrutiny* is to provide criteria, from the realm of general intelligence, for determining which specialists can be trusted and how far'. But why, one might well ask, should one expect to find messages from 'the realm of general intelligence' in a journal of literary criticism like *Scrutiny* rather than in, say, the *English Historical Review* or *Mind* or the *Economic Journal*, or the journal of any other professional group who, like the literary critics who wrote in *Scrutiny*, were largely but not exclusively based in universities and who addressed topics that were arguably equally pertinent to arriving at such criteria? But in Leavis's view, all these other disciplines, including, most culpably, philosophy, had retreated into self-consciously 'value-free' technicality, with the result that it now fell to criticism alone to provide the idiom for the judgements made by Arnold's 'other tribunal'.

Although there is obviously no single or simple line of continuity that connects the concerns of Arnold or of Leavis with the pronouncements of the more prominent literary critics and theorists in the present, I hope I have said enough at least to suggest why debates about the nature and consequences of specialization and professionalism have tended to rage most fiercely in relation to the discipline of 'English'. As Bruce Robbins, Gerald Graff, and others have argued, literary criticism has been the chief inheritor of the problematic status of culture—at once set apart from the normal processes of everyday life but also the source of authority for standing in judgement on those processes; at once the locus of an otherwise lost wholeness but also the subject-matter of one specialism alongside others. As a result, one can see how the dialectical tension between the specialized and the general, which I have been discussing, plays itself out in microcosm *within* the field of literary study.

But, returning to a broader view of the matter, I also want to suggest that this recurrent lament about the growing divide between academic specialists and the 'non-specialist public' has functioned as a figure or trope for the expression of a range of other concerns. When the form that has been familiar to one generation for conducting part of its general cultural conversation starts to change, the cries of 'foul!' are often symptomatic rather than accurate causal diagnoses. For instance, changes in the structure and economics of periodical publishing seem frequently to generate jeremiads about cultural decline in which academic specialization is fingered as one of the culprits. Similarly, I suspect that some of the concern about the disappearance of 'the general public' in the latter part of the twentieth century has in practice been a reactionary response to the spread of more popular or democratic cultural forms into areas where the concerns of the traditional educated class had previously held a monopoly. It has surely become harder for those who were beneficiaries of the most prestigious forms of education in the middle decades of the twentieth century to continue to take for granted, in the way their Victorian counterparts did, that their particular range of acquired pursuits are coextensive with 'culture', and that change tends easily to be felt as decline even though the audience for many of those pursuits may in fact be thriving and expanding. The logic of the opposition between 'specialist' and 'general public' projects the latter as singular and as endowed with a common range of assumptions and allusions, with the result that some, at least, of what have been construed as 'threats' to that public have surely been, rather, expressions of its increasing diversity and dividedness. This point has recently been made in a more emphatic and polemical, perhaps

too polemical, way by Gerald Graff when referring to contemporary disputes within the university: 'What really makes the antitheory traditionalists so angry', says Graff, 'is that educational
definitions, issues and decisions that they for so long had the power
to determine as a matter of course now have to be defended by
argument—and against a whole array of new groups that previously had no say in the matter. For the traditionalists, this new situation is "relativism", but an older word for it would be
"democracy" '.

III

This last point is, I think, the clue to a much larger development
that also marks a new stage in this concern. A further reason, it
seems to me, why the 'specialist/generalist' dichotomy does not in
any simple way map onto the 'academic/public' dichotomy (to
adapt the terms I have just used in speaking of Leavis) is that the
academic world now constitutes a far more substantial part of any
'non-specialist' audience than ever before. What we have seen in
the course of the last two or three decades is the rise of what I want
to call 'the academic public sphere', a sphere whose existence
complicates the inherited picture of an increasingly impassable gulf
between specialist and public.

The material preconditions for this development obviously
include the huge expansion of higher education that has taken
place since about 1960 in nearly all Western countries. I shall not
pile up statistics to support this point, which is anyway not in
dispute, but two figures may help to bring home the sheer size of
the academic world at present. In the United States, according to
the most recent estimates, approximately 60 per cent of the age
cohort now participate in some form of tertiary education, and the
number of full-time professors is about 600,000; in Britain, as I
mentioned in Chapter 14, 30 per cent of the age cohort will soon
be entering higher education, and of course the number of universities has been practically doubled in the 1990s by the reclassification of the former polytechnics. Now, we know, of course, that
these figures cover a multitude of sinners, and I do not for one
moment suppose that even this large constituency represents the
only public worth trying to reach. But it is certainly true that the

sheer size and diversity of the academic world, broadly defined, is in itself a new and relevant circumstance.

At the same time, the structural relation of universities to their parent societies has also altered in recent years. What appears to be happening—and the process has gone furthest in the United States—is that increasingly the university is coming to be seen as the arena within which reflection on the cultural and intellectual life of society, and even much of the primary activity of that life, is largely *expected* to take place. To take one practical illustration of this point: one reason why so many of the candidates for being 'public intellectuals' in the United States at present are academics is that even those who did not start out as career academics, frequently come to be offered enticing deals and prestigious chairs once they have started to make a mark in some field of cultural analysis or commentary. (There are signs of a similar pattern emerging in Britain also.) This is, in turn, related to an expansion of the range of things it is now considered legitimate (though not, of course, by everybody) for universities to teach and study. When there are courses and chairs in almost every aspect of contemporary life and popular culture, it is inevitable, as I suggested in earlier chapters, that a high proportion of those who write about these things will be academics. By the same token, the university comes to seem a natural base from which to engage in cultural criticism— indeed, in the intellectuals-unfriendly environment of American society it can come to seem the *only* base—and so an increasing number of those who are recognized as 'intellectuals' will be found within its walls. To cite just one prominent example, Cornel West recently urged his readers to think about 'the degree to which the waning of public spheres in this society tends to displace politics into the few spheres where there is in fact some public discussion— spheres like the academy', where 'so much of American intellectual life . . . now has been monopolised by default'.

This is why, surely, universities were so much at the heart of the Reaganite-Thatcherite *Kulturkampf* of the 1980s and early 1990s. A century or even half a century ago, right-wing denunciations of left-wing dogma would only have given a relatively minor role to institutions of higher education, but contemporary right-wing ideo- logues may, in a sense, be correct in thinking that engaging with the dominant liberalism of academia is now for them a priority. One of the ways in which these attacks (which have been more common in the United States) are misguided, of course, is in their conspiracy theories about how a power-hungry stratum of radical professors are indoctrinating the young with subversive and relativist ideas derived from Nietzsche and Foucault, and that if we could only get back to studying the classic canon all would be well. For among the forces helping to bring about the changes and fashions within American universities in the last couple of decades or more is the way that an increasingly diverse range of groups in an increasingly multicultural and rights-conscious society are increasingly making their aspirations felt in the arena in which that society's intellectual and cultural life is increasingly carried on. The ideal of the tweed-jacketed harmony of the Ivy League universities cannot, fortunately, be restored just by narrowing the reading lists. Britain is a very different society with a somewhat different academic culture, but here, too, the vast recent expansion of higher education has, along with other difficulties it may have brought in its train, made academia more and more the arena in which a range of the larger society's concerns are fought out.

So, I have been suggesting that it is a mistake to think about this matter in starkly binary terms—that is, in terms of that familiar opposition between addressing ourselves only to other specialists or addressing ourselves to 'the general reader'. Perhaps we are anyway now disposed to be a little sceptical of the term 'the general reader' and to recognize that it is more often used polemically than descriptively. Certainly, the general reader of publishers' dreams—that intellectually omnivorous creature of indeterminate employment who reads (and *buys*) a large number of serious books on a wide range of topics, whether primarily 'academic' or not—may well be a mythical beast, though, as I suggested in the Introduction, we have to recognize the ways in which we are all 'general readers' part of the time. But, if we are to liberate ourselves from this misleading opposition, what I am now suggesting is that we *also* need to question the other half of the dichotomy. The vast expansion of higher education and the transformation of its place in the cultures of the major Western countries has created a situation in which there are now several extensive and overlapping audiences that are largely populated by those involved in one way or another in the academic world, and in any given case they cannot all be regarded as consti-tuting a 'specialist' audience. To bring home this point, let me just offer a brief and unashamedly homespun taxonomy of the more obvious kinds of audiences different kinds of writing by academics can be aimed at and may reach.

First, there are fellow-specialists in the strict sense, people who will have read some of the sources cited in one's footnotes, people who might be chosen to review one's work in the most specialized professional journal, people who might buy the monograph in hardback.

Second, there are other members of the same discipline or sub-discipline, those who may read some but not all of the same journals and attend some but not many of the same conferences, those to whom methodological manifestos, position-papers on the 'state of the field', and so on are often addressed.

Third, there is a larger swathe of people, drawn from more than one neighbouring discipline, who share some further common feature or interest—medievalists, feminist theorists, people working on 'developing countries'; writing that reaches such people tends to be cited in the opening paragraphs of their own books and articles, whether by way of claiming descent, justifying revisionism, or displaying the breadth of one's reading.

Fourth, there are academics in quite other disciplines who are curious about developments in different fields, or who are on the look-out for ideas or approaches they might import to their own work, or who once took a course or minor field in this area and still have an interest, or who remember the name of a visiting lecturer who came to their university and was impressive, and so on. This may be the audience that is primarily reached through the pages of journals such as the *Times Literary Supplement* or the *New York Review of Books*, though both these and some similar publications are also read by a certain number of entirely non-academic readers.

Fifth, there is a yet more diverse readership, which is none the less still largely academic, of people commenting on the present state of academia, writing about current intellectual paradigms, reflecting on the changing relations between the disciplines, pronouncing on government policies towards universities, and so on. (Publishers, bookshops, and libraries have no trouble deciding where to place writing addressed to my first four categories: work addressed to this fifth audience usually defeats them and gets assigned to 'education' or, despairingly and archaically, to 'philosophy'.)

Sixth, there is the whole range of student readers: mostly graduate students in the case of the more advanced writing, and mostly undergraduate students in the case of textbooks, works of synthesis, introductions to editions and anthologies, etc. Students, of course, quickly become former students, but they do not thereby necessarily become former readers.

Only after this point, as we move further outward still, do we meet the first category of readers who can properly be called wholly 'non-academic', and obviously this is itself a capacious category that needs to be broken down further, but for the moment it can include everybody else from the reflective, politically concerned, professionally employed, reader of *Prospect* to the most recreational reader of biography and military history. It is not obvious where, along the spectrum formed by these categories, the 'non-specialist public' for any given piece of writing begins.

One recent development that I take to be confirmatory of my argument that academia now furnishes an audience large enough and diverse enough to reproduce many of the properties of the larger 'public sphere' has been the emergence of deliberately non-specialized but still self-consciously academic journals like *Contention* or *Common Knowledge*. These journals function as arenas within which people who have one identity as specialists in some particular field can engage in some kind of public conversation on intellectual matters with those who have different specialist identities. The relation between, say, *Common Knowledge* and the *Journal of Ecclesiastical History* is very much the relation between 'general' and 'specialized' played out in a new form.

These developments also mean that whereas in the latter part of the nineteenth century one could find scholars who were specialists but not professionals, one is now seeing the growth of a small class of superstars who are professionals without being specialists. That is to say, figures in the nineteenth century like the historian E. A. Freeman or the philosopher Bernard Bosanquet were vigorous proponents and exemplars of more specialized work in their respective disciplines, though they both spent the greater part of their writing lives as gentlemen of private means. In the late twentieth century the academic world supports (in both senses) figures like, say, Richard Rorty or Stanley Fish who, though they may have begun as more or less conventional specialists, are now able to pursue a career which is in one sense wholly academic but which has ceased to consist of the practice of a specific discipline, at least in the sense in which graduate schools understand and inculcate that practice.

All these developments taken together certainly indicate a change from the situation that obtained fifty years ago, let alone a hundred and fifty years ago. But do they count as a decline? Where Arnold's implied reader could be represented as a well-connected upper-middle-class man spending the hour after lunch in the library of his club reading an essay on the function of culture in a fashionable magazine like the *Cornhill* before returning to his task of revising the regulations for education in the Punjab, the contemporary cultural critic's implied reader might be represented as an upwardly mobile ethnic-minority woman spending her lunch-hour in the library of her university reading an essay on the function of cultural criticism in a fashionable journal like the *London Review of Books* before returning to her task of revising the regulations for the summer-school course for social services managers. It does not seem to me obvious that the historical shift from the first type of reader to the second is best described as a 'narrowing' of the audience or as the loss of contact with a 'non-specialist public'.

Since this is a sensitive and complex topic, and since I am well aware that I have been able to do little more here than sketch one or two lines of approach, let me conclude by stating my own position in the baldest terms. Let me, to begin with, just make four basic points by way of clarification. First, I am not adding my voice to that chorus which decries specialization itself or which represents academic disciplines as organized conspiracies against human emancipation. Specialization is, it should be needless to say, essential to the advance of knowledge, and disciplines empower as well as constrain. Second, I think we should be sceptical of those nostalgic accounts which see a golden age of the 'educated reading public' in some vaguely located past. Different periods have seen different types of both opportunities and constraints for addressing different types of audience. Third, I therefore think, to repeat a point made earlier, that in trying to understand our present situation we should reject the binary opposition between 'addressing the general reader' and 'addressing other specialists in an ivory tower'. There is no single thing called 'the non-specialist public': individuals who are specialists in relation to one context are non-specialists in relation to another, and there are many more than just a single contrasting pair of contexts. As I suggested in the Introduction, this last point applies to all of us, and it applies to us not just as readers but, potentially at least, as writers, too. Fourth, and following directly from that last point, although I believe, as I have tried to make clear in this chapter and in this book as a whole, that we must now recognize the extent to which changed circumstances have created something we could call an 'academic public sphere' and that in so far as we do reach this audience on matters of general concern to it we are going much further towards fulfilling the aspiration to reach a 'non-specialist public' than the familiar clichés about ivory towers suggest, I would emphasize, none the less, that the academic world, even on the most expanded definition of that term, is certainly not coextensive with 'the educated public', and there are good reasons, including prudent self-interest where attitudes and policies towards higher education are concerned, for continuing to attempt to reach other elements in that public.

I do not, therefore, endorse either of what seems to me a related pair of opposing snobberies: on the one hand, that self-consciously high-minded disdain for what is sneered at as 'journalism', a term sometimes dismissively used by academics to embrace any writing other than a heavily footnoted contribution to a learned journal; and on the other hand, that attitude which equates intellectual significance with media exposure, and which presumes that high-profile book launches and occasional opinion pieces in the national press are the real markers of importance. Needless to say, it is for most of us not too difficult to avoid the second of these, though we can all no doubt think of a few academics who seem to display an unseemly eagerness to seize such opportunities as do come their way. But the seductions of the first, to which most of us are more susceptible, include that kind of drawing-the-wagons-up-in-a-circle mentality that is so appalled by the simplicities and vulgarities of discussion outside the walls that it maintains, usually in a somewhat high-principled tone, that serious scholars should simply get on with real scholarship and leave these frothy questions to journalists and pundits. However, if academics, among other people, do not address these questions, then we are letting what may eventually be highly consequential social attitudes be influenced by, among other people, those who may well be more ignorant, more tendentious, or more partisan in any given case. I do not mean blithely to underestimate the difficulties here, including the danger that the media we must use to reach such audiences have a way of imposing their agenda on us rather than vice versa. But one final advantage of an informed historical perspective is that it reminds us that ours is not the first generation to confront difficulties of this kind. And I am not persuaded—not yet, anyway—that ours is the first generation that has no chance of overcoming them.

ACKNOWLEDGEMENTS

ALTHOUGH sections of each chapter in this book are here appearing in print for the first time, the greater part of its contents consists of revised versions of essays that were first published in other forms. For permission to draw upon this material, I am grateful to the editors of the following publications: *Times Literary Supplement*, *London Review of Books*, *Dissent*, *Times Higher Education Supplement*, *Guardian*, *Cambridge Review*, *Irish Review*, *Utilitas*, *Victorian Studies*, *Le Débat*, *Le Monde*.

As always, I am deeply and diversely indebted to those friends whose judgement I regard as the most searching, but also the most rewarding, 'tribunal' my writing has to face. Whatever jokes in doubtful taste or other imprudent expressions of literary high spirits readers may now find in this book should be taken as evidence of my own pigheadedness rather than of any critical slackness or excessive indulgence on the part of John Burrow, Peter Clarke, Geoffrey Hawthorn, Ruth Morse, John Thompson, or Donald Winch.

REFERENCES

IN the interests of brevity, this list includes only works actually referred to or quoted in the text; it is not intended as a list of 'sources' nor as a guide to further reading on the topics discussed.

CHAPTER 1

Keith Thomas, *Man and the Natural World: Changing Attitudes in England 1500–1800* (Allen Lane, 1983).

John Brewer, *The Sinews of Power: War and the English State 1688–1783* (Unwin Hyman, 1989).

J. W. Burrow, *A Liberal Descent: Victorian Historians and the English Past* (Cambridge University Press, 1981).

David Cannadine, 'British History: Past, Present—and Future?', *Past and Present*, 116 (1987).

Mary Moorman, *George Macaulay Trevelyan: A Memoir* (Hamish Hamilton, 1980).

G. M. Trevelyan, *An Autobiography and Other Essays* (Longmans, 1949).

A. J. P. Taylor *English History 1914–1945* (Oxford University Press, 1965).

Peter Clarke, *Hope and Glory: Britain 1900–1990* (Penguin, 1996).

CHAPTER 2

David Gervais, *Literary Englands: Versions of 'Englishness' in Modern Writing* (Cambridge University Press, 1993).

Patrick Wright, *On Living in an Old Country: The National Past in Contemporary Britain* (Verso, 1985).

Robert Colls and Philip Dodd (eds.), *Englishness: Politics and Culture 1880–1920* (Croom Helm, 1986).

Eric Hobsbawm and Terence Ranger (eds.), *The Invention of Tradition* (Cambridge University Press, 1983).

Robert Gittings, *The Older Hardy* (Heinemann, 1978).

Stefan Collini, *Public Moralists: Political Thought and Intellectual Life in Britain 1850–1930* (Oxford University Press, 1991).

Kenneth Baker (ed.), *The Faber Book of English History in Verse* (Faber, 1988).

CHAPTER 3

Élie Halévy, *The Growth of Philosophic Radicalism* [1901–4], trans. M. Morris (Faber, 1928).
—— *A History of the English People in the Nineteenth Century*, vol. i: *England in 1815* [1912], trans. E. I. Watkin (Ernest Benn, 1926).
William Thomas, *The Philosophic Radicals: Nine Studies in Theory and Practice 1817–1841* (Oxford, 1979).
Isaiah Berlin, *Personal Impressions* (Hogarth Press, 1980).
Julia Namier, *Lewis Namier: A Biography* (Oxford University Press, 1971).
Lewis Namier, *The Structure of Politics at the Accession of George III*, 2 vols. (Macmillan, 1929).
—— *1848: The Revolution of the Intellectuals* (British Academy, 1944).

CHAPTER 4

Gertude Himmelfarb, *On Liberty and Liberalism: The Case of John Stuart Mill* (Knopf, 1974).
John Stuart Mill, 'Coleridge' [1840], *The Collected Works of John Stuart Mill*, vol. x (University of Toronto Press and Routledge and Kegan Paul, 1969).

CHAPTER 5

John Clive, *Thomas Babington Macaulay: The Shaping of the Historian* (Secker and Warburg, 1973).
Virginia Woolf, 'Mr Bennett and Mrs Brown' [1924], *The Essays of Virginia Woolf*, ed. Andrew McNeillie, 6 vols. (Hogarth Press, 1986–).

CHAPTER 6

John Stuart Mill, *The Early Draft of John Stuart Mill's 'Autobiography'*, ed. Jack Stillinger (University of Illinois Press, 1961).
M. H. Abrams, *The Mirror and the Lamp: Romantic Theory and the Critical Tradition* (Oxford University Press, 1953).
John M. Robson, *What Did He Say? Editing Nineteenth-Century Speeches from Hansard and the Newspapers* (University of Lethbridge Press, 1988).

CHAPTER 7

Anthony Trollope, *An Autobiography* [1883] (Oxford University Press, 1961).

D. Carroll (ed.), *George Eliot: The Critical Heritage* (Routledge, 1971).
Gordon Haight, *George Eliot: A Biography* (Oxford University Press, 1968).
F. R. Leavis, 'Lawrence Scholarship and Lawrence' [1963], *Anna Karenina and Other Essays* (Chatto, 1967).
Henry James, 'The Life of George Eliot' [1885], *Literary Criticism: Essays on Literature, American Writers, English Writers* (The Library of America, 1984).

CHAPTER 8

Nora Barlow (ed.), *The Autobiography of Charles Darwin 1809–1882* (Collins, 1958).
Bertrand Russell, *The Autobiography of Bertrand Russell*, 3 vols. (Allen and Unwin, 1967–9).
—— 'A Free Man's Worship' [1903], in *The Collected Papers of Bertrand Russell*, vol. xii (Allen and Unwin, 1985).

CHAPTER 9

R. H. Tawney, *Religion and the Rise of Capitalism: A Historical Study* (Murray, 1926).
—— *The Radical Tradition: Twelve Essays on Politics, Education, and Literature*, ed. Rita Hinden (Allen and Unwin, 1964).
—— *R. H. Tawney's Commonplace Book*, ed. J. M. Winter and D. M. Joslin (Cambridge University Press, 1972).
—— *Equality* [1931], with introd. by Richard Titmuss (Allen and Unwin, 1964).
Ross Terrill, *R. H. Tawney and his Times: Socialism as Fellowship* (Harvard University Press, 1973).
A. W. Wright, *R. H. Tawney* (Manchester University Press, 1987).
Alasdair MacIntyre, *Against the Self-Images of the Age* (Duckworth, 1971).

CHAPTER 10

Isaiah Berlin, *Against the Current: Essays in the History of Ideas* [1979] (Oxford University Press, 1991).
—— *Personal Impressions* (Hogarth Press, 1980).
Robert Kocis, *A Critical Appraisal of Sir Isaiah Berlin's Political Philosophy* (Edwin Mellen, 1989).
Claude J. Galipeau, *Isaiah Berlin's Liberalism* (Oxford University Press, 1994).
John Gray, *Isaiah Berlin* (HarperCollins, 1995).

CHAPTER 11
Alan O'Connor, *Raymond Williams: Writing, Culture, Politics* (Blackwell, 1989).
Terry Eagleton (ed.), *Raymond Wiliams: Critical Perspectives* (Polity Press, 1989).
Richard Hoggart, *Life and Times*, vol. i: *A Local Habitation*; vol. ii: *A Sort of Clowning*; vol. iii: *An Imagined Life* (Chatto, 1988–92).

CHAPTER 12
Friedrich Nietzsche, *Untimely Meditations* [1873–6] (Cambridge University Press, 1983).
David Lodge, *Changing Places: A Tale of Two Campuses* (Penguin, 1978).
—— *Small World: An Academic Romance* (Secker and Warburg, 1984).

CHAPTER 13
Richard Hoggart, *The Uses of Literacy* (Chatto, 1957).
Raymond Williams, *Culture and Society, 1780–1950* (Chatto, 1958).
E. P. Thompson, *The Making of the English Working Class* (Penguin, 1963).

CHAPTER 14
Brian Harrison (ed.), *The History of the University of Oxford*, vol. viii: *The Twentieth Century* (Oxford University Press, 1994).
Arthur Engel, *From Clergyman to Don: The Rise of the Academic Profession in Nineteenth-Century Oxford* (Oxford University Press, 1982).
A. H. Halsey, *The Decline of Donnish Dominion: The British Academic Profession in the Twentieth Century* (Oxford University Press, 1992).
George W. Stocking, *Victorian Anthropology* (Collier Macmillan, 1987).
Perry Anderson, 'Components of the National Culture' [1968], *English Questions* (Verso, 1992).

CHAPTER 15
John Carey, *Original Copy: Selected Reviews and Journalism 1969–1986* (Faber, 1987).
—— *The Violent Effigy: A Study of Dickens' Imagination* (Faber, 1973).
Noel Annan, *Leslie Stephen: The Godless Victorian* (Weidenfeld and Nicolson, 1984).
—— 'The Intellectual Aristocracy', in J. H. Plumb (ed.), *Studies in Social History: A Tribute to G. M. Trevelyan* (Longman, 1955).

CHAPTER 16

Samuel Johnson, 'Thomas Gray', *The Lives of the English Poets* [1779–81], ed. G. Birkbeck Hill (Oxford University Press, 1905).

Jürgen Habermas, *The Structural Transformation of the Public Sphere* [1962], trans. T. Burger and F. Lawrence (Harvard University Press, 1989).

C. P. Snow, *The Two Cultures*, with introd. by Stefan Collini (Cambridge University Press, 1993).

Matthew Arnold, 'The Bishop and the Philosopher' [1862], *The Collected Prose Works of Matthew Arnold*, ed. R. H. Super, vol. iii (Michigan University Press, 1962).

F. R. Leavis, *For Continuity* (Minority Press, 1933).

Gerald Graff, *Professing Literature: An Institutional History* (Chicago University Press, 1987).

Cornel West, 'The Postmodern Crisis of the Black Intellectuals', in Lawrence Grossberg, Cary Nelson, Paula A. Treichler (eds.), *Cultural Studies* (Routledge, 1992)

Index

I am grateful to Dr Alicia Corrêa for assistance in compiling this index.

Coleridge, S.T. 87, 138, 143
  essay on by John Stuart Mill 137
  and Wordsworth, *Lyrical Ballads*
    125
Colley, Linda 79, 83
Columbia University 127
Combe, George 155
Comédie Française 46
Commentary 87
Committee of Vice-Chancellors and
    Principals (CVCP), on measures
    of productivity in research
    241, 242, 243–4, 249–50, 251
  see also 'bibliometric methods',
    limitations and errors of 244–6
Common Knowledge 322
Communist Party 211
Compagnon, Antoine, on Proust 52
Comte, Auguste 134, 201
Conrad, Joseph 172
Conservatives 15, 32, 61, 66, 79, 82,
    87, 93, 106, 108, 124, 132,
    250, 302
  and Victorian values 104–5, 108,
    110, 111
  denunciation of Victorian 'elitism'
    109–10, 111
  in the United States 87, 91, 94
  Party (1988) 103
  radicalism of 106, 107
Contention 322
Copernicus 137
Corbin, Alain, 'Paris-province' 53
Cornhill Magazine 323
'Coronation Street' 266
Corrie, G. E., Master of Jesus College,
    Cambridge 274, 277
Coss, J. J. 127
Country Diary of an Edwardian Lady
    102
Covent Garden, Royal Opera House
    196
Coventry 155, 158
Crawley, Josiah 146
Croce, Benedetto 22
Cromwell, Oliver 57
Crosland, Anthony 299
Cross, J. W. 157
  *George Eliot's Life as Related in
    Her Letters and Journals* 151–2,
    155, 159–60
Crossman, Richard 178
'cultural materialism' 212, 217, 221

'Cultural Studies' 217, 221, 227, 253
  definitions of 253–4, 259, 262
  popularity in the United
    States 255
  foundation of 255
  roots of in literary criticism 255–6
  theoretical disciplines assimilated by
    257
  British vs. American styles of 257,
    265
    see also United States
  importance of class as a determi-
    nant of life-chances in 257–8
  definition of 'culture' in 258–9
  as an interdisciplinary enterprise
    260–1
  many methodologies of 262
  weaknesses of 263–5, 268
  as academic subject and social
    therapy 268
*Current Research in Britain: The
  Humanities* (British Library)
    234, 237

Danton 11
Darwin, Charles 86, 161
  early letters of 161–2
  Shrewsbury schooldays 162
  Beagle voyage 162, 164, 163
  wife of 162
  Edinburgh days 163
  Cambridge days 163, 164
  scholarly notebooks of 165
  as a transmutationist 165
  The Origin of Species 163, 166
  Autobiography 167
Darwin, Robert Waring, father of
    Charles Darwin 161
Davenant, William 61
de Gaulle, General Charles 40
Descartes, René 41, 52
Dickens, Charles 97, 102, 290, 291
Dictionary of National Biography 63
Dilthey, Wilhelm, on
    Geisteswissenschaften 312
Dimbleby, David 14
Disraeli, Benjamin 79
Dodd, C. H. 272
Donne, John 290
Donnithorne, Arthur, in *Adam Bede*
    156
Drake, Sir Francis 13
Drayton, Michael 61

humanities (*cont.*):
236, 237, 238, 239, 247
divide between specialist and non-
specialist in 310–13
Arnold as the general cultural legislator 313–15
Leavis on critic as generalist
315–16
Hungary 13
Hunt, Thornton Leigh 154
Huxley, T. H. 292, 314

illegitimacy 88, 89
Illinois, University of 127
India 13, 20, 114
India House 126
Industrial Revolution 179, 180, 181,
192
Inglis, Fred 268
Raymond Williams 211, 212, 217,
218
assessment of 212–13, 217
intellectualism 289–90
definition of 290; anti- 289–90, and
see John Carey's *The
Intellectuals and the Masses*
intellectuals:
as opposed to the 'non-specialist
public' 308–9:
responsiveness towards that public
310; *and see* 'non-specialist
public'
growth in number and diversity of
318–19, 320, 324
as 'general readers' themselves 320,
324
categories of 321–2
Ireland 57
famine (1846–47) 140
Irish Free State (1922) 57
Israel 82
see also Palestine
Italy 201

Jackson, Brian 227
Jackson, Henry 273
Jackson, Robert 250–1
Jacobites 10
Jamaica 266
James I (James VI of Scotland) 57
James II 11
James, Henry 224, 225, 266
on Cross's *Life* 159

on George Eliot 160
on Trollope's *Autobiography* 150–1
writing style of 224
Jaurès, Jean 40
Jeanne d'Arc, Saint. 40, 46
Jefferson Lecture 87
Jenkins, Roy 302
Jews 78, 81, 195
in Britain 82
Johns Hopkins University 127
Johnson, Samuel 62
Lives of the English Poets 307, 308
Jonson, Ben 60
Journal of Ecclesiastical History 322
*Journal of English and Germanic
Philology* 234
Journal of Microbiology 311
Joyce, James 292
Judaism 61
July Monarchy, in France 47, 126

Kafka, Franz 225
Kahn, Richard, Lord 300
Kaldor, Nicholas, Lord 300
Kant, Immanuel 238, 258, 312
philosophy of 71, 209, 299
Karl, Frederick, *George Eliot: A
Biography* 154, 155–60
comparison with Gordon Haight's
biography 156–7
Keats, John 61
Keble, John 61
Kensal Green cemetery 58
Kermode, Frank 207
Keynes, J. M. 30, 112, 114
Keynesian economics 299
'Khâgne, La' 48
King's College, Cambridge 271, 298
Kingsley, Charles 152
Kinzer, Bruce 142
Kipling, Rudyard 63
Knesset 82
Knowles, Dom David 272
Kocis, Robert, on Isaiah Berlin 196
Kristol, Irving 87
Kristol, William 87
Kulturkampf 319

La Juive 69
Labour government 20, 108, 177, 178,
191, 212, 299
denunciation of Victorian 'elitism'

Portobello Road (London) 101
Potter, Dennis 227
Pound, Ezra 315
Priestley, J. B. 112
Prior, Jim:
　Employment Bill of 301
Productivity-Speak (Prodspeak):
　definition of 237–8
　demands of 238–9
　limitations of 238–40, 250,
　see also 'bibliometric methods'
Prospect 322
Prost, Antoine, 'Les Monuments aux
　morts' 44
Protestantism, in England 12, 74
Proust, Marcel 52, 69
psychoanalysis 257, 284
Public Interest, The 87

Quakerism 168
Quaritch, book dealers 150
Quayle, Dan, Vice-President of the
　United States 91
Queen's College, Oxford 63

Radcliffe-Brown, A. R. 280, 285
　impact on social anthropology 283,
　287
　The Andaman Islanders 281
Ranger, Terence, see Hobsbawm, Eric
Rathbone, Eleanor, 112, 114
Rawls, John, 301
　A Theory of Justice 188
Reagan, Ronald 319
Rebérioux, Madeleine, 'Le Mur des
　Fédérés' 44
Reformation, in England 12, 28
Reginald Brown, Alfred, see Radcliffe-
　Brown, A. R.
Reims 44
Reith, John, Lord 112, 114
　ideals of 206
'research productivity' 242
'research selectivity' exercise
　limitations of 246
　Citation Index 246–7
　research, and publication of 237–8,
　248
　categories of 244–5
　definition of 237
　demands of 235–7, 241, 247
　in humanities, definition of 243–4,
　249

in the sciences 244
in the United States, limitations of
　productivity associated with
　248–9
peer reviews of 245–6
systematic analysis in 252
Restoration, in France 41, 47, 126
Revue de Métaphysique et de Morale
　70
Ricardian economics 73
Richards, Audrey 285
Richards, I. A. 281
Riga 77, 195
Right-wing political parties 267
　see also Conservatives
Rio de Janeiro 163
Rivers, W. H. R. 283, 284
Robbins, Bruce 317
Robbins, Lord 302
Robertson Smith, William 283
Robespierre, Maximilien 11
Robinson, Armitage, Dean of
　Westminster Abbey 62
Robinson, Joan 299
Robson, Ann P., on John Stuart Mill
　140–1, 142
Robson, John M. 130, 131, 142
Romantic cultural criticism 256
Romanticism, German 138, 199
Romantic poetry 124, 125
Rorty, Richard 322
Rose, Norman, Namier and Zionism
　79, 80
Rossini, Gioacchino 125
Rousseau, Jean-Jacques 11, 44, 46, 52
　symbolism of in French national
　history 46
Royal Anthropological Institute 288
Royal College of Science (Dublin) 284
Royal Commissions 298
　affecting Cambridge 273, 274, 275,
　276, 279
Royal Opera House, see Covent
　Garden
Rugby school 192
Ruskin College, Oxford 95
Ruskin, John 230
　influence of on Tawney's The
　Aquisitive Society 183–5
　Unto This Last 184, 188
Russell, Bertrand 112, 167, 287
　letters of 162, 167–8:
　　see also Nicholas Griffin, The